CW01508998

from Hillsborough to Lambeth:

CORRUPTION AND COVER-UP

OF

CHILD ABUSE

AND RACISM

IN LAMBETH

by

Brian Pead and Michael Bird

INVENIRE PRESS

1

Illustrations:

All photos © Invenire Press unless otherwise stated.

Front cover: Phyllis Dunipace, former Executive Director of Children & Young People's Service at Lambeth, receives the OBE from HRH Prince Charles (8 February 2011); © Press Association, Photo by Lewis Whyld

Back cover: locations, clockwise: the Old Library Centre, West Norwood; the Redfearn Centre, Vauxhall; the White Bear Pub and Theatre, Kennington; road sign for the South London Employment Tribunal Court;

Back cover: personnel, left to right: Anya Hiley, Connexions Personal Advisor; Cathy Twist, Assistant Director, Standards Division, Lambeth; Annabel Field, part-time English teacher at the OLCVS and part-time actress.

First published in Great Britain 2012

Invenire Press Limited, PO Box 5983, Southend-on-Sea, Essex SS1 9PL

ISBN   978-0-9574301-0-5 (paperback)

"You have enemies? Good. That means you've stood up for something, sometime in your life."

SIR WINSTON CHURCHILL

For Emily, Lauren and Joseph so that you would one day learn THE REAL TRUTH.

For those who died at Hillsborough and their families who also suffered because of police corruption and a cover-up by self-serving politicians.

Introduction

On Wednesday 12 September 2012, the world finally learnt THE REAL TRUTH about the Hillsborough Disaster. It was **not** the fault of Liverpool fans. For almost a quarter of a century, the Government, the legal system, the police and the press had conspired to lie to the public and to create a 'smoke and mirrors' campaign which would keep the ordinary person busy in fighting for justice and clearing their names whilst simultaneously diverting the public's attention away from the authorities' sickening agenda of lies, of doctored evidence, of changed statements and of the condemnation of innocent people by the government-controlled press (which likes to claim that it is 'free'.)

As David Moyes, the Everton manager, stated on 17th September 2012, the public could no longer trust the very authorities on which we all, as human beings, rely. He rightly castigated the police and the government and the press. He left no-one in any doubt as to his feelings about the tragedy in 1989.

Brian Pead, the renowned and respected author of books on the entire history of Liverpool Football Club from 1892, had attended the game at Hillsborough and witnessed the unnecessary deaths. From the moment the tragedy occurred, he (and others) witnessed the police lies and the cover-up by members of Margaret Thatcher's government and successive governments. As a football historian, he wrote about the contempt that those within the Football Association and Premier League have for the 'ordinary fan'. As long ago as 27 March 1899, there had been a serious problem in an FA Cup semi-final second replay tie between Liverpool and Sheffield United at Fallowfield, Manchester. The game had to be abandoned at half-time because there were far too many spectators in the ground. Brian Pead's exhaustive research of this game showed that the footballing authorities had not concerned themselves with crowd safety but only about the size of the gate money. There was inadequate policing and that which existed was seriously called into question.

The referee had taken the players off the field of play after the crowd spilled on to the pitch. Eventually the players came out again, but once the gate money had been removed from the ground to a place of safety, it was reported that the officials did not then care what the crowd did.

There had been crushes at various entrances to the ground. The prestigious *Pall Mall Gazette* castigated the large crowd for encroaching on the pitch, but it had no option due to the crush.

In yet another echo of Hillsborough, the Sheffield Daily Telegraph commented that the Fallowfield ground was not fit for purpose and that the fiasco was a sad reflection on the wisdom of the Football Association who sent the teams to play there. The newspaper added that "...those who knew the ground trembled for the game from the very announcement of its selection as the venue for the semi-final tie..."

On 17 April 1989, Simon Barnes of The Times wrote an article [p.16] entitled 'Why the dead are the victims of contempt' and he was strongly critical of the state of football. 'Why make the football grounds pleasant? Cram them in, take as much money as you dare to charge, that's the way. Spend a million quid on a player, spend the legal minimum on ground safety and spend next to nothing on comfort'. Echoes of Fallowfield, Manchester in 1899. This article was referred to in the Hillsborough Report on page 343.

There can be no excuse for such neglectful behaviour by the authorities in either 1899 or 1989. Had the great Bill Shankly - a man of the people - still been alive, it is Pead's belief that there can be little doubt he would have worked diligently to support the families and friends of those who died at Hillsborough to fight for Justice.

For eighteen of the twenty-three years it has taken the people of Liverpool to obtain some form of justice, Brian Pead watched from the sidelines. He read all of the police lies. He knew that evidence had been altered. He knew that the press had been misdirected by the police and members of parliament, who cast a long and dark shadow over Justice in this country.

Then, on 8 December 2006, the course of Brian's life altered dramatically. He had reported on child abuse and racism in a Pupil Referral Unit in which he was the Head teacher. Yet, just three weeks after dismissing the female Deputy Head for grooming young girls and racism, Lambeth Council unlawfully suspended **him** and then re-employed **her** in an all-girls' school.

Since that fateful December day, he has been beaten up in the street by police officers whilst waiting at a bus stop, he has been subjected to two unlawful criminal trials, he has been wrongly labelled a sex offender, he has been subjected to more than six civil trials in less than a year, he has been wrongly imprisoned at maximum security prison, Belmarsh, and moved between Belmarsh and Wandsworth prisons every 5-6 days, he has been vilified in the press and evidence has been fabricated against him and evidence that would have proved his innocence has been altered or destroyed.

Brian Pead's experiences whilst working at Lambeth have been a mirror of what happened since Hillsborough. The police, the politicians, the legal system and the press come out of this story with no credit whatsoever. The widespread corruption and cover-up that was Hillsborough was repeated on a man whose only crime was to uncover corruption and report it to the local authority and the police.

This story is the story of an innocent man whom the world was told was guilty – of a crime with no victim. This story is also of a man who – like his hero, Bill Shankly, before him – refused to believe that there is a lost cause. This is the story of a man of indomitable spirit.

The families of those who died at Hillsborough were lied to.

Brian Pead's family has also been lied to. His beloved grand-children no longer have contact with him because of the actions of corrupt police officers at Scotland Yard, ineffective members of parliament and members of the legal profession who have brought disgrace upon that often revered vocation.

Just as in Hillsborough, this is the story of a fight for Justice. One man's fight for Justice. Of putting right the terrible wrongs that have been committed in his name.

But this is also the story of three innocent grand-children ... so that, like the families of those who died at Hillsborough, they would one day learn THE REAL TRUTH and not 'THE TRUTH' as promulgated by despicable people working for the authorities.

So, this book is for Emily, Lauren and Joe. Every word has been typed with love ... so that the REAL TRUTH may set you free.

The families and friends of those who died at Hillsborough vowed to fight for Justice – no matter how long it would take. On his first arrest, Brian Pead vowed to get the truth to his grand-children – no matter how long it would take.

The purpose of this book is to bring factual information - not lies and conjecture - to the public's attention, and to overturn two miscarriages of justice – his unlawful dismissal by Lambeth Council and the perverse judgment of an Employment Tribunal. The authors – like those at Hillsborough – expect several people to be brought to justice and to face criminal trials.

The authors present facts in this book. Each fact can be supported with robust evidence, the provenance of which can be established. The reader is free to draw his or her own conclusions.

If the issues in this book affect you or someone you know, please write to Invenire Press at invenirepress@hushmail.com . This is secure email which uses encryption for your safety.

CONTENTS

1

pieces of the jigsaw

On Friday 2 December 2011, the BBC ran a news item about a Head teacher in Lambeth having been awarded the sum of £100,000 in compensation for unfair dismissal in an 18-day tribunal hearing.

He had resigned in 2010, claiming constructive dismissal from Henry Fawcett Primary School.

Both parties – the Head teacher, James Walker, and Lambeth Council – "...agreed to draw a line under the matter..."

James Walker had been suspended in November 2008.

-o-

In March 2008, a former Lambeth Head teacher, Brian Pead, lost an Employment Tribunal case against Lambeth for unfair dismissal in a one-day tribunal hearing. The verdict was perverse.

-o-

On 20 May 2008, Brian Pead was arrested by Bexley Police on allegations of indecent exposure, voyeurism and stalking. He was offered a 'Caution' (off the record and without the tape playing) but insisted he was innocent and so was charged with Exposure.

-o-

On 4 June 2008, police from Scotland Yard unlawfully trespassed on Pead's house and arrested him on an allegation of inciting a child to engage in a sexual offence.

After being in police custody for more than thirteen hours, he was released without charge.

-o-

On 26 November 2008, Classroom Teachers.co.za ceased its programme of sending South African teachers to the UK.

-o-

On 4 June 2007, Rosa Vaz, a Lambeth Human Resources officer, admitted that "...We [Lambeth HR] wouldn't know if agency staff in any schools were CRB checked or not..."

-o-

On 13 November 2006, Brian Pead informed his line manager, Barry Gilhooly, that a white South African teacher calling herself Maryn Murray, had been racist towards young black male pupils and had offered young white girls bribes to go to the gym with her after school hours and asked one of them to go shopping with her and round to her flat. Alone.

-o-

On 15 November 2006, Brian Pead calls the Classroom teaching agency and instructs them to call Murray and tell her that her services are no longer required.

-o-

On 8 December 2006, Barry Gilhooly and Rosa Vaz call at the Open Learning Centre for Vocational Studies housed in the Redfearn Centre in Vauxhall and frogmarch Pead out of the building, telling him that he is suspended, but giving him no reasons why.

-o-

On 13 December 2006, under Gilhooly's instructions, officers from Lambeth Council ransack Pead's office at the OLCVS. All evidence is removed. Locked filing cabinets are removed. All paper files are removed. The computer is removed. Only a desk and chair remain.

-o-

On 19 December 2006, Pead receives an email from Nadia Al-Khudhairy of King's College Psychiatry Department informing him that his pupil referral unit is "...the best in London..." and asking him whether he would like to write a paper for a psychology journal on his successful methods of combining teaching and therapeutic interventions.

2

seeds of destruction

In 2001, having lost more than a quarter of a million pounds in an online educational venture based on four books he wrote with Ann Armin entitled 'National Curriculum Homework Sheets which were published by First and Best in Education, Brian Pead went back to work as a supply teacher, until an offer to become the Head of a new Pupil Referral Unit (PRU) in Lambeth presented itself.

With considerable experience of management, of teaching, of special needs pupils and of classroom discipline, he attended four separate interviews with Barry Gilhooly, an Assistant Director of Education with Lambeth Council.

For personal reasons, Brian Pead requested that he be known as Brian Johnson in this venture. The two men spoke about the need to have the name Brian Johnson added to his Criminal Records Bureau (CRB) checks and Pead willingly submitted to this normal procedure. He had been subjected to Enhanced Disclosure checks since their inception in March 2002 and had never gained a criminal record in his 52 years.

Gilhooly was to be his immediate Line Manager. Pead knew that it was important for him to establish a good rapport with Gilhooly, but this was an extremely difficult proposition, since Gilhooly was a secretive, aloof person with few 'people-skills'.

Nonetheless, in spite of this potential problem, Brian Pead accepted the post as Head teacher of the PRU, which was to be known as The Old Library Centre Virtual School and, as its name suggests, it was housed at the Old Library in West Norwood, a beautiful Victorian edifice built in 1887, and currently being used as a community centre.

The term 'virtual' was a misnomer, since it suggested that the school was an online enterprise. It was not. The PRU was housed in two 'classrooms' within the Community Centre. Each morning the desks and chairs would have to be set out and after each day's teaching, they would have to be stacked up and locked away because the rooms were being used for other activities by the local community.

3

major responsibilities

In any post, of course, there will be an agreed set of responsibilities that both parties – the employer and the employee – will be working towards. These responsibilities underpin the contract. Brian Pead studied these carefully. Following a Freedom of Information Act request to Lambeth Council, the list of responsibilities is reproduced here in its entirety because it is the basis of this entire story of corruption and cover-up. The most relevant and critical responsibilities are in bold type. The emphases are the authors':

MAJOR RESPONSIBILITIES:

1 To be responsible for the range of duties and responsibilities for headteachers contained within the Teachers Pay and Conditions document.

2 To be responsible for the production of the Virtual School development plan in consultation with the staff and the Authority reflecting both national statutory requirements and Authority priorities.

3 To provide sound and informed advice to the Authority on all matters relevant to the Unit. This will include providing regular reports to the Authority as required.

4 To be responsible for the management and organisation of the Virtual School and the effective use of all resources including the deployment of staff and the care and maintenance of buildings and equipment. This will include the evaluation of teaching and learning appraisal, recruitment and associated administration, teachers' salary assessment, disciplinary, capability and sickness procedures.

5 To manage the Virtual School's budget and to be responsible for maintaining effective monitoring and budgetary controls in line with the Council's financial procedures. This will include dual registration funding, Standards Fund activities and charges to schools for advice and temporary pupil placements.

6 To be responsible for the development of the curriculum as appropriate to meet the needs of pupils at the Virtual School and consistent with national requirements and Authority policy. To ensure that the curriculum is broad and balanced, relevant, differentiated, coherent and that pupils' learning experiences are organised in a progression which supports high achievement for each individual child.

7 To be responsible for the arrangements within the Virtual School for conducting national assessment and to report the results to parents/carers the DfES and the Authority. To ensure the maintenance of appropriate systems for assessing pupils' needs, recording pupil progress an (sic) for good communication with pupils and parents/carers.

8 To be responsible for the general discipline within the Virtual School and the welfare and social development of pupils including child protection.

9 To monitor and review the work of the Virtual School and its staff and to be responsible for the provision of any necessary programmes of staff development and in-service training.

10 To involve parents/carers appropriately in the life and work of the Virtual School and to work co-operatively with the range of interest groups that make up the Virtual School community.

11 To take a lead in developing and operating of the Authority's policy on the reintegration of excluded pupils. This may include attending placement panels and undertaking appropriate follow-up actions and developing innovative and effective links with local schools.

12 To develop the work of the specialist EBO Advisory Teacher Team. This will include ensuring that the team provides high quality advice to schools in a responsible and flexible manner.

13 To act as key site manager taking responsibility for all matters of health and safety including compliance with statutory and Authority requirements.

14 To work co-operatively with other colleagues and the wider multi-disciplinary team and to contribute to the general development of the service at a senior level.

15 To ensure that the 1996 Education Act and Code of Practice is implemented in full within the Unit.

16 To meet with parents and colleagues as appropriate and organise staff meetings.

17 To attend and provide INSET and training as required maintaining a high level of subject knowledge in the areas of curriculum and emotional and behavioural difficulties.

18 To make full and appropriate use of information technology with training if required.

19 To implement the borough's equal opportunities policy fully and to work actively to overcome and prevent discrimination on the grounds of race, gender, disability, class or age in any part of the service.

20 To carry out such other duties as may be required from time to time to meet the needs of the service.

The above list of major responsibilities was studied by Brian Pead carefully before he signed a contract to manage the Unit.

He had carefully noted at (2) that the Unit would reflect both national statutory requirements and local authority priorities. Being the type of character that he is, he ensured that he was fully conversant with the national and local authority requirements.

At (4) above, he had ensured that he was solely responsible for the deployment of staff. He had an issue with Gilhooly from the outset because the line manager had presented Pead with three members of staff whom Pead had never met, had not interviewed and yet was being asked to manage. Pead preferred to recruit his own staff but, rather like a football manager who takes over at a new club, he knew that sometimes you take on staff whom you have not recruited and who will not be suited to the manager's system. But a wise football manager will always give the players an opportunity to impress and this is what Pead decided he must do.

Pead had managed people from the age of 18. After leaving school at 17, he took on the job of Retail Manager at MacFisheries. He was given a company van and his remit was to drive around the southeast of England and take over from the manager of any particular branch when that manager went on holiday. This peripatetic role required enormous strength of character and people skills – the staff at a shop would generally not like an unknown manager leading them until their own manager returned from holiday. However, in his years in management for MacFisheries, he never encountered a single complaint, despite being responsible for managing people much older than himself.

He left that role to go to university to train as a teacher in 1982.

Brian Pead, therefore, had years of experience of managing people. He had learnt what makes a good leader and what makes for a happy team. He was also extremely capable of assessing a staff member's character and individual strengths and weaknesses.

At (5) above, Pead was pleased that he would have control over the budget, since he hated the waste that often comes with running a Local Authority establishment. Parsimonious by nature, he felt that he would be able to divert monies that might be wasted towards more critical needs.

He was pleased that he would be responsible for the development of the curriculum (6). He knew that some subjects would be a waste of time in the Unit, and so he wanted to focus only on those subjects that would engage the pupils' attention and help them to learn. He also wanted the pupils themselves to suggest subjects that they would like to study.

At (7) above, he knew that he wanted the first cohort of students to leave the OLCVS with at least one nationally-recognised qualification. He set this as one of his goals for the end of the first year.

He was particularly pleased with (8) above because he had – through some 23 years of teaching – come to realise that the curriculum content of a school or pupil referral unit mattered little in his view. He felt that society would benefit more readily from pupils leaving school who were emotionally equipped to take their place in the wider context of society outside of the school gates and his training as a counsellor ensured that he was equipped with the skills that would enable him – and his staff – to deal with the highly complex emotional needs of the pupils.

Following on from (8), he took full responsibility for developing the training needs of his staff (9). He was happy to devise a programme of training to help his staff deal with difficult pupils and he was also extremely keen to help staff deal with their own emotional needs around helping such pupils. Pead saw this as a two-way process. He did not like the way many schools expected staff to deal with difficult pupils without training the staff in how to deal with them. His view was that his role was to train the trainers. He also felt that it was his responsibility to ensure the safety of his staff. Working constantly with such challenging and difficult pupils can be draining on one's own emotional reserves, so he ensured that his staff would be able to look after their own emotional needs as well as those of the pupils.

At (16) above, Pead was pleased that he was responsible for organising staff meetings. He had some radical views on not only the content of such meetings but also the process of meetings.

Perhaps the responsibility that pleased him the most was (17) – to provide INSET training as required and to maintain a high level of subject knowledge in the areas of curriculum and emotional and behavioural difficulties.

As a young man in a children's home and having been sexually abused in that home, Pead knew only too well how events in one's life can lead to emotional difficulties. He had had the strength of character to overcome his own life-changing traumas, but he knew that many people in life do not possess the capacity to overcome their challenges. Brian Pead wanted to help these disadvantaged pupils to overcome whatever life threw at them and to deal with it in a positive way, rather than let it destroy their life forever.

Throughout his 23 years of teaching, he had never encountered discipline problems. Colleagues would often ask him how he achieved such excellent classroom control. Being such a humble man, he was bemused by such questions. To him it was obvious how to achieve good classroom control – most teachers, he found, did not either (a) study classroom control techniques or (b) have a natural flair for leadership. Pead had both. Although he always enjoyed excellent classroom discipline in his lessons, he was also humble enough to continue to study assiduously all things about classroom discipline. He was continually adopting, adapting and improving his own performance. Rather like Sir Alex Ferguson who would win the Premier League title then want to win it again the following season, Brian Pead would enjoy an academic year of success in the field of classroom discipline then want to do even better the following academic year. Year after year. He continually honed his skills in this area. He knew (because they told him so) that pupils felt safe in his classes. They always knew where 'the line' was. Humour played a significant part in his teaching – but the pupils in his classes always knew how far they could go and no more. Classroom discipline underpinned his entire teaching ethos. He believed that once good discipline was in place, then learning could take place. It could not be done the other way around.

Pead was also pleased to see clause (19) with regard to the council's equal opportunities policy. He was happy to work actively to overcome and prevent discrimination based on the grounds of race, gender, disability, class or age. He had felt strongly throughout his life that discrimination on any level was pernicious and that it ought to be eradicated. As he was about to embark upon a position working in the London Borough of Lambeth, he was particularly conscious of race discrimination and he knew that he would not tolerate this whatsoever.

Thus an agreed set of responsibilities had been worked out. An initial hurdle had been cleared. But Brian Pead was still cautious. He would not accept the post unless he was confident that he had the necessary skill set in order to make a success of the job. He did not want his name associated with a venture that would be something of a 'white elephant'. Having established considerable brand awareness in his name through his books on Liverpool Football Club, he did not want his name tarnished with a project that might not work. Pead was an astute man and he would not accept just any post – it had to match his skill set and it had to be something he was sure he could make a success of. Had this not been the case, he would have walked away at the negotiation stage. Thus he turned to the Competency Based Person Specification document authored by Lambeth.

He scrutinised this document carefully.

Two main areas drew his attention.

> "...High level knowledge of current developments in education generally including the National Curriculum, key stage testing and the ability to manage the planning, delivery and coordination of a curriculum offer which is appropriate to the individual requirements of pupils. This includes pupils with special educational needs, in particular, emotional and behavioural difficulties and individual education planning..."

Having taught English and Special Needs for 23 years, he felt – and Gilhooly felt – that he fulfilled this criterion. His role as a trainee counsellor could only add to the skillset that was necessary for this role with pupils with emotional and behavioural difficulties.

> "...High level knowledge and understanding of assessment and record keeping and its use to promote the educational and personal development of pupils

within the Unit and the ability to initiate, develop, evaluate and monitor strategies to raise levels of pupils' achievement..."

As the creator and Managing Director of www.einsteinonline.co.uk, an educational programme for primary aged children that tracked a child's work online throughout his or her entire school career, Pead felt that he had the necessary knowledge to fulfil this criterion.

"...High level knowledge and skills regarding effective strategies for working with pupils who have emotional and behavioural difficulties. This will include the ability to advise colleagues throughout the borough in all aspects of working with pupils who have emotional and behavioural difficulties..."

Note the importance of this paragraph. It is fundamental to this story. The postholder was required to possess "high level knowledge and skills" with regard to working with "pupils who have emotional and behavioural difficulties". A range of "effective strategies" was also required.

Brian Pead had, as has been previously shown, never experienced behavioural problems from the pupils in his charge. He had carefully adopted a role which would ensure that potential problems were 'nipped in the bud', sometimes with the use of humour or sometimes with a firm "No".

Pupils in his charge always knew where they stood and thus – although some might try to push the boundaries as far they could – they ultimately knew they would not succeed. There would only be one winner – and that would be Brian Pead.

Thus Brian Pead felt that he had the required skills that the role demanded. He had the relevant knowledge and the relevant experience. And Barry Gilhooly also felt this; otherwise he would not have offered Pead the job.

"...Willingness and ability to maintain a high level of specialist knowledge in the areas of emotional and behavioural difficulties and educational management attending training as appropriate. This will include the ability to develop innovative solutions/approaches to issues arising..."

This particular competency might have been written specially for Pead. He had always enjoyed excellent classroom discipline and his training as a counsellor meant that he had 'the inside track' on what made pupils behave the way that they did. Most teachers are re-active to pupils' behaviour. Brian Pead was pro-active. He let his pupils know from the moment they walked into his classroom what his expectations were. Most teachers employ the word 'you', as in "You will do this" or "You will do that". Brian Pead did not. He chose to use the word 'we', as in "We will do this" because he knew that it was important that pupils felt that their teacher was part of the rule-making process and that he would have to abide by the rules just as much as they would. Yet he rarely explicitly voiced these expectations. They were implicit in everything he did and everything he said. It was his manner, his tone of delivery and his body language that he employed to excellent effect. Some of this was instinctive – some of it had been thought through.

Thus Pead and Gilhooly both felt that the former possessed the necessary skills to make a success of the Unit and a contract was duly signed on 12 August 2005, backdated to 1 August 2005 since Pead felt that he had already been involved in several meetings and much research up to this point and he felt quite strongly that he wanted payment for his time.

The initial contract was until 31 December 2005. This was, therefore, only a one-term contract. Pead wanted a longer period of time, but he was also concerned that Gilhooly had apparently not thought the project through properly and it gave Pead the ability to withdraw from the project at an early stage if things were not going as he felt they ought to.

Brian Pead shared the information on matters concerning the OLCVS project and Lambeth's disciplinary process which is referred to throughout this book with John Callow as a friend and had requested his opinion on matters concerning the OLCVS project and Lambeth's disciplinary process based on feedback from the Head teacher or written information he had requested Callow to read.

Callow, Pead's wise old friend, was of the view that there was something amiss with such a short contract. Had Management or Lambeth really expected the OLCVS to be a long-term project, then surely it would award contracts commensurate with that longevity. Or, on the other hand, if Management wasn't sure that Pead was, after all, the right man for the job, then why offer it to him in the first place? Either way, this strategy of a one-term contract did not fit with a long-term project.

The PRU had no permanent home. It had no staff, no equipment of its own, no budget and no direction.

It had ostensibly been created by Lambeth in response to forthcoming local elections. Lambeth had – and still has – a high percentage of NEET pupils: Not in Education, Employment or Training. These pupils are often school refusers or they have been thrown out of school or they are new immigrants into the country. That they were difficult pupils to teach was not in question.

Brian Pead thus had tremendous odds against him in creating this venture. Gilhooly presented him with three members of staff, Duane Maddison, Jennifer Foster, and Eloise Whitmore. Pead had never met them before they walked through the door to start day one of the OLCVS.

4

duane maddison

Duane Maddison is a charismatic Guyanan, with dreadlocks and colourful clothes and he was employed by Gilhooly to work as a Learning Mentor to the pupils. Brian Pead assessed him to be an extremely capable man and Maddison was able to gain the trust of the pupils almost immediately. He had over 20 years' experience in working with disadvantaged pupils in Lambeth, Wandsworth, Merton and Camden, as well as working nationally in the Midlands to help young people and middle-aged people and practitioners to empower themselves to achieve their goals and aspirations. Maddison has enabled his success to be accessible for those wishing to establish their footprint in the world.

SKILL SET & EXPERIENCE

- Highly experienced & trained Mentor

- CPCAB Trained Counsellor.

- Numerous years' experience devising programmes for Schools, Colleges, Youth Clubs and Youth provisions.

- Professional facilitator for practitioners and working groups.

- Inspirational and Motivational Leader and facilitator.

- Highly I.T. literate.

- Over 25+ years' experience working in the Arts.

- Experienced teacher and classroom management advisor.
Source: <http://amennoir.weebly.com/about-an-consultancy.html>

5

jenny foster

Jennifer Foster was used to working with primary-aged pupils. In her own way, she was highly skilled with that age group. However, strategies that work with younger aged pupils are not necessarily transferrable to older pupils. Put simply, you do not treat a 15 year old the same way you would a 5 year old. It seemed to Brian Pead that although she was a capable mentor of primary-aged pupils, she did not possess the emotional flexibility to adapt to an older group of pupils. Indeed, on her own admission, she cited this difficulty when she later chose to seek employment elsewhere.

6

eloise whitmore

Eloise Whitmore was employed by Gilhooly as the secretary of the PRU. Her official title was School Administration Officer. Within a few days it became obvious to Pead that Whitmore did not possess the gravitas necessary for that role. He assessed her to be something of a bull-shitter. She had a raucous laugh and tried to bluff her way through when asked penetrating questions about the job.

She alleged to have had a degree in psychology, though her performance in the role did not show this. Most importantly, she had no qualifications whatsoever for this specific role. In his time as a teacher, Brian Pead had had considerable dealings with school secretaries of all ages. One of the best he ever worked with was Joan Stekelenberg at Colyers Primary School in Erith, Kent. With a wicked sense of humour and an astute mind, Joan was a thorough professional. Now, in West Norwood, he had been presented with a woman aged around 28 who had no experience whatsoever of being a school secretary and her curriculum vitae showed Pead that she had drifted from job to job and from role to role, never spending more than six months in any one job.

Early on, Brian Pead asked Whitmore to type out a one-page letter to parents. With great eagerness, Whitmore went upstairs to the computer room and typed out the letter. It took her more than an hour.

When she presented the letter to Pead, it was full of errors. He knew that these were not mere typing errors but rather they were errors in spelling and punctuation.

So he then corrected the letter, and asked her to re-type it. Away she went to re-type it before coming downstairs to the office (which still had no furniture of its own) to show Pead the letter.

What he saw horrified him. The previous errors had been corrected, but other – different – errors had crept in.

Again he corrected the letter and asked her to re-type it.

A third draft was presented to him. He corrected it for a third time and she went away to re-type it for a third time.

And a fourth.

And a fifth.

Part of Pead's major responsibilities (paragraph 4 in the document of the same name) was to ensure the capability of staff. He assessed Whitmore as being incapable of holding down such an important role in the Unit.

What on earth was Gilhooly doing in employing this woman? And why did he think she was capable of holding down a job as the 'school administration officer' when it was already clear to Pead that she was not capable of fulfilling the role?

Pead mentioned this to Gilhooly in a rare management meeting. "Give it a little time," Gilhooly urged.

Immediately, this did not make sense to Pead. Here he was attempting to create a school from nothing and Whitmore was impeding the progress of that building programme. And his Line Manager was not supporting him, but rather trying to ensure that Whitmore would remain in employment.

Nor did it make sense that Gilhooly did not present Pead with a budget, despite it being asked for on numerous occasions.

Despite these difficulties, over the coming weeks Pead ensured that he created something that would pass as a school in order that pupils could be admitted. Gilhooly was a silent partner in the enterprise. He would often holiday in Goa.

7

anya hiley

Another person who was to be associated with the OLCVS was Anya Hiley, a Connexions Personal Advisor. She was around 30 years of age and unmarried. She worked out of a top floor office at the Old Library, two floors above the pupil referral unit.

As part of his networking, Pead invited her for a coffee and chat in the café on the corner near the Old Library.

Unknown to Hiley, Pead had undertaken research into the role of a Connexions Personal Advisor before he even met her. He did this so as to have an understanding of her role.

Connexions described the role thus:

> "...Lambeth Connexions Personal Advisors will provide a youth support service, which will meet the needs of individual young people aged 13-19 ensuring that they are motivated to engage in education, training and employment. The Personal Advisor will work with clients with special needs up to the age of 24 years.
>
> We work with Young People who face homelessness to Teenage Parents and everything in between. If you have the ability to work with Young People facing challenging times we would like to hear from you.
>
> You will also work with Young People in Schools as well as in the Community.
>
> Applications are invited from suitably qualified and experienced people. Ideally you will need to hold a relevant qualification relating to working with young people. Extensive experience working with the client group will also be considered. You should have the ability to relate to young people in order to befriend, motivate, empathise and positively influence them..."

He also familiarised himself with the main duties and responsibilities of an advisor:

1. To engage with young people to identify and address their needs which affect their education, training and employment.

2. To utilise and support education and training institutions and employers in meeting the needs of young people.

· Personal Advisors will establish working relationships and maintain contact with other professionals in the local area to ensure a joined up approach in meeting the needs of young people.

3. To work with a network of voluntary, statutory and community agencies to remove barriers to learning and employment for young people.

4. To work with families, parents and carers to engage young people in education, training and employment opportunities.

5. To manage information to facilitate the process of meeting the needs of young people.

6. Work with other agencies, to broker access to specialist agencies including education providers, Youth Services, Social Services, Health Authorities, Youth Justice organisations and voluntary and community groups. Link young people to these organisations according to their individual needs and accompany them on visits, to interviews and events.

7. Work with a caseload of young people who require intensive, individual support, befriending and mentoring. Maintain contact with young people forming caseload, and monitor the progress of all young people referred to the Connexions service. Keep accurate records of all contacts.

8. Offer advice to other professionals and to parents and carers for example in situations when a young person is moved into care or is placed on a pastoral support programme.

9. Liaise across organisational barriers providing comprehensive reports to support the transition of students.

10. Carry out all duties in accordance with London Borough of Lambeth's Equal Opportunities policy, actively promoting equality and seeking to prevent and overcome disadvantage and discrimination.

11. Use information technology to research information, produce reports, and correspondence, keeping statistics and engage young people in researching their future options and assessing their potential and abilities.

12. To represent the Central London Connexions Pilot – Lambeth Project as necessary within and outside the borough as appropriate, necessary and relevant.

13. To undertake such other duties, as required commensurate with the grade of the post.

14. To take responsibility, appropriate to the post for tackling racism and promoting good race, ethnic and community relations.

Brian Pead examined these duties carefully. He wanted to understand Hiley's role and perhaps find ways in which he could support her if that were necessary.

He also researched the Person Specification. It seemed to him that Connexions (strapline 'Youth on the move') required a high standard of professionalism and its Advisors to network and engage with partner organisations in a mature manner.

When Pead met Hiley in the café, he was not at all impressed. He asked a few penetrating questions connected to her job and returned to the OLCVS with a sigh of resignation. This woman, he believed, did not have a very good understanding of her role and it appeared to Pead that she had little awareness around the needs of the pupils.

Although not impressed by Hiley, he reasoned that she was what she was and that he would try to find a way to work with her.

He was particularly struck by (7). It seemed to him that it was vital for a Connexions advisor to be able to understand the young people whom they came into contact with and to be able to encounter young people without judging them.

It appeared that Hiley – and all other Connexions Personal Advisors – would be required to work with young people who needed intensive and individual support. They might also need befriending. A further aspect to Hiley's role was to maintain contact with young people and to monitor their progress. Keeping accurate records was essential.

Brian Pead examined clause 7 carefully. He thought long and hard about the role and noted that it gave a lot of power to Personal Advisors. If one were minded to befriend pupils for less than honourable purposes, this would be the perfect job. One could – ostensibly legitimately – get very close to pupils, monitor them over a long period of time and 'befriend' them. Or groom them under the guise of 'befriending' them.

It is possible that not every Connexions Personal Advisor in the country would use the information they held on pupils honourably. One or two might use that knowledge as power over young people. Others might pass on their contact details to paedophiles and sex offenders. Yet others might abuse young people themselves, whilst others might well work on behalf of sex traffickers in obtaining the personal details of extremely vulnerable young people. 'Youth on the move' could well be interpreted as moving vulnerable youngsters around the UK under the guise of 'helping them'.

The vast majority of personal advisors in the UK are probably doing a perfectly good job. But in every barrel, there is always at least one rotten apple.

8

first steps

The OLCVS opened its doors to students on 12 September 2005. The pupils were all in the age range 14 to 16 and they were an incredible mix of highly capable pupils and those of lower intelligence. They came from extremely varied backgrounds. Sixty per cent of the pupils had English as an Additional Language (EAL). However, there was a common bond that united them all – they had either all been rejected by mainstream schools, been labelled as 'unteachable' or were 'unwanted' by Lambeth. Pead knew, however, that he could work with these pupils. Strangely, there were slightly more female pupils than males. There was a significant contingent of Brazilian and Portuguese black males.

As the previous century had drawn to a close, Pead was closely monitoring the situation in South Africa. Whilst at university he had been moved by an excellent book entitled 'Mine Boy' by Peter Abrahams. Published in 1946, it was one of the first books to look at what life as a black person meant in South African society during the days of Apartheid. Abraham's father was from Ethiopia and his mother was classified by South Africa as a mixed race person, a "Kleurling" or Coloured. The author was born in Vrededorp, nearby Johannesburg, but left South Africa in 1939. He worked first as a sailor, and then as a journalist in London. One of South Africa's most prominent writers, his work deals with political and social issues, especially with racism. Pead eventually wrote to Abrahams, who had re-located to Jamaica, about the book and racial abuse. Pead is against all forms of human abuse.

With this strong moral compass, he vowed to run the OLCVS based upon the words of Nelson Mandela in his Inaugural Address in Pretoria on 9 May 1994:

> "We enter into a covenant that we shall build a society in which all [...], both black and white, will be able to walk tall, without fear in their hearts, assured of their inalienable right to human dignity – a rainbow nation at peace with itself and the world."

Brian Pead taught this rainbow nation himself, despite being the Head of the Unit. Duane Maddison and Jenny Foster would act as classroom assistants, although this was not their specific role. It seemed to Pead that Gilhooly had not thought this through. The OLCVS had been created to address the fact that Lambeth Council was not meeting the needs of these pupils and it was a political move, designed to ensure that in the forthcoming local elections in May 2006, Lambeth could be *seen* to be doing a decent job. The reality was far from different.

Maddison and Pead quickly established a positive rapport with the pupils. In her own way, Jenny Foster created some positive relationships with mainly female pupils but Eloise Whitmore was not able to establish such positive relationships because many of the pupils could see that – in their opinion - she was false.

Brian Pead worked hard. Living in Sidcup, Kent, he would rise around 5.30am and walk to New Eltham train station and alight at London Bridge, where he would take a second train to West Norwood. He would arrive around 7am, open up the community centre and set out the desks and chairs. Pupils would drift into the community centre from around 8am. Pead would work until 6 or 7pm. Allowing for a two-hour journey home, his day was full.

He combined this position with studying for an Advanced Diploma in Humanistic Integrative Counselling at the Centre for Personal and Professional Development. He had already gained a Diploma in this subject area, but he wanted to undertake the Advanced Diploma because he knew that it demanded a more rigorous, academic approach to counselling and a considerable amount of reading about different therapeutic approaches and theories. On this course he encountered some of the 'heavyweights' of counselling: Sigmund Freud, Melanie Klein, Carl Jung, Bill Rogers, Fritz Perls, Donald Winnicott, Wilfred Bion, Heinz Kohut and Christopher Bollas.

There were two main themes on the Advanced Diploma course: transference and counter-transference and psychosexual issues. There was a great deal of reading around these subjects. Brian Pead was fascinated by both themes. From an early age, he had been part of groups in a children's home, as a manager and within his dysfunctional family and marriage. He had been particularly interested in the interaction between the different members of whichever group he was involved in. He was acutely aware not only of his own role within each group, but he also gained increasing awareness of the transferential and counter-transferential issues between members of the group. And having been abused between the ages of 5 and 11, he naturally had a deep interest in psychosexual matters.

9

reference

A day after the OLCVS opened its doors to pupils, Lambeth received a reference from John Beach, Managing Director of Global Recruitment Solutions. Brian Pead had been registered with Global since 2003 and he had worked with the agency regularly throughout the two years. He had met with John Beach – a former Head teacher himself – on a number of occasions.

Questions have to be asked: Why did Lambeth employ Brian Pead before obtaining satisfactory references for him? He is an innocent man who has no criminal convictions and he is no danger to children. However, what if this had not been the case? What if he had been a dangerous man? Why did Lambeth install him in such a powerful position without having made the necessary checks? How often are Lambeth doing this? How many children are being put at daily risk through such lax measures? How many children have been abused simply because Lambeth HR does not conform to statutory child protection safety measures?

John Beach wrote a glowing reference and added that:

> "...In the time that I have known Brian he has never given me any cause to doubt his complete honesty and integrity [...] Brian has been given the usual criminal checks and they have been clear [...] I believe that Brian Pead will be an excellent appointment to this post. Besides being well qualified and experienced, he is always enthusiastic about the work that he does..."

John Beach was in no doubt that Pead was a man of great integrity who was well qualified for the post and that all the enhanced criminal checks would show that he had no convictions whatsoever in his 52 years of life.

Another part of the background checks that local authorities can activate are an application to the Teachers' Pension scheme, which will have an up-to-date account of a teacher's entire career. Lambeth HR applied for this printout on 26 August 2005. This record confirmed Brian Pead's name, date of birth, national insurance number and his qualifications. It also confirmed that he gained a First Class honours degree in the Bachelor of Education exams in 1986. It confirmed that his specialist subject was English and that he was trained to teach in both the primary and secondary sectors of education. The record also shows the last employer and the amount of pension contributions that a teacher has made. This document is evidence that everything that Brian Pead had stated on his job application could be confirmed by the Teachers' Pension Association. He had not lied at all.

It also showed that he had never used any other names in his teaching career.

For personal reasons – not illegitimate ones – he had sought permission to be known as Brian Johnson. This permission had been granted. The name was CRB checked.

10

is goa safe for the children?

On July 28th 2006 at the Hotel Fidalgo in Panjim on the Indian island of Goa, representatives of the ChildLine India Foundation (CIF) met with non-Government organisations and Government representatives to discuss "Is Goa Safe for the Children?" There were 48 participants. Representatives from CIF were Naushad Hasan Ansari, Nishit Kumar, Benoy T.D., Chitrakala Acharya and Surabhi Shrivastava.

The CHILDLINE India Foundation conducted a study on the issue related to child sexual abuse/paedophilia and sex related tourism. The objective was to study the perception of allied systems about the issue of paedophilia, challenges faced by Government Organisations and Non-Government Organisations while intervening in the cases of paedophilia and how the issue can be addressed. This study was based on in-depth interviews conducted with representatives from the different allied systems of Goa. During the course of the study 20 stakeholders were interviewed, which included Government and NGOs representatives. It was felt that it was important to disseminate the findings of the study with various stakeholders working in the area of child protection so that collective solutions to the existing challenges could be arrived in consultation with the state administration. The major objective of the consultation was to disseminate the findings of the study, to elicit support from stakeholders at different levels of interventions; to draft recommendation for action; present a strategy paper to Goa State Administration.

The workshop commenced with the introductory address by Ms Philomena Serrao, Nodal Director, CHILDLINE Goa. She introduced the chief guest Mr. T.S. Sawant, Director, Women and Child Welfare Government of Goa and other panel members sitting in the hall.

Mr. Nishit Kumar, Head: Awareness and Advocacy, CHILDLINE India Foundation, introduced the programme and also shared the current scenario of child sexual abuse, issues and challenges. This was followed by a brief sharing of the Anchorage case of Mumbai by Ms. Chitrakala Acharya, Head of Services, CHILDLINE India Foundation. The panel members were:

1. Ms. Anita Haladi, Member State Commission for Women and Children
2. Mr. Newman Fernandez, Principal, St. Xavier's College, Mapusa, Goa.
3. Ms. Nishta Desai, Consultant, Child Rights in Goa, Goa.
4. Ms. Shobha Tumaskar, Director of Prosecution, Goa.
5. Ms. Chitrakala Acharya, Head: Services, CIF, Mumbai.

A phone call on 1098 (the Indian ChildLine number) in 2000 reported the abuse of children in the Anchorage case, which unearthed the incidence of child sexual abuse in the shelter run by two ex-British Royal Navy members Duncan Grant and Allen

Waters. It took CHILDLINE and its associated partners five years of struggle and on Saturday, 18 March 2006, the court delivered a verdict convicting the two to a sentence of 6 years of imprisonment for offences related to unnatural sex and the abuse of children.
Source: Childline India Foundation

11

first steps in counselling

Pead had commenced his counselling studies in 2003 at the Sidcup Adult Education Centre in Birkbeck Road. He had found the course somewhat easy because he was regularly attending philosophy and psychology talks and discussions in London run by Inner Space <http://www.innerspace.org.uk/>.

Having completed Level 2, he then progressed to the next level but found the quality of teaching to be extremely poor. With years of teaching experience behind him, Pead believed that the tutor was not a good teacher and that she often "winged it" and was too repetitive in her methods. He resolved to leave the Sidcup Adult Education Centre and began researching other organisations in which he felt he would acquire a better education in his counselling studies.

Brian Pead takes his education – and the education of others – extremely seriously. From his youngest days in the children's home in Harpenden, he knew that education was his route out of poverty and towards a better life.

He chose to further his education at the Centre for Professional and Personal Development (CPPD) in Hornsey, north London. This meant that Pead would have a two-hour journey from his house to the college instead of a twenty-minute walk to the Sidcup centre, but this did not deter him because the quality of his education was important to him.

Student counsellors have to secure placements as part of their training, so that the focus is not entirely on academic theory but also on meeting real clients in real situations.

Pead researched several possible placements and one drew his attention: the Community Drug Service (CDS) in Wallington, Surrey. The agency worked with some extremely difficult clients who presented with chaotic lives. Some were hardened heroin addicts. Never having taken drugs in his life, this appealed to him because it would increase his knowledge around the subject of drugs and dependency.

He underwent an initial interview at CDS with Michael Bird and Vera Andrew, who, despite her name, was in fact, Russian. Both were experienced counsellors. They were seeking to fill four volunteer posts and in that process they interviewed fifteen people.

Of all the interviewees, Michael Bird felt that Brian stood out because of his understanding of the client group and the difficulties that they face, how difficult the client group find it to be socially accepted and how they feel marginalised by their choices to use illicit substances to make it through each day.

34

Both Bird and Andrew felt that Pead presented in an extremely professional manner. He asked more questions about the agency and the agency's goals than any other volunteer. This stood out as one of the main reasons for CDS appointing him. The questions he asked were challenging and were designed by Pead to elicit a response from his interviewers. This suggested to Bird and Andrew that he was really interested in the agency and what it did. This was unique amongst the volunteers, since none of the other volunteers wanted to know anything about the agency – their goal was merely to secure a counselling placement.

Vera Andrew was also impressed with the fact that Brian wanted to work at CDS and not just any agency to make his counselling hours up.

According to Michael Bird, this interview can be seen as indicative of what sets Brian Pead apart from most people. His fierce intelligence and sense of self enable him to ask searching questions. He wants the best for himself and those he loves or cares about. He wants the best for the homeless, or those using illicit substances.

At the CPPD counselling school, Pead was the only male counsellor in a group of 18. He was the last student to obtain a placement because of the way in which he works. He had decided that he would find a placement which would challenge him, which would enable him to learn a great deal and in which he felt his clients would most benefit from him. It took him several months to secure a placement. His supervisor, Clare Manifold, would often suggest to him that he needed to "hurry up and find a placement because all the other student counsellors have secured one", but this did not affect Pead in any way whatsoever. "I'll find the right one for me, and as yet the universe hasn't provided one for me, but I'm confident that it will come along soon," he told Manifold in one of their supervision meetings.

All of the other students in the group had already secured counselling hours. CPPD required students to complete 150 hours of one-to-one sessions with clients as part of their training. Some of his peers had already accrued up to 30 hours of working with clients. Pead had none, yet he was not going to join just **any** agency – it had to meet certain conditions.

In the event, Pead completed his 150 hours (and many more besides) before any of his peers. Some of his peers had rushed into "any old agency" so that they could complete their required hours, but they had not researched either the agency or the type of clients and this led to those who had rapidly accrued 30 or 40 hours suddenly finding that their clients no longer attended, or that the agency was employing further volunteers and reducing the number of hours each volunteer could work.

Pead does not operate in this manner. He is methodical and painstaking in his research – his first book, which took more than 20 years to complete, exemplifies this – and he had taken the trouble to look into the type of work undertaken by the Community Drug Service in Wallington. He had even taken a train there, to stand opposite the building and to observe the type of clients who entered or left the building. He had walked around Wallington town centre, spoken with local people and generally 'got a flavour of the place'. He had found out as much background information as he could before he even set foot in the building for his interview.

His slow, painstaking, thoughtful approach to his life often infuriates others, particularly those people who want to rush into a project. Pead believes that a more considered approach will bear fruit in the longer term and save a great deal of unnecessary work. And so it proved here.

Although he had completed his 150 hours before any other student, he was mindful of the fact that it was not a race. He had painstakingly researched the agency and the type of clients that that agency helped. He then researched the behaviour patterns of that client group before he even met any clients, so that he could build rapport and understanding quickly. He instinctively knew that once he had secured this knowledge about the client group, he would build up his client hours rapidly.

This incident alone shows Pead's enormous strength of character. In the past, unintelligent and uninformed people have chosen (usually for their own benefit) to view his strength of character as being "big-headed" or "aloof", but he is not. In fact, he is an extremely humble man. He learnt a great deal about humility throughout his life, but in particular when he spent time alone with Bob Paisley, the former Liverpool FC manager who wore cardigans and carpet slippers and who swept up the leaves in his own garden rather than employ a gardener. Humility is something that Pead actively strives for in his life.

During the interview with Bird and Andrew, Brian Pead brought up the fact that he wished to use the name of Steve Goodfellow and explained his reasoning. They fully understood why he felt the need to protect himself in such an environment and they added that he would need to include the name of Steve Goodfellow on the CRB checks that the agency undertook on his behalf. Again, this demonstrates Pead's transparency around his use of names.

Following the interview, both counsellors felt that they would be pleased to offer Pead the role. Another decisive factor was that Michael Bird was going to be Pead's supervisor and he instinctively felt that Pead's knowledge and experience would mean that he would not require considerable supervision.

One of his tutors at CPPD had told the students that she had once had a client who set up a tent in her front garden so as to be "closer to me." This event had been recounted in a discussion about counsellor self-disclosure and the tutor reported that some counsellors had chosen to work under a different name in order to protect themselves from unwanted attention from unbalanced clients. This appealed to Brian Pead, whose unusual surname would be easily traceable to any chaotic client. Some of these clients are highly manipulative and highly skilled at obtaining information. They have learnt to be, because otherwise they would not be able to "score".

One client whom Pead encountered was a recovering hardened heroin addict and, at the height of his addiction, the client memorised the entire bus timetable of a particular bus route that took him to a particular park to obtain his drug of choice. No matter what time of day or night his need arose, this client knew precisely what time the bus would arrive to take him to the park. In any other scenario, this man was intelligent enough to, perhaps, be managing Marks and Spencer or ICI or some other corporation. But he had chosen a path of drugs and employed his considerable intelligence towards securing a steady supply of narcotics.

Working with such clients, Pead resolved to use a different name. He spoke about this with his daughter, Sorrel, and with a number of friends. One friend suggested the name of Steve Goodfellow, and this was chosen as his counselling name.

Having taken the post as Head teacher of the Pupil Referral Unit in Lambeth and again working with pupils with often chaotic lives, he discussed using the name of Brian Johnson with Barry Gilhooly. He also informed Gilhooly that a condition of accepting the post as Head Teacher would be that he would be able to leave two hours early on a Tuesday afternoon and attend lectures at CPPD in Hornsey to continue his counselling training. Both men agreed that counselling was a useful additional skill to have when working in the Pupil Referral Unit, since almost all of the students had emotional difficulties and these were causing blocks to their academic as well as emotional progress.

Thus, upon accepting the post, it had been agreed that Pead could use a different name in order to protect himself and that he could continue his counselling training. Naturally, the name of Brian Johnson was checked by the Criminal Records Bureau (CRB), and Pead always added it to his birth name when the checks were made on a regular basis. He did, of course, have to be CRB checked when working at his counselling placements and he always declared both names, as well as the name of Steve Goodfellow.

Many members of the public may find the use of multiple names as highly unusual, but in counselling circles it is not necessarily that unusual. It does not automatically follow that someone using multiple names is 'up to no good'.

The police, however, often promulgate the idea that sex offenders use multiple names. They may well do so, but in promulgating such ideas to the general public, the police have sown a seed of doubt in the public's minds that anyone using different names must be a sex offender. They rarely make the link that John Wayne was born Marion Morrison, that Elton John is really just plain Reg Dwight and that the person born as Harry Rodger Webb uses the name of Cliff Richard. The worlds of film and popular music are heavily populated by people who use a different name from their birth name. Why, then, is it never suggested that they have employed a different name in order to commit acts of sexual abuse?

12

if you can bear to hear the truth you've spoken
TWISTed by knaves to make a trap for fools

Pead had ensured that his employers and agencies for which he worked and also his tutors at CPPD all knew of his uses of different names. He was completely transparent about this. He had also discussed with his daughter the possibility that he would permanently change his name from Pead by Deed Poll. He was open with her about this, and he also considered her feelings in the matter. She was living with her partner and had two children by him, but was unmarried and still using her name of Sorrel Pead and occasionally the name of Sorrel Birch, especially when dealing with her children's schools. Countless thousands of women throughout the land operate in this way, particularly in respect of their children's schools.

On Friday 26 May 2006, Brian Pead attended an individual supervision meeting with Clare Manifold, an official CPPD supervisor. Counsellors meet their supervisors on at least a monthly basis in order to discuss a counsellor's work. There are several benefits from such meetings. The main benefit is that the work of the counsellor is discussed and the supervisor is then able to check that standards are being met and that the BACP code of ethics is adhered to. These meetings help to provide checks and balances.

Another benefit is that if the counsellor is encountering certain difficulties with a client or clients, he or she is then able to discuss strategies to enable the work to move forward.

Yet another benefit is that theoretical approaches can be discussed, and Clare Manifold knew that Brian Pead had a voracious appetite for theory as well as practice.

The Centre for Personal and Professional Development insisted – quite rightly – that its students would undertake both individual supervision and group supervision.

At this time, Pead undertook his individual sessions on a Friday evening (since he was already in London when working at the OLCVS) and his group sessions on a Saturday morning.

Clare Manifold's house in Belsize Park is a rambling affair which houses a vast collection of elements of her life and which reflects her open personality, intelligence and wisdom. She would supervise counsellors in a room at the very top of her house.

This particular meeting commenced at 7.15pm, after Pead had completed a full day's work at the OLCVS in West Norwood.

Every supervisor – just like every counsellor – will have a different way in which they conduct supervision sessions. Clare Manifold and Brian Pead discussed ways as how best to run the meetings which suited their individual needs. They agreed that each would come to the session with points for discussion, and that each session would start with them both creating the agenda in the 'here and now'.

Brian Pead's first agenda item was his use of names. This was discussed with Clare Manifold, who offered him useful advice and suggested that he add the name of Steve Goodfellow to the CRB form when he was next to be checked. Both Brian Pead and Clare Manifold made meticulous notes of their meetings. Brian Pead still has in his possession notes from meetings with Clare Manifold. It is therefore clear that his use of multiple names was not the work of a furtive individual. He had had discussions about his use of names with his tutors at CPPD, his peers, his daughter, his friends and colleagues. There was nothing secretive or sinister about this behaviour. It was all undertaken with considerable transparency.

There would shortly come a time, however, when Lambeth Council and Gilhooly attempted to make great capital out of Pead's use of various names.

13

volunteer counsellor

Pead was offered a role as a volunteer counsellor at the Community Drug Service in Wallington, Surrey and started with three male clients on Monday 7 August 2006.

His first client was homosexual and he was struggling with this, since his family was extremely religious and unable to accept his sexuality. For the first fourteen hours – that is, over a period of fourteen consecutive weeks – the client would enter the room with a book, throw it down on the coffee table so that Pead could see it (the client was trying to impress his counsellor with his knowledge) and proceed to cry, holding his head in his hands in a foetal position and sob like a baby.

Week after week.

The weeks slipped into months. The same pattern was acted out each week. This client would have been an extremely challenging client for even the most experienced of counsellors. This was Pead's first client in that agency. It seemed to Pead that his client was experiencing deep psychological pain in which he felt unloved and unheard and unaccepted. Pead decided to "hold" his client – simply be there every week for him, speak whenever a moment arose, but generally simply listen and be available to the client in a way in which his family was not.

After working with this client for eighteen months, he not only came to accept himself as he was – homosexual – but he also went on to train (on Pead's suggestion) as a counsellor himself. These two men had been on an immense journey. With no previous knowledge of the gay community, Pead learnt a great deal about the psychology of homosexual relationships from this client.

The authors are, naturally, unable to name the clients that Brian Pead (counselling as Steve Goodfellow) encountered for reasons of confidentiality. However, it can be confirmed that he had four clients over a period of eighteen months.

This was, in itself, extremely unusual. Four is a relatively small number of clients over such a long period of time in an agency dealing with such a chaotic clientele.

The reason for this small number was that his clients *kept returning* – this is, again, highly unusual for such distressed clients. The normal behaviour patterns established by such clients is that they attend three or four sessions and then drift away from the service, often never to be seen again, or, if they do return, it is often many months or years later.

Yet Pead – a student counsellor – had created such conditions that his clients kept returning. If a client was unable to attend due to other (external) pressures such as work or other commitments, they would always call Pead and apologise and they would always return the following week.

This unusual pattern of high attendance became noted in the agency. Other student counsellors would ask Pead why his clients always showed up and theirs didn't. Pead didn't like to discuss this because, although he was aware of the reasons why his clients kept returning, if he discussed it, it would appear that he was an egotist, when, in fact, the opposite was true.

In fact, the conditions that Brian Pead set for his clients in making them feel comfortable, welcomed and supported were well beyond the level of any other student counsellor according to his agency supervisor, Michael Bird.

He ensured that he would arrive in the counselling room at least fifteen minutes before the scheduled appointment. He would arrange the furniture in the small room so that each person had sufficient personal space. He sometimes lit a candle. Occasionally he would play relaxing music in the background. He would ensure that the lighting was sufficient, and that the room was adequately warm. He would read through his client notes, to refresh his memory of their previous sessions and to look for patterns of behaviour or themes running through their work together.

When the client arrived, Pead would ask if they wanted a cup of tea or coffee. His first thought was to put the client at his or her ease, and to normalise the situation as if it were two friends meeting for a chat.

Clients also commented on his trust and balanced self-disclosure. Pead would put his clients on their trust. He refused to work with any client who arrived under the influence of drugs or alcohol. He told his clients that he would terminate his work with them on the spot if they ever arrived in this condition, as he felt it was disrespectful to both him and themselves.

Occasionally, he would disclose elements of his own life where it was judged to be appropriate. (For this reason, the use of the counselling name Steve Goodfellow was obviously a sensible safety device).

There is much discussion and divergence between counsellors with regard to self-disclosure. Many counsellors do not like to self-disclose and the reasons for this are varied. Some counsellors like to offer something of themselves in sessions, whilst others believe they should remain "distant" or "aloof" or even provide a "blank canvass".

Whilst respecting all of these views, Pead does not subscribe to them. His view is that if he occasionally shares some examples of his life or his pain with clients, it somehow has the effect of reducing his client's pain because they can hear how another human being has suffered, and that "other" is now sitting opposite them as a counsellor. It can even be inspiring.

Bird felt that Pead's level of ability as a trainee counsellor was far beyond that of many counsellors with many years' counselling experience behind them.

Through their supervision sessions together, Bird found Brian Pead to be a very open and self-inquiring student counsellor who took his supervision very seriously and his learning, therefore, of himself as a counsellor grew significantly during the eighteen months he was at CDS.

Michael Bird and Brian Pead would meet in supervision sessions to discuss the clients that Pead was seeing at CDS. They explored psychosexual topics because all of his male clients – Pead only encountered male clients at CDS – had issues around sex. One was homosexual and was initially unable to accept his sexuality. Another client, aged 24, was married to a woman significantly older than him at 42 who used sex, or the withdrawal of sexual relations, as a means of control and a third client who had been sexually abused by an older female cousin when he was in his early teens. A fourth client saw all women as "slags", which was clearly an unhealthy view to adopt.

When dealing with adult clients, the issue of sex will almost always present itself during sessions. A counsellor who fails to educate him- or herself around psychosexual matters would be a poor counsellor. Michael Bird encouraged Pead to research these areas for Pead's better understanding of his clients.

Occasionally, Bird and Pead would meet in the kitchen at CDS and, over tea and a Pret sandwich, Pead would seek Bird's counsel on a particular issue with his client.

Throughout the year, Pret support hundreds of charities by giving their unsold sandwiches to them at the end of each day. The Pret Charity Run operates LPG vans that deliver over 12,000 fresh meals to numerous shelters in London every week. Many charities across the UK collect directly from Pret shops at the end of each day, too.

In total, Pret donates over 2.4 million products to charities for the homeless across the UK every year believing that "...It's much better our natural food goes to people who really need it at the end of the day and not in the bin..."

Pret prefers to work on long-term arrangements with charities to ensure that as much food gets to the homeless as possible. Over 90% of their shops in the UK give their food to a homeless charity, but tragically a few do not, due to their location or because Pret struggles to find volunteers to collect from them.
Source: <www.pret.com/pret_foundation_trust/charity_run.htm>

Pead also sought permission and written consent from all of his clients to record their sessions together. They always agreed. He would therefore listen to these sessions as he travelled home from the agency, or to work the next day. He would analyse his comments to clients, or look for things they had said that he had missed in the moment and he would berate himself if he felt that his work was not of the highest possible standard. These tapes were also made available to Clare Manifold so that she, too, could analyse his work and offer a constructive critique wherever necessary.

But, Michael Bird believes, what sets Pead apart from most other people is that he is prepared to be unpopular in order to deliver the best outcome for those he is working with. He was prepared to be an unpopular teacher with his colleagues because of his insistence on delivering the best teaching to his pupils. Similarly, he was prepared to be unpopular with his counselling peers because of his insistence on delivering quality counselling sessions to distressed human beings. In other words, he was quite willing to sublimate his ego in order to help others.

Not many people are able to do this – they seek the popularity of others and sublimate their desire to be the best they can be in order to "make friends" with others. Pead feels that this lacks integrity and that the friendships created in such conditions are false.

He was quite prepared to upset other counsellors because of his insistence on working in the same room each week so that his clients could feel safe and secure in familiar surroundings.

On one such occasion, he was berated by a colleague because he refused to change the room which had been allocated to him. He knew this room represented safety and security to his clients and for this reason he insisted on keeping the room.

His colleague, however, insisted that he was "unreasonable" and "dogmatic". Even when he presented her with his reasons for wanting to maintain his sessions in that room, she still felt that he was acting out of an ego position rather than seeing that Pead's focus was on the wellbeing of his clients. She was unable to learn from him. She was the one, in fact, who was acting out of her ego, yet she was projecting this on to Pead, who was merely being compassionate towards his clients.

Pead is always prepared to make his working relationship more difficult because of his clients or, in former days, his pupils. He does not actively seek confrontations, but situations will occur in the course of his working life in which his desire to meet the needs of his clients or pupils will mean that he will assert their rights on their behalf. His methods are not the 'normal' methods used by his colleagues or peers, but they are always highly successful. Just as he had refused to label 10 and 11 year old pupils he taught at Gravel Hill Primary School in 1999 as 'stupid' or having 'special needs' (they went on to achieve the highest-ever SAT results in the history of the school), he would alienate other staff because he would put pupils and clients before others and before himself.

Brian Pead goes outside the boundaries of 'norm'. This takes tremendous courage. It invites criticism. It invites hostility. It invites attacks, and this puts enormous risks upon himself as he seeks to get to the best possible place for the other person.

Although not a practising Buddhist, Brian Pead subscribes to many of their philosophical perspectives. He has read a large number of books on the subject of Buddhism. He lives by the Buddhist credo:

"Do not believe something just because wise men say so. Do not believe something just because it has always been that way. Do not believe something just because others may believe so. Examine your self. Experience your self."

When he was Chairman of Sidcup Round Table in 1993, Pead set great store in the Round Table maxim of "Adopt, Adapt, Improve."

Brian Pead was working full-time at Lambeth, attending CPPD on the Advanced Diploma course and he was also undertaking a complete refurbishment on his semi-detached house in Sidcup. He was also undergoing weekly supervision on an individual and also on a group basis. He would be travelling between West Norwood in south London and Belsize Park and Hornsey in north London. He would also be travelling to Wallington in Surrey for his counselling placement and he was organising building materials for his home. His workload was unremitting.

A good friend, John Callow – whom he met at Sidcup Adult Education Centre whilst they both were undertaking the Level 3 counselling course – was working as a telephone advisor in a charitable agency which focused entirely on clients who had been sexually abused and/ or raped. Both Pead and Callow visited another trainee counsellor's house on a weekly basis and shared intimate details of their Personal Learning Journals between January 2006 and May 2006. They got to know each other well during this period and that Easter they went to Malta for a break, the holiday cementing their friendship. They were also both members of the Esporta Leisure Centre in Sidcup <http://www.esporta.com/>.

Callow had been employed by British Telecom as a manager installing cabling systems which would provide broadband and television to BT customers. At the age of 55, Callow had years of management and surveying experience behind him.

Brian Pead would often inform John Callow of his doubts surrounding the job at Lambeth. Callow's years of experience helped him inform Pead that it appeared to be an enterprise set up not to help pupils without an education but as a 'front' for something else. Both Pead and Callow knew that it is not feasible to set up a school without a home, without a budget, without staff and without any equipment. The Old Library Centre Virtual School was – to some extent – operating in a world of virtual reality.

Brian Pead would challenge Barry Gilhooly about the OLCVS. It was under-funded and under-staffed, yet there was a tremendous need to not only deal with the pupils' academic needs, but also their often severe emotional needs.

Pead was equipped to deal with these needs, but he needed assistance. Gilhooly finally relented. Eloise Whitmore was assigned the task of calling a teaching agency and securing the services of a supply teacher for the subject of Information and Communication Technology (ICT).

14

south african smile

A Marion Murray arrived at the OLCVS in November 2005. When Pead briefly interviewed her, he found out that her name was not, in fact, Marion, but Maryn. She was a white South African and spoke English and Afrikaans. She apparently had qualifications in ICT and had recently left a girls' school in Ealing where she claimed to have been Head of ICT. The school was called St. Augustine's Priory Catholic School for Girls. She claimed that she started working there in September 2000. Murray claimed that in February 2005 she applied for a sabbatical which started in September of that year. She presented as an open and friendly individual.

Brian Pead was astute enough to know that how someone presents themselves to the outside world upon a first meeting is rarely their true self. It will usually be a mask which they use to protect themselves, to draw attention to or away from themselves, or simply to get other people to like them. To some extent, everybody wears a mask in public. Some people's masks are used to defend them to such an extent that you never actually learn much about them, however long you spend in their company. At the other extreme, some people appear to be fully open and transparent and not actually wearing a mask and the other person who encounters them is led to believe that the person is open and transparent, but the wise person will see that this apparent openness and transparency is, in itself, a mask to deflect attention away from whatever the mask-wearer is hiding.

Pead had managed people from the age of 18. He was now 52 years of age and had thus been in management positions for almost 35 years. In all that time he had managed thousands of people and learnt something about group and individual dynamics.

Maryn Murray had presented as a grinning, open personality. If she was fully congruent Pead knew that this would be close to her true personality. If, on the other hand, she was not being congruent, she would be the 'smiling assassin'. Only time would tell which was her true self.

Initially she conducted herself well, and appeared to make some positive relationships with pupils, but it soon became apparent that there was a mismatch between her attitude to female pupils and male pupils, especially black males. As is his custom, Pead made a note of this mismatch.

fraser hall

With Brian Pead having to take more of a back-seat so that he could oversee the OLCVS from a general's position rather than forever dwell in the trenches, Fraser Hall walked through the doors from a different teaching agency.

Hall was a 25 year old New Zealander with a "can-do" attitude. He had come from a good family and was particularly close to one of his grand-fathers. Hall's wisdom was beyond that of a normal 25 year old and Brian Pead felt that this was because of the quality of Hall's relationship with his grand-father. As a grand-father himself, Pead understood this type of relationship.

Hall taught Maths. He initially struggled to understand the emotional depth of the students he encountered, but he discussed this with Pead and after a few days the situation settled down for the New Zealander, who would employ humour wherever he could.

Hall worked prodigiously and independently, though he was also a team player. Brian Pead saw something of his younger self in Hall and the two men shared many happy conversations together.

When Pead acquired an inter-active whiteboard, Hall made excellent use of this to engage the students in some brilliant lessons. He planned lessons well, marked all of the work efficiently and was generally a great addition to the team.

It was a great shame to Pead when Hall announced that he would be leaving the Centre in December 2006 to return to his native country upon the death of his grand-father.

16

extension to contract - 1

On 8 December 2005, Barry Gilhooly signed form LPS4, which was an extension to Brian Pead's contract. The original contract expired on 31 December 2005, but Gilhooly had extended it until 31 March 2006.

Brian Pead felt that this was still unreasonable, given the amount of effort he had put into creating and developing the Unit, but he accepted the extension and tabled a motion with Gilhooly to discuss the award of a one-year contract when they next met.

Such was Lambeth's tardiness when it came to paperwork that the extension was not signed off until 21 December 2005.

a field with dreams

Another member of staff whom Pead engaged was Annabel Field, a teacher of English and part-time actress. Although Pead had been the sole teacher in the first few months of the OLCVS, he knew that in order to expand the unit he would have to employ others to undertake the teaching responsibilities whilst he oversaw the 'bigger picture'. Alicia Harris introduced Annabel Field to Brian at the OLCVS in January 2006. Brian had met Alicia at the Library in West Norwood. She was of a similar age to Annabel Field – around 25-26 – and yet she never questioned Brian's motives.

In November 2005, Pead asked Field to teach a lesson in English to his pupils. Pead was to observe. If he liked what he saw, he would hire her. If he didn't, she could go on her way. He liked what he had seen and she started work at the OLCVS in the following January.

Alicia Harris and Annabel Field had met at the Guildford School of Acting (GSA).

"...The GSA has grown from the Grant-Bellairs School of Dance and Drama which was founded in London in 1935. It moved to Guildford at the beginning of World War II and operated from premises opposite the Yvonne Arnaud Theatre, the Founders Studio. In 1964 the Guildford School of Acting was constituted as a private charitable company whose objectives were to provide vocational training for actors and stage managers..."
Source: <http://www.conservatoire.org/home/index.php?dept=21&id=417>

Annabel Field was a 25 year old woman who was lost in her dreams. She could not make up her mind whether she wanted to teach, or whether she wanted to act. Indecision was her greatest enemy. Yet, despite this relatively common trait, she nevertheless possessed great passion, though failed to realise that passion alone is rarely enough to become successful. Other qualities are necessary – particularly that of commitment. Yet Pead liked and admired her. She had integrity and no little courage. He felt that one day she could become a formidable woman. He knew that her passion would be noted by the pupils, especially the females, and that they would be carried along on this tide of passionate creativity. He felt that, as long as he monitored it from a distance, it would be no bad thing. Annabel could also use her acting skills to enthuse her captive audience. And, Pead hoped, she would inspire some of the pupils to share her love of English and Drama.

Pead often had to mentor her, almost like a wise father on occasions. Sometimes her passion would run away with itself and she would be reduced to tears of frustration, particularly when the pupils didn't actually share her passion for Shakespeare or classical literature.

18

the field good factor

After three months working in the OLCVS, the indecisive Annabel Field had finally made a decision. She emailed Brian Pead:

From:	annabel field
Sent:	17 April 2006 16:35:58
To:	brian johnson
Subject:	update!

Dear Brian,

Hello! I hope you've had a fantastic holiday whatever you did - Tunisia or not! I know I'm going to see you tomorrow but I thought I'd e-mail you cos (sic) lots has happened in the last couple of weeks and I want to keep you up to date! As predicted after our chat - this has been a very reflective holiday for me!

To cut a long story short the gist of it is that I'm moving out of London in the next couple of weeks. I know that this is not ideal in terms of the exam groups and I'm sorry for that. I did intend to stay on but to be honest, the chance has suddenly come up this weekend to move to Bath and I feel that I have to take it as soon as possible in an effort to quosh (sic) my recent restless state!

I am sorry to make things difficult for you guys - I do feel bad but hey I'm sure there is someone ready and waiting to take on the job without having crazy burning ambitions to act at the same time!

I know that I'm gonna see you but just to let you know at this point that I have really enjoyed working at the school - and its definately (sic) been my most positive teaching experience in London. Thank you for all your support to me!

I'll see you tomorrow and I'll certainly aim to get the English work as organised as possible over the next week or so.

Laters!

Annabel

It is evident from this email that Annabel Field had enjoyed a positive relationship with Brian Pead. She had referred to their 'chat' in a positive way.

49

She provides a reason for leaving her post – a move to Bath to pursue an acting career.

She is also considerate enough to tell Brian that she has enjoyed working at the school. She goes on to say that it has been her most positive teaching experience in London. She then specifically thanks him for all his support and uses an exclamation mark for added emphasis.

She signs off on a positive note: "Laters!"

It is important to note that Annabel Field sent this email completely unsolicited.

19

turkish delight

On 26 April 2006, just nine days after receiving Annabel Field's positive email and news that she was to leave the OLCVS, Pead attended a Life Coaching seminar in London. There he met a Turkish Muslim woman called Ipek Yÿlmaz who went by the name of Elif. The number of people who use multiple names or who are only known by their nickname is a common feature of this book.

Although only 25 to Pead's 52, they soon became lovers. She was a highly intelligent woman whom Pead admired. She had come to England to develop her English speaking skills. They shared many intellectual debates and she particularly liked his intelligence and ability to see outside of the box, as she put it.

20

theatre invite

Annabel Field breezed into the OLCVS office bursting over with excitement. She had just landed the role of Lizzy Price in a play called 'The Horse Dealer's Daughter' at the White Bear Theatre in Kennington. She invited all of the staff to come and watch her act.

21

cracks

At this time, cracks in the team were beginning to manifest themselves. Pead knew this to be normal. A wise manager predicts what might happen at this stage and then closely observes. Pead was a student of all things psychological since his days in speech therapy after he was first sexually abused at the age of 5, upon learning about the concept of 'quis custodiet ipsos custodes?' (who will guard the guards themselves?) at the age of 11 in his first Latin lesson with Mr Campion at Hinchley Wood Secondary School in Surrey and as a manager for more than 35 years.

The psychologist Bruce Tuckman first came up with the memorable phrase "forming, storming, norming and performing" back in 1965. He used it to describe the path to high-performance that most teams follow. Later, he added a fifth stage that he called "adjourning". Others often call this stage "mourning" since it better describes the emotions surrounding the disbanding of a group.

Teams initially go through a 'forming' stage in which members are positive and polite. Some members might be anxious, as they haven't yet worked out exactly what work the team will involve. Others are excited about the task ahead. A manager and leader will play a dominant role at this stage, while other members' roles and responsibilities are less clear.

This stage is usually relatively short, and may only last for the single meeting at which people are introduced to one another, though this is rarer. At this stage there may be discussions about how the team will work, which can be frustrating for some members who simply want to get on with the team task.

Brian Pead took it upon himself to fully explain to his team the specific roles that they would be required to undertake. He knew this to be essential if he was to 'get them on board' and performing to their potential.

Soon, the 'honeymoon period' is over, reality sets in and the team moves into a 'storming' phase. The manager's authority may be challenged as others jockey for position and their roles are clarified and they become more secure in themselves. The ways of working start to become defined and the wise leader will become aware that some members may feel overwhelmed by how much there is to do, or uncomfortable with the approach being used.

It became obvious to Brian Pead that Eloise Whitmore was not only a loose cannon, but also someone who was ill-equipped to perform the role of a school secretary. Compounding these difficulties was the fact that she possessed, in his opinion, a destructive personality, viewing anything outside of her sphere of knowledge as "odd" or "freaky" or "weird". She had little awareness of herself or others. She began to question everything, needlessly.

Brian Pead is a man who questions everything. He usually gets along with such like-minded people, but only if their questioning is constructive and adds to the team's knowledge. Eloise Whitmore challenged everything in a destructive way. Even when Brian Pead explained to her and other members of the team his reasons for managing as he did, she would still continue to ask "Why?" in the manner of a rebellious teenager. This naturally became tiresome, since it used up a lot of time which could have been put to more constructive use.

According to Tuckman, some members of the team may react by questioning how worthwhile the goal of the team is, and by resisting taking on tasks. This is the stage when many teams fail, and even those who remain focussed on the task may feel that they are on an emotional roller coaster, as they try to focus on the job in hand without the support of established processes or relationships with their colleagues.

There was a three-month review of Eloise Whitmore's work as part of her probationary period. Brian Pead arranged to meet with her in order to discuss this review. He patiently explained to her that she had failed and he sensitively provided her with examples of why she had failed, and also the things she needed to address with immediate effect.

She was not at all happy with the review, confronting Pead in an aggressive manner. She did not appear to think that there was anything wrong with typing out the same letter on five occasions before finally producing a version that could be sent out to parents. Nor did she appear to think that there was anything wrong with lacking the skills necessary to operate as a school secretary. She merely denied that she was under-performing and refused to take responsibility for herself.

Brian Pead had followed all of Lambeth Council's policies and procedures. In fact, he had 'gone the extra mile' and had been exceedingly patient with Whitmore, explaining ways in which she might be able to pass her second probationary period.

Whitmore failed to address the situation and then became nasty towards Brian Pead, often not speaking with him unless it was absolutely necessary.

Pead sought the counsel of Lambeth's Human Relations department, and he asked to meet with Rosa Vaz, head of that department. They met in a café near to the OLCVS during Pead's lunch break. Rosa Vaz came to the conclusion that Eloise Whitmore was not able to conduct herself in a professional manner and that she was unable to fulfil her role.

Immediately afterwards, Eloise Whitmore sought the advice of her union, the GMB <http://www.gmb.org.uk/home.aspx>. The General Municipal Boilermakers Union called a meeting with Brian Pead and he, in turn, asked that he be accompanied by Rosa Vaz.

The meeting took place in an upstairs room at the OLCVS on a warm spring day. The Union representative, Robin Irwin, was a particularly obnoxious character who had clearly made up his mind about Pead before the meeting even started. Within a few minutes, he accused Pead of wanting to dismiss Whitmore on the basis that she was of child-bearing age. At no point in their previous discussions had this point ever been raised. Thus it was clear that the GMB union was attempting to seek compensation if Whitmore were dismissed. Pead did not agree with the fact that her being of child-bearing age was at all relevant to these proceedings. In fact, he didn't possess the knowledge of whether she could even have children!

Brian Pead tried to focus the meeting on the relevant issues – that Whitmore did not possess the necessary gravitas for the role of school secretary, nor did she possess the appropriate ability to perform her role and her under-performance was impeding the progress and development of the pupil referral unit.

At this point in the meeting, Whitmore claimed that she was never aware that she would have to undertake a period of probation, yet this had been made clear to all the staff in their letters of engagement from Lambeth Council. However, Whitmore was being supported by an aggressive and bullying union representative who then accused Pead of bullying Whitmore.

As the meeting drew to a close, Whitmore and her representative left the room and Pead and Vaz discussed whether to maintain Whitmore's employment, or dispense with her services for good. It was agreed between both parties that – under the circumstances – it would be better to release Whitmore, Pead seeing that she offered nothing constructive and Vaz seeing that the introduction of Whitmore's child-bearing age was a potential disaster for Lambeth in the future.

The outcome was that this debacle – originally created by Barry Gilhooly who employed her without consulting with Pead and when she was clearly not able to undertake the role – finished with Whitmore being awarded the sum of £8,000 for her dismissal in an out-of-court settlement! Thus she had been a wholly destructive force, she had underperformed, she was not qualified for the role and she walked away with a cheque for £8,000. This was Lambeth tax-payers' money, unwisely spent.

Gilhooly's lack of judgment was apparent to Pead and a number of his friends and colleagues. It should be noted that Pead's friends are made up of a wide and a diverse group, both male and female and of all ages from 18 to 85.

Although his friends are extremely diverse, they share one common trait – they are not afraid to challenge Pead in his thinking or in his actions. Which is precisely why he chooses them as his friends. He is not at all attracted to people who might be described as 'yes-men or women'.

Another trait shared by Pead's friends is one of intelligence, whether that is intellectual intelligence or – even more likely – emotional intelligence. For a better understanding of the term emotional intelligence or EQ, visit: <http://danielgoleman.info/topics/emotional-intelligence/>. Pead likes his friends to challenge and inspire him, to teach him and help him see things that he might have missed. In return, he provides the same 'service' for them.

Pead's friends and colleagues were extremely disparaging towards Lambeth. Their collective years of experience informed them that Lambeth Council was not investing properly in the Pupil Referral Unit both in terms of finance, but also in terms of a permanent building, a settled staff and the tools to undertake the job properly.

annabel field aka lizzy price

Between Tuesday 9 May and Sunday 14 May 2006, Annabel Field played the part of Lizzy Price in a play called "The Horse Dealer's Daughter". This new play by Jeremy Robinson was, as Robinson himself describes, "...inspired by a short story by D.H. Lawrence. Set in 1916, a doctor saves a young woman from drowning in a lake, culminating in a classic Lawrencean scene of the rebirth of the body and the soul through the healing power of love..."

With a running time of one hour and fifteen minutes, the play had first shown at the Brook Theatre in Chatham before moving to the White Bear Theatre in Kennington. It was promoted by the Ocean Magic Theatre Company. Annabel Field had mentioned this to all the staff and asked if any of her colleagues would like tickets. Pead said that he would like two tickets (for which he paid the full price of £10 for each ticket).

The White Bear Theatre describes itself thus:

"...The White Bear Theatre was established in 1988 and focuses on new writing and Lost Classics. It exists to nurture talent, extend possibilities and offer a space where risks can be taken. People who have cut their teeth at The White Bear include: Joe Penhall, Emily Watson, Tamsin Outhwaite, Kwami Kwei Armah, Vicky Featherstone, Torben Betts, Lucinda Coxon..."
Source: <http://www.whitebeartheatre.co.uk/about-the-white-bear-theatre/>

Brian Pead and Elif Yÿlmaz had arrived at the White Bear Theatre early on Saturday 13 May 2006, so bought drinks and sat outside on the benches on the pavement to the front of the pub. Soon afterwards, Annabel Field arrived and Brian introduced his companion to her. Annabel hugged Brian upon seeing him.

When Brian and Elif actually entered the theatre where the play was to be enacted, they saw a room of about 8 metres square.

LondonTown.com had visited the pub and theatre and reviewed the venue thus:

"...It's easy to spot who's at the White Bear for the pints and who's there for the Pinter but somehow the two aspects unite comfortably under one roof. While the pub is a genuine local, complete with TV screens and no frills food, the regulars happily co-exist with the theatre-going visitors [...]

Since 1988 the White Bear Theatre has been bringing people to [...] this South London boozer. It has received numerous awards including Time Out Best Fringe Venue, Peter Brook Empty Space Award for Best Up and Coming Venue, and the Carling London Fringe Awards for Best Actor and

Best Production. Some of their highly regarded theatrical shows have transferred to the West End.

Precisely because of its small scale - it has around 40 seats - the audience get to experience the drama all the more intensely. During a particularly energetic battle scene, for example, you'll be close enough to can (sic) see every bead of sweat. As you would expect, the productions vary wildly in quality, but prices are reasonable, and when it's good, the sheer intimacy means that it's very good indeed..."

Source: <http://www.londontown.com/LondonInformation/Entertainment/White_Bear_Theatre/7442/>

This completely independent review of the White Bear Theatre had been in the public domain on the LondonTown.com website, which was London's first full service internet site for visitors to London starting over 15 years ago.

It is an important review for reasons which will be discussed later.

The review calls the theatre a "...small room..." It states that there are "...around 40 seats..." It states that members of the audience will "...be close enough to see every bead of sweat..." on the actors' faces in an energetic battle scene.

These facts – long in the public domain – were to become extremely important.

So that he could stretch out his legs, Brian and Elif sat together in the front row, holding hands. The audience that evening was sparse and no other audience members were on either side of them. No members of the cast or audience were introduced to Brian or Elif.

After the play, Brian and Elif met Annabel in the pub. They all shared a round of drinks before Brian and his companion caught a train to Sidcup. As they left the theatre, Annabel hugged Brian and thanked him and Elif for coming to watch her performance.

It is important to note here the following:

(i)   that neither Brian nor Elif was introduced to anyone else on that evening

(ii)   that Annabel thanked Brian and Elif for attending the play

(iii)   that Annabel hugged Brian as he left the pub

(iv)   that this event occurred in May 2006.

An innocent and enjoyable night out at the theatre was to have serious repercussions for Pead some months later when the Machiavellian Murray was fed back with this information by Field.

the low-cut top conversation - 1

With Eloise Whitmore now gone, Maryn Murray sought to take her position as school secretary. She was by now teaching ICT (Information and Communication Technology). When not teaching her subject, she worked on the new office computer that Pead had finally managed to requisition. Pead had asked her to create a database of all the pupils, with full contact details and he also wanted their academic progress charted. Murray claimed that she had the capability to create this database.

One lunch-time, a female pupil by the name of Chloe Gordon came into the office where Pead was sitting eating his sandwiches and Murray was sitting at the computer.

Chloe Gordon was 14 years of age. She was a bright, blonde-haired young woman with some attitude. She had a mind of her own, which Brian liked and respected. She was 'street-wise' and not unintelligent. She had not really had a settled time throughout her entire secondary school career. Despite being a reasonably mature young woman, Chloe had something of a short fuse at times and Brian worked on this. She could be entirely reasonable one moment and then 'fly off the handle' the next moment. In spite of this, she and Brian established a positive working relationship.

Chloe, Pead knew as she entered his office, was agitated. Something had upset her.

"Sir," she said, "I've just been to my hair-dressing job and the manageress has asked me to wear a low-cut top."

Pead thought for a moment. His first instinct is always to protect himself and he felt relaxed because there was a female teacher – Maryn Murray – in the room.

"Ok, so what do you feel about that?" he replied.

"Well, I don't want to," she responded.

"Do you know why she has asked you?"

"Yes, I suppose if I flash 'em, it'll get me more tips and bring in more customers, but I don't want all the men perving over my boobs, Sir!"

"Right," said Pead, "if you don't want to wear low-cut tops in your job, what are the consequences?"

"I'll lose my job! And I need the money!"

"Ok, and what are the consequences to you if you *do* wear low-cut tops?"

"I'll feel bad and degraded and feel that I only got the job because of my boobs and not because I want to be a hairdresser!"

"Hmmm," said Pead, before pausing. "So, you either lose your job because you won't wear the low-cut tops, or you'll feel awful about yourself if you keep your job and have to wear the low-cut tops?"

"Yes, exactly!"

"So then, what do you propose to do about it?"

Pead was always keen to assist pupils in their thinking, but not think for them. He believed that Chloe was more than capable of making this decision on her own, but she needed to work through her self-doubt and find her own voice. He had done a lot of work with Chloe in respect of her finding her own voice and not being led by others, sometimes with more powerful personalities than her own.

Pead thought that this event – which lasted no more than five minutes – was the end of the matter, but it was to play a significant role in his life several months later.

24

space invader

Brian Pead was a keen observer of everything that occurred in the Unit he was running. Like a male lion protecting his pride of cubs, he would observe every pupil as he or she entered the building and he was highly in tune with their mood that day. On occasions he would make a comment or two that would ensure that an angry mood would be placated before that anger would have an opportunity to erupt in the classroom and thus become a destructive force. Pead would use the anger and explain to pupils that it was ok to feel anger, but that it has to be channelled correctly if it is not to be a destructive force in one's life. Most of the pupils had strong reasons to be angry about their lot in life and Brian Pead understood this. He had come from a similar background and knew only too well the feelings associated with such under-privileged beginnings. Yet he had managed to harness his own anger into a positive life force.

One morning, Talya Cuthbert arrived at the Centre and Pead detected that she was not 'her usual self'. He knew that Talya was a person who had to be handled sensitively. In that way, she was no different from the other pupils. Something was clearly troubling her but Pead knew that he would have to give her time to settle into the day and her usual routine. He chose his moment at break-time later that same day.

"Hey, Talya, you don't seem your usual self today. Anything wrong?"

He would often speak to pupils (and staff) in this somewhat invitational way. He would let them know that he had seen that something might be wrong and gently ask if anything was the matter. The pupil or member of staff then had the choice of whether to answer or not, or how far to go in terms of talking about the problem, or – rarely – that there wasn't a problem anyway. An extremely empathic man, Pead was rarely wrong about the students or staff in his care.

"Well," began Talya, tentatively, "it's Miss Murray."

"Go on."

"It's hard to put my finger on it, but she bothers me."

"Ok, can you describe your feelings about her?"

"Well, she keeps invading my space, my personal space."

"How, exactly?"

"If I don't understand something when I'm working on my laptop, she'll come right over to me and lean right in, right close, as if she's trying to get closer to me physically. I move away and she moves even closer in on me. I hate it!"

"Have you mentioned it to her, Tal?"

"No, I told my mum about it last night and she said I should mention it to you first."

Pead thought about his pupil's words. Then he asked a question that he had come to ask many times: "What would you like me to do, Tal?"

He always gave the problem back to the pupil. He believed that one of the ways for the pupils to overcome their lack of self-esteem or to gain control back in their lives was to empower them. He would listen. He would ask the odd question or two to gain greater clarification – and then he would always ask the pupil what he or she wanted done about a situation, if anything. In Pead's world, they had to have the power and take responsibility for their own lives – within reason. Pead knew it was useless giving power to a pupil who was unable to cope emotionally with that power.

But Talya was not this type of pupil. She was an extremely mature, spiritual and thoughtful person of fifteen years of age.

"I want it to stop."

"Sure, I get that, but how?"

"I suppose I could mention it to her next time she does it."

"Sure. Good idea. Anything else?"

"Could you have a quiet word in her ear, too?"

"That's what you want from me?"

"Yes please."

And the matter was resolved. Talya Cuthbert knew that Brian Pead's manner was never to make a great deal out of human matters and that he mostly resolved all issues with a 'quiet word in someone's ear'. This ability to defuse any situation was a key ingredient to the successful running of the Unit.

So Pead approached Murray about it when the most opportune moment presented itself. Murray immediately went on to the defensive, as was her manner. Behind the wide grin and flashing white teeth was a bullish temperament that didn't take kindly to any form of criticism. She always had to be right. She would often wag her finger at members of staff during meetings and several had mentioned it to Pead.

Murray did not like it being suggested to her that she should think about how close she got to pupils' personal space. She objected to the fact that she had ever invaded any pupil's space and this was indicative of her lack of sensitivity around others.

Brian Pead – who had been teaching for almost a quarter of a century – had long ago worked out that he would not invade a pupil's personal space and that all pupils had a different tolerance to this. He dealt with the issue by ensuring that all pupils knew implicitly that **he** didn't want his personal space invaded and in his career it never became an issue for either him or his pupils. His boundaries were strong.

He had tried to gently coach Murray about this and had been careful to ensure that he had not reprimanded her but merely brought it to her attention as something to think about.

Murray – on the other hand – had seen this as a rebuke. She did not take kindly to the conversation. It challenged her deluded and narcissistic perception of herself as a person who could do no wrong.

the racist afrikaner

Further cracks began to show in Maryn Murray's demeanour around the referral unit. One or two male pupils made comments that she was dismissive towards them on the afternoons when he went to his counselling school. In a typical while-the-cat's-away-the-mice-will-play scenario, she would treat the young men differently from the way she treated young women. She also used these opportunities to try to impose her authority over the entire unit, when she had no need to do anything other than merely continue to steer the ship in the direction that Pead was ably captaining it.

Brian Pead knew that all pupils are capable of making mischief about members of staff. No single member of staff is exempt from this process, including himself.

However, he had built up significant rapport with these young males. They hailed from Brazil and Portugal and were, in the main, decent young men. Pead made notes of their concerns and asked them to be patient whilst he quietly went about his business. He also asked them to report any further instances in which they felt abused or victimised by Maryn Murray.

Brian Pead also sought the wise counsel of Duane Maddison, whom he trusted to give an accurate account of events without injecting his own bias on those events.

Maddison agreed that Murray was somewhat indifferent and dismissive towards these young black males and that she was more often seen in the company of the female students.

Another member of staff whom Pead admired and trusted was Sandra Roach. He regarded her as a wonderful black woman with considerable presence. A single mother with a son, she worked hard to provide for them both. She had initially come to the unit as a Teaching Assistant after Jenny Foster left to return to the primary sector. She confirmed that Murray acted differently around the male pupils (especially the black ones) and the young white female pupils (especially the blonde ones).

Pead and Sandra Roach struck up an immediate rapport based on mutual respect. She was a gregarious woman, who swiftly gained the trust and respect of the pupils, principally because she had a son of a similar age to the pupils and thus was able to 'mother' them and discipline them – when necessary – all in the same professional manner.

For her part, Sandra Roach found Brian Pead to be dependable, reliable, hard-working, conscientious and honest. She also noted that he had seen in her – just as he had seen in the classroom assistants at Gravel Hill Primary School – that she possessed far more qualities, both as a human being and as a Teaching Assistant, than she was being asked to use.

Brian Pead had seen in her ways in which she could develop herself and thus earn more money, which would benefit both her and her son.

Pead offered all of his staff weekly supervision. This usually took place in a café just a few yards from the Old Library building in West Norwood. He would give them up to forty-five minutes and no more. This was to help develop their ability to manage time, to be relevant and to focus their minds on the tasks in hand.

Over a period of just a few weeks, Sandra Roach grew significantly in stature. She said that she always felt comfortable in his company and that she was happy to be a part of his team because he never judged people, he was always open and transparent and because he gained the utmost respect from his pupils and gave it in return.

Roach would say that students felt comfortable in Brian Pead's company and that they trusted him and were able to discuss with him their own personal issues. She also liked the fact that Pead could identify potential areas of growth in all the staff and pupils.

Sandra Roach often commented on the attendance figures at the OLCVS. In the first year – despite having no permanent home, no proper staff initially, no furniture or equipment - Brian Pead managed to gain a pupil attendance record of 82%. And this was achieved with a client group of disaffected pupils who were school refusers, or who had been rejected by mainstream schools as 'unteachable'. In Brian Pead's view, no-one is unteachable. He has taught things to hardened criminals, to disaffected pupils and to pupils who challenged him with "You can't teach us nuffink, Mister!" Brian Pead does not shy away from a challenge. He knew that such a challenge was really a cry for help to be taught, so that they might make something of their lives.

Maryn Murray did not like her one-to-one weekly meetings with Pead. He would ask her challenging questions about her role, set her realistic targets and try to assist her development in the psychology of discipline. She would often claim to be busy in order to avoid meeting with him. It was clear that she found these meetings uncomfortable – she was the only member of staff who did – and that she found them uncomfortable because she was astute enough to know that Brian Pead was learning more and more about her with every question that he asked. She had something to hide, but at this point in time, Pead was not yet aware of it. He merely asked her to consider how she responded to the male pupils and told her that if she ever wanted to learn more ways in which to deal with pupils in terms of discipline, or simply how to speak to them without alienating them, he was always available. She never partook of his offer.

Despite being incredibly busy as the Head of Centre and also in his personal life away from the Centre, doubts about Murray were niggling away at Pead. Something didn't quite add up.

She claimed to have had a permanent contract as Head of ICT at St. Augustine's School in Ealing, earning £38,000 per annum.

This school is a fee-paying girls' school.

Murray claimed she had been granted a sabbatical to "explore other career opportunities".

Who would leave such a position?

Why would someone leave a girls' school with relatively good behaviour and well-motivated pupils to join a pupil referral unit with de-motivated boys and girls?

Did the fact that the pupils at the OLCVS were vulnerable have anything to do with Murray's decision?

Yet – by taking the position at the OLCVS – Murray was now on a daily contract. Why would anyone walk away from a £38,000 p.a. permanent contract to work in a pupil referral unit which was hardly exploring other career opportunities, since it was still in the educational field?

Research has since shown that when Murray claimed to have asked for a sabbatical from St. Augustine's in Ealing this was at exactly the same time that the child protection policies at the school were later shown to be wholly inadequate. Child abuse was found to have been endemic at St. Benedict's School in Ealing and at Ealing Abbey. So rife was it that on 25 October 2011, the Ealing Gazette ran a story under the headline: "...Vatican orders child abuse inquiry into Ealing Abbey..." A synopsis of the story, by Michael Russell, read:

> "...THE VATICAN has ordered an inquiry into sexual abuse at Ealing Abbey, the first of its kind in Britain, **after decades of mistreatment of children.** A number of priests and lay teachers at St. Benedict's School in nearby Eaton Rise, have been linked to the scandal, the subject of three previous inquiries..."

The emphasis is the authors'.

Had Murray – a lay teacher claiming to be 'deeply religious' - **really** been given a sabbatical, or had she been forced out because of the storm around child sex abuse raging in Ealing at this time? Had she decided to run for cover in a different borough?

another *fait accompli*

In June 2006, Gilhooly visited the pupil referral unit and met with Pead. Gilhooly said that the OLCVS was going to move to new premises, the Redfearn Centre in Vauxhall.

This was yet another of Gilhooly's *faits accomplis*. He presented Pead with members of staff without consulting with him, and he now presented a new building without having had the decency to consult with Pead.

Pead visited the building that month, in order to become acquainted with it, so that he could start the process of planning for the Unit's second academic year.

Pead naturally reported his findings to his staff. He also said that it would be good practice for the staff to spend a day discussing endings – in leaving the Old Library Centre behind and leaving some thoroughly decent people who worked in the Community Centre behind. Sherine and Dwayne Thompson, Mercedes, Veronica, Paul Maddox and Alphonso Harris were all of West Indian or African extraction and they worked hard within Lambeth to establish a thriving community centre. Brian Pead had established positive and respectful working relationships with them all.

Maryn Murray was extremely uncomfortable about the day. She never liked discussing her emotions and the workshop on Endings provided such an opportunity. Every other member of staff participated fully, and though Pead knew that each person would get out of the day only what they put into it, it was nevertheless a worthwhile exercise.

But not for Maryn Murray.

Pead never asked any member of staff to say or do anything they didn't feel comfortable with. But Murray was positively guarded throughout. She blocked all attempts to engage her. She created significant barriers to positive exchanges.

As the first term drew to a close, the subject of staff contracts loomed large on the staff agenda.

27

contractual problems

The concerns around staff contracts had been an issue almost throughout that first year. Brian Pead (who only had a one-term contract of his own) asked Barry Gilhooly to issue contracts to Duane Maddison, Maryn Murray, Jennifer Foster, Fraser Hall and Sandra Roach. On 7 May 2006, as the first academic year drew to a close, Pead wrote to Gilhooly via email:

Dear Barry,

I hope you're well. I'm writing to you with regard to one specific area that I feel requires our immediate attention - that of staff contracts. I have worked hard at trying to build a staff team which is motivated, skilful and effective. I've recruited some excellent people and we also have Duane, who has been there from the beginning and who continues to do an excellent job, despite not receiving a bona fide contract, but rather extensions to a one-term contract.

I am turning my attention to the strategic development of the Virtual School, and am trying to build on the successes we have thus far experienced. But I keep coming up against a block - that of continuity of employment and staff contracts. With the acquisition of Colin, we now have a situation where the newest recruit has greater security of tenure than any other staff member, including myself.

I feel sure that you will agree that this is an unacceptable situation which we now need to resolve. We have spoken in the past about the posts being advertised, and staff applying for their own jobs. I have met with Duane and Maryn, and they fully understand the process that must take place. It was my understanding when we last spoke that this was a process that you would activate through H.R. Perhaps I misunderstood.

Whatever the reason, I am now seeking clarity about this situation. I am particularly keen to retain the services of Duane as learning mentor, though I have spoken with him about a new role of Head of Student Well-being, which I feel meets the needs of the students, parents and the school more readily than that of learning mentor per se.

I would also like to appoint Fraser Hall (Maths teacher) and Sandra Roach (LSA) on to contracts.

Once these contracts are in place, I believe that the Virtual School will be in a position to grow and develop in a sustainable way. I am cognisant of how busy you are, but I would appreciate you giving this your immediate attention. If it requires some action on my part, please advise and I will take the necessary action with immediate effect. The negative impact upon staff morale is something I am working hard to avoid, but goodwill lasts only so long and I would hate to lose valuable staff in any event, and in particular when Lambeth has identified a need to retain effective staff.

I look forward to your reply.
Kind regards
Brian

Only Fraser Hall received a contract. Colin Hill had significant security of tenure with a permanent Lambeth central contract. Gilhooly and Lambeth were reluctant to issue contracts, however. In discussions with his friend John Callow, the latter voiced his concerns about Lambeth's intentions to continue to fund the OLCVS, since any organisation would ensure that contracts were in place for staff it wished to retain. Callow warned Pead to be 'careful' – something appeared to be seriously amiss with this project. "Nothing adds up, Brian," Callow told his friend, with considerable prescience.

It is important to note that Pead wrote to his line manager on 7 May 2006 and stated that he had informed his staff – particularly Maddison and Murray – that there was a specific process of advertising the posts that all staff had to go through.

On 1, 8 and 23 March 2006, the English consultant to Lambeth, Marion Richards, visited the OLCVS to look at how the subject of English was being taught and how it was received by the pupils. In her report of 31 March 2006, Richards stated that "...Brian would like to appoint a full-time English teacher for September 2006. I agreed to support with the appointment procedure..."

This is clear evidence that Pead was not in the habit of promising contracts to staff, but that he liaised with his line manager, Human Resources and Lambeth consultants to discuss the appointment procedure.

28

hiley email

On 5 June 2006, Anya Hiley of Connexions, who worked out of a top floor office at the Old Library Centre in West Norwood, sent an email to her line manager, Glenice Lake.

The email read thus:

> "...I am concerned that Brian Johnson of the OLCVS uses different names. I am also concerned that he engages in long conversations with young white blonde females and that he is grooming them. I can think of no other reason for these conversations..."

This was an important email in this story.

The allegation has no legal or other basis. There are no names mentioned. There are no dates for these alleged conversations. There are no times provided. Hiley does not even provide the names that Brian Johnson uses.

In short, this email has no merit whatsoever. A reasonable recipient of such an email – adopting a professional attitude – would firstly meet with Brian and seek information.

But Glenice Lake is no professional. She obviously panicked and pre-judged the situation and merely took Anya Hiley at her word. Hiley had been appointed as the Connexions Advisor to the OLCVS, but according to Pead she was not doing her job properly and was neglectful towards the male pupils. He assessed her as being something of a dreamer with no understanding of the process of change. She certainly had no understanding of the lives of the pupils at the OLCVS.

Lake received the email and immediately forwarded it to the Executive Director of Education at Lambeth, Phyllis Dunipace. One has to question the emotional intelligence of Lake. Her lack of professionalism is a worrying factor for someone in her position.

Dunipace then forwarded the email to Barry Gilhooly, who – unknown to Pead – secretly met with Hiley. A decent and transparent line manager would have called Hiley to a meeting with Pead and Gilhooly – but he failed to keep this transparent. He was a person who preferred to have 'information' on people in case he needed to use it at a later date.

Thus Hiley was unprofessional by not speaking with Pead in the first instance. Lake was unprofessional for the same reason, as was Gilhooly.

It was left to Gilhooly to ask for evidence. Hiley was unable to provide any. She had no names, no dates, no times. It was, apparently, just a 'feeling' that she had.

Gilhooly rightly told Hiley that without any evidence he was unable to take any further action.

He appeared not to ask her how she had come by the information that the man known to her as Brian Johnson was using a different name. It is evident that this information had come from Murray – with whom Hiley had aligned herself.

Furthermore, Gilhooly also failed to ask Hiley how she could allege that Pead engaged in long conversations with blonde-haired girls when, in fact, she worked two floors above the OLCVS and she was rarely in the building.

Nor did Gilhooly ask the most sensible question: "What purpose did Hiley have in sending this email?"

Pead had recently admonished her for her lack of professionalism by constantly postponing careers advice meetings with the 'tougher' young males. When they re-booked their meetings, she always gave them dates weeks in advance and then would cancel them again near to the date of the meeting. Hiley did not like interacting with males.

Hiley was never reprimanded for spreading malicious and libellous rumours.

extension to contract - 2

On 18 May 2006, Alicia Reynolds of Lambeth Human Resources prepared form LPS4 (serial number 42144) upon instructions from Barry Gilhooly. The purpose of this form was to give Pead a one-year contract to commence on 1 September 2006 and to finish on 31 August 2007.

Gilhooly signed this form off on 20 July 2006. Lambeth required him to provide reasons for this extension to Pead's contract.

Gilhooly: "...Brian is a valuable member of staff who has contributed effectively to the service we provide in the Children and Young People's Service – Inclusion..."

This was a month after the Hiley malicious email.

Since the numbers on roll at the OLCVS had increased significantly due to the refugee and asylum seekers who attended, Pead was also given a pay increase from £40,374 to £49,038. This increase also reflected Pead's management of the extra staff needed to teach the asylum seekers.

A further form entitled 'Human Resources Essential Expenditure Approval Form' followed a natural path in the chain of command. On this form Gilhooly was required to complete a box which asked for the reason that recruitment is **deemed essential** (the authors' emphasis). Gilhooly wrote: "....Brian is a valuable member of staff who has contributed effectively to the service we provide..."

From Gilhooly the form went to Chris Ashton, Gilhooly's line manager. However, Ashton did not actually sign the form, Gilhooly performing this task on Ashton's behalf. From Ashton's desk it went to Phyllis Dunipace, the Executive Director of Young People's Service for Lambeth and it was copied to Farrukh Akbar. Dunipace ratified the contract extension and salary increase on 9 August 2006.

All seemed to be going well for Brian Pead. He had been awarded a significant increase in his salary, he had been given a one-year contract and the development of the OLCVS was making good progress.

Yet, within just three months he would be unlawfully suspended from the job that he loved. How could such a catastrophic chain of events occur when everything pointed to a period of sustained progress at Lambeth?

What was the catalyst for such incredible events?

30

a grand-father's love

The summer of 2006 was a good one for Brian Pead. On 19 May his grand-son, Joseph, was a gift for the family and Brian was delighted. They had a lot of fun together. Pead spent much of that summer in the company of Joe and his two grand-daughters, Emily and Lauren Birch, aged 7 and 5 at that time.

They enjoyed each other's company. The love between a grand-parent and his or her grand-children is often easier than between a parent and his or her offspring, because there is some distance between them. The love is unconditional.

From their earliest days, Brian Pead involved himself in their lives on an almost weekly basis. He taught them English and Maths and French, took them to museums and the cinema, and they would enjoy reading to him, or him reading to them. He would make up rhymes about their names in the manner of "Emily Birch went to church to sing a happy song, Emily Birch went to church but didn't stay for long..." and, just so that Lauren would not miss out, he would insert her name instead of Emily's, and they had a lot of fun with words. Most children love words and rhymes and Pead also loved words and the rhythm of words. The grand-father and his grand-children were made for each other.

At this time, Brian was also Chairman of the Friends of Scadbury Park, in Chislehurst, Kent, a site of special scientific interest: http://www.scadbury.net. He would often take them there. It was not far from their house in Sydney Road, Sidcup.

He also took them rock-climbing, believing that it would develop their physical and emotional selves.

Pead did not buy them valuable presents. He believes that the greatest gift you can give a child is your time and for them to know that are loved for who they are. Thus he made as much time as he possibly could in order to be with them and spend many happy hours in their company.

31

plans

Also during the summer of 2006, Pead made plans for the second academic year. He wanted to expand the unit still further and he wanted to increase the number of pupils on roll, increase the number of teachers and broaden the curriculum.

All of the pupils on roll in West Norwood had passed at least one nationally-recognised qualification. This in itself was a major achievement. Coupled with an attendance record of 82%, the Unit was clearly working under Pead's strong leadership.

He was also having plans drawn up to redevelop his house. Built in 1936, it had been extended to the side and rear, but inside it was tired-looking and Brian Pead felt that it needed a major overhaul. He had previously dabbled in plastering, plumbing, roofing, carpentry and electrical work, but he wanted to strip out the entire internal structures and re-build it from the inside out.

His counselling work was gathering pace, and his hours at the Community Drug Service in Wallington were rapidly increasing. He had also acquired a second placement at Whitefield School in Barnet, but this did not provide him with the satisfaction that he achieved when working with adults.

Just as his counselling hours increased, so did his supervision hours. He was an incredibly busy man. He was involved with individual sessions with Clare Manifold on a Friday evening and also in monthly group sessions on Saturday morning. Occasionally he would travel to Belsize Park on a Friday evening, travel back to Sidcup to sleep and then back on the Saturday morning to Belsize Park, for a three-hour group supervision session commencing at 9am.

32

supervision

Clare Manifold's supervision group consisted of three students – Brian Pead, Raman (from Sri Lanka) and Pippa, who died suddenly and before her time soon after the group ended.

On Saturday 1 July 2006, Manifold asked each student counsellor to write an account of how they experienced their peers after having worked together for a year in group supervision. Pippa wrote of Brian that he is "...very brave. He is open and it is quite remarkable how open he is. Brian is open to suggestions and learns by experience. It is fascinating to observe how he operates. He listens intently and sees everything. Although he listens to the opinions of others, he draws his own conclusions. He is the best example of how a person can be..."

Pippa worked as a Receptionist in a doctor's surgery in north London. She was a bright and lively woman. She is sorely missed, not only by her immediate family but also by Brian Pead, who shared many emotionally intimate moments with her as they studied together. They trusted each other implicitly.

Raman, a Tamil-speaking Sri Lankan, was a highly intelligent man who worked hard within the Tamil community to help the under-privileged with legal concerns. He and Brian shared a mutual respect, since Brian is always concerned about using his intellect to help others.

Raman's review of his year's supervision with Brian was that "...he has a natural interest in humanity. He is sensitive and honest with his views. He is incredibly insightful. He is a natural counsellor. He is open to feed-back and critical debate. He has the ability to separate professional discussion from personal friendship..."

These people had worked with Brian Pead extremely closely for over a year. They had encountered him each week at the CPPD counselling school, and each month they worked together in group supervision for three hours. Both Raman and Pippa had written about and discussed Brian Pead's qualities.

In March 2006, Manifold herself had written in a report that Brian Pead "...is a clear and thoughtful communicator, he uses counselling techniques such as active listening and reflection intelligently, he is able to perceive transferential and counter-transferential material, he is both able to receive and give feedback appropriately and is empathic and professional in terms of, for example, boundaries and agenda-keeping.

...He has shown himself to be a reliable student, committed to his counselling studies and the counselling process..."

By way of explanation, transference "...refers to an unconscious process in which the client projects on to the therapist both positive and negative qualities belonging to another significant person in the client's life and behaves towards the therapist as if he or she was that person..." (Ernesto Spinelli, 1994)

Counter-transference is that which arises in the therapist as a result of the client's influence on the therapist's feelings. Counter-transference can be reactive (syntonic) or proactive (illusory). Reactive counter-transference is a counsellor's emotional response to what the client brings to the encounter (in counselling-speak, this is often referred to as 'the client's stuff'). Proactive counter-transference is a counsellor's emotional response based on what the counsellor him or herself brings to the encounter (his 'stuff'). Some counsellors – Pead included – often referred to it as 'your shit' or 'my shit'. Knowing the difference between whose 'shit' is getting in the way of the relationship usually makes for a more positive relationship.

Brian Pead was particularly adept at sorting out what was 'his stuff' or 'the other person's stuff' in encounters he had, both in and out of the therapy room. He has a significant level of awareness of his own 'stuff' and, as a peer was later to point out, was emotionally intelligent enough to differentiate 'his stuff' from the 'other person's stuff' in most encounters. This ability had been honed through years of management, years of reading about psychology and years of attending psychology and philosophy talks at Inner Space in London. Clare Manifold was impressed with the level of awareness that Pead had around these concepts, writing in his end-of-year report that he "...is able to perceive transferential issues..."

She also wrote that he "...is open to self-exploration, uses his journal well and is happy to look at issues raised in our sessions. [...] he is open to both give, which he does with sensitivity, and receive. [...] He is willing and interested in examining the cultural heritage (of people he encounters). [...] His strengths are good boundaries, evident intelligence and a serious commitment to the work. He forms trusting relationships, gives insightful feedback and is a generous contributor..."

It is important to note that Clare Manifold referred to Pead using his journal. This reference was made to the fact that a requirement of the Diploma Course – and subsequent Advanced Diploma – was that each student counsellor must maintain a journal. It is not a log. It is not a diary. It is a random collection of the thoughts and experiences of the trainee counsellor which is designed to raise the counsellor's level of awareness around what happens to him or her on a daily or weekly basis. Whilst not being a diary *per se*, it will often be written in the form of a diary and it may well be written on consecutive days in the manner of a diary. Equally, there may be periods of several days between entries, or perhaps even longer. Each trainee would complete his or her journal in their own way. There were no hard and fast rules, except that it must be completed and that it must focus on the events that occur within the trainee's life which evoke feelings, whether strong feelings or mere fleeting feelings that are often ignored by us all as we go about our daily lives. It is often these fleeting glimpses of feelings that we experience that, if recorded, and reviewed from time to time show us patterns about our behaviour or feelings (or the way that we interpret them) that can provide vital information for therapeutic progress and understanding of one's self. Pead was in the habit of writing his journal on an almost daily basis, since he was fascinated by the way in which the fleeting emotional responses he had to events or people in his life would form a "bigger picture" of who he was.

Some three years later, his journal writing would become a topic of discussion at a criminal trial at Southwark Crown Court. This criminal trial was a direct consequence of his work at Lambeth.

Clare Manifold, of course, could not have known this when she produced the report. Her CV is impressive. She is a Master of Philosophy, has an MA in the Psychology of Counselling, a Diploma in Adult Education, a Diploma in Cognitive Therapy, is a BACP accredited counselling supervisor and is UKCP registered.

But – back at the OLCVS – Maryn Murray was not of the same opinion of her manager as Clare Manifold, Raman and Pippa were.

the gathering storm clouds

Towards the end of the first academic year at the Old Library in West Norwood, the research department of the Psychiatry Department of King's College, London had arranged through Lambeth Council to visit the OLCVS to identify those pupils who were at risk of developing addictive behaviours towards drugs, alcohol and sex, or a combination of these. The work of the researchers at King's College was known as the Preventure Programme and can be found at the following URL: <www.kcl.ac.uk/iop/depts/addictions/research/legacyprojects/PreVenture.aspx>.

The programme had been created by Dr Patricia Conrod, who "...is a clinical psychologist and Clinical Lecturer at the National Addiction Centre. Her research focuses on cognitive, personality and biological risk factors for alcohol and drug misuse and the factors that mediate the co-occurrence of addictive behaviours with other mental disorders. Her experimental research focuses on factors that make people more susceptible to seek out behavioural reinforcement from drugs of abuse. She has published several studies demonstrating that personality factors determine the type of reinforcement experienced from substances of abuse. More recently, her research findings have led to the development of new approaches to substance abuse treatment and prevention that target personality risk factors for substance misuse..."
Source: <http://www.iop.kcl.ac.uk/staff/profile/default.aspx?go=10342>

King's College described the programme thus:

"...The Preventure Project is a school-based programme currently being conducted in schools in London boroughs. It is a prevention programme which aims to reduce risk-taking behaviour by targeting anxiety sensitivity, sensation seeking, negative thinking and impulsivity which are known risk factors for early onset substance misuse. The programme uses psycho-educational manuals within interactive group sessions with students aged 13-16.

The group sessions focus on motivational factors for risky behaviours and provide students with coping skills to aid their decision making in situations involving, anxiety and depression, thrill seeking, aggressive and risky behaviour (e.g. theft, vandalism and bullying) drugs and alcohol misuse.

The Preventure programme significantly reduced shoplifting rates in comparison to the control group (24% v 33%). This reduction in shoplifting was most pronounced in those students who participated in the Impulsivity intervention. The prevalence of shoplifting reduced from 45% to 26% for the intervention group compared to an increase of 45% to 53% for those in the control group.

The programme significantly reduced truancy rates in students who participated in the Anxiety Sensitivity intervention, with truancy rates reduced to just 5% compared to 28% in the control group.

The Preventure programme reduced depression scores in students who participated in the Negative Thinking intervention in comparison to the control group, and it reduced panic attack rates in those who participated in the intervention showing lower rates of experiencing panic attacks (20%) in comparison to the control group (29%). This was most significant in students who participated in the anxiety sensitivity intervention, with rates reduced from 35% to 18%.

In terms of programme developments, data from the first wave of schools was collected for 12 month and 18 month follow-up. This was analysed for new findings and to enable the researchers to see if the positive results could be maintained.

Additional research is being conducted utilizing the Preventure programme with adolescents at higher risk of substance misuse and associated emotional and behavioural problems such as students attending Pupil Referral Units and the children of parents who misuse alcohol..."

Brian Pead was fascinated by this programme. He had long understood that prevention is better than cure, and, in his time working at Gravel Hill – and other – primary schools, he had seen the power of early interventions. In his time at university in the 1980s, he had learnt in Sociology that it is far better for Governments to invest money in younger-aged children than other age-groups so that, by preventing, for example, criminal behaviour at an early age, the cost to society would be reduced, both in economic and social terms.

Leading the group of three research therapists was Nadia Al-Khudhairy, an intelligent and sensitive woman who enjoyed the atmosphere of the pupil referral unit at West Norwood where she commenced her research. When the OLCVS moved to Vauxhall in the autumn term of 2006, she visited again to acquire more data about the pupils.

Brian Pead and Nadia Al-Khudhairy discussed the Preventure Programme at great length. As a trainee counsellor himself, and as the creator of Einsteinonline.co.uk, he understood the power of this research programme. In August 2005, Pead had undertaken a course on the Psychology of Addiction and was awarded a Merit by Birkbeck, University of London. He immediately saw, therefore, that the work being undertaken by Nadia Al-Khudhairy and her team was of considerable significance.

He could not have known, however, just how important Al-Khudhairy's work was to be to him.

a new home at last!

The Old Library Centre Virtual School moved from West Norwood to the Redfearn Centre in Vauxhall during the summer of 2006.

Pead was relatively pleased that the venture finally had a more permanent home where the desks and chairs would not have to be set out each day and stacked up each night. Although the building was used as a Community Centre, the OLCVS – now re-named by Pead as the Open Learning Centre for Vocational Studies – had the exclusive use of it throughout normal school hours. The Centre itself was run by Denise Campbell-Downie.

Pead was also pleased that he had retained the services of Duane Maddison, Fraser Hall, the exuberant New Zealander who had joined around February 2006 to teach Maths, and Sandra Roach. The number of pupils on roll was to substantially increase with the introduction of around 30 refugee and asylum seeker pupils from all corners of the earth, many of whom who did not speak English. Derek Langan was recruited by Lambeth to teach these pupils within the pupil referral unit, but in a separate area of the same building. Langan was 'old school', and something of a gentleman.

Another member of staff was Colin Hill, who was employed by Lambeth and paid on a central contract, so he did not cost the OLCVS anything from its virtual budget. (Pead had continued to ask Gilhooly for a copy of the budget, but one was never forthcoming.)

When Pead had asked for extra staffing, Gilhooly offered him the services of Colin Hill, who was around 50 years of age and considerably experienced, having worked in similar Units before. However, he came with 'baggage'.

Gilhooly told Pead that Hill had been the subject of sexual allegations, but that no charges had been brought against him. Gilhooly added that Hill was 'an alcoholic'. "But you're good with people, so if anybody can get the best out of Colin, I'm sure you can," said Gilhooly, attempting flattery on a man who couldn't care less about being flattered because he doesn't rely on the opinions of others in order to respect himself.

By way of a 'sweetener' Gilhooly told Pead that he was giving him a substantial raise in his salary.

Thus Gilhooly had paved the way for a checkmate on Pead in later months.

Brian Pead observed Colin Hill closely. His view was that Hill was a man with a great deal of experience, but who was not always able to control his enthusiasm. He would get an idea into his head and immediately want to follow it through. Pead saw that he would have to be carefully managed, though he also felt that Hill was possibly a useful addition. There is always a trade-off when managing such people. On the one hand, a manager might wish to take advantage of such enthusiasm and willingness but, on the other hand, if this took up a considerable amount of management time, then it might not be beneficial to the Unit in the longer term.

Hill told Pead that his partner, Naine Woodrow, was a potter. This was something that Pead had briefly dabbled in at Sidcup Adult Education Centre, but he was not very competent. He did, however, admire those who had such a skill and it was arranged that Brian would visit Colin and his partner in Clapham at the North Street Potters.

> "...The North Street Potters is a busy urban pottery set in the heart of Clapham, South London. Founded in 1978, it is an Aladdin's Cave full of handmade pottery at affordable prices.
>
> A large range of hand thrown tableware, decorative and sculptural pieces is made in the shared studio behind the shop..."
> Source: <http://www.northstreetpotters.com/>

Pead visited the pottery and had an enjoyable time meeting Colin and his partner, Naine, and watching pottery being made. It was Pead's way of seeing a different side to Colin Hill - in his own environment. It all added to Pead's perception of Hill.

Almost as soon as the new term got underway, Maryn Murray broached the subject of staff contracts. None of the staff (except for Pead, the Head of the Unit and, bizarrely, Frazer Hall, the Mathematics teacher who was leaving at the end of the year) had a contract. Gilhooly was stalling. John Callow smelt a rat, telling Pead, "Be careful, Brian. Nothing about this enterprise rings true!" His words were to gain power as the storm clouds gathered.

Murray spent a large part of her time seeking allies, in the manner of Brutus planning the assassination of Caesar. She attempted to forge alliances with Maddison and Langan in particular.

Sandra Roach acted as Pead's 'eyes and ears' and would report back all that she saw. Pead valued her wise judgments. She had the ability not to gossip – something which Pead abhors – but to report accurately her perception of events.

When she did not receive the contract that she coveted, Murray then went behind Pead's back directly to Barry Gilhooly. She had failed to realise that it was Lambeth – not Pead – who were refusing to issue contracts. She lacked the intelligence to realise that Lambeth were stalling on the issue of contracts and this was because of Gilhooly's influence.

Gilhooly had no right to undermine Pead by having a secret conversation with Murray about the issuing of contracts. He ought to have told Murray that she should meet with Brian or he should have arranged for her to meet with HR so that they could explain the position.

However, Gilhooly used this incident in order to control the chess pieces. He made capital out of the fact of Murray's discontent. He knew that he would be able to use her antipathy towards Pead at a later date if he needed to.

Gilhooly emailed Pead with the following:

"...Dear Brian,

Thank you for meeting with me today to discuss this matter. I suggested that you meet with Maryn to talk through the following issues:

1. her accusations and how she feels they should be resolved
2. your response to her accusations and your suggestions for ways forward
3. the fact that the main focus is on the smooth running of the OLCVS, particularly in relation to students' welfare and progress
4. that she told me her main anxiety was around job security until the end of the summer term
5. that HR have suggested to me that she carries on with her agency contract until that time as it would cost Lambeth a fee if we were to put her on a Lambeth contract.

Maryn may wish to have someone with her when she meets with you. It would be helpful to offer her that facility.

As her line manager it falls to you, not HR, to deal with this situation. Please contact me (or HR) at any time if you need and further advice or support. Many thanks.

Regards,
Barry..."

This is a significant email because it provides incontrovertible evidence that Murray went above Pead's head in an attempt to obtain a permanent Lambeth contract. It provides evidence that Pead had sought his line manager's advice as well as advice from HR at Lambeth with respect to his handling of the contract situation at the OLCVS.

Although Gilhooly claimed that he was available for support, he was rarely available to meet and his PA, Beverley Williams, was always fending off calls on his behalf to ensure that he was often "out of the office" or "in meetings".

As Gilhooly's PA, she obviously had the 'inside track' on a lot of unsavoury conduct that Gilhooly was involved in.

35

squaring the circle

Pead introduced 'Circle Time' as the main feature of each day at the OLCVS. Because of the large number of students, the cohort had, once again, to be divided into two groups – those attending from 9am-12 and those attending from 1pm-4. Registration would be taken within Circle Time. Pead was aware that anybody entering a group situation brings with him or her 'stuff' from their experiences of the day thus far, or 'stuff' from family situations or from their past. Thus, he used this time to see what the pupils were bringing to the Unit that morning or afternoon.

Some pupils would comment on how busy the roads were, or how crowded the bus was, or on the weather. Others would comment about how bad they felt because they had told their mum to "Fuck off!" as they were leaving the house. Yet others would comment on being hungry. Or of having had a row the previous night with their boyfriend or girlfriend.

Pead introduced this process in order to defuse strong feelings. He created a safe environment for feelings to be aired, so that pupils could 'get if off their chests' before they started their lessons. He knew that, if it had been dealt with prior to lessons, discipline problems were unlikely to arise in the lessons themselves. Which is precisely how it played out.

Although there was a scheduled time for the start of the first lesson (9.20 for the morning session or 1.20 for the afternoon session), Pead would sometimes allow Circle Time to spill over into lesson time. This was not because he was weak with regard to boundaries, but because if a particular scenario evolved during Circle Time, he would allow it to be played out, particularly if one pupil's angst was caused by the actions of other pupils. Pead often used the restorative justice principles of the New Zealand Maoris which he had studied. In other words, the pupils learnt to police themselves. And, because they were involved in their own justice, they were more willing to buy into it and adhere to it.

As a Group Therapist, Brian Pead was particularly adept at leading Circle Time. Duane Maddison, who was also used to running groups in youth clubs, was also an able leader and Pead would sometimes ask him to lead a group. On these occasions, Pead would simply sit back and observe all the interactions and dynamics between the protagonists within the circle.

Because she was so well respected, Sandra Roach would sometimes take Circle Time. The female students liked this in particular, so Pead was able to provide a balance to these sessions. Fraser Hall sometimes took the group process, but – being 25 and closer to the pupils' ages than any other teacher – he was not too keen on running the group. Very occasionally, Pead allowed Colin Hill to take the session, but he would sometimes be encouraged to lose focus by the more astute and streetwise pupils.

Maryn Murray was the only member of staff who refused to take a group. In truth, this suited Pead because she did not possess the emotional intelligence – despite her 30 years – to run such a group. She lacked self-awareness and one of the pre-requisites of a group leader in such a process is that he or she must have considerable self-awareness so that he or she can effectively lead the group without ever becoming involved in its machinations.

october 2006

Having met with Clare Manifold, his supervisor at CPPD, in which the use of the counselling name Steve Goodfellow had become an agenda item, Brian Pead emailed Alicia Reynolds at Human Resources, Lambeth:

"...Sent: 10 October 2006 14:51

Subject: CRB form

hi Alicia,

if memory serves me correctly, my CRB form is due for an update.

Barry is aware that I do counselling outside of my role with the OLCVS, and that I use a different name, Steve Goodfellow.

My counselling supervisor has suggested that we add the name of "Steve Goodfellow" to the CRB form under my birth name of Brian Pead.

What do you think?

Hope you are well,
kind regards
Brian..."

This is a significant email for a number of reasons. It shows that Pead was aware of his need to keep his CRB checks up to date and accurate.

It also provides irrefutable evidence that his line manager, Barry Gilhooly, was aware of the name of Steve Goodfellow.

The email shows that Pead had been discussing his use of names with his counselling supervisor (Clare Manifold) and a person up to no good would hardly be so transparent about his use of names.

Pead seeks the advice of Alicia Reynolds when he asks, "What do you think?"

Staggeringly, Pead did not receive a reply to this email until 9th February 2007, some four months later.

37

bullying

On Sunday 5 November 2006, Brian Pead sent Rosa Vaz an email in which he stated that he was being bullied by Maryn Murray, especially with regard to a contract. Pead also stated in the email that Murray had claimed to be keeping a dossier on him. Pead sought the intervention of Human Resources as his complaint was an official complaint.

"...the only [other] thing my father bestowed upon me at birth was a name, Rolihlahla. In Xhosa, Rolihlahla literally means 'pulling the branch of a tree', but its colloquial meaning more accurately would be 'troublemaker'."

Nelson Mandela, Long Walk to Freedom, 1994.

apartheid and abuse

On Wednesday 8 November 2006, Brian Pead was approached by three young, black Portuguese-speaking pupils named Mauro Brito, Jose Mario Pontes Centeio and Miguel Neves, who asked to speak with him in his office. He invited them in and asked if they minded if Sandra Roach joined them. They did not object.

The young men had specifically chosen this day - a Wednesday - to speak with Brian because Murray no longer worked on Wednesdays.

The pupils – who all enjoyed an excellent relationship with Pead based on mutual respect and discussions about football and boxing – patiently explained that Maryn Murray had been racially abusing them and treating them with disrespect. Similar complaints had been made against her previously but Pead had not, at that stage, been able to gather sufficient evidence against her.

This, however, was a different situation. The young men were able to provide concrete examples, and Sandra Roach was herself able to corroborate their allegations against Murray.

The pupils said that they wished to make an official complaint about Maryn Murray.

They said that throughout this term she had been racist towards them all by calling them 'stupid' in front of the whole class. The young men said that she also made fun of them and mocked them if they got an answer wrong. They added that she never did this if a white boy got an answer wrong and certainly not if a white girl did.

They claimed that "...she seems to like the white girls and shows favouritism towards them by smiling a lot and she always spends more time with female pupils. She seems to flirt with the girls and praises them a lot and never praises us even though we work very hard in her lessons because we actually like ICT and Art and want to do well in these subjects but she never seems to respect us at all..."

The young men said that Murray "...tries to make us feel small in front of the whole class..." and that "...she has made us feel bad about ourselves because we are black..."

They added that other pupils and staff had noticed this behaviour and Sandra Roach corroborated this. "...We are making a complaint about her racism towards us..."

Pead made notes, and read out the notes to the young men. A set of complaints against Murray was agreed in writing. Murray had racially abused the young men in respect of her attitude towards them – asking them "Are you stupid? Can't you understand what I'm saying?" Calling them 'stupid' was also wholly unacceptable.

Brian Pead would never support such an attitude in his Unit, nor in his life. He had worked hard to create a happy Unit based on mutual respect and he would not tolerate such language and attitudes towards any pupil, let alone these three decent young men.

After signing statements outlining the racial abuse, the pupils left the office content in the knowledge that they had been listened to and content that their complaints had been officially logged in writing.

After they left, Pead discussed the problem with Sandra Roach, his wise assistant. It was agreed that action needed to be taken and that a close eye had to be kept on Murray. Pead was still leaving the Unit at 2pm on a Tuesday in order to attend lectures on the Diploma course, and Murray – as Deputy Head elect – was thus in charge of the Unit whenever Pead was at college.

further evidence of murray's inappropriateness - 1

A day later, on Thursday 9 November 2006, a young female pupil asked to speak with Brian in his office.

Although overlooked entirely by Lilian Baylis School and therefore not a 'private area', Brian's office was known by the pupils to be a safe sanctuary. Pupils would often ask to speak with him on personal matters. Pregnancies, drugs, sexually transmitted diseases, bereavement and many other issues were discussed in the safety of his office.

Gemma Mandry was an impressive 14-year-old with a penchant for Maths. She had a voracious appetite for Maths and wanted Brian to set her reams of homework – which she always completed. She was a spirited young woman, who had already seen a lot of life and was 'street-wise'. She had a number of personal issues which she felt safe enough to share with her Head teacher.

One of Gemma's endearing qualities – as strange as it might sound – was that she had a propensity to swear. She usually meant no harm by this; it was just what she had grown up with and she would utter such statements as "Where's my fucking Maths book?" or "How do you do these fucking sums?"

There was no malice in her use of expletives. On the rare occasions that she did lose her temper, she would add greater emphasis to her use of expletives, but swearing was just a normal way of life to her (and many of the other pupils). Whilst Brian did not encourage swearing, he also knew that – with pupils like Gemma – what was really important was that she attended every session. Gemma was thoughtful and cared about her education, she was clean, she helped others with their Maths, and she was generally a very nice person to be around. If he had continually tried to punish her for swearing, he would simply have alienated Gemma and she would be lost to the education system, whereas she was now in it and performing well. It is a trade-off all parents will understand – you cannot continually admonish your child for every mistake that they make. Gemma had a best friend – Talya Cuthbert, who was another remarkable young woman.

For obvious reasons of confidentiality, it is not possible to discuss the main issues spoken about between Brian and Gemma.

However, what can be put into the public domain is that Gemma Mandry made extremely serious complaints against Murray, with Sandra Roach once again present.

Mandry told Pead that Murray had offered her £50 worth of gym vouchers if she would go to the gym with her after school hours and if she (Mandry) would stop swearing. This was clearly a very serious allegation on at least three counts:

(i)   it showed that Murray was making improper suggestions towards Mandry to meet her after school hours
(ii)   it showed that Murray had offered Mandry a bribe
(iii)   it demonstrated that Murray was grooming young women.

Again, Pead logged these allegations and asked Mandry to sign a statement against Murray, which she did.

Thus Pead had significant evidence against Maryn Murray of a racist, bullying and sexual nature.

40

yet further evidence of murray's inappropriateness - 2

On Tuesday 14 October 2006 another female student asked to speak with Pead. Her name was Ashleigh Mills. She was a blonde-haired fifteen year old, who was very good at English. Her home life was unsettled, and at this period in her life she was extremely vulnerable.

She told Pead that Murray had made improper suggestions towards her, asking her to accompany her on shopping expeditions and to visit her flat alone.

Again Pead noted these allegations and asked Ashleigh to sign a statement. She did this.

Pead now had further damning evidence against Murray. He was duty-bound to take action and report it to his line manager, Barry Gilhooly.

Thus Pead called Gilhooly and said that he needed to meet with him urgently in his office.

41

grand master gilhooly

When Gilhooly arrived, Pead explained about the allegations against Murray and showed Gilhooly the signed statements. Gilhooly agreed that the evidence was, indeed, incontrovertible and damning.

Pead said that he had no option but to dismiss Murray. He sought Gilhooly's counsel with regard to the legal position about dismissing her. It transpired that Murray was only on a daily contract via her teaching agency, and Gilhooly instructed Pead to call the agency and ask them to inform Murray that her services were no longer required. Brian Pead made the call and logged it in the telephone calls book that he had established in September 2005 when setting up the Unit.

And in making that call, he was, quite literally signing his own death warrant on his position at Lambeth and his life was to spiral rapidly towards destruction as Lambeth – with Gilhooly as the Grand Master of a game of local authority chess – sought to destroy an innocent man in an effort to cover up corruption and collusion at a high level.

42

disinformation

In the military, disinformation is the deliberate spreading of false information to mislead an enemy or opponent as to one's position or course of action.

In politics, disinformation is the deliberate attempt to deflect voter support of an opponent, disseminating false statements of innuendo based on the candidate's vulnerabilities as revealed by opposition research.

In both cases, it also includes the distortion of true information in such a way as to render it useless. Disinformation may include distribution of forged documents, manuscripts, and photographs, or spreading malicious rumours and fabricated intelligence. Its techniques are often to be found in commerce and government, where it is used to try to undermine the position of a competitor or an enemy of the State.

Disinformation was used at the Hillsborough Disaster when the police deliberately put out false information to the press that the Liverpool fans had committed crimes and were, therefore, the architects of their own fatal destinies.

The Metropolitan Police Service, members of Lambeth Council, the judiciary, senior politicians and corrupt barristers have all used disinformation to impugn the character of Brian Pead.

He has been libelled in the press. He has been accused of being a sex offender when he is not. He has been slandered by a policeman to his neighbours – who, all being somewhat short of intelligence – believe whatever the police say or show them. They never stop to ask the police to prove that documents shown to them are genuine.

The principle exponents of the art of disinformation were the Nazis. In 1933 Goebbels became Adolf Hitler's propaganda minister, which gave him power over all German radio, press, cinema, and theatre. Goebbels possessed a brilliant insight into mass psychology. By a strange quirk of fate, Brian Pead had studied the Nazi Party's rise to power during his English degree from 1982 to 1986. He had studied the play *Rhinoceros* by Eugene Ionesco, a Romanian-born French playwright, which was a commentary on the German invasion of France. His research into the play and the Nazi Party led him to study the psychology of groups and the masses. Brian Pead is now a group therapist.

Most people in the UK today want to believe that they live in a democracy and that the police and elected politicians are honest and 'doing a good job'. This extreme form of naivety is dangerous. It allows the UK government and the police force – an instrument of government – to perpetrate crimes and breaches of human rights under the very noses of the people they are meant to serve. The UK Government fills our newspapers and television screens with human rights abuses in China or Burma or some other far-flung regime while the reality is that Britain is guilty of just as many abuses of human rights on a daily basis. They are rarely brought to the public's attention. It is only when a major tragedy like Hillsborough occurs that can sometimes shine a light on the dark forces operating in Government and Scotland Yard.

The way Brian Pead has been treated is nothing short of the worst excesses of Hillsborough, where he attended on that fateful day. Although he immediately knew that the police had lied and deliberately misinformed the public, little did he know how he would one day become the subject of a similar campaign against him by Lambeth officials, by senior police officers at Scotland Yard and by members of Her Majesty's Government.

But it is not just Brian Pead who suffered at the hands of these masters of the dark arts. Three innocent children – his grand-children – have also suffered as they were separated from the love of their grand-father. Brian's daughter, Sorrel Birch, was told that her children would be taken away from her if she continued to maintain contact with her father. Emily Birch, aged 13, Lauren Birch aged 11 and Joseph Birch, aged 6 are as much the victims of the dark forces as Pead himself.

43

lack of police involvement (1)

It would have been normal practice for Gilhooly and Lambeth to notify the police that Murray had been demonstrably racist, that she had abused a position of trust and that she had been grooming young female pupils.

At the very least, it would have been appropriate for the police to have interviewed Murray. The authors have sufficient evidence, they believe, for a charge and conviction against Murray, yet the Metropolitan Police Service did nothing.

Why didn't the police interview her?

The answer is simple: had they interviewed her, they would have been duty bound to also interview the male pupils and the female pupils. Parents and carers would have been involved. The reputation of Lambeth Council might have been called into question. Yet this alone cannot be sufficient reason for the police failing to become involved.

The authors strongly suggest that the police were not called because the police were aware of Murray's placement at the OLCVS. Murray did not have qualified teacher status. Neither did Hiley. Yet Gilhooly had been responsible for placing Murray at the OLCVS and for putting Hiley in the Connexions role connected with the OLCVS. Gilhooly had also placed a wholly inadequate person – in the form of Eloise Whitmore – as the School Administration Officer. Why would Gilhooly place such people in the OLCVS? Why would he place them there if he genuinely wanted the OLCVS to be a success?

The authors allege – and there is considerable evidence to suggest that they are right – that Murray was placed in the OLCVS to gain access to young girls for herself and others. The 'others' might well be senior Lambeth officials, senior police officers and politicians, given how each of these groups has sought to destroy or impugn Brian Pead. Otherwise, why would they go to such extraordinary lengths to implicate an innocent man?

The authors are aware that the groups mentioned in the previous paragraphs – who are all expert in disseminating disinformation – will attempt to further impugn the reputation of Brian Pead. They have already threatened to have him sectioned under the Mental Health Act. This is a typical response to anybody who threatens their security. Just as the police and Government ministers tried to impugn the dead Liverpool supporters at Hillsborough, the police and government ministers have tried to impugn Brian Pead for uncovering institutionalised corruption and a cover-up of that corruption of immense proportions.

Examine Lambeth's reaction to the news that Pead had been given evidence of Murray's racist behaviour and grooming of young female pupils.

96

Lambeth **reinstated** Murray. The same Murray who had committed such offences. The same Murray who had not been CRB checked by Lambeth HR.

Not only did they reinstate her, but Gilhooly then placed her at Norwood School for Girls in Crown Dale, West Norwood, SE19 3NY.

This school is approximately one kilometre from the original OLCVS building. The Connexions Advisor to the Norwood School for Girls was Anya Hiley.

Why would Murray be reinstated? Why would she be placed in an all-girls' school when evidence existed to show that she had been inappropriate around young female pupils?

Why would Murray be allowed to link up again with Hiley? Both Murray and Hiley claimed to be deeply religious but it is conceivable that they were using the Alpha Course and their alleged religion to gain access to vulnerable pupils and other young people.

Both Murray and Hiley had considerable and unfettered access to vulnerable pupils. They also had unrestricted access to the private and confidential contact details of these pupils.

Were Murray and Hiley ingratiating themselves with female pupils (or even male pupils, for that matter) for their own sexual gratification and that of others?

Wikileaks has shown that there is evidence in the public domain that suggests that the police control child pornography in the UK, just as they did with adult pornography in the 1970s, according to the former Flying Squad commander, John O'Connor.
Source:
<http://mirror.wikileaks.info/wiki/an_insight_into_child_porn/#Small_reflection_on_the_history_of_the_industry>

In an article in *The Independent on Sunday* 10 July 2011, in an article entitled 'The suspects are in charge of the case', O'Connor wrote:

> "...Scotland Yard is facing its worst corruption crisis since the 1970s, when senior police officers were found to be controlling London's pornography industry. The investigation and subsequent purge left many detectives out of a job and in some cases serving prison sentences. The gloom that surrounded the Yard in those days is similar to the atmosphere that pervades it today.
>
> Each day reveals more details of misconduct by the press and the police..."

That from a former Flying Squad Commander.

Corruption is endemic within the police and Government ministers are not beyond reproach following the MP allowances scandal. O'Connor added in his article that "...Nobody in authority was prepared to recognise the endemic nature of this corruption and each case was dealt with as a stand-alone incident..."

He continued in his condemnation of his former employers:

> "...At risk is the reputation and integrity of the service. It cannot afford to get it wrong again. The problem is that senior officers did not recognise the extent of the corruption. [...] They must accept their responsibility for what has happened. It is astonishing that with so many resources being spent on anti-corruption, they could not see it when it was right under their noses..."

The authors can add little to that robust criticism of Scotland Yard by one of its most high profile former employees.

the post-apartheid era

Having dismissed Murray on 15 November 2006, the atmosphere at the pupil referral unit became instantly more pleasant. The scheming Murray had had a pernicious effect upon the OLCVS, like a creeping cancer eating at a healthy body.

Pead was content that he had acted swiftly and decisively to rid the OLCVS of a teacher who was racist and who acted improperly towards pupils in a number of ways. Pupils reacted positively when they learnt that she would not be returning to the Unit.

Throughout November, Pead continued his counselling placement at the Community Drug Service in Wallington. He was fast approaching his target of 150 hours, since he was volunteering on Wednesday evenings as well as Monday evenings.

In the period August 2006 through to December 2006, Brian Pead was regularly attending self-improvement courses run by Inner Space, as well as spending time with his beloved grand-daughters and new grand-son.

On Sunday 13 August 2006 he attended a course run by Gopi Patel in Islington on the subject of humility, patience and tolerance.

On Wednesday 30 August he attended further training provided by the Community Drug Service in Wallington.

On Thursday 31 August, he took his grand-daughters, Emily and Lauren, to Avery Hill Park in Eltham. They spent time running the 100 metres and Emily ran it in 20 seconds, which was a very good time for a seven year old. Pead's best time was 14.85 seconds, which was a reasonable time for a 53 year old.

On Friday 1 September he attended an Inner Space lecture entitled *Don't Get Mad, Get Wise.*

On Saturday 8 September he travelled to Belsize Park for group supervision with Clare Manifold, Pippa and Raman.

On Friday 15 September he attended Inner Space at Hop Gardens to listen to the talk entitled *Freedom from Worry.*

On Friday 22 September he attended the Inner Space lecture entitled *Living Outside The Box* by Jim Ryan, an excellent speaker.

On Sunday 24 September, he attended the Inner Space lecture at Islington entitled *See, Feel, Think, Do.*

On Wednesday 27 September he attended group supervision at CDS in Wallington.

On Friday 29 September he attended the Inner Space talk entitled *Just a Minute*.

On Sunday 1 October, he went to Islington to attend the Inner Space talk entitled *Boiling Point*, given by Barry Woodhouse.

On Wednesday 4 October he attended individual supervision with Karen Lacey, his new supervisor at CDS, who had taken over from Michael Bird as Brian's personal supervisor.

On Friday 6 October 2006 he attended the Inner Space talk entitled *Heart Maintenance*.

Over the weekend of 4 and 5 November, Pead attended a weekend course at the CPPD < http://cppd.co.uk/> on the subject of Family Constellations. It was an excellent course and he had both enjoyed himself tremendously on the course and also learnt a great deal more about family dynamics.

He was also counselling at Whitefield School in Barnet during this period, but since volunteer counselling hours in a school do not count as adult hours or count towards the 150 hours he was required to accrue, Pead was not too happy with this particular placement, since he was not trained as a child counsellor.

It is evident that Brian Pead led a full and interesting life. His time was completely taken up with his full-time job, his counselling studies, group and individual supervision at CDS, group and individual supervision at CPPD, time with his grand-children and twice-weekly visits to talks given by Inner Space. He focused on his own self-development as well as trying to help others at the pupil referral unit known as the OLCVS and in his counselling placements.

He was also working on plans to refurbish his house and garden. It is important to note just how busy Pead was throughout this period. It demonstrates his mind-set over a considerable period of time.

With Murray now out of the picture at the OLCVS, it seemed that Pead was set fair to continue to develop the Unit. But the Machiavellian Murray and Grand Master Gilhooly had been plotting Pead's downfall. It was not long in coming.

suspension

Friday 8 December 2006 had started out just like any other day at the OLCVS in Vauxhall.

But it was to end in dramatic fashion.

Brian Pead instinctively knew something was wrong when – around 2pm – he saw Barry Gilhooly and Rosa Vaz enter the Redfearn Centre. He could not have predicted the events that were about to unfold.

Gilhooly asked to meet with Brian in his office. Brian thought that, with Rosa Vaz in attendance, the reason for the visit must be something to do with the dismissal of Maryn Murray for her racism towards young black males and for her sexual grooming of young females. Pead had heard nothing back from Gilhooly since providing his line manager with reports on Murray's conduct. He entertained fleeting thoughts that Gilhooly had come to tell him about the ways that Lambeth were going to reprimand Murray and report her to the police and various teaching authorities and to ensure that her behaviour would be recorded on her CRB checks and that she would be added to List 99.

But the reality of the situation was nothing like that at all.

Gilhooly opened. Pawn to King4. This opening gambit allowed him to introduce other pieces as soon as he wanted to mobilise them. "Brian, you're suspended."

Brian felt check-mated in one move. (For those who do not play chess, the minimum number of moves in which to obtain checkmate is four.)

His normal fighting instincts took over. "What do you mean, I'm suspended?"

"We can't tell you why."

"What do you mean, you can't tell me why? I have a right to know. You can't legally suspend me without telling me why. I want to know why."

"We'll put the reasons for your suspension in a letter and send it to your home."

"That's not good enough. I want to know why I'm being suspended or I'm going nowhere."

Pead look at Vaz. She sat, hands on her knees, a picture of timidity. She looked as though she would rather be anywhere in the world at that moment than in this office in Vauxhall.

Gilhooly raised his game. "If you don't leave now, we have the authority to call the police."

"The police? You can't be serious," retorted Pead.

"Brian, gather together your immediate belongings and leave with us. You'll receive a letter explaining the reasons for your suspension, but some very serious allegations have been made against you."

"Serious allegations? By whom?" demanded Pead.

"We're not at liberty to say," lied the blank Gilhooly.

Gilhooly gave Pead a letter from Lambeth entitled Suspension from Work. It is reproduced in full below:

Dear Brian Pead,

RE: SUSPENSION FROM WORK

I am writing to confirm the decision that has been taken to suspend you from duty with immediate effect on full pay pending an investigation into allegations of gross misconduct.

Since these allegations, if proven, could constitute serious or gross misconduct under the School's disciplinary procedure and rules, you will be suspended from duty on your normal rate of pay with immediate effect whilst a thorough investigation takes place. A thorough investigation will take place, and you will be suspended from work on full pay with immediate effect whilst the investigation takes place, or until further notice.

I must emphasise that this is a precautionary suspension pending investigation into the matter. The suspension in itself does not constitute disciplinary action and does not mean that your case has already been judged. Every effort will be made to complete the investigation as quickly as possible. If at any stage during or at the end of the investigation, or if applicable, at any stage of the disciplinary process, it is considered that this suspension should be lifted you will be informed immediately.

Following the completion of this investigation you will be advised whether or not a disciplinary hearing will take place.

During the period of your suspension you are required to comply with the following instructions:

You must not make contact with any work colleagues or Staff/Members of the Council, Governors, pupils or parents at the Open Learning Centre for

Vocational Studies, on any work matters or matter in connection with your suspension or the investigation. If you need to make contact, for whatever reason, with your work colleagues, or any other employee, you must in the first instance telephone either Barry Gilhooly, Assistant Director, Inclusion on 020 7926 9794 or Rosa Vaz, Schools Principal Human Resouces (sic) Officer on 020 79269972 to obtain permission. However, you may contact an employee if she or he is your recognised trade union representative or work colleague who will be accompanying you at any subsequent hearing or managerial meeting. You must make your own arrangements for, and advise management immediately of, your decision on whom you wish to support you at any future hearings or meeting.

You must not enter any Lambeth Council office or buildings (including Lambeth's education establishments: schools (sic) colleges etc) unless instructed by management to do so. If you are a resident or service user of the Borough of Lambeth and are in receipt of Council services, such as housing, social services, education, or wish to use Council facilities such as libraries, parks, leisure facilities, please notify Rosa Vaz immediately so that she is aware that you need to have access to these premises.

During the period of suspension you must remain available for work, (sic) during the office hours that you normally work, (sic) and you will be expected to make yourself available for any meeting, which may be arranged as part of the investigation. You may also be required to give work-related assistance to management as appropriate. Should you need to take annual leave, or be unavailable for any reason, approval must be obtained from your manager in the normal way. For the period of your suspension, should you fall sick, you are required to comply with your normal sickness reporting requirements, including immediate notification to Rosa Vaz or Barry in Human Resources on 020 7926 9972 and the provision of certificates as necessary.

[Page 2 of 2]

If this matter proceeds to a hearing under the disciplinary procedure, you will be given prior notice of the date, time and place of that hearing and information relating to the matter or matters to be considered there. At these meetings you are entitled to representation by a trade union or professional association representative or you may wish to bring along a workplace colleague.

Enclosed is a copy of the Council Disciplinary Rules, Procedure and the Staff Code of Conduct. I refer you to section 6 of the Disciplinary Procedure on your right to be accompanied.

You are required to hand in your Council ID card, any security card you have and all Council/school keys, or office equipment that you may have in your possession, to your Line Manager.

Please note that any breach of the conditions of your suspension may lead to further disciplinary proceedings being taken against you.

Should you have any queries about your suspension, please contact Rosa Vaz on 020 7926 9972 or Barry on 020 7926 9794.

Yours sincerely

pp Claire Cobbold

Head of Human Resources

cc: Rosa Vaz, Schools Human Resources

Encl: Disciplinary Rules
           Disciplinary Procedures
           Staff Code of Conduct

There are a number of considerations to make here.

Firstly, the letter is in itself an unlawful letter. It fails to provide Brian Pead with the reasons for his suspension. It merely makes reference to "...allegations of gross misconduct..." That phrase is as wide-ranging and ambiguous as to be unlawful. It is extremely bizarre and is akin to the police arresting someone because they might have "broken the law" without ever specifying precisely which law they might have broken.

The second paragraph states that a "...thorough investigation will take place..." However, despite such assurances, and despite it being his legal right to a fair hearing, no such fair hearing ever took place.

The third paragraph states that the case has not been pre-judged, but, again, this was not borne out in reality, as will become evident in the following pages. Also in the third paragraph is a reference to the fact that – if at any stage it is considered that this suspension should be lifted – Pead would be advised of this decision. However, when Lambeth Council was put in possession of facts which completely undermined the allegations, they still continued to pursue Pead as far as they could.

Paragraphs 4, 5, 6 and 7 inform Pead of certain instructions, principally that he must not contact any colleague, parent or pupil and he must not visit any Council building, including his place of work.

These Draconian measures are not lawful. However, Lambeth Council employs these tactics on a number of occasions.

Brian Pead is, of course, a meticulous keeper of notes. His years of research have taught him to keep careful records. He owns the world's largest private collection of newspaper reports on Liverpool Football Club from 1892.

He kept paper records as well as data records on his workstation in his office. Accordingly, he had carefully stored the complaints against Maryn Murray and the dismissal of Eloise Whitmore and all of the records necessary in running a pupil referral unit.

He would naturally need access to all of this material in order to defend the allegations against him – which he was not yet aware of.

By banning him from entering his place of work, Lambeth Council prevented him from defending himself. That is clearly an unlawful act. An organisation cannot suspend an employee on the grounds of allegations of misconduct and then prevent that employee from accessing his records and files or from contacting his colleagues. Yet this is precisely what Lambeth Council did.

The letter was signed by Rosa Vaz, on behalf of Claire Cobbold. These names are important. The name of Barry Gilhooly is also of significance.

Pead – who had never before been suspended or investigated in his 35 years of employment - was frogmarched out of the Redfearn Centre like a prisoner under the Gestapo. But this was not Hitler's Germany. Nor was it the Russia of gulags and the KGB. Nor was it the Stasi of the East Germans, when Germany was a divided country. This was Britain in the 21st century and Pead's human rights had been smashed into smithereens. He was not allowed to say goodbye to any member of staff or any pupil. He had been suspended on full pay without even being told the reasons for that suspension.

His first action was to inform John Callow, who had steadfastly told Brian that nothing good would come of this appointment at the OLCVS.

Callow informed Pead – who already knew this to be the case – that the suspension might be unlawful, since he had not been given any reasons for it. All that was said was that 'serious allegations' had been made against him, but even these had not been communicated to Pead. Nor had the name of the person making the allegations been communicated to him.

"This is farcical!" Callow said.

"But I've done nothing wrong, so what on earth could these allegations be about?"

In response to the suspended Head teacher, Callow hypothesised that they didn't even know whether the allegations were genuinely made or maliciously made, or whether Lambeth were inventing them just to get rid of Pead because they had, for example, a desire to close down the Centre for some political or economic purpose.

"But there can't be anything to be said against me," said Pead, "because I've done nothing wrong."

"Brian, you know as well as I do that people can make anything up about anybody, so wait and see what the situation is."

46

further human rights abuses

Whilst the letter handed to him by Gilhooly forbade Pead to make contact with his staff, it did not state that *they* could not make contact with him and Sandra Roach called him the following week to inform him that officials from Lambeth had entered the building and stripped his office bare.

All his box files were removed. All his filing cabinets were emptied. His computer was removed. Personal possessions were unlawfully removed. Only his desk and chair remained.

Pausing, we need to reflect on precisely what happened to Pead. He had been frogmarched out a building by his line manager and the Lambeth Schools Human Resources manager.

He had been suspended without being told of the reasons for his suspension.

He had been banned from entering any Lambeth building.

He had been banned from contacting any member of staff.

He had been banned from contacting any pupil.

He had been banned from contacting any parent.

His office had been ransacked and all of his files removed.

Copies of all of his emails with Barry Gilhooly were removed.

He had been marginalised, and unlawfully at that. Lambeth Council was isolating him and removing all of his evidence.

It was clear that some dark forces were at work. However, neither Pead, nor his colleagues or friends could have predicted quite how dark those forces were.

lack of police involvement (2)

Having had such allegations made against him, Brian Pead spoke with his trusted ally, John Callow. Neither man – with a combined age of over 110 years – could understand why, if Lambeth took these allegations seriously, they had not informed the police with a view to his being interviewed **at the very least**.

Thus there had now been two separate occasions when the police **ought** to have been called by Lambeth – it was their statutory duty to inform the police – yet they had failed to do so.

What on earth was going on?

Serious allegations – according to Gilhooly – had been made against Pead. Despite the fact that he knew himself to be innocent of all charges, and knowing that he had evidence in his office which would completely exonerate him, he still believed that he would be invited to an interview with the police at the very least.

Thus the police had failed to interview Murray, who had demonstrably been racist and made inappropriate requests of pupils, and they had failed to interview Brian Pead, who was now the bearer of spurious – yet potentially serious – allegations against him.

Why would the police **not** become involved?

The answer could lie in the fact that, just as in the Murray situation, if the police arrested Brian Pead it would be necessary for the pupils and their parents to be called as witnesses.

By dismissing Murray for improper behaviour around children, Pead had unwittingly signed his own death warrant. She had been working on the inside and obtaining the full contact details of extremely damaged and vulnerable children and she was working closely with Anya Hiley in this regard.

Murray **had** to be reinstated so that she could carry on her work in obtaining the full contact details of vulnerable children, so that she – and Hiley – could befriend them before handing them over to others higher up the 'food chain'. Bearing in mind the extreme lengths that Lambeth Council went to dismiss an innocent man, the 'others' might well have been senior police officers, Lambeth officials or even politicians.

And the need to reinstate her – in an all-girls' school (just like St. Augustine's) – meant that they had to do four things to Pead: (i) dismiss him (ii) impugn his name and reputation (iii) ensure that he could never work as a teacher again and (iv) keep him busy with criminal trials, civil trials and fighting to clear his name. While his head was turned towards fighting to clear his name, he was not looking towards

Murray and questioning her and her motives. She was, in effect, being given *carte blanche* to abuse hundreds more children while Pead's attention was entirely focussed on clearing his name and surviving the loss of his job.

The plan outlined in the previous paragraph is just one example of the dark forces at work. Those in power often refer to the ordinary people as 'mushrooms' – in other words, you keep them in the dark and feed them shit (in this case through the media such as radio, television and the newspapers). For this reason, governments the world over fear the Internet. This sometimes faceless entity has incredible power when ordinary people work together in such places as forums in order to achieve justice. And it is because the Internet can be such a powerful tool for informing the masses about what is *really* going on as opposed to what the government *tells* you is going on, that disinformation is spread by the government that there is a paedophile behind every mouse click, for example. The idea is to frighten the mushrooms so that they never see the light of day for fear of confronting a sex offender. One of the most powerful tools known to the ordinary person has to be metamorphosed by the government into a menacing creature about to bite your head off. Better to hide under the duvet and live than to click on the net and find out the truth about society and the cover-ups and disinformation that abounds in the so-called democracy that is known as the UK.

It was Eleanor Roosevelt, the late President's wife, who said, "...You cannot make me feel bad about myself without my permission..."

Brian Pead never gave his permission to Lambeth officials, to the police, or to corrupt MPs when they were doing everything in their power to impugn him. Pead's internal locus of control is firmly intact.

allegations outlined but not specified

On the 13 December 2006, Brian Pead received a letter from his line manager, Barry Gilhooly, dated 12 December. It is reproduced below:

BY RECORDED DELIVERY AND FIRST CLASS POST

PRIVATE & CONFIDENTIAL

12th December, 2006

Dear Brian Pead

Disciplinary Investigation

I write further to our meeting on Friday 8th December 2006 and Claire Cobbold's letter dated 8th December in relation to your suspension from work at the Open Learning Centre for Vocational Studies.

Your suspension is pending an investigation into allegations of gross misconduct including the following:

1. Irregularities in not following procedures when students taking exams;

2. Inconsistency in the treatment of particular students;

3. Inappropriate language to a student;

4. Not adhering to Council Recruitment and Selection procedures;

5. Unfair treatment of staff members;

6. Causing distress to members of staff through inappropriate management style;

7. Bringing the Council into disrepute whilst attending a play.

These allegations will be investigated by a senior Lambeth officer and a Human Resources Officer. Further details will be sent to you by the beginning of next week.

You will be required to attend a disciplinary investigation meeting with the investigating officers. Details will be sent to you in due course. This investigation is not a disciplinary hearing, (sic) it is to enable us to establish the facts, to hear your version of events and for you to raise any other issues which you consider relevant, so that it can be determined whether or not there is a case to answer.

You have the right to be accompanied at the meeting by a work colleague, trade union or professional association representative, (sic) you may not be accompanied by anyone else.

[Page 2 of 2]   The investigation is being carried out under the Council's Disciplinary Procedure, (sic) copy of which has been given to you. You have also been provided with copies of the Council Disciplinary Rules and Staff Code of Conduct.

Should the allegations be substantiated, I must forewarn you that further disciplinary action may be taken.

Please do not hesitate to contact me should you have any queries regarding this matter.

Yours sincerely (sic)

Barry Gilhooly
Assistant Director, Inclusion
Cc Claire Cobbold, Head of Schools Human Resources

The number of grammatical errors in the letter from an Assistant Director of Education was worrying. Even more worrying was the inaccurate information that it contained: in the final paragraph of page one, Gilhooly claimed that Pead could not be accompanied by anyone other than a work colleague, trade union representative or professional association representative. This was a complete fabrication. Pead was entitled to employ the services of a barrister or solicitor if he so wished in order to defend himself against unwarranted allegations.

It should be noted that Pead still had not received particulars of the allegations against him – these were generic headings with no details whatsoever. Thus Lambeth continued to breach employment law.

Callow and Pead pored over the allegations. They looked at each of them in turn while Pead made copious notes.

1.   *Irregularities in not following procedures when students taking exams.*

Pead had worked hard to ensure that all of the pupils had been entered into nationally recognised exams at the end of the first academic year. He had worked together with Colin Hill and between them they had some 50 years' experience of entering pupils into exams. It did not seem feasible that procedures would not have been followed.

2.   Inconsistency in the treatment of particular students.

Pead knew that he treated all pupils with respect. He tried to think of any particular scenarios in which he might have treated certain pupils differently from others. No situations sprung to mind. Several questions arose. Who were these pupils? Who had made the complaints? No details had been provided by Gilhooly.

3.   Inappropriate language to a student.

Brian Pead never spoke inappropriately to any pupil throughout his entire career in teaching. In fact, the opposite was true. He had built his entire career on mutual respect. He spoke to all pupils – male and female – appropriately and with respect. But again questions arose – who was this student? Why had he/ she made complaints? What language was he supposed to have used? Who judged it as being 'inappropriate'?

4.   Not adhering to Council Recruitment and Selection procedures.

This was a perplexing allegation. At all times Pead liaised with Rosa Vaz or other staff at Lambeth Human Resources. All of his conversations and emails between him and Human Resources had been logged. This paper trail was held in box files and on his computer. It was incomprehensible to think that he had not adhered to Council recruitment and selection procedures when this aspect of running the Unit had been the ultimate responsibility of Human Resources. That is one of the functions that a human resource department is set up for – to deal with issues of recruitment.

5.   Unfair treatment of staff members.

It was incomprehensible to Pead that any allegations had been made against him by any of his staff. He always held weekly management meetings with all of his staff and none of them had ever raised a complaint of unfair treatment.

And, naturally, in all of these management meetings he had used agendas and he then produced Minutes of all meetings, which were subsequently signed off by each member of staff.

And Pead kept paper copies of these meetings and recorded minutes in his office and on his computer.

6.   Causing distress to members of staff through inappropriate management style.

Callow and Pead discussed this allegation. The suspended Head was, to some extent, working blind in that no specific examples had been provided and no members of staff had been named.

It was also perplexing because – in over 30 years of management – he had never before received any complaints about his management style. And he had devised a system of weekly management meetings for the very reason that if any issues with regard to his management ever arose, they could be recorded and dealt with immediately before becoming insurmountable issues.

7. *Bringing the Council into disrepute whilst attending a play.*

This did not make sense. How on earth could the reputation of Lambeth Council have been brought into disrepute by his attending a play? In what ways was he supposed to have brought the Council into disrepute?

Not a single allegation made sense. Any single one of them could have been brought up in the weekly full staff meetings or the weekly individual line manager meetings that Pead held with his staff. But perhaps the most bizarre of the allegations was his visit to a play in Kennington.

What was even more bizarre was that – as pointed out by John Callow – Lambeth Council had still not provided Pead with particulars of the allegations. They continued to breach employment law.

In a further breach of employment law, Pead was not to receive details of the allegations against him until after the Christmas holidays.

allegation 1

It was not until the third week of January 2007 that Pead received specific details of the allegations – all of which had been made by Maryn Murray in an 8-page report. Or at least, to the naïve mind, the reader was led to believe that Murray was the sole author of the document. The authors are in possession of evidence which suggests that Murray had only a marginal role in the creation of the document and that Dunipace had commissioned a third party to create it and to make it appear as though Murray were the sole author. Bearing in mind that Pead had been instructed by Gilhooly to dismiss Murray on 15 November 2006, it was beyond comprehension that Lambeth Council should give any credence whatsoever to Murray's allegations, particularly when she had been dismissed for incidences of racism against black males and inappropriate sexual conduct by grooming young white females.

This 8-page report was then circulated by the woman undertaking the investigation, Cathy Twist. This was a name that was to become a thorn in not only Pead's side, but also that of James Walker, the Head who had been suspended by Lambeth Council in 2008 in similar circumstances to Pead.

A full copy of Murray's report can be found on the website www.lambethchildabuseandcoverup.com. For the sake of brevity, it is précised below:

1. Identity
2. Professional Conduct – students
3. Professional Conduct – staff/ general
4. Meeting Conduct

1. Identity

Murray claimed that Brian Pead had used three different names whilst at the OLCVS. He clearly did not. He had, as has been discussed elsewhere in this book, sought permission to use the name of Brian Johnson whilst Head of the pupil referral unit.

Murray herself used a different name – that of Marion Murray – in her work, but failed to bring this to the attention of Lambeth.

She also alleged that Pead had presented himself as younger to students than to adult staff. She cited an instance where – in her view – Pead had told a male pupil that it was his birthday and told the pupil he was 38.

This was not true at all. What had actually happened was that Sean Gayton and Brian were playing a game of snooker during the lunch break, and Brian had, indeed, told his opponent that it was birthday and therefore Sean should let him win the game. This was clearly said in jest. The pupil asked how old Brian was. Brian said, "Guess", and Sean said, "38". Brian winked at Sean and said, "That'll do me!"

No-one had been deceived. In any event, even if the incident had occurred in the way that the Machiavellian Murray had reported, one is forced to ask "So what?" Who would care whether Pead was 38 or 83? What did it matter? Pead used humour a lot in his work with these disadvantaged pupils and it worked well and formed part of the mutual respect between pupils and Head teacher.

What Murray was doing, of course, was sowing seeds of doubt in the minds of the readers of this ridiculous report.

She also made statements including

> "...Brian Johnson hands out business cards with the name of Steve Goodfellow on them and he operates a counselling service from the school..."

This was clearly nonsense. Any manager – including Gilhooly – would know that Pead had worked hard to establish a flourishing, successful and happy unit. He had been given a wage increase because of his hard work and achievements at the Unit. He had no time to operate a counselling service from the building. But what really proved that Murray was lying was that there was CCTV in operation in the Old Library Centre in West Norwood and the Redfearn Centre in Vauxhall and everybody entering either building was captured on it. All visitors also had to sign in at Reception. It would have been impossible for anybody to run a separate business whilst in the environment of the OLCVS without it being noticed. Furthermore, this had never been brought to Pead's attention before.

In respect of Pead's use of alternative names, Murray wrote:

> "...I am not aware of any more identities, but am concerned about whether all his identities have been CRB checked and whether his counselling status is legitimate..."

This allegation was actually laughable. Pead had significant documentation around his CRB checks, and Lambeth had agreed to allow him to use of the name of Brian Johnson.

And one telephone call to the Centre for Professional and Personal Development in Hornsey, north London would have proved that his counselling status was, indeed, legitimate.

Yet Cathy Twist, allegedly in charge of a "...thorough investigation..." failed to take these simple and necessary steps.

Making matters worse, Twist – how apt that name is – sent a copy of Murray's 8-page report to ALL of the people she intended to call as witnesses in her 'investigation'.

In the Hillsborough Report published on 12 September 2012, Chapter 12 on page 341 is entitled, *Behind the headlines: the origins, promotion and reproduction of unsubstantiated allegations.* The report discussed how false information (disinformation) can be promulgated around the world extremely quickly.

At 2.12.2 of the Hillsborough Report, it stated: "...As it became increasingly evident that people were trapped, dying and injured in the central pens, Chief Superintendent David Duckenfield told Football Association (FA) representatives that Liverpool fans had broken into the stadium and rushed down the tunnel into the packed central pens causing the fatal crush. 2.12.3 His untruthful allegation was broadcast internationally..."

This is one way in which the police – an instrument of government – seek to impugn those who dare to challenge their authority. This is what Twist did to Pead. She unlawfully promulgated to Pead's staff a fabricated document containing several serious allegations, none of which had been substantiated. For Chief Superintendent David Duckenfield read Cathy Twist. For Cathy Twist read Chief Superintendent David Duckenfield.

Note how the police try to include a sexual element in any allegations. At 2.12.7 of the Hillsborough report (p.341), it states that "...They [Liverpool fans] were portrayed as predominantly ticketless, drunk, aggressive and determined to force entry. In the throes of the disaster it was alleged that they had assaulted police officers, urinated on officers and the dying, stolen from the dead and verbally sexually abused a lifeless young woman..."

There was no evidence ever produced to substantiate these wild allegations about Liverpool fans at Hillsborough. There was no evidence ever produced to substantiate these wild allegations about a Liverpool fan – Brian Pead.

Ineptitude is one thing. On compassionate grounds, it is possible to forgive people who are inept. But corruption is quite another thing. The corrupt Cathy Twist failed to conduct an investigation according to the standards of a reasonable person.

Perhaps the most astonishing factor behind all this smoke and mirrors was the fact that one of Lambeth's very own consultants was operating under a very different name. Ermina Waters was an ICT consultant within Lambeth Education. The tall and elegant woman would travel around the borough and offer advice to schools about how to improve their ICT offering to pupils. She came into contact with literally thousands of pupils throughout the year.

The feminine and quietly spoken Ermina Waters was, however, hiding a deep secret:

"...Even as a young child Ermina knew she was different. Brought up in a male dominated house, she enjoyed the company of girls and female pursuits.

Ermina is married and her wife was pretty shocked at first, but once she realised how important this is to Ermina's happiness she was very supportive.

Their children are 9, 13, 17 and 18. They saw Ermina dressed as a woman around the house and gradually got used to it. The move to 'dressing up' full-time was a gradual one.

Ermina has been living as a woman for a year and says its (sic) been wonderful. She is an ICT consultant, which means that she trains people in computers. Part of her job is to teach school children, and she says her employers, the children and the teachers have all been terrific. There are only around 5,000 transsexuals in the UK, so the chances are that Ermina is the only one many of the children have met. She feels a deep contentment in her new life..."
Source: <http://www.bbc.co.uk/radio4/hometruths/0233ermina.shtml>

It is remarkable that Lambeth vilified Brian Pead for his legitimate use of different names and yet allowed a transsexual to work in its schools without informing staff, pupils or parents.

Important questions have to be asked: Ermina Waters' real name is Paul. Were both of his names CRB checked?

And, in fact, Ermina Waters would sign all official Lambeth reports on the OLCVS as "Mina Waters" – thus she was using three different names. Were all of these names CRB checked?

Who knew that Waters was really a man? (There is, of course, an argument that says it is not at all important: as long as a person is doing a job for which he or she is being paid, then a person's sexual identity has nothing to do with anyone else unless there is a sexual proclivity towards children.)

More worryingly, Waters established a close relationship with Murray – whom had been dismissed for sexual impropriety with young white females.

On the BBC website, it says that Waters "...enjoyed the company of girls and female pursuits..."

As responsible authors, the question has to be posed - Was the reason for the father-of-four Waters' dressing up as a woman and working in schools an elaborate disguise concocted in order to gain access to "...the company of girls and female pursuits..."?

In asking the question, the authors cast no aspersions upon Paul Waters. Yet these sensitive questions need to be asked in the best interests of children.

Further information about Ermina Waters can be found on the following website <http://www.englishinengland.org.uk>:

> "...Experience: I've taught in mainstream Secondary schools for 20 years and worked as a Teaching and Learning consultant for eight years with Cambridge Education, Southwark and Lambeth..."

Thus Paul Waters began his teaching career in schools over 28 years ago and in that time had significant access to children.

For whatever reasons, he then began dressing and operating as a woman, used a different name, and continued to have considerable access to young girls in particular, something he had craved since childhood.

He has, on his own admission, also moved around a lot, particularly in London.

As Ermina Waters, he then began a close friendship with Maryn Murray and was then instrumental in reinstating Murray after she had been dismissed by Pead for inappropriate behaviour towards young girls, whom Murray categorised as "unattractive", "attractive" and "very attractive". This type of classification is typical of a woman with paedophilic tendencies.

Why had Waters changed his sexual identity? Was it merely a case of some form of dissociation with one's gender? Or was it, perhaps, an elaborate disguise to ensure that he could more readily gain the trust of children and then abuse them?

Why did Waters choose to align herself with Murray? Why did Waters reinstate Murray when Waters was in possession of the fact that Murray had offered bribes to, and been grooming, young, white girls?

Why was Waters never called as a witness in Pead's disciplinary hearing?

Murray's diatribe against Pead continued:

> "...he has very little knowledge of normal school procedures, eg. Exam procedures, curriculum development, planning etc which often surprised me in light of his claims to be a teacher with a vast amount of experience..."

At no point has Pead uttered the words that he is a teacher with a vast amount of experience. He is not a man given to making such extravagant claims. He merely lets the facts speak for themselves. Some of the facts are provided below:

1. won the Elsie Haydon Carrier prize in 1986 for Excellence in Teaching
2. in secondary schools between 1986 and 1998, he had taught English; taught Special Needs; ran football teams; ran the school library; been on dozens of school trips abroad; had produced Variety Shows and radio shows with pupils; ran the school newspaper; been involved in teacher exchanges in

       Germany; and – with parental permission - had undertaken private tutoring in his own home and private tutoring in students' homes

3.   in primary schools between 1998 and 2000 he had taught all subjects for 10 and 11 year olds
4.   secured the best SATs results in Gravel Hill Primary School's history
5.   developed a comprehensive homework system based on the national curriculum which had been published as a series of four books
6.   awarded 7 out of 7 'Excellent' grades in OfSTED inspection for the quality of his teaching, including planning and preparation

Murray's comments were clearly without foundation. However, both she and Twist appear to have overlooked the fact that Pead had attended four separate interviews with Gilhooly for the post of Head Teacher of the OLCVS. Gilhooly had been confident about Pead's ability to hold down the post. Gilhooly worked in the same building and on the same floor as Twist. She had only to stroll along the corridor to speak with Gilhooly and establish that Murray's claims lacked credibility.

In a remarkable allegation, Murray wrote that Pead had

"...frequently claimed that he had been headhunted by Lambeth and insinuated, when speaking with colleagues and students, that he is extremely wealthy..."

As Callow and Pead pored over this document, they laughed at the incredible stupidity of these comments. If we were to assume that Pead had been headhunted by Lambeth, why on earth would Lambeth headhunt a man who – according to Murray – lacked the ability to be a head teacher?

Pead never speaks about being headhunted by any organisation. He never speaks about his level of wealth. He views his financial position as his own business.

More importantly – if we were even to give credence to Murray's assertions – so what? So what if Pead had said that he had been headhunted? So what if Pead did tell people about his financial position? Who cares? And quite what does that have to do with allegations of gross misconduct?

allegation 2

Professional Conduct – students

If the first set of allegations – if, indeed, that is what they were – stretched the imagination to extremes, Murray's assertions with regard to Pead's professional conduct towards students forced one to suspend one's disbelief entirely.

Murray wrote: "...Anya Hiley and Brian had a disagreement about a (not so attractive) female student, Melissa Whitrod...."

Pead showed this report to some of his counselling peers. They were all shocked at the language used by Murray. Who on earth – they queried – would describe female pupils as (attractive) or (not so attractive) when writing a report? And what was Twist doing in giving this report a single moment's credible thought? It had clearly been penned by a woman who had been dismissed and whose sole intention was to seek some form of retribution.

Pead's counselling peers also commented on the fact that if a person is writing a report and refers to the female pupils as (attractive) or (not so attractive), this is indicative of the author's own sexual proclivities, not those of Pead.

His peers commented that Murray appeared to be "a sick woman".

Murray went to assert that "...As far as I know, Melissa did not sit her exams..."

This is a strange comment to make in a report. A credible person would conduct the necessary research – if Pead had prevented Melissa Whitrod from taking her exam, this would have shown up in the examination records of all of the pupils. The facts are that Melissa **did** sit her exams and thus Murray's wild accusation that he treated a (not so attractive) pupil differently from the (attractive) pupils has no credibility whatsoever.

Twist could easily have established whether Melissa had sat her exams or not. This information was obviously supplied by Pead to Lambeth Education. Every school in every local authority provides full details of the examinations undertaken by each pupil. It has a statutory requirement to do so. Thus this information was readily available to Twist, who chose to ignore it.

The question then has to be asked: why did Twist ignore such obvious evidence that Murray's allegations had been created maliciously as a direct consequence of her having been dismissed? Both Callow and Pead knew that Twist's handling of the affair did not make sense.

But events would soon transpire that showed that Twist was hiding a dark secret.

In Murray's report, her diatribe against her former boss continued.

> "...During the GCSE exams, there was another incident where a student, Kerrie Hamilton, **also a very attractive female student** (whom Brian often pulled out of her classes to engage in long conversations in private) arrived very late for her exam. Once again, she received preferential treatment in that she was allowed to sit her exams in the office..."

To the less educated reader of Murray's 8-page report on Pead, the above paragraph has clearly been designed to (a) cause him damage and (b) fool the reader into thinking that Pead had acted improperly towards the pupil. The facts do not bear this out, for the following reasons:

(i)   Kerrie Hamilton **did** arrive late. The rules around the execution of exams allow for latecomers to be allowed to sit the exam. Pead therefore followed the rubric from the examination authority

(ii)   Kerrie Hamilton was on the "At Risk" register

(iii)   Pead had a number of one-to-one conversations (no more than four or five in the year) with her around the private issues that had put her on the register. This information was completely confidential

(iv)   at no time did she receive preferential treatment. She would not have wanted this in any event. Brian Pead helped her considerably, just as he helped thousands of students throughout his teaching career.

For the second time in her report, Murray had used terms such as "attractive" and "not so attractive". With regard to Kerrie Hamilton, however, Murray has created a further category of students when she describes Kerrie Hamilton as "very attractive".

Whenever Pead spoke with pupils in one-to-one meetings, this was always done at the Old Library Centre in West Norwood in his office. What Murray failed to put in her report was that the wall of Pead's office was made up entirely of glass, with two large glass doors. He would sit in a chair opposite whichever pupil he was speaking with. The OLCVS had CCTV throughout the building, as one might expect in a community centre. Thus Brian Pead could be seen on CCTV at every opportunity as he walked throughout the building or if he was in his office. The CCTV recordings were taped each day and stored in a locked cupboard. Thus there was full transparency about Pead's work. He had very good reasons to discuss vital and private information with Kerrie Hamilton in his office. It formed part of his duties as a Head teacher, but Murray has attempted to make capital out of such events. In any event, Kerrie Hamilton never made any complaints against Pead and, furthermore, when she left the OLCVS after its first year, her parents came into the school and thanked Pead for all that he had done for her, particularly in the area of raising her self-esteem.

Cathy Twist had all of this information available to her. Yet she continued to let the investigation move inexorably forward.

Murray's twisted and perverted mind knew no bounds. Her report continued to illustrate her mind-set.

> "...Ashleigh Mills, **very attractive**, female, year 10 student. Brian engaged in long conversations with her, after school and sometimes pulling her out of lessons. On occasion this took place outside the school office in a more private area of the centre. He offered her an office job at the school as an admin person and said she could gain a qualification through it..."

Again Murray uses worrying terms such as "very attractive". Since Pead never described pupils in this way, these terms can only have come from Murray's own depraved mind.

Furthermore, Ashleigh Mills was a Year 11 pupil. Brian did sometimes engage in hour-long conversations with her, but what Murray maliciously omits is the fact that her aunt was often in attendance. If a person was to provide an accurate report, why would that person omit to include the fact that some conversations took place with family members present?

It is true that Pead offered Ashleigh Mills an admin job at the school. She had asked for such a post, and Pead and Colin Hill had discussed the possibility of introducing vocational qualifications. After some research, they found a vocational qualification in administration.

> "...ASDAN qualifications, which are explicitly designed to supplement a core curriculum, and develop skills for learning, skills for employment and skills for life, have an important role to play in supporting the development of "generalised skills".
>
> ASDAN's curriculum programmes can also be deployed to accelerate the acquisition of literacy and numeracy.
>
> At Key Stage 4, schools should be free to offer any qualifications they wish from a regulated Awarding Body, whether or not these are approved for performance measurement purposes, subject to statutory/health and safety requirements.'
>
> This recommendation encourages Head teachers to innovate, and meet the personalised needs of learners, with courses, programmes of study and qualifications that best suit their needs, abilities and requirements..."
> Source: <http://www.asdan.org.uk>

Thus it can be seen that Pead was, by offering Ashleigh Mills (and others not named by Murray) this qualification in office administration, providing her with a nationally recognised exam opportunity.

Yet Murray has included this event in a malicious way. She attempted to show that Pead had ulterior motives towards Ashleigh Mills – which was completely untrue. In any event, Pead was dating his Turkish companion and was happy in that relationship. He had even introduced her to his daughter and grand-children.

It is also true that on occasion Pead met with Ashleigh Mills outside of his office. If his office was being used by other members of staff, Pead would sit with pupils to have discussions in another area of the centre. What Murray fails to include in the report is that this 'other area' was a mere five yards from his office on the ground floor of the community centre and was covered by CCTV. Had Pead been 'up to no good', he would hardly have conducted conversations in such an area.

Murray continued:

> "...Brian praised Ashleigh and told everyone how wonderful she was. Whilst I regarded her highly, giving her preferential treatment seemed inappropriate..."

It is a fact that Ashleigh's English was of a reasonably high standard and, of course, Pead would have commented on this. He never called her 'wonderful'. It is not a word he chooses to use about people. Nor did he give her 'preferential treatment', since the admin job was also offered to other pupils. Yet Murray omits to include this important fact in her report.

The reason that Murray included the term 'preferential treatment' was so that Lambeth Council could suspend him on such grounds.

The reason they would want to do this will soon become evident.

Worryingly, Murray failed to include in her report the fact that she had asked Ashleigh Mills to go on shopping expeditions with her at weekends and to visit her flat. This was no doubt why she referred to the pupil as 'very attractive'.

These dark forces filling Murray's head would continue to force themselves out into the open.

the low-cut top conversation - 2

Cathy Twist knew of the reason for Murray's dismissal from the OLCVS – that she had been racist and bullying towards young black male pupils and that she had been guilty of the sexual grooming of Ashleigh Mills and Gemma Mandry.

Yet Twist continued with the investigation, when any self-respecting manager would have thrown the report in the bin and ensured that Murray had been reported to the relevant authorities, including the police.

Murray then goes on to record details of Brian's interactions with Chloe Gordon. This has been written about in chapter 23, but the following is Murray's twisted interpretation of the scene.

> "...Chloe Gordon, a **very attractive** female, Year 10 student ... I was present when Brian and Chloe had a conversation. She was working part-time at a hairdresser's salon and was mentioning that her workers' (sic) uniform top was cut too low and that she did not want to wear it. Brian said that she should as she could get more tips if she wore a low cut top. Chloe said that she knew, but felt uncomfortable showing her cleavage. I intervened and told her not to listen to Brian as I thought that conversation to be completely inappropriate between a Head Teacher and a 14/15 year old girl..."

Murray completely distorts the conversation and her version of it bears no relation to reality. She has a great wish to be seen as a 'rescuer' by claiming that she intervened, but she did not. She then informs the readers of the report that she felt the conversation to be 'inappropriate' as if she were the only arbiter of what is, or is not, 'appropriate'. She is also unsure whether the pupil was 14 or 15. If this had really occurred in the way that Murray implied, she would surely have recorded the age of the pupil since she had access to that information. And she claimed that she had kept a 'dossier' on Pead 'from day one'.

But who would actually include the description of the pupil as "...**very attractive**..."? Who is the arbiter of beauty? What does it matter whether Chloe Gordon was very attractive or very unattractive? At no time did Pead ever discuss such matters with any member of staff because he did not view pupils as 'unattractive' or 'very attractive' or, for that matter, 'ugly' or 'handsome'.

These labels have been put on the pupils by Murray's warped mind. She therefore projects them on to Brian in order to protect herself, lest people should find out about her innermost desires towards young female pupils.

Clearly there is a discrepancy between Pead's version of events and Murray's version. In such cases, the wise investigator would simply take the most sensible step of calling Chloe Gordon as a witness to the proceedings so that she might give **her** account of the conversation.

This is, in fact, a legal requirement for employers.

In situations where it is one employee's word against another where, for example, an employee has made an allegation of misconduct about another which they strongly deny, an employer ought to take advice from the Court of Appeal.

Civil courts work on the age-old test of reasonableness – in other words, in each situation, what would the reasonable man (now the reasonable person) do when in possession of the same facts?

Thirty or so years ago, in the case of *British Home Stores* v *Burchell* 1980, the Employment Appeal Tribunal laid down the three-stage test - known as the 'Burchell Test' – which an employer must follow to establish whether an employee has committed an act of misconduct. It says they must:

1. believe the employee was guilty of misconduct.

2. have 'reasonable grounds' for holding that belief, e.g. an allegation or other evidence.

3. carry out a 'reasonable investigation', taking into account all the circumstances, before imposing disciplinary sanctions including dismissal.

It is worth noting that at no point could Cathy Twist have believed that Pead was guilty of any misconduct, since the allegations made against him by Murray – **after she had been dismissed by him on the advice of Gilhooly** – were clearly the work of a perverted fantasist.

This particular (Burchell) case is still good law. Thus, if an employer takes a decision to dismiss an employee but is unable to satisfy the tribunal that the Burchell Test was met, the Tribunal is likely to make a finding of unfair dismissal.

In the case of *Salford Royal NHS Foundation Trust* v *Roldan* 2010, the Court of Appeal was asked to consider how far an employer must go during an investigation to satisfy the Burchell Test. Here, one nurse (D) had made an allegation of patient abuse against another, Roldan (R). Roldan, a Filipino, was an experienced registered nurse. The Trust conducted an investigation and decided to dismiss nurse Roldan for gross misconduct. Under its procedures it also notified the police, although no criminal charges were actually brought.

Roldan subsequently issued a claim for unfair dismissal on the basis that she had not been the subject of a fair disciplinary investigation. The matter ended up in the Court of Appeal, which found firmly in her favour.

Although the court noted that the Trust had acted promptly, in that it had not allowed the allegations to hang around for months (unlike in Pead's case), it criticised its investigatory procedures, particularly in light of the seriousness of the allegation. Firstly, it pointed out that it had accepted D's version of events 'without question' - this was dangerous as she was the only witness and Roldan denied any wrongdoing.

Because there was conflicting evidence, the court said the Trust should have made real attempts to determine what happened by locating independent witnesses, for example patients or other staff.

Cathy Twist failed in precisely the same way in her 'investigation'. Murray had made allegations, Pead robustly denied them. In such circumstances, the Court of Appeal would have expected her to call independent witnesses. There was no shortage of independent witnesses – Murray had named more than a dozen pupils in her allegations against Pead. **Not a single pupil was called as a witness in an abuse of process.** Chloe Gordon was never called to inform the panel that the conversation had not been as Murray described.

Why would Twist **not** call Chloe Gordon as a witness?

In the above case, Salford Royal NHS Foundation Trust also failed to 'test' the physical evidence, i.e. the layout of the area where the alleged misconduct was said to have taken place. This was relevant to the strength of D's evidence.

This case is also relevant to Pead's case, as will be explained in a separate chapter.

The Court of Appeal indicated that where there is conflicting and unproven evidence from two employees, employers are not automatically obliged to believe one over the other; if no independent witness can be found, the safest option is to conclude that there is, in fact, no case to answer.

This option was, of course, available to Twist and Lambeth Council – but for their own dark reasons, they continued with the allegations against Pead.

As a point of good practice, the court also said that where disciplinary action might result in a 'black mark' against an employee's name, for example by having criminal charges brought against them (regardless of whether it results in a conviction), the employer must ensure the evidence is accurate before they rely on it. If they don't ensure that the evidence is accurate, it will be almost impossible to satisfy the Burchell Test and the employer will have acted unlawfully.

Despite there being considerable legislation under employment law to indicate that Twist should drop all charges against Pead, she maintained her unrelenting and irrational pursuit of an innocent man.

52

the low-cut top conversation – 3

On 24 September 2012, the authors approached Chloe Gordon and asked her for her version of events.

She remembered the conversation she had had with Brian Pead and she sent him a message via Facebook at 20:29. The message is reproduced below:

> "...I do remember this conversation, but it's not like she said it was in her report. You were just a lovely teacher and made me feel safe and determined to learn. There was nothing out of line..."

Chloe Gordon provided these comments of her own volition. She was not coerced in any way whatsoever. She was not remunerated for her comments. Her account shows that Pead had been telling the truth all along – and that Murray had lied about the conversation.

The comments by the 21 year old show that she ought to have been called as a witness by Twist and Mary White, a Human Resources 'consultant' brought in to assist Twist. Both women are guilty of perverting the course of justice by not calling the pupil and of misrepresentation to an Employment Tribunal.

53

cassandra trimmings

Murray claimed that Pead had shown favouritism towards another "...**very attractive** female pupil, by the name of Cassandra Trimmings..."

Murray claimed that Brian allowed Cassandra to take an examination early because she had to attend a Probation meeting with her boyfriend.

Cassandra Trimmings was a highly intelligent young woman of fifteen years of age. She had been from school to school and had never really settled. Yet despite these obstacles, she had nonetheless acquired a great deal of knowledge and she was emotionally beyond her chronological age, as often occurs with such nomadic people.

With no father in her life, she and Pead struck up a healthy relationship. She saw in him some of the qualities missing in her life, and, in turn, he had seen in her a courageous young woman with a lot to offer society. It was, of course, purely platonic and this relationship of mutual respect occurs hundreds of millions of times in schools across the world. And Cassandra trusted him and his world view.

The OLCVS was a registered examination centre. In order to become registered, a centre has to meet certain criteria, such as having a safe to store exam papers and scripts. Brian Pead and Colin Hill worked hard to ensure that the OLCVS met all the necessary criteria so that it would be registered as an official exam centre. All exam boards issue rules which have to be met, of course, by all of the registered centres. These rules range from mobile phones not being allowed in the exam room to whether calculators can be used in a Maths exam, for example. Both Hill and Pead had been involved in organising and invigilating numerous examinations over many years – Murray had no such experience. In fact, she did not even have Qualified Teacher Status.

Murray claimed that Trimmings was allowed to sit her examination early and in a separate room from the main examination hall. However, when Colin Hill was interviewed on 25 January 2007 and asked whether Pead had allowed this to happen, Hill replied: "...I am the Exam Officer at the Centre. The legal requirements and responsibilities for exams were known at the Centre. Concerning the situation with Cassandra, this didn't actually happen as she didn't actually sit the alleged exam. I have no knowledge of her sitting an exam in the Centre office. Cassandra sat one paper and was marked absent for the other paper. I don't know how this misunderstanding occurred. Kerrie Hamilton made the late time frame for an exam and was given the full time to sit the exam although I don't think she needed it. Also, Rickkardo Crawford-Burrows arrived late for one exam and was also given the full time to sit his exam. There is photocopied evidence of students who sat exams. **The incident with Cassandra never happened as Murray claimed...**"

Early on – 25 January 2007 – Twist was in possession of facts that proved that Murray had lied in her 8-page submission. At no point did she inform Pead of this. Nor did she dismiss Murray's other claims.

Yet Murray – without qualified teacher status – made a complaint **after she had been dismissed by Pead for racism and inappropriate behaviour towards young females**. Murray claimed in her report that "...Brian never had this type of relationship with any male student and never engaged in these hour-long conversations with any of them..."

This was completely untrue. In fact, Brian's log of private conversations (he recorded all such conversations on his computer in his office before printing them off and storing them in a locked filing cabinet) shows that he had had such conversations with male students. Whilst it is true to say that he had marginally more conversations with female pupils, this is simply because females of that age are usually more willing to discuss their feelings than young men of that age, who are often struggling to be seen as a "man" or a "tough guy" who can handle anything. Indeed, in his book *Emotional Intelligence*, Daniel Goleman writes: "...Parents, in general, discuss emotions – with the exception of anger – more with their daughters than their sons..." and cites as his source the excellent review in Leslie R. Brody and Judith A. Hall, *"Gender and Emotion"*, in Michael Lewis and Jeannette Haviland, editors, *Handbook of Emotions* (New York, Guilford Press, 1993).

Goleman adds: "...Girls are exposed to more information about emotions than are boys: when parents make up stories to tell their preschool children, they use more emotion words when talking to daughters than to sons; when mothers play with their infants, they display a wider range of emotions to daughters than to sons; when mothers talk to daughters about feelings, they discuss in more detail the emotional state itself than they do with their sons—though with the sons they go into more detail about the causes and consequences of emotions like anger (probably as a cautionary tale).

Brody and Hall, who have summarized the research on differences in emotions between the sexes, propose that because girls develop facility with language more quickly than do boys, this leads them to be more experienced at articulating their feelings and more skilled than boys at using words to explore and substitute for emotional reactions such as physical fights; in contrast, they note, "boys, for whom the verbalization of affects is de-emphasized, may become largely unconscious of their emotional states, both in themselves and in others." (Brody and Hall, *Gender and Emotion*, p.454.

At age ten, roughly the same per cent of girls as boys are overtly aggressive, given to open confrontation when angered. But by age thirteen, a telling difference between the sexes emerges: Girls become more adept than boys at artful aggressive tactics like ostracism, vicious gossip, and indirect vendettas. Boys, by and large, simply continue being confrontational when angered, oblivious to these more covert strategies. (Girls

and the arts of aggression: Robert B. Cairns and Beverley D. Cairns, *Lifelines and Risks*, New York, Cambridge University Press, 1994). This is just one of many ways that boys—and later, men—are less sophisticated than the opposite sex in the byways of emotional life.

When girls play together, they do so in small, intimate groups, with an emphasis on minimizing hostility and maximizing cooperation, while boys' games are in larger groups, with an emphasis on competition. One key difference can be seen in what happens when games boys or girls are playing get disrupted by someone getting hurt. If a boy who has gotten hurt gets upset, he is expected to get out of the way and stop crying so the game can go on. If the same happens among a group of girls who are playing, the game stops while everyone gathers around to help the girl who is crying. This difference between boys and girls at play epitomizes what Harvard's Carol Gilligan points to as a key disparity between the sexes: boys take pride in a lone, tough-minded independence and autonomy, while girls see themselves as part of a web of connectedness..."

Not for Twist, then, the notion of consulting sound academic research.

adrian henry

One example of Brian's interaction with male pupils can be seen in the following letter, dated 18 February 2008, from Adrian Henry, an intelligent and articulate black pupil with an outstandingly charismatic personality and considerable level of decency. He is now studying at the University of Greenwich in London.

"...I am a former student of Mr Johnson and I think he is a very nice and honest person. When Mr Johnson started to teach me from 2005 to 2006, he really open (sic) my eyes to what I could achive (sic) in life. Even to this day his words still means (sic) a lot to me. When everyone else gave up on me, he would tell me never to give up and that I can be anything I want to be. He also had one to ones with us as well so that we could set aims and objectives as to what we wanted to achive (sic). I personally think Brian is a good teacher and many of his former students would agree with me.

Yours sincerly (sic)

Adrian Henry..."

There was significant evidence to show that all of Murray's allegations were ludicrous and malicious. Yet Cathy Twist continued her deadly pursuit of Pead.

Murray added a further allegation against Pead. She claimed that a male pupil, Rickkardo Crawford-Burrows, had been treated "...totally differently from the above-mentioned girls..." in that Pead – it was alleged – had attempted to have Crawford-Burrows removed from the Unit and that Pead did not want to enter him for the GCSE exams.

The absurdity of these claims is staggering.

Firstly, Pead and Crawford-Burrows got along well. The fourteen-year-old pupil was tall for his age – at over six feet one – and walked as if he owned the building, with a slight swagger. But Pead liked him, because he could see that beneath that initial cockiness was a decent young man struggling for an identity. Pead knew that Rickkardo had the potential to become involved in deviant behaviour on the streets, but that could be said of millions of such 14-year-old young men.

Pead and Crawford-Burrows often had differences of opinion in the manner of a father attempting to keep his son on the 'straight and narrow'. This was nothing out of the ordinary.

Where Murray's report was so wide of the mark, however, was that Pead had – in association with Colin Hill – been researching a better unit for the young man's energy. Pead was **not** 'trying to get rid of him' and it was minuted at a staff meeting that Pead was researching a unit that would more readily meet Rickkardo's needs, because Pead felt that the OLCVS was, to some degree, holding him back by not providing a daily, full-time education. Besides, Rickkardo wanted to be an electrician, and Pead conducted research on the pupil's behalf to try to find him a school that had a significant vocational bias. Pead found a unit that would have helped Rickkardo how to wire a plug and train to be an electrician. In his interview of 25 January 2007, Hill confirmed that Pead was researching courses that offered training in electrical qualifications, adding "...I would differ with the allegations made by Maryn regarding Rickkardo..."

Thus Hill has also disproved another allegation of Murray's. The entire 8-page document had been fabricated. Yet Twist persisted in hunting down her quarry. She was acting on orders from Phyllis Dunipace, the Executive Director of Lambeth.

The fantasist Murray also claimed that Pead had argued with Annabel Field, the English teacher and part-time actress, about entering Rickkardo for the GCSE.

It had long been a goal of Pead's that he wanted **every** pupil to leave the OLCVS with at least one nationally-recognised qualification. He was not the kind of man who would want to say "Every pupil except one left with a GCSE". Murray's suggestion was manifestly ridiculous.

However, what makes her claims even more ludicrous was that Rickkardo **was** entered for the GCSE examination.

The official examination centre records provide evidence of this claim. And these records were available to Cathy Twist in her 'investigation'. Hill told Twist during his interview that "...there is photocopied evidence of students who sat exams..."

Thus another allegation had been shot down in flames.

It did not matter whether Pead liked Rickkardo Crawford-Burrows or didn't like him. It didn't matter whether Pead had or had not been trying to remove him from the school. It didn't matter whether Pead argued with Annabel Field about entering Rickkardo for the exams or not – all of this nonsense was merely a smoke screen to present Pead in a bad light and to ensure that Lambeth Council had sufficient reason to dismiss him.

The question now becomes "Why would Lambeth Council want to dismiss a man who was doing an excellent job, who had created a school out of nothing, who had built a happy and safe environment for all the pupils and who had ensured that all of these disaffected pupils had gained at least one nationally-recognised qualification?"

The answer was some time in coming and was nothing short of sensational.

55

further complaints

Meanwhile, Murray's report continued.

Under the heading 'General Conduct: Staff/ General', Murray made a number of extravagant and false claims. Her particular use of language should be noted. It reflects her mind-set.

"...There has been a higher staff turnover than I have experienced at previous schools. In this regard the following is of concern:

- People who have left within less than a year after expressing concerns about Brian:

  Ellie Whitmore

  Jenny Foster

  Annabel Field

  Maryn Murray..."

John Callow and Brian Pead looked critically at this list. Eloise Whitmore had been dismissed by Lambeth because she failed her probationary period. She was not capable of holding down the job. Therefore, it has to be asked, what had this to do with Brian Pead? He had managed her and found her to be ineffective and incapable. Therefore he was, in fact, doing **his** job properly.

In chapter 3, entitled major responsibilities, at Paragraph 4 it stated that part of Pead's role was to be responsible for the deployment of staff and 'capability'. By failing Whitmore in her first probationary period, he had found her incapable and he was merely fulfilling his role as Head of the unit.

Jennifer Foster had left because she had no permanent contract from Lambeth and also because she wanted to return to primary education. Brian had liked her and noted that she was no doubt an excellent Learning Mentor at primary level. Most people find a level at which they feel comfortable and can succeed. Jennifer Foster was exactly like this. Her appointment as a secondary school Learning Mentor was another example of Gilhooly's mismanagement. Brian Pead told her to her face that he was sorry she was leaving but that he understood her reasons why. Gilhooly's insistence on only offering termly extensions to one-term contracts was inhibiting the growth of the OLCVS. Pead wrote Foster an excellent reference – which he showed to her and invited comments from her before posting it off. He wished her well on the next step of her career and on her journey through life.

Again, what had Jenny Foster's return to primary level got to do with Brian Pead?

Annabel Field had sent Pead an email in which she said that she had an opportunity to act in Bath and so she took that life-enhancing opportunity and left the OLCVS on amicable terms, just as Jenny Foster had done. This had nothing to do with Pead's management of her. In fact, the email of 17 April 2006 is evidence that she had had her best teaching experience in London at the OLCVS.

And then Murray herself. She had been dismissed – with agreement from Gilhooly – for being racist against black male pupils and for the sexual grooming of white female pupils, including offering bribes and asking girls to visit her flat and go on shopping expeditions with her. Of course Pead dismissed her.

Yet this document had been put together in such a way as to cause the naïve reader to believe that there were problems with Pead's management style. The evidence shows otherwise.

And then the real reason for Murray including all these female names becomes clear when she adds: "...they were all young females..."

From a psychological perspective, this shows that Murray was not only a fantasist, but also severely damaged and delusional. To suggest that Whitmore (28), Foster (45), Field (25) and Murray (30) were **young females** was stretching reality too far. To include the phrase in a document in which the author has already used the phrase **young females** when referring to girls aged 14-16, is nonsense. Either the 14 to 16 year olds are young females, or the 25-45 year olds are young females. Both cannot be true.

Murray's use of the term young females was simply (a) to present Pead in a bad light and (b) indicative of her mind-set. She had already been dismissed by Pead for her inappropriate advances towards young white females and yet in her report – compiled some weeks **after** her dismissal – she attempts to hide behind the allegations that she is throwing at Pead.

Although Murray's allegations appeared to be serious, Callow questioned whether any of them could be reasonably substantiated.

Upon greater examination, not a single allegation had any merit; there was substantial evidence to disprove all of the allegations, but Cathy Twist continued in her pursuit of Pead.

Murray made a number of wholly unsubstantiated claims against Pead in relation to his treatment of Eloise Whitmore, Jennifer Foster and Anya Hiley. **Note that not a single person made any complaints against Pead other than Murray – after she was**

dismissed by him. No member of staff, no pupil, no parent or carer, no Lambeth advisor and not even Gilhooly had made a single complaint about Pead. They had all had ample opportunity in which to do so. There were enough official mechanisms in place in which to make a complaint and to have it properly dealt with. All of these allegations had come from a single person – Maryn Murray – after she had been dismissed for inappropriate contact with children.

Anya Hiley was a Connexions Advisor who worked out of a small third floor office at the Old Library Centre in West Norwood. Initially, she and Brian struck up a reasonable working relationship.

However Hiley, in her role, had access to the private details (name, addresses, and telephone numbers) of hundreds of children. She claimed to have seen Pead engaging in hour-long conversations with female students. How could she have done so? She worked on the third floor and the OLCVS was on the ground floor. Furthermore, was she timing conversations if she happened to come upon them? How would she know when a particular conversation started and ended? Furthermore, she often worked outside of the building entirely. Her lies exactly mirrored those of Murray. By aligning herself with a woman who had been dismissed for gross misconduct against children, the unmarried Hiley's motives towards young females also have to be called into question.

Why would Hiley seek to defame Pead? What possible motives would she have? Clearly, her experience of the OLCVS was at a considerable distance since she worked on the third floor of the Old Library. Yet Hiley – who claimed to be deeply religious – was clearly not averse to lying to protect her friend, Maryn Murray. Was Hiley, therefore, working in partnership with Murray to groom young girls?

56

a detached perspective

Brian had several positive working relationships with staff at the West Norwood Old Library Centre. A large number of the community centre staff were of Afro-Caribbean descent, and Brian enjoyed their charisma and what they added to his life. He had chats with various staff about the type of hair that Afro-Caribbeans have, the type of fish they like to eat and even recipes for goat meat curries. He enjoyed their lively and spirited attitude to life.

One such member of staff was Alphonso Harris, a Lambeth Detached Youth Worker. Alphonso and Brian were of a similar age and enjoyed all types of discussions about all aspects of life that men in their age range share.

> "...I was part of the Lambeth Detatched (sic) team that occupied the Old Library Centre in Knights Hill, West Norwood. From Sep 2005 – July 2006, The (sic) ground floor was occupied by an organization referred to as the Virtual School, run by Mr Brian Johnson.
>
> Brian appeared to have a very positive impact on what appeared to be some very difficult students; they seemed to interact well. From my position as a very frequent user of the building I could tell that all the students liked and admired Brian.
>
> As a fellow member of staff, I can honestly say me and Brian shared many conversations and I found him to be genuine and honest. We never had a cross word and he was down to earth, practical and ran the centre with a very professional attitude. His outlook was bright and all his students admired and respected him.
>
> Alphonso Harris, Detached Youth Worker..."

Thus we have a man aged a little over 50, who used the building frequently and who shared many conversations with Pead, stating for the public record that he found Pead to be genuine and honest. Harris goes further still, and states that Pead ran the Centre very professionally and that all his students admired and respected him.

Why would Harris' statement be so different from Hiley's and Murray's account? Harris was a frequent visitor to the centre and therefore saw Brian on a far more regular basis than Hiley did. Why would Harris not refer to the alleged "...hour-long conversations that Pead had with young, 'attractive' girls..."? Why did Harris not refer to the allegation that Pead treated female students differently from male students for, after all, Harris was a vastly-experienced youth worker? Why did Harris not refer to the allegations that Pead would meet with female pupils in the more remote areas of the centre?

Why did Twist fail to call Alphonso Harris as a witness?

And how can the views of pupils, parents and centre staff be so diametrically opposed to the views of Murray and her partner-in-crime, Hiley?

the botswanan simon cowell

One parent who was impressed with Pead's running of the OLCVS was a Mr Sesinyi, father of the then 14 year old Cathy. According to Pead, his daughter was an amazing young woman. Intelligent and vivacious, she had a maturity beyond her years. She and her father and Brian established an excellent working relationship. They were something of kindred spirits. Cathy's father referred to her as "my ever-smiling daughter" and she was, indeed, always smiling and showing her beautiful white teeth.

Keabetswe Sesinyi was a pop star in his native Botswana, under the name of Mr Dee. He had produced an album entitled *Mist of Darkness*, in which he had composed all of the music, written all of the songs and completed all of the arrangements. The album was recorded at the MDM Studio in Gaborone, Botswana.

He was an extremely talented man, who was also humble. He and Pead established an excellent relationship based on trust and mutual respect. Sesinyi said, "...I work and click better with down to earth people..."

Sesinyi owned some land on the outskirts of Gaborone, the capital of Botswana. He wanted to build a soccer stadium and establish a school on the land. He approached Pead and asked him if he would be interested in becoming involved in the project and run the school. Had he had any issues with Pead's running of the OLCVS, he would hardly have invited Pead to run the school in Botswana.

Sesinyi and Pead visited the Botswanan Embassy in London to meet with the Minister for Overseas Development and to discuss Sesinyi's project.

Sesinyi is currently the Simon Cowell of Botswanan television. He is the Executive Producer of the popular local talent show My Star, a reggae maestro and a music producer. Born in Mmankgodi, Keabetswe Sesinyi, popularly known as Master Dee in the music industry, has braced himself to overcome challenges that many could not face in order to do what he believes is the best for those hoping to break into the big time.
Source: <<http://www.thevoicebw.com/2012/05/04/scouting-for-talent/>>

evidence ignored

A significant number of statements were collected in support of Pead. All of these statements completely contradicted the wild and spurious allegations of Hiley and Murray.

But perhaps the most interesting of Murray's attacks on Pead came in regard to his alleged treatment of Annabel Field.

Murray claimed the following:

> "... Annabel Field felt that she was being bullied by Brian. He had several very private and personal conversations with her, which I understand that he led through his style of probing. She once commented to me that she felt that she was his 'subject' as if he was going to use her in a counselling study. She mentioned to me that she felt violated and vulnerable after being in conversation with Brian..."

Upon a first reading, this provides a picture of a somewhat bullying line manager and an employee who was a victim. It is, of course, all nonsense. Murray clearly was not in possession of the email sent by Annabel Field in which she had thanked Brian for his support (see chapter 18).

This email evidence was presented to the investigatory meeting by Brian Pead to Cathy Twist, who clearly ignored it.

Furthermore, a psychological analysis of Murray's mind-set makes for interesting reading. She is what is often referred to as a 'Rescuer' – someone who believes they can sort out every problem for everybody else. The payoff for this is that they believe they will be admired. Murray had a deep need to be admired because of her narcissistic personality disorder, but had no idea about how to actually be a recipient of such adoration. She had what is known as omnipotent feelings – that she was almost God-like in status. Her hubris knew no bounds. She made several references throughout this 8-page document to the fact that she attempted to mediate, but she had displayed no such skills whatsoever. In fact, when trying to sort out a contract, she displayed no mediation skills at all – merely relying on a position of "This is what I want". Those skilled in mediation will know that that particular point of view lacks the vital ingredient of mediation – that of understanding the differing positions of all parties in the mediation process. Murray lacked empathy. In fact, she displayed sociopathic qualities of always wanting her own way, without ever seeking to learn what the other party wished to achieve or even acknowledging that the other party had needs of their own.

"...There was one particular conversation between Brian and Annabel where she told him that he was 'mind fucking/head fucking' her. (They both told me this on separate occasions). She explained that he would mention things to her without wanting to give examples even though she would ask him for concrete examples. He would suggest things or insinuate things in a negative way without justifying where he was going with the conversation. Annabel and Brian had a very long conversation that particular late afternoon/evening. Again, I can remember both of them mentioning it the following day. Brian told me that he had a very deep conversation with Annabel and that it was the type of conversation she should be having with a boyfriend. I asked him why he allowed the conversation to go that far. I picked up that he felt uncomfortable. Annabel in turn told me that she did not want to share certain things with him, but before she knew it she did..."

Brian Pead never had a conversation with Maryn Murray about Annabel Field. Any conversation he has with people is private and confidential. He would not have mentioned to Maryn Murray a private conversation that he may or may not have had with Annabel Field.

Furthermore, had Annabel Field felt uncomfortable, or that she had been 'mind-fucked' by Brian Pead, why did she not include this in her email in which she thanked him for his support to her?

Murray's report makes certain claims against Pead **on behalf of Annabel Field,** yet the latter made no such complaints herself. This is further evidence of Murray's disturbed mind-set. She believed that she was powerful enough to speak on behalf of everybody else – without ever seeking their permission, or without ever suggesting to them that if they did, in fact, have an issue with Brian Pead, they should mention it to Pead himself.

This disturbing mind-set was evident throughout her report. Her disturbing attitudes towards sex and young women were also evident.

the horse dealer's daughter

Note the following allegation:

> "...On one particular occasion Annabel invited all staff to attend a play that she was performing in. Brian went with a young female. After the performance Annabel had a conversation with a fellow cast member. The cast member told Annabel that his wife was sitting next to Brian (whom she knew was Annabel's boss) and the female. During the performance Brian and the female performed sexual acts, one of which she described as the female giving Brian a 'hand job'. Annabel was embarrassed and shocked and told me about this very soon after the performance..."

This section in Murray's report is particularly disturbing on a number of levels. It is worth examining in some detail.

It has been cleverly authored. The paragraph commences with a fact – that Annabel Field did, in fact, invite all of the staff to attend a play in which she was appearing.

That is the clever part. It fools the reader into thinking that the **entire** paragraph must be true because it starts with a fact that several people know to be true. Thus all of Brian's colleagues – when reading this paragraph – would immediately start to believe that the whole paragraph must be true because they had first-hand knowledge that they, too, had been invited to attend the play. This is often how disinformation works.

Immediately Murray then turns that fact into mere hearsay "...Brian went with a young female..."

Since Murray did not attend the play, how would she know that Brian attended the play himself, and how would she know that he had attended with anyone else, male or female? One can only assume that Annabel Field had told her at some point. Yet surely Annabel would not have referred to Brian's companion as a "...**young female...**" since she was the same age as Elif, 25. Who, in fact, refers to 25 year olds as young females?

The fact is that Brian attended the play with a 25 year old female companion who enjoyed his company. He does not have to answer to anyone about whom he had chosen to take to the theatre. He often took his grand-daughters to the cinema. They were at the time aged 8 and 6 – in other words, young females. No doubt Murray would have made extensive capital out of the fact that Pead spent many hours in the company of young females – his grand-daughters!

Murray claims that after the performance, Annabel Field "...had a conversation with a fellow cast member. The cast member told Annabel that his wife was sitting next to Brian – whom she knew to be Annabel's boss – and the female..."

The cast member is not named. This immediately casts doubt upon Murray's allegations. This unnamed cast member is allegedly married – where is the evidence? Furthermore, this unnamed wife of the unnamed cast member somehow automatically knew that Brian was Annabel's boss. No date was provided in respect of when Brian attended the play.

Murray now expects her readers to believe that the unnamed cast member's unnamed wife sat through an entire performance of *The Horse Dealer's Daughter* in a room in which – according to the LondonTown.com website – it is possible for audience members to see beads of sweat on the cast members' faces, observed sexual acts between Pead and his companion and then saw him being masturbated **and said nothing to anyone else about these alleged acts at the time.**

It is incomprehensible that these events occurred. They, of course, existed only in the dark recesses of Murray's disturbed pathology. That Cathy Twist – the investigating officer appointed by Lambeth Council to investigate this report – should give the report a single moment's credence is also incomprehensible. Why, then, did Cathy Twist continue such a ridiculous 'investigation'? Before this question is answered, we must return to Murray's allegations:

> "...During the performance Brian and the female performed sexual acts, one of which she described as the female giving Brian a 'hand job'..."

This needs to be examined in two parts. Firstly, there is an allegation that Brian and his companion (whom it should be noticed has now been elevated from a 'young female' to a 'female') performed sexual acts. This is in the plural. These sexual acts are not specified. Why aren't they specified? What, indeed, is a sexual act? Is it copulation? Is it fellatio? Is it cunnilingus? Is it 'fingering'?

Any investigator worth that title would have sought specific answers to these questions. **Twist sought no such answers** and thus the allegations are just that – completely unspecified and unfounded nonsense.

Secondly, the unnamed wife of the unnamed actor allegedly told Annabel Field who allegedly told Maryn Murray that the female gave Brian a 'hand job'.

Thus we have hearsay evidence four times removed. The actor, the actor's wife, Annabel Field and finally Maryn Murray. The chain of hearsay was about as long as Bill Brewer, Jan Stewer, Peter Gurney, Peter Davy, Dan'l Whiddon, Harry Hawk, Old Uncle Tom Cobbleigh and all...

However, let us assume for one moment that this unlikely event **did** actually occur. There is substantial evidence in the public domain that shows that the White Bear Theatre performed plays in a small room and catered for a maximum audience of 40. The room is so small and the audience so close to the actors that beads of sweat on the actors' faces can be seen by the members of the audience.

Now let us imagine that during this performance, a woman in the audience starts to masturbate another member of the audience. This act would have been impossible to miss by anyone acting in the play and by other members of the audience.

Clearly this act did not happen.

However, for the purposes of exposing the corrupt Cathy Twist and the malignant Murray, let us continue to assume that it did occur.

The unnamed actor's unnamed wife witnesses these sex acts, only one of which is a 'hand job'. Why didn't she complain? Or shout out? Or draw anyone's attention to it?

If she really had mentioned it to her husband, who allegedly mentioned it to Annabel Field, who allegedly mentioned it to Maryn Murray ... why didn't she take the very simple step of calling the police on her mobile phone during the performance so that Brian Pead and his female companion could have been arrested? Or, given that this unnamed wife was so allegedly upset, why didn't she complain directly to Pead or his companion and tell them to stop? Or complain to the Theatre Manager? Or Director – Jeremy Robinson – who was on hand? Or complain to the manager of the pub?

And was this unnamed wife sitting alone or with friends or companions? If she was sitting with others, why did she not complain to them, and why did they not complain on her behalf?

The reason is that **it simply did not happen.**

At this point we must return to the famous "Burchell Test". It has been an established part of employment law in England and Wales since the 1980 *British Home Stores* v *Burchell* case, which established a legal precedent.

This three-stage test of reasonableness demanded that employers must:

(1) believe the employee was guilty of misconduct

(2) have "reasonable grounds" for holding that belief (i.e. an allegation **or other evidence**)

(3) carry out a "reasonable investigation", taking into account all the circumstances, **before** imposing disciplinary sanctions including dismissal.

There is already enough evidence that has been presented in this book that demonstrates that Cathy Twist could not have reasonably believed that Brian Pead was guilty of misconduct. There was sufficient evidence to show that Maryn Murray – having been sacked by Pead for inappropriate behaviour around children – had lied in the 8-page report. Cathy Twist failed to carry out a reasonable investigation, particularly in view of the fact that – if proven – the allegations would cause Pead to lose his position and never be able to teach again and that he might also be the subject of a police investigation.

In the recent case of *Salford Royal NHS Foundation Trust* v *Roldan* (2010), the Court of Appeal was asked to consider how far an employer must go during an investigation to satisfy the Burchell Test.

The Court said that an employer should make real attempts to determine what happened by locating independent witnesses. It also said that an employer should "look around" at physical evidence, by, for example, visiting the scene where alleged misconduct occurred. Why, then, did Cathy Twist not visit the White Bear Theatre in Kennington? After all, her office in Canterbury Crescent, Brixton is no more than a short bus ride away. Buses 3, 59, 133, 159, and 415 run from Brixton Station to the Oval and Kennington tube station is just two minutes from the White Bear Theatre. The bus services are very good and operate every six minutes or so. It is little more than a mile between Lambeth Education offices and the White Bear Theatre. Had Cathy Twist taken the tube from Brixton on the Victoria Line to Stockwell (just one stop away) and then taken the Northern Line to Kennington that was just two short stops away, the journey from Lambeth Education offices to the White Bear Theatre would have taken her around thirteen minutes. Even allowing for disruptions or delays, the maximum time it would have taken her was twenty minutes to inspect the room about which Murray had made her allegations.

Yet, despite it being a reasonable action (as defined by the Court of Appeal and not the authors of this book) Cathy Twist failed to make that journey.

ipek yẙlmaz

The tale of corruption surrounding Twist and Murray is compounded upon a reading of the following email. It is from Ipek Yẙlmaz, known as Elif, who accompanied Brian to the White Bear Theatre in Kennington.

Her email was sent directly to Brian, who had naturally contacted her to let her know that her name had been sullied by Maryn Murray. The email was sent on 6th February 2007 at 19:42:14 via Hotmail, some nine months after she had visited the theatre. It has not been redacted or altered in any way.

"...My name is Iperk (sic) Yẙlmaz. I am 26 years old and live in Turkey. From March 2006 until January 2007, I lived in London whilst studying there. I met Brian in London whilst attending a Life Coaching seminar and we became very good friends.

On 3 February 2007, Brian contacted me to make me aware of the allegations in question as they not only involved himself, but also brought my name into disrepute. As a result, I have decided to write the following and wish it to be presented to a panel in any hearing in which Brian may find himself in respect of these allegations.

On one night out, we visited the White Bear public house in Kennington, London, where a colleague of Brian's was appearing in a play, The Horse Dealer's Daughter. I was introduced to Annabel Field (Brian's colleague) by Brian as she arrived at the pub. I was surprised by the size of the Theatre, as it was in the back room of the pub, with only 2 rows of seats as I recall.

Neither Brian nor myself was introduced to any other member of the cast, so I am not aware of how the alleged cast member's wife would even know who Brian was, (sic) and nor could she have known that he worked for Lambeth.

Furthermore, the allegations that "...during the performance Brian and the female performed sexual acts..." is completely untrue and I am concerned to have my name and character linked to these allegations in this way. I am also concerned that the allegation has been made but contains no concrete facts – for example, what specific sexual acts are alleged to have taken place? The most we did was to hold hands.

145

Notwithstanding this, I understand from Brian that Miss Murray has also alleged that I gave Brian "...a hand job..." during the performance. I am astounded at such an allegation for the following reasons:

1) The allegation is completely untrue
2) It would be against my religion to perform such an act in such a public place
3) Had the allegations been true, it would have been possible for everyone in the theatre and all the actors and actresses to have witnessed the act, since it was a small 'theatre' – completely open and with no stage. Since the play was performed on the floor of the room, with actors and actresses moving around with high frequency, it would have been possible for every person present to have witnessed this alleged act.
4) Both Brian and myself waited behind after the performance and had a drink together while waiting to say goodbye to Annabel and congratulate her on her performance.
5) When we met up with Annabel in the pub after the performance, at no point did she bring the matter of this alleged incident to either Brian's or my attention. At no point did she look "...embarrassed..." or "...shocked..." as the allegations claim, and in fact I recall her and Brian hugging one another as we left – hardly the action of someone who was embarrassed or shocked.
6) If such an incident had indeed taken place, I would have thought that the police would have been called, and they were not called
7) I should also have thought that we would have been asked to leave the theatre and no such request was made
8) I should have thought that the "...cast member..." would have been named and note that his name was not included in the allegations against Brian
9) However, even if this incident had occurred, and even if this particular cast member did say the things he was alleged to have said, I would have thought that the cast member would have spoken with Brian about the incident and no such conversation took place
10) I am also wondering why Miss Murray waited 8 months to inform Lambeth of this alleged incident when she was apparently told about the incident "...very soon after the performance..."

I wish to repeat that I did at no time engage in sexual acts with Brian in this theatre and I more specifically did not perform "..a hand job..." on him.

I am considering taking legal action against Miss Murray as this allegation is completely untrue. It is offensive to my culture and to my family that it has even been suggested that I would behave in such a way.

Yours sincerely,
Ipek Yÿlmaz..."

This email from Ipek Yÿlmaz was given to Cathy Twist during her initial investigation. She failed to act upon it. She did not call the Turkish woman as a witness, even though Yÿlmaz would have been willing to fly to England to clear her own name and in defence of Pead. Twist failed to conduct a reasonable investigation as set out by the Court of Appeal.

Twist was in possession of documents – incontrovertible evidence – that showed that Murray had clearly lied. Once a manager or investigator is in possession of knowledge that a person making allegations has lied, he or she is bound to conclude that if that person – in this case, Murray – had lied about the masturbation in the theatre, then it is likely that the rest of her report was also lies (which it was).

Being in possession of such information about Murray, why, then, did Twist pursue the investigation? This will be revealed later.

Yÿlmaz made a number of intelligent comments in her email. Perhaps the most pertinent is that relating to chronology. Pead and Yÿlmaz visited the play in May 2006, some eight months prior to this report being authored.

Why did Murray wait so long to bring such a claim? If it were true, why did she not inform Lambeth Council in May? After all, she had already stated in the 8-page report that she was not averse to going over Pead's head straight to Gilhooly. She admits that she did this in respect of her contract, so why didn't she do this in respect of such serious allegations of sexual impropriety? Why did she not contact Gilhooly in May 2006 about this alleged offence? On Murray's own admission, she became aware of such information "...very soon after the performance..." Thus it is inconceivable that she failed to inform Lambeth of this alleged misconduct until some eight months later **and after she had been dismissed by Pead.**

It should not be forgotten that the visit to the theatre by Pead and his companion occurred not in May but in "...January or February" according to Murray.

Ipek Yÿlmaz was **never** contacted by Cathy Twist or anyone else from Lambeth Council. Yet her evidence corroborates Pead's version of events. Her evidence is itself corroborated by LondonTown.com around her description of the size of the theatre.

There was sufficient evidence in the public domain which corroborated Pead's versions of events and which showed that Murray's report had been authored by a lying fantasist who had dark desires towards young white female pupils.

Cathy Twist was supporting Murray's version of events. Why would she support Murray when she was in possession of evidence which proved that Murray had been lying all along?

What dark, deep secrets involving children was Twist, herself, hiding?

By pursuing Pead in her relentless quest to dismiss him, who was she protecting from his ability to unearth corruption and expose it? He had exposed Murray's inappropriateness with children, and reported his findings to his line manager, Barry Gilhooly. Now Pead found himself at the epicentre of a smoke and mirrors campaign which was designed to try to label him as a danger to women and something of a sexual deviant.

Why were these allegations being brought against him? Why were they being pursued when evidence existed that proved his innocence on every allegation? Who was master-minding this circus? And who – or what – was the mastermind hiding?

murray's allegations continue

On page 5 of the 8-page report, Maryn Murray continues her tissue of lies:

"...On my first day at the OLCVS, Brian gave me his home telephone number and invited me to go walking with him in a park/ woods near where he lives. I did not take up the offer as it made me feel uncomfortable..."

The reality is that – just as Annabel Field had invited all of the staff to watch her perform at the White Bear Theatre, Brian – as Chairman of the Friends of Scadbury Park in Chislehurst, Kent – had also invited all of the staff (via a staff meeting) to attend one of the guided walks in the site of special scientific interest, with him as a guide. The Friends of Scadbury were keen to develop the park and wished to increase the footfall through the beautiful site. Walks were graded according to difficulty.

The <http://www.scadbury.net> website includes details about these guided walks:

"...Walks start at the car park in Old Perry Street, Chislehurst at 10.00 unless another start time is shown.

Thur March 22nd 2012, 10am
Meet: Car Park, Old Perry St
Guided Walk around Acorn Trail 4km grade 2 plus byo picnic

Thur April 19th 2012, 10am
Meet: Car Park, Old Perry St
Guided Walk around Acorn Trail 4km grade 2 plus byo picnic

Wed June 6th 2012, 10am
Meet: Car Park, Old Perry St
Guided Walk through Meadows with botanist Judith Johns

For Further Information Phone 01689 826535

Walks usually take about 2-2½ hours. Bring something to drink if it's a hot day. Make sure you wear suitable clothing and footwear for the weather conditions on the day of the walk.

Please note that guided walks are attended at your own risk and that Bromley Council and the Friends of Scadbury cannot accept liability for any accident or loss..."
Source: <http://www.scadbury.net/walks.html>

Murray was never invited there on her own with Pead. Nor would he have given her his home telephone number. He naturally gave members of staff his mobile phone number so that they could contact him in the event of an emergency because the OLCVS did not – in its first few weeks at West Norwood – even have a telephone line connected, such was Gilhooly's lack of foresight and management.

Pead naturally needed to know if staff were going to be away from work due to illness or arrive late due to the traffic or cancelled public transport. Providing all of the staff with his mobile number was the only option he had in the circumstances.

> "...Brian also gave me his business card and offered me life coaching. He told me to keep the card private..."

This never happened. It has already been established elsewhere in this book that Pead was an extremely busy man. He simply would not have had the time to provide life coaching to Murray, and he certainly did not have the inclination. Nor does it make sense that – had he actually given her a business card in respect of life coaching – that he would ask her to keep it private, since any respectable business person wants maximum exposure and not to operate in secrecy.

> "...I was very guarded in my dealings with Brian from very early on. I did not find it appropriate nor wanted to engage in any conversations about my private life. I felt he had a 'trained' way of leading people in conversation towards the direction he wanted it to go..."

This paragraph was designed to add further antipathy towards Brian Pead. However, trained psychologists would suggest that it shows more about the mind-set of Murray than it ever does about Pead.

She was an extremely guarded person. She was acting in inappropriate ways, such as bullying black male pupils and offering bribes to young white female pupils, as well as inviting them to visit her flat and to go on shopping expeditions with her. She would, in an attempt to cover up her behaviour, become extremely guarded in case she let slip her ulterior motives. Working with Pead, a trained counsellor and experienced manager, must have been a tense situation for her, in case he saw through her incongruent behaviour.

> "...During the following week whilst I was doing Supply Teaching at the school, Brian invited me out for dinner and drinks, but I never accepted these invitations..."

At no point did Pead ever invite Murray out for dinner and drinks, or to spend time alone in her company. She, of course, offers no proof, and this allegation is yet another example of her propensity to invent events and write about them as if they were real.

> "...Brian also gave me a poem that made me feel very uncomfortable and which I found inappropriate..."

Good managers will find various ways in which to bring a team together. Some take their staff on 'bonding' experiences like paintball wars or go-karting or outdoor pursuits. Pead did not have a budget and so he was unable to draw on funds for such activities.

He therefore used some relatively basic techniques including the reading of poems in order for staff to share their reactions or feelings and learn more about one another. Almost all of the staff enjoyed these encounters – or at least the feedback they gave was extremely positive – except for Murray. Anything that focussed on her having to give anything of her 'self' to others was met with extreme resistance. Pead was sensitive enough to know not to force any member of staff to participate in any activity in which they felt uncomfortable or unable to comment. Murray, however, was motivated to resist **all** of the activities which involved her in sharing any of her self. Pead knew that she was hiding something. People who are constantly on their guard as Murray was, usually have something they are frightened to share with others. Her defence mechanisms were unusually complex and almost impenetrable. Pead had noted Murray's propensity to defend herself to the extreme.

> "...There was a sexual undertone in many of his conversations..."

This was not the case. This is not the way in which Pead manages. Besides, had it been the case, why did Murray not complain to Pead's line manager or her teaching agency about this?

Why did she wait until **after** she was dismissed by Pead and until **after** he had provided Gilhooly with information and evidence about **her** inappropriateness around children?

> "...Duane Maddison suggested that I should take some of the circle time openings for the students to see me as well in my role as Deputy Head. Brian opposed this. He would frequently text me when he was not there requesting Duane or Colin to take circle time..."

Again, this does not have any merit. Firstly, Murray herself told Pead that she did not want to take Circle Time. She feared being exposed and thirty 14 to 16 year olds would have exposed her at some point.

Secondly, apart from Tuesday afternoons, Pead was always at the OLCVS and so her use of the word 'frequently' is not borne out in fact.

Thirdly, Murray refers to the fact that Pead texted her. Why, then, would he give her his private home telephone number, as she alleged, when she obviously – on her own evidence – had his mobile number?

Murray's twisted perception on normal, everyday events knew no limits.

a pupil's perception

Talya Cuthbert was one of the nicest pupils that Brian Pead had ever met. She was immaculate in her appearance and obviously took great pride in how she looked. She would always arrive at the OLCVS with her hair pulled tightly off her face and in a pony-tail. Her clothes were always clean and well pressed. She had come from a loving and caring family, which was rare amongst the pupils in the Centre.

She was particularly good at Art, and often drew. One of her greatest attributes – Pead felt – was her incredibly dry sense of humour. Talya Cuthbert displayed a maturity far beyond her fifteen years. She also had a strong moral compass, no doubt as a result of her mother who worked tirelessly to help Talya with her education. She would often visit the Unit to discuss Talya's work with Brian. Mrs Cuthbert and Pead established a positive working relationship and they were both intent on providing their best for Talya, whose best friend at the Unit was Gemma Mandry. Watching Talya and Gemma together was an education to Pead in itself. In his view, they were like two thirty-something women with all their mannerisms and wise sayings. And both shared a similar sense of humour.

The level of Talya's maturity can be seen in her letter about her experiences at the OLCVS when Pead was there and immediately after he left. It should be remembered that she was fifteen years of age. Her letter has a detachment about it more reminiscent of an older person.

Her letter is published below in its entirety, save for her address and telephone number. Any emphasis by way of underlining is Talya Cuthbert's and not the authors'.

"...To whom it may concern,

I am a former student of the Open Learning Centre for Vocational Studies. I had been struggling to find a school place as they either saw my last school report and decided I had nothing to offer them or their waiting lists were simply too long. For a short while I attended a centre for children in the same position. However the work they gave me to do was aimed at children much younger than I was and I didn't see the point in completing it. Instead I asked the teacher for work that I would find more challenging but he said he didn't have any. The teachers basically left the kids to it as they had no control over them. Students were getting bullied & robbed right under the teachers' noses and nothing was said or done. So after only a few days I refused to go back as it was obvious I would not benefit from being in that environment. My mother was very upset because it was starting to look as if I would never be back in education.

Then, a friend who had also been out of school for years recommended I contact the Open Learning Centre for Vocational Studies. She had just come back from the induction day and every comment she made about the centre was positive. I remember how enthusiastic she was about going back. I had lost hope in finding a school or centre where I would be able to progress with my studies. My friend encouraged me to contact the centre despite the fact that there probably weren't any spaces left as it was halfway through the year.

My mother rang the centre and arranged an interview with the head teacher Brian Johnson for the following week. I tried not to get my hopes up as I felt sure this would just be another let down. I was very nervous going to the interview but when I arrived I was met by the head teacher (Brian Johnson) who instantly put my mind at rest as he was so friendly and helpful. He was the first teacher not to make assumptions about me after reading my last school report. He very kindly took a chance and let me attend on a trial basis. I left the interview feeling happy and confident that I would settle in. My first impression of him was that he was a genuine good person who had the best interests of the students at heart. And during the time I was there, Brian proved that my first impression was spot on.

On my first day I was pleasantly surprised at the atmosphere. The students all listened and got on with the work they were given. No one was being bullied and if a student got stuck they would raise their hand and straight away a teacher would come to help. I liked the fact that the Head teacher found a good balance between being a teacher and a friend. For example children are told to tell a family member or teacher they trust if they have a problem. It was obvious that all the students had that trust in Brian as he listens without judgement and gives you good honest advice. I think one of the reasons he is such a good teacher is because he has experience in counselling which means he picks up on things that other teachers never do.

He also encouraged students to pursue their talents and interests and gave them jobs to suit their skills. For example I love drawing so he gave me the job of making posters for the different subjects we did. My friend Gemma enjoys maths so he would give her extra maths work to do at home. Another student liked playing snooker so Brian gave him the job of organising a tournament. He let every student know that he believes in them, which ordinary teachers don't ever take the time to do. This is just one of the many reasons why it would be so unjust if

Brian had to stop teaching because of false allegations made against him.

The fact that Brian helped me to finally understand algebra the first time he explained it to me is proof of his excellent teaching skills. My parents wanted to give me the best start in life they possibly could so they worked hard to pay the tuition fees for me to attend a private school for years. While I was there, different teachers had attempted to teach me algebra but failed to explain in a way that I could understand. Brian understands that while one method of teaching might be best for one child, another child may respond better to being taught a different way. I was so happy the moment algebra made sense and it all clicked into place. My mother knew how hard I found algebra so she was really proud of me when I told her I finally understood. Brian explained it so well he made it seem easy and I know if it had just been explained like that to me the first time then I would have understood straight away.

Whenever there was a falling out between students Brian would gather them together in his office and let each student have their say on what had happened. He somehow always managed to mediate the situation without taking sides and then resolve the dispute. Whenever a student would misbehave and he would tell them to stop, nine times out of ten they would. The reason for this is because the students all have a lot of respect for Brian as he has a lot of respect for us. None of the other teachers there had the students respect except for Dwayne. Marryn (sic) obviously couldn't cope with a child misbehaving. She would get easily irritated and act as if she was having a panic attack which only made the boy who was misbehaving act up more. The way in which she spoke to the students was very patronising. I felt she lacked the appropriate communication skills to deal with teenagers and personally think she's in the wrong profession. I barely spoke to her because of this and could never remember her name.

On one occasion she was being very patronising to a Portuguese boy in the class constantly asking if he understood after he'd made it quite clear that he did. The students all found her quite controlling but even more so when she was promoted to Deputy Head. She wanted everything to be done her way and she'd often try and convince Brian that her teaching method was better than his. I also remember that she acted differently around Brian. I got the impression she had a crush on him but at the same time she would constantly undermine him.

I heard that she claimed Brian allowed Gemma and I to go outside to smoke which is completely untrue. In actual fact it was the same rule for everyone – no one was to go out for a cigarette. However Gemma and I would sneak out anyway. When Brian saw us he would tell us off and tell us to go back inside which we did. He never gave us his permission.

One day Brian didn't come in to the centre and when the students asked where he was Colin said that he couldn't make it that day. A few days passed and Colin kept saying the same thing. We all knew that Brian wouldn't just disappear without good reason. The next morning students started asking a lot of questions about why Brian hadn't been coming in. Colin told us that no one from the centre was allowed to contact Brian and he was not allowed to contact us and that he was not allowed to tell us any more than that. That made it clear that a complaint must have been made against Brian. Although I did not have a clue as to what the complaints were I knew that they could not be true. Everyone knew what a nice honest man Brian is so I was confident that he would return to the centre. But weeks passed and he still hadn't come back. The level of teaching had gone way downhill. For some bizarre reason Colin was made Head Teacher which was ridiculous as he so obviously wasn't up to the job. The centre began to fall apart and the majority of the students who had been happily attending no longer saw the point in going.

Colin told Gemma and I that we were not allowed to return to the building until further notice after an incident started by a new girl (who was extremely disruptive) got out of hand. Colin lost all control of the situation and ended up ringing the police who came charging in and made a scene which all would have been avoided if only Brian was there. He never would have let it escalate to the point where the police had to be called.

Eventually Collin (sic) contacted Gemma and I to tell us that he had made the decision that we would no longer be able to attend classes at the OLCVS but we would be allowed to come in for tutorials with Dwayne (sic) to help us get into college or find a job. I told Collin (sic) that I would be very grateful if they would still allow me to sit my GCSEs. He replied that it was too late as the students had already sat them. He said I could have come in to do them but this is hypocritical of him as he stated in the letter sent to both my mother and I that I was not to return to the centre until further notice. This made me extremely upset as I could not go to the college of my choice without any GCSEs. I know the situation would not have ended this way had Brian been there.

Brian Johnson is the first teacher to ever gain my respect and trust. Every child should have a teacher like him. He made a big impression on each and every one of his students by letting us all know that he has faith in us. I can still remember the look of utter disappointment on everyone's face when told Brian may not be returning to the centre. Everyone has a talent and Brian's is teaching, (sic) it would be a travesty if he ever has to stop.

Yours sincerely,
Talya Cuthbert..."

This letter – authored by a fifteen year old female pupil at the OLCVS – provides a clear picture of what really occurred at the Unit.

Talya Cuthbert provides background as to how she ended up at the OLCVS – a personal recommendation from a friend. She notes in her letter that Pead was "...friendly and helpful..." and that he "...did not make assumptions about me..."

She states that her first impression of him was that he was "...a genuine good person who had the best interests of the students at heart..."

Talya Cuthbert describes the atmosphere at the OLCVS as hardworking and that there was no bullying. She says that the pupils were helped a great deal to understand their work. She found Pead to be "...a good balance between being a teacher and a friend..." and adds that "...it was obvious that all the students had (that) trust in Brian as he listens without judgement and gives you good, honest advice..."

However, Talya Cuthbert is perceptive when she adds that "...I think one of the reasons he is such a good teacher is because he has experience in counselling which means he picks up on things that other teachers never do..."

Maryn Murray referred to this about Pead, too, but presented it in such a way that **he** claimed he picks up on things others never do, whereas he never made such claims. However, the Machiavellian Murray was astute enough to know that Pead was picking up on things about her that were not right. In an effort to deflect the spotlight away from her deceit and inappropriate behaviour towards children, she authored a document – with the help of Gilhooly and on the instructions of Dunipace, Executive Director of Education for Lambeth – which was designed to engineer his dismissal from the Unit.

Cuthbert's letter also draws the reader's attention to the fact that Pead encouraged **all** students to pursue their talents and interests and gave them jobs to suit their skills.

Why, then, did Murray present a report in which she claimed Pead only offered jobs to female students when in Cuthbert's letter it is clear that Pead offered a male student the job of organising a snooker tournament because that particular sport was the student's passion?

Cuthbert explains that Pead's ability to teach her algebra was first class. But this should come as no surprise, because – unknown to Cuthbert - he had won an award for excellence in teaching and was awarded 7 out of 7 'Excellent' grades by an independent OfSTED inspection team for the quality of his teaching, which was proven to raise standards whilst encouraging self-respect and discipline.

The fifteen-year-old Cuthbert also explains how Pead would ensure that discipline problems were kept to a minimum because he never took sides and he also allowed both parties to have their say without judging. She used the word 'mediate' in respect of his ability to ensure good discipline throughout the Unit.

Cuthbert describes Murray as a teacher who was unable to cope with a pupil misbehaving, saying that she would get "...easily irritated..."

What is of particular interest is that Cuthbert refers to Murray's patronising manner towards some pupils. This is clear evidence her attitude was not good towards young males. She writes: "...On one occasion she was being very patronising to a Portuguese boy in the class, constantly asking if he understood after he'd made it quite clear that he did..."

In an earlier chapter, it was shown that three black Brazilian and Portuguese male pupils made statements against the racist Murray. Pead had many friends of African, West Indian or Indian descent and he would not tolerate for one moment any racist comments.

Cuthbert writes that "....The students all found her quite controlling..."

This is how Pead found her, too, particularly when she attempted to negotiate a contract. Colin Hill found Murray "...strident..."

Perhaps one of the most insightful comments in her letter was Cuthbert's description of the working relationship between Pead and Murray: "...I also remember she acted differently around Brian. I got the impression she had a crush on him but at the same time she would constantly undermine him..."

This is of particular importance. Murray's attack on Pead in her report made numerous references to alleged sexualised conversations between her and Pead. These never occurred. Murray claimed that Pead had invited her out to the woods. This never occurred. Murray claimed that Pead had invited her out for drinks and a meal.

This never occurred. Murray claimed that Pead gave him his home telephone number. This never occurred. Murray claimed that Pead offered her Life Coaching. This never occurred. Murray claimed that Pead had been given a 'hand job' in a theatre. This never occurred.

Talya Cuthbert also provided her account of the smoking incident in which Murray claimed that Pead had shown favouritism towards females by allowing them to smoke. A non-smoker himself, he would not have allowed **any** pupil to smoke.

In her letter, Cuthbert writes that Colin Hill was not capable of running the Unit and cites a complete breakdown in discipline when the police were called to a knife fight.

Cuthbert also makes reference to the fact that Pead had been unlawfully isolated by Lambeth.

Questions have to be asked why Cuthbert was not allowed to sit her GCSE exams. Was it because Lambeth knew that Pead was professionally close to Cuthbert and her mother? Was it because Cuthbert was best friends with Gemma Mandry, who had made a statement against Murray in which she stated that Murray had offered her a bribe and asked her to join her at the gym? Was Cuthbert's education and future destroyed by Lambeth who were attempting a cover-up of racism, bribery and inappropriate behaviour by Murray towards young female pupils?

But what is even more worrying is that this letter was never acted upon by the corrupt Cathy Twist, who is guilty of misfeasance in public office.

Yet more worrying is that Twist did not call Cuthbert as a witness, even though she had been named in Murray's report.

In fact, Murray mentioned six different pupils in her report, **yet Twist failed to call a single pupil or parent as witnesses to the investigation.**

Thus the entire investigatory process was not lawful or fair.

The question needs to be asked why Twist failed to call even one pupil in order to establish the veracity of Murray's wild and ridiculous claims. It is obvious why she did not. Had pupils or parents been part of the investigatory process, it is obvious that Murray's claims would have been immediately disproven.

Twist needed to maintain the notion that Pead was guilty. And she needed to keep Pead busy in defending himself, in an attempt to deflect his attention away from going public about the abusive Murray.

discrepancies in murray's account

There were significant discrepancies in Murray's account of the allegations and Twist's perverse distortion of all the interview transcripts.

Twist had obviously worked hard to patch together a series of fifteen separate allegations by taking – completely out of context – single sentences by staff.

This chapter focuses on the major discrepancies which led to an unfair hearing and Twist perverting the course of justice. It is based on an account that Murray gave to Cathy Twist on the 10th Floor Meeting Room at International House on 19 January 2007. Twist was present, as was Mary White, a Human Resources consultant. Gerlize de Villiers - whom Murray claimed was her sister – was also in attendance. Karina O'Neill took the notes.

Research on de Villiers shows that she attended Stellenbosch University in South Africa from 1986-1990, where she did a Bachelor of Science Honours degree in Maths and Psychology.
Source: <http://www.yatedo.fr/p/Gerlize+De+Villiers/normal/07bccf09d761fb98d3b97d94f600ea5c>

From 2000 to 2001, she worked as an HR Business Partner at Cable & Wireless. She describes her role as providing "...a comprehensive internal HR consultancy service in support of overall business strategy..."

From 2001 to 2004, she worked at KPMG, describing her role: "...to shape and promote the evolving people agenda, manage HR calendar processes within budgets and timescales in close collaboration with business leaders and provide operational and strategic HR support in a complex matrix structure..."

From 2004-present she worked as HR & Business Operations Director in De Villiers Walton and describes her role thus: "...Define, implement and manage the HR and Business Operations framework for a professional services organisation including all governance and controls (People, Process, Client), financials, statutory and contractual elements associated with the day-to-day running of the company and the deployment of SAP Consultants across multiple engagements..."

De Villiers is named as the Company Secretary of Enterprise On Demand Limited, a post she commenced on 18 March 2011.
Source: https://www.duedil.com/company/07570058/enterprise-on-demand-limited/people

The 8-page document allegedly authored by Murray alone appeared to have had input from de Villiers. Little wonder, then, that she distanced herself from any further involvement in the allegations.

But what was de Villiers doing between 1990, when she left Stellenbosch University and 2000 when she joined Cable and Wireless?

Murray claimed that she had been promised a contract in February 2006, yet Pead emailed Gilhooly on 7 May 2006 in which he stated that he had been discussing contracts with Murray and Duane Maddison and that they both "...understood the due process..."

Twist had been given a copy of this email by Pead. It demonstrates that Murray had lied when she claimed that she had been promised a contract three months before Pead sent his email.

Twist asked Murray how she became aware of the issues in her complaint. Murray claims that she became aware of issues through "...a chain of events, observations and personal experience. Where I was sitting in the office I could hear conversations around me. People made comments to me..."

Murray does not provide names. She also claimed that Pead had private conversations with pupils out of her hearing. Indeed, she complained that he would pull pupils out of her lessons in order to speak with them.

When asked whether she had received any formal complaints from staff or pupils, Murray says no.

Murray claimed that Annabel Field confided in her about Brian Pead before she left to work in Bath. Field's email to Pead disproves this.

When asked about Pead's identity, she claimed – quite rightly – that he only used the name of Brian Johnson at the OLCVS. This was also corroborated by Barry Gilhooly and other staff.

Murray then claimed that Pead took the books that he had written on Liverpool into the Centre for pupils to read.

This is a complete fabrication. Brian Pead, as the author of nine books – five of them on the history of Liverpool Football Club – is naturally provided with first edition copies of his books whenever one is published.

He has first edition copies of his Liverpool books in his library at home which are all signed by Liverpool managers and players over a considerable number of years. On Friday 20 April 2012, Brian Pead attended a show at the Southport Floral Hall in which he met the former Liverpool players Ron Yeats, Ian Callaghan, Chris Lawler and Ian St. John and all the players signed his books. The show's producer, John

Keith, also signed his books. These books are worth a considerable sum of money. Not only are they valuable first editions in their own right, but they contain the autographs of hundreds of Liverpool players. Is it conceivable that Pead would take these books into the Centre for boisterous young men of 14-16 to read?

Murray did not have Qualified Teacher Status (QTS). Pead spoke with Gilhooly about this and he suggested that Pead help her to obtain it. Yet Murray – not even a qualified teacher on her own admission – claimed that Pead did not have experience as a teacher. He never told her about the awards he had won for teaching, which are mentioned in other chapters.

Pead had grown highly suspicious about Murray, who claimed to have been Head of the ICT department at St. Augustine's School in Ealing, yet she wasn't even a fully qualified teacher. This did not make sense to Pead. Nor did it make sense that Gilhooly was keen to help her acquire qualified teaching status. Brian Pead wanted only the very best staff around him. Gilhooly had given him a Learning Mentor who had never previously worked with secondary-aged pupils, a school secretary who had never before performed in that role and who could barely type a letter and now he was promoting Maryn Murray who was not even a qualified teacher. If one is to assume – and assume it we must, at least for the moment – that Gilhooly wanted the OLCVS to be a success, why would he play fast and loose by staffing the Unit with inadequate or inept people? This simply made no sense whatsoever to either Brian Pead or John Callow and other friends of Brian's. It appeared that the people Gilhooly had populated the OLCVS with were somehow connected. Gilhooly had not put them there without reason – they clearly had some purpose to fulfil. But what was that purpose?

Twist later told a Disciplinary Panel that Pead "...had been working as a Life Coach at the OLCVS..." yet Murray stated in her interview that he didn't see private clients at work.

At this point, there are already numerous discrepancies in Murray's statement and Twist's interpretation of Murray's statement. More smoke and mirrors. Any Investigating Officer conducting a genuine investigation would have called a halt at this point, because it was obvious to even the least impartial person that Murray was fabricating the whole thing and that Twist was then further distorting Murray's words. Twist asked Murray whether she had ever received any complaints from students regarding Brian Pead. Murray replied, "...Not formally, just in conversation..."

Again, there can be no case to answer. People say things about other people all the time. Pupils criticise their teachers all the time. Much of it has to be taken with the proverbial pinch of salt. Unless hard evidence is collated, anything said remains hearsay and is inadmissible.

Murray cited the name of Mohammed Hamza and claimed that he had made complaints against Pead. If that were the case, why he was not called as a witness? Could it be that his mother respected Brian Pead and would later thank him for all his hard work with her son and her daughter, Kadisha?

Murray claimed that Cassandra Trimmings was not properly invigilated when she sat a Maths exam early in the office (which was used by all members of staff). However, the truth is that Cassandra Trimmings did not even sit the Maths GCSE exam. Even more worryingly, Twist failed to obtain the list of examination grades for each pupil – this list would have shown that Trimmings did not sit the Maths exam and that **Murray had lied**.

Murray also claimed that Kerrie Hamilton had arrived "...long after the cut-off point for late entry to sit the exam..." yet she provides no times and also failed to raise this issue in a staff meeting (had it actually occurred the way she said it did).

In her statement, Murray stated that she knew that the mother of Ashleigh Mills had "...mental health problems..." yet failed to understand why Pead and Mills should be engaged in sometimes lengthy conversations.

When asked by Twist, "Which elements of Pead's conversations with Ashleigh Mills were inappropriate?" Murray replied, "...I didn't know what his motives were for his conversations with Ashleigh. Observing these conversations made me feel uncomfortable. He had a non-professional way of interacting with her..."

This is nothing but unsubstantiated hearsay. It should be remembered that Murray is being interviewed two months after having been dismissed because of racism, bullying and inappropriate sexual advances to white female pupils. She would say anything to deflect attention away from herself.

It is extremely worrying that Murray declared she didn't know what Pead's motives were in speaking with Ashleigh Mills in the same breath that she said she knew Ashleigh's mother had mental health problems.

Twist asked Murray, "...Would you say that the tone and manner of their conversations were inappropriate?"

Murray replied: "...Yes."

Twist asked no further questions. Even an inexperienced investigator would be forced to ask Murray to describe the tone and manner that were allegedly inappropriate. No such investigatory questions were asked by Twist and the entire process was a breach of Lambeth's duty of care towards Pead. Twist was wholly negligent in failing to ask such obvious and necessary questions.

Murray claimed that Pead actually told Chloe Gordon to wear a low-cut top. This is, of course, a fabrication and it would have been easy for Twist to call Gordon as a witness and either prove or disprove this allegation. Twist failed in her duty as an investigator. Nor did Twist even inform the parents of Chloe Gordon that her daughter had been named in a report about the clothes she was or was not wearing. Lambeth owed the Gordons – and Chloe – a duty of care to have informed them about this malicious report. They were denied an opportunity to have their say.

When asked by Twist whether other people were around when Pead engaged in one-to-one conversations with pupils, Murray replied, "...There were other people around..."

This clearly demonstrates that Pead was meeting with pupils for all the right reasons. Other people were always around. The OLCVS office had a glass wall and glass doors which meant that everybody could see what was happening in the office at all times. CCTV was in operation.

When asked about staff leaving, Murray told Twist that Eloise Whitmore was dismissed, that Jenny Foster was looking for another job and that Annabel Field left not because of Brian. Yet Twist manipulated Murray's words and told a panel that all of these staff had left as a direct result of Brian Pead's management style.

Murray claimed that Whitmore had made complaints about Pead to her, that Hiley did the same and that, later, other (unnamed) staff made complaints to her.

Yet none of this was logged. No times or dates or noting down of the content of these alleged complaints was ever produced. No complaints were ever raised in staff meetings. Murray never mentioned these alleged complaints to Pead as one might have expected her to do.

Murray also claimed that one (unnamed) male member of staff had complained to her that Pead treated female staff differently from male staff. No evidence of this allegation was ever produced.

When asked about the play at the White Bear Theatre, note carefully how Murray informs Twist of the incident: "...Only Brian attended. It would have been January or February 2006..."

Clearly it would have been a basic task for Twist to establish the date of this play. She could have asked Annabel Field herself. She could have visited the theatre, a mile or so away from her office. She could have picked up the telephone and called the theatre. She could even have used Google to find out.

Yet Twist did none of these. Yet she had been tasked with conducting a full, thorough and fair investigation.

The UK Theatre Web (UKTW) website is operated and owned by Dynamic Listing Ltd. UKTW has been around (formally) since 14 February 1995 providing information about what's on in the performing arts in the UK. The original service developed out of a joint web/gopher site offering "What's on in Oxford and London" which had been running since late 1994. In its early incarnation the website was all hand-crafted but it soon switched to being database driven. The database contains a total of 818,887 archived listings of which 8,083 are for current/future events.

There are 139,738 productions and/or tours in the system. The database makes reference to 152,352 people, groups, organisations and companies mentioned.
Source: <http://www.uktw.co.uk/archive/>

The UKTW website identifies each specific play in any theatre in the UK and issues an identifier for each play. The Horse Dealer's Daughter is identified in their database as T01790624196 (WHBEAR06).

Furthermore, it provides the dates of each production which, in this instance, were from Tuesday 9 May 2006 to Sunday 14 May 2006.

This was yet another example of Murray – who allegedly kept notebooks on Pead's behaviour from the first day that she joined the OLCVS because she was made to feel 'uncomfortable' – getting facts significantly wrong. She also fails to tell Twist why she did not report the alleged masturbation in the theatre for some eight months and not until she had been dismissed.

The official Lambeth records do not show at what time this meeting ended. However, the authors are in possession of her statement which is signed M.Murray. This is highly unusual. Why would Maryn Murray – also calling herself Marion Murray (were both names CRB checked by Lambeth HR?) – not use her full name? What was she hiding?

The meeting re-convened at 4pm on Monday 22 January 2007 on the 10th floor of International House in Brixton. A notable absentee was Gerlize de Villiers – why was she not in attendance? No reasons were given, yet this is normal practice when someone who was at the first meeting is not available in a continuation of that meeting.

A worrying fact is that Damien Murray was the note-taker.

This meeting could not have lasted long because the transcript was only 2½ pages in length.

64

murray bombshell

With no evidence against him that would stand up to even the most basic scrutiny, Lambeth had suspended Pead on 8 December 2006, without informing him of the reasons why.

With substantial evidence to prove that Pead was innocent of all charges, they maintained his unlawful suspension.

However, in January 2007, Pead received a telephone call from his trusted colleague and confidante, Sandra Roach. She told him that she had just heard that Murray **had been reinstated by Lambeth and was now working as an ICT consultant in Norwood School for Girls in Lambeth.**

The reality of the situation is quite clear: Brian Pead had gathered significant evidence of racist behaviour by Murray and sexual impropriety towards young, white female pupils.

He had shared this evidence with Sandra Roach in the first instance and then with Barry Gilhooly, his line manager.

Pead had recorded his findings on his computer in his office and printed off the files and stored them in a locked filing cabinet in his office.

He had thus 'protected his arse' by informing at least one other person – Sandra Roach – of his findings, as well as Barry Gilhooly. 'Who will guard the guards themselves?' resonated in Pead's mind.

Murray had been dismissed and so she ought to have been. She had no business working in schools.

Gilhooly failed to take any action against her. Pead was not happy about this and told Gilhooly as much.

Just three weeks **after** Murray is dismissed, Pead is suspended without being told of the nature of the allegations against him.

His office is ransacked, and all evidence is removed. Locked filing cabinets are removed. All paper files are removed. The computer is removed. Only a desk and chair remain.

And then – **with Lambeth knowing that Murray was a danger to children** – she is reinstated and allowed to work again in schools. Despite having been racist towards black males. Despite having bribed young white female pupils. Despite inviting girls to go shopping with her. Despite asking girls to visit her flat.

Despite being in possession of all this knowledge against Murray, Lambeth Education reinstated her and gave her unfettered access to thousands more children.

And Pead's career was in danger of being ruined.

The normal expectations would be that Pead would still be in his role as Head of the OLCVS, and that Murray would have been reported to the police and the General Teaching Council and the Independent Safeguarding Authority and barred from working as a teacher with immediate effect.

Yet none of this occurred.

What did Murray know that Lambeth was so scared of that would invert the normal expectations of such events?

And if Murray had been guilty of making inappropriate advances towards children, had Gilhooly and Twist been involved? Was Murray the conduit through which Gilhooly and Twist gained access to children?

What other logical reason can there be for Lambeth reinstating a woman when they were in possession of hard and robust evidence that she had acted inappropriately on a number of levels?

65

a brilliant model

On Friday, 8 December 2006, Brian Pead had been frogmarched out of the Redfearn Centre by Gilhooly and Rosa Vaz, who had suspended him without providing him with any reasons for the suspension.

On Tuesday 19 December 2006 – a day before his daughter's 32nd birthday – Pead received a birthday present of his own, an email from Nadia Al-Khudhairy of King's College.

This email is reproduced in its entirety below:

"...From: Al-Khudhairy, Nadia <Nadia.Al-Khudhairy@iop.kcl.ac.uk>
Sent: 19 December 2006 10:55:38
To: <brian.johnson89@hotmail.co.uk>
Subject: FW: A Brillant (sic) Model that should be considered by other PRUs

Dear Brain (sic)
I wanted to write to you to let you know how impressed I was with the model you and your team have developed. As you are aware I have been visiting and working with PRUs all over London. I have now visited approximately 20. I have been more surprised on most of my visits how little focus is placed on assisting pupils in their emotional and behavioural needs. Most pupils in PRUs appear to me to come from difficult backgrounds and have emotional and behavioural difficulties. However, most models in PRUs appear not to address this.

In your PRU, I found it interesting to see how you focused both on the pupils (sic) educational needs as well as emotional/behavioural needs. I was impressed to see how circle time was used to address any possible problems that could erupt or how you discussed difficult emotional issues. The affect of this approach was reflected in how during the 3 weeks I was working in your PRU there were no fights nor verbal arguments. I contrast this to most of the other PRUs I have worked in where there is a fight or verbal arguments daily. This was also reflected in my one to one work with the pupils, who clearly had an insight and understanding about themselves.

I have been struck how a the (sic) majority of PRUs have no input from Counselling Psychologist or Counsellors. I think the way that you have integrated counselling themes in enabling pupils to reflect on their behaviour and how it impacts on others whilst also maintaining your aim to teaching is impressive.

The problem in most PRUs is that they just focus on teaching the pupils with minimal focus on emotional needs. By addressing the emotional needs and the complex problems in their life's (sic), you are giving them the calmness and stability within themselves to learn.

I write to enquire if you have thought of writing a paper and presenting it to a journal on your approach. I do think it is much needed and one that could be replicated in other schools.

I would like to take this opportunity to thank you, the staff and pupils for welcoming me to your school and taking part in our work.

Yours sincerely,

Nadia Al-Khudhairy
Research Therapist
King's College..."

Clearly this email is of tremendous significance. It was authored by a wholly independent research therapist – a person with a good deal of knowledge about human interaction and the dynamics between people.

Al-Khudhairy states that she had visited at least twenty Pupil Referral Units all over London.

She writes that in other PRUs there is little focus on assisting pupils with their emotional and behavioural needs. She identifies that most pupils in PRUs come from difficult backgrounds and have emotional and behavioural difficulties.

Al-Khudhairy comments on how Pead focussed on the pupils' educational as well as emotional and behavioural needs. She writes that she was impressed with Pead's use of Circle Time to address any possible problems that could erupt. She also praises Pead's ability to discuss difficult emotional issues with the pupils.

Al-Khudhairy comments that she observed that there were no fights or verbal arguments in Pead's PRU. She contrasts this to most other PRUs that she has worked in where there are fights or verbal arguments on a daily basis. When Al-Khudhairy engaged with OLCVS pupils on an individual basis, she comments that she found the pupils insightful and that they had an understanding about themselves. This was a direct consequence of the processes and procedures that Pead had initiated.

Al-Khudhairy also comments how well Pead had integrated counselling themes in enabling pupils to reflect on their behaviour and how it impacts on others whilst also maintaining his aim to teaching. She writes that most PRUs focus only on teaching pupils with minimal focus on emotional needs. By addressing the emotional needs and the complex problems in their lives, she writes, Pead was giving them the calmness and stability within themselves to learn.

Al-Khudhairy says that she is writing to inquire whether Pead would be interested in writing a paper about his running of the PRU for publication in a psychological journal or magazine.

This email from Al-Khudhairy contrasts vividly with the 8-page report compiled by Murray. Al-Khudhairy viewed Pead's PRU as the best in London.

Why, then, was this email not taken into consideration by Twist? Why was Al-Khudhairy not called as an independent witness, as recommended by the Court of Appeal?

What possible motives did Twist have in denying credible evidence such as Al-Khudhairy's in favour of Murray's ill-considered diatribe?

66

procedure

Lambeth selected Cathy Twist to conduct the investigation. She had visited the OLCVS just prior to the May elections in 2006 and only stayed for an hour or so to meet with Brian Pead.

She was not, therefore, a wholly impartial investigator. But breaching Employment Law regulations is not something that concerns Lambeth Council.

The process was a relatively simple one. Twist had to interview Murray – who made the allegations – and Pead, who was on the receiving end of the allegations.

All of the staff at the OLCVS ought to have been interviewed – they weren't.

All of the pupils who were named in Murray's report ought to have been interviewed – none of them was.

Parents of the pupils named in the report ought to have been interviewed – none of them was.

Third parties such as other workers at the community centres in West Norwood and Vauxhall ought to have been interviewed – only one was.

Counselling colleagues of Pead's ought to have been called, but none were called.

The manager of the White Bear Theatre ought to have been contacted – but wasn't.

Nonetheless, Twist went through the motions and called Maryn Murray in to interview on 19 January 2007.

By this time, Murray had been reinstated and was working as an ICT Consultant at Norwood School – another all-girls' school. Mina Waters – the transsexual ICT consultant for Lambeth – had been instrumental in securing the position for Murray. But Gilhooly and Twist also ensured that Murray would be 'looked after' once she had made the complaints against Pead.

That Murray was reinstated made her an unreliable witness – she would hardly change any of her report now that she was within the 'inner circle' of Gilhooly, Twist and Waters.

If, as Pead and Callow believed, there was no case to answer because it was clear that the report had been fabricated by a woman who had been dismissed for racism and sexual grooming, the matter would be dropped and Pead could return to the OLCVS.

However, if Twist firmly believed – on all the available evidence – that there was a case to answer, it would go to a Disciplinary Hearing and panel.

In either scenario, Lambeth were dragging their feet – Pead had been suspended on 8 December 2006 and the first witness was not interviewed until 6 weeks later. Lambeth's own policies stated that such hearings would be completed within 13 weeks from start to finish.

By way of comparison, in the Roldan case against the Salford NHS Trust, nurse Roldan was suspended on 22 September 2007 and the Trust **completed** the task of interviewing witnesses by 26 September 2007.

Roldan's Disciplinary Hearing took place on 12 October 2007 and she was dismissed the same day.

This meant that the entire process had been concluded in a little under three weeks.

murray - first interview

Murray was interviewed by Twist on 19 January 2007.

One of the staggering statistics with regard to this interview is that Murray was asked 42 questions in 75 minutes. This interview of the person who had prepared an 8-page report on Pead was shorter than the interviews of Field, Hiley and Whitmore – who had constantly lied throughout their testimonies. Murray's interview was also shorter than Jenny Foster's interview.

Of all the interviews undertaken by Twist, the average length of interview was 66 minutes, making Murray's interview only nine minutes longer than the average. (For a more detailed analysis of all of the interviews, refer to chapter 135.)

Remarkably, however, while the average percentage of open questions was only 19% - an indication of Twist's narrow questioning – Murray was asked 43% of open questions and no leading questions at all. Twist had allowed Murray free and unfettered access to vent her spleen. Twist cast her line and baited the hook and Murray obligingly took the bait and made things up as she went along.

The authors have analysed the interview questions and answers robustly. We provide (with our commentary) some of the questions and Murray's replies below in order to provide a flavour of the inept Twist and the lying Murray:

Twist: Can you please confirm which name you used for the alleged perpetrator and what was his position?

Murray: Brian Johnson, Head of the OLCVS.

> Commentary: It is clear that Murray has shot herself in the foot with this reply. In her vitriolic 8-page report against Pead, she claimed that he had used three separate names whilst at the Unit, but here she says he only used the one name – this was corroborated by every other person interviewed.
>
> Note Twist's use of the word 'perpetrator'. This is, of course, generally used in relation to sex offenders. Twist has no right to use this word in relation to Pead. Not only is it leading terminology, but it is also inaccurate and slanderous. She attempts to mind her back with the use of the word 'alleged'.
>
> At no point does Twist ask Murray to discuss why she had said that Pead used three names at the OLCVS and has now said that he only used the one

name. Twist – had she been a genuine investigator – would have asked Murray to discuss this discrepancy.

Twist: Did you receive any formal complaints from any of the people named in your complaint?

Murray: No.

Commentary: There is, therefore, no case to answer and Twist knows this. Murray has confirmed that she never received a single formal complaint against Pead. If she did ever receive an informal complaint this has no bearing on the case against Pead whatsoever.

A genuine investigating officer would by now have asked Murray why she waited until after she was dismissed before making complaints about Pead, but Twist fails in her duty of care and negligently fails to ask that vital question.

Twist: Did you think that Pead was carrying out non-Centre work as a life coach at work?

Murray: I don't know if he was running his business from school. As far as I'm aware he didn't see private clients at work.

Commentary: It is clear that Murray has now provided a response which completely contradicts her original 8-page report in which she stated that Pead **had** ran a life coaching business whilst running the OLCVS – a completely ridiculous notion.

Note how Twist again fails to point out this contradiction to Murray – yet it would have been vital in the interest of justice for Twist to point out this to Murray.

Twist: Did you ever receive any complaints from students concerning Brian?

Murray: No, not formally.

Commentary: Thus there is no case against Pead. Despite her 8-page diatribe against Pead, Murray has now stated in the same interview that she never received any complaints against Pead from either other staff or pupils. This renders her entire document null and void. It has no merit whatsoever, since there were never any allegations against him.

Then Murray – at the height of her hubris – lies. She stated that on 5 June 2006, Cassandra Trimmings sat her Maths exam in the office and that Pead had given her preferential treatment by allowing her to do this.

> Commentary: The official school exam records – copies of which are sent to the DfES and to the Local Authority – show that Cassandra Trimmings did not sit her Maths exam.

> There is no case to answer, therefore.

Murray's case against Pead is slowly disintegrating with every response she makes and the following extract from her interview ensures that yet another brick in her wall of hatred against Pead is dislodged:

Twist: In relation to the alleged preferential treatment from Brian Pead to a female student, Ashleigh Mills, were their conversations in private?

Murray: A number of times they had private meetings. I didn't want to listen into their conversations but I did hear Brian asking her about her home life. [...] Their conversations were not in complete privacy as the Centre is open plan.

> Commentary: It is self-evident that conversations which can be overheard or which are not in private areas are not, by their very nature, private. Yet, in the 8-page document, Murray had claimed that Pead had engaged in 'private' conversations with 'attractive' and 'very attractive' female pupils.

> It is, actually, of no consequence whether the female pupils were 'attractive' or 'ugly' – the fact is that there were no private conversations in private areas because both Centres are open plan with CCTV in operation.

> There can, therefore, be no case to answer.

Yet the farce is perpetuated by the incompetent and corrupt Twist:

Twist: Would you say that the tone and manner of Brian and Ashleigh Mills' conversations were inappropriate?

Murray: Yes.

> Commentary: At no point does Twist ask Murray to elaborate on this. Once Murray has said that the conversations were – in her mind at least – 'inappropriate', a genuine investigator would ask the interviewee to elaborate

and explain in what ways she thought the conversations were inappropriate. Twist fails to ask this basic question.

Twist: Did you mention this to anyone?

Murray: No.

> Commentary: There can be no case to answer. At no point has Murray ever mentioned that **she** thought these conversations were 'inappropriate' until **after** she was dismissed by Pead.

> Furthermore, Twist fails to ask Murray why she failed to mention this to anyone (until after she was dismissed by Pead).

Twist: Were his conversations always where other people could hear them?

Murray: There were other people around [...] Usually, there would be other people in the office. Other staff members may have observed his conversations.

> Commentary: It is difficult to imagine a more farcical scenario. Brian Pead has been accused by Murray – after being dismissed by him – that he had 'inappropriate' conversations in private areas of the Centre with female pupils.

> At no point can she produce evidence of these alleged 'inappropriate' conversations. Then she says that, actually, there were no private areas in the centre. Then she says that usually there were other people around in the office, and that other staff may have observed these conversations.

> It is evident from Murray's own testimony that Pead has done nothing wrong – certainly nothing that he can be dismissed for.

> Yet Twist has no other outcome than dismissal in mind.

The absurdity that was masquerading as an investigation continued under Twist's corrupt management:

Twist: Did you receive any complaints from staff members concerning Brian?

Murray: No.

> Commentary: Again, there can be no case to answer.

Twist: Do you think that male staff members felt discriminated against by Pead?

Murray: One male member of staff noted that Brian spoke differently to females.

Commentary: This is absurd on at least two levels: (one) Twist asks Murray for her view about male members of staff. Murray has already just said that no members of staff – and that must include the males – had ever complained about Pead. Therefore the question is redundant. It does not matter what Murray **thinks she knows,** what matters is what she can prove and (two) Murray fails to identify the name of this male member of staff. Twist fails to ask her to identify the man - if he ever existed.

Murray claimed that she kept logbooks and diaries about Pead **from her first day at the Centre**. Yet there are alarming gaps in her document. She makes general statements such as 'one male member of staff complained' but never provides real proof by naming the individual. Twist exacerbates the charade by never asking her to supply details – that would be too much to ask: Twist wants only one outcome.

The meeting ended at 4pm. They were scheduled to meet again on Monday 22 January 2007.

Following a Freedom of Information Act request, Lambeth Council supplied a copy of the interview that is the basis of this chapter. The interview notes were not signed off by Murray. They were not dated. This breaches protocol.

However, Lambeth Council did forward a second copy of this interview which **was** signed and dated by Murray – 22 June 2007. This is fully **six months** after the interview.

Lambeth Council's own policies and procedures state that the **maximum** length of time that a disciplinary hearing will last for is 13 weeks.

The second copy of the interview notes that Murray **did** sign was a completely different set of notes from the original one sent by Lambeth. It is self-evident, of course, that there can only be one set of interview notes which has been agreed and signed off.

murray - second interview

Murray's second interview was on Monday 22 January 2007 in the 10th floor meeting room at International House in Brixton.

Twist was again asking the questions and Mary White was the HR consultant. Damien Murray was the note taker.

The entire tone of this meeting was for Twist to provide Murray with a platform to vent her considerable frustration about having been dismissed by Pead for racism towards young black males and the grooming of young, white female pupils.

The angry Murray enjoyed having such a platform. It provided her with yet another opportunity to twist the knife into Pead.

In further worrying breaches of protocol, there are no times recorded for this interview. It had been timetabled to commence at 4pm, but no record exists of the start or finish of this interview. Or whether it really ever took place.

Furthermore, there are two entirely separate copies of the transcript in existence, both of which have been differently annotated by Murray.

One copy in existence is dated by Murray on 22 June 2007 and the other copy is signed off on 2 July 2007. There should, of course, only be one official copy. Twist was playing fast and loose with official protocol in her unprofessional handling of the case.

A robust examination of these two documents makes for interesting reading. The copy signed by Murray on 22 June 2007 has been substantially annotated by her, with scrawlings all over the three pages.

However, the second copy – signed by Murray on 2 July 2007 – had far fewer (and different) annotations, yet the corrections from the first draft had not been made.

These documents are inadmissible evidence because they are flawed.

When asked by Twist if staff meetings had agendas, Murray replied, "...Minutes started in September. I felt that I had to read the Minutes each time to ensure that it was a true depiction of what was discussed..."

This reply demonstrates Murray's absurd thinking and paranoia. Pead had established good practice in ensuring that Minutes of each meeting were taken. They were then typed out as a first draft and left in each staff member's pigeon-hole for their comments. Once these had been returned and any alterations or amendments made, a final copy would be signed off and held in Pead's office for any member of staff to examine whenever they wanted to.

There was no need for Murray's paranoia. In attempting to strike out at Pead, she was, in fact, merely confirming that he had instigated good practice with regard to the recording of Minutes.

The question from Twist had little to do with the allegations. She was, as usual, merely trawling for information.

This interview provided nothing for Twist. So she tried a different approach.

Twist: Do you have any examples of your timesheets which were signed by you and not by Brian?

Murray: Yes, I'll try to find some at home.

Thus it was evident that Twist would try to add a charge of misappropriation of Lambeth funds to his other charges. There never had been any misappropriation of funds. Whenever a timesheet was signed by him – or by Murray – a duplicate copy remained with Pead for filing in his office. He would always examine this to check that it was correct before the copy was filed away. No member of staff had ever signed for more days than they had actually worked. There had, therefore, been no misappropriation of funds, but Twist would use this against Pead because she had no other evidence against him.

Murray had been asked eleven questions. All eleven were closed questions.

What is particularly worrying from a point of view of protocol was that Murray never signed off a completed copy of the record of this meeting. When she did sign off two entirely different copies, this was a full **six months** after she had been interviewed. This is a breach of employment law and a breach of Pead's human rights.

Furthermore, the chronology is also worrying. It demonstrates that Pead was being interviewed without having had sight of the notes of those who had been interviewed before him. This was grossly unfair, since Twist had already sent out Murray's allegations to all of Pead's staff before they had been interviewed by her. Pead had not been afforded the same treatment. It was somewhat ironic since the basis of the allegations by Murray was that **he** had been meting out unfavourable treatment.

Murray had been asked 53 questions in two interviews. She had produced an 8-page document of spurious allegations against Pead. Rosa Vaz, who worked in the HR department at Lambeth and whom Pead had met briefly on only 3 or 4 occasions, was asked 48 questions – just 5 questions less.

Eloise Whitmore had been interviewed for 120 minutes. In total, Murray's two interviews lasted no more than 95 minutes. Whitmore had been dismissed after three months for failing her probation. Murray had worked with Pead for a year.

How Twist could claim that this was a fair and thorough hearing is beyond common sense.

69

further breaches by twist

It is evident that, having interviewed Murray – who made the allegations – Twist was duty bound to then interview Brian Pead.

However, she failed to do this. Instead, she interviewed Anya Hiley who was not even a member of Pead's staff.

Then she interviewed all of Pead's staff.

Then – on 19 April 2007 – she first interviewed Pead. This was an appalling lapse and breach of Lambeth's own policies on the efficient disposal of such proceedings.

anya hiley interview

connexions personal advisor

Hiley was interviewed in Meeting Room 8 at International House, Brixton on Thursday 25 January 2007.

According to Lambeth documents, the interview commenced at 9.30am and finished at 10.50am.

Twist and White were also present and notes were taken by Karina O'Neill.

In the 80-minute interview, Hiley was asked 32 separate questions. Of these questions, only 22% were open questions. Therefore 78% of the questions were closed, leaving no room for greater clarity or context. Twist did not want to allow for this. She had an agenda – to dismiss Pead at any cost. Her questions were designed to remain narrow in order to receive extremely narrow responses. Eighteen per cent of questions asked were completely leading questions, starting with a full description of the allegation before actually asking a question.

This is completely improper. An investigator would normally ask a few closed questions in order to establish the interviewee's name, job title and so on, but then open out the interview so that he or she could obtain full and frank responses.

But Twist could not afford this option. She knew that Pead was innocent, but she had to obtain a guilty verdict at any cost. He knew too much.

Hiley was asked why she stopped contact with Pead and she replied: "....I felt, on a personal level, uncomfortable with him and I didn't want to spend time with him..."

Yet this woman – who aligned herself with Murray and her interest in young, white female pupils – was supposed to be a professional, working for Connexions and doing the best for the students at the OLCVS.

However, she was a weak advisor according to Pead. She failed to meet the male pupils – especially the 'rougher' boys – and she appeared to favour the 'nice' girls.

She worked out of a small office on the top floor of the Old Library Centre in West Norwood, but was hardly ever in the Centre. Hiley claimed in the interview to have worked for Connexions for four years. If this was true, Pead felt that she had learned little about how to handle the client group that composed of the students at the OLCVS.

Twist asked Hiley about the staff turnover at the OLCVS. The implication by Twist was that there had been a high turnover of staff, but this was far from abnormal – research by the Institute of Directors shows that in any organisation's first year, as many as 75% of the original staff will leave for a wide variety of reasons. Whitmore failed her probation. Foster wanted a move back to primary. Field left to pursue an acting career. This was hardly the stuff of a 'high turnover' of staff.

Twist – in a rare open question - asked Hiley how she knew that there was a high turnover of staff, but Hiley failed to answer the question.

Hiley claimed that Whitmore had been side-lined by Pead. This raises a number of issues. Firstly, how would a woman working two floors above the OLCVS even know this if it were true? How would she have seen this?

Secondly, Whitmore never made any complaints of being side-lined. She had ample opportunity during her probationary interview with her Union representative Robin Irwin present, but she never complained. The only complaint came from Murray on her behalf after Murray had been sacked.

The questions asked by Twist and the responses by Hiley were nothing short of farcical due, in the main, to a lack of searching questions.

Twist asked Hiley on what date Eloise Whitmore left the Centre.

Hiley's response: "...I'm not sure. I think it was December 2005. She seemed to leave secretly. People generally knew that it had something to do with Brian..."

Of course it had something to do with Brian Pead – he was her Line Manager and she had failed her probationary period. And Whitmore - on her own admission – had left on 19 January 2006. Hiley claimed to have noticed that Pead had 'side-lined' Whitmore, yet was unable to answer a simple question about when Whitmore left the OLCVS.

However, Hiley was then asked to describe her relationship with Pead. It had to be remembered that Hiley is not a *bona fide* witness – her best friend, Murray, has just been dismissed by Pead for racism and the sexual grooming of young, white girls. Hiley was not even employed by Pead. She worked for Connexions two floors above the OLCVS. These facts alone do not make for a credible witness.

Hiley's description of her relationship with Pead is interesting. The emphases are the authors':

"...Initially I had contacted Brian via an email to introduce myself and my role at Connexions to him. I met with him and he was very enthusiastic. **Even on** that first meeting he made observations about me. For example, Brian said that he could see that I was not happy in my current role. **I thought he was an insightful person. I thought it was uncanny how he sensed things about me and I was intrigued as to how he could sense these things.** He said that he was a life coach and he offered to life coach me. Initially I had fairly regular contact with him at the Centre. I felt that initial meeting had had a dual purpose which was both professional and personal. I met Brian for coffee outside of the Centre twice. Brian was very complimentary and mentioned that I would make an excellent counsellor. I didn't give him very much personal information. We talked a bit about my faith and upbringing. We both suggested books to each other regarding spirituality. I was a little wary about his level of interest in me. I thought he wasn't genuine and I decided I didn't want to spend more time with him and I didn't take up the offer for him to life-coach me. I would still see him around the site every day, **we had a professional relationship.** I was aware of my personal boundaries around him and so I didn't answer his personal type of questions, for example, what I did at the weekend. Brian has an analytical and probing style. He once told me he had had a vision about me but I didn't respond to this. I was vigilant in not letting him get close to me. **He didn't make unwelcome overtures to me and I didn't see him do so with others...**"

According to Hiley's own testimony, it would seem that the relationship got off to a good start. She claims that he was insightful. She claims she was vigilant in not letting him 'get close to her', yet she also goes on to say that he never made unwelcome overtures to her, or with others.

Why, then, did she choose to distance herself from Pead? Was it because (a) he knew her too well and that disconcerted her because she had a secret to hide? and (b) he had asked her several questions about how she would support his pupils and she was unable to come up with answers that would suggest to him that she was 'on top of her job'.

Pead wants the best for himself and those around him. His opinion of Hiley was that she was lazy and unprofessional.

At all times, Pead was professional with her. Hiley admits that much. At no time did she complain to him about any questions he may have asked. In offices all over the world, people ask one another "So, have you got anything lined up for the weekend?" or a hundred similar questions. There is nothing out of the ordinary in that. Those sorts of questions can hardly be described as 'intrusive' unless the person has something to hide, or says that they do not wish to answer such questions. Hiley had not said that she did not wish to answer such questions.

And Hiley had something to hide. She withdrew from Pead because she had seen that he was insightful. She didn't want him finding out her secret.

Twist asked Hiley if Pead had used any name other than Brian Johnson at the Centre. She said that he had not. This therefore completely contradicted Murray, Whitmore and Foster. It corroborated Maddison, Langan, Hill, Roach and even Gilhooly and Reynolds.

During this interview, it is clear that Hiley engaged in a number of conversations with Murray. Little wonder that neither of them achieved a lot of work since they were gossiping all day.

Hiley claimed that when Murray told her that Pead had a counselling name, she immediately emailed her line manager – Glenice Lake – and Lake then forwarded the email straight to Phyllis Dunipace, Executive Director of Education at Lambeth.

Note the extreme escalation. The management skills of Lake have to be called into question. **At no point did either Hiley or Lake consult with Brian Pead.** Any professional would have asked for an 'off the record' meeting in the first instance in order for the person to have an opportunity to explain themselves before taking it further if, indeed, it needed taking further.

However, the point also has to be made that Hiley and Lake were Connexions staff and thus had nothing to do with the OLCVS itself. It was, in short, none of their business. Pead could have called himself any name he wanted.

It can also be seen that hysteria – as first described by Sigmund Freud – abounded within the Connexions office. Allied to a lack of professional etiquette, this made for a dangerous cocktail. Imaginations ran wild.

The next question from Twist highlights the rampant neurosis that was Hiley.

Twist: What were your concerns with Brian's behaviour?

Hiley: It's hard to say. I don't have evidence of unprofessionalism, but a worst case scenario was my concern. **I was worried that he may be grooming women.**

Thus Hiley pointed out that Pead was professional. She stated that he was 'insightful'. She said she was amazed how he knew so much about people. She said that he had never used other names around her. So quite where did this allegation about 'grooming' women come from?

On her own admission, Hiley and Murray saw a lot of one another outside of the Old Library Centre. In fact, Murray even invited Hiley to lunch in the OLCVS without asking any of the staff, who were naturally concerned at her lack of consideration for their feelings and particularly concerned that there were not enough seats for everyone because Hiley was sitting at the table.

Hiley was being used by Murray. Murray was grooming the young, white girls. Hiley aligned herself with Murray.

This makes Hiley a witness lacking in credibility. But Twist did not care. Hiley was being primed and she was providing the answers that had been neatly typed out for her on the table in front of her.

Twist asked Hiley if Pead had used inappropriate treatment towards female staff. Hiley, who had previously stated that Pead was 'professional', claimed that he spent a lot of time in 1-to-1 conversations with 'attractive' female staff and students.

Notice Hiley's use of the word 'attractive'. What are the chances of two women – supposedly independent – using the same adjective when merely being asked to describe the **treatment** of staff?

Twist had simply asked if Pead had treated female staff inappropriately. What motivated Hiley, then, to comment on the looks of the staff members?

In fact, all of the staff who were interviewed after Hiley stated that there were allotted times for individual professional development meetings with Pead. All received equal treatment – male and female. Besides, Pead wondered, who were these supposed 'attractive' staff? He had not noticed any. He was, as Hiley pointed out, professional.

Then Twist asked Hiley if she had witnessed Pead giving favourable treatment to female staff, to which Hiley replied, "...No, not first-hand..."

Which renders her account invalid. She had never seen Pead giving favourable treatment to female staff.

Twist then asked if Hiley had ever received any complaints from students or other colleagues, and Hiley's response is staggering: "...No..."

Thus Hiley had never received a single complaint from either a pupil or a member of staff about Pead. This was all in her head. Her concerns about his possible 'grooming of women' were at best a malicious thought and at worst a psychotic episode.

From September 2005 to July 2006, Hiley had never received a single complaint.

And she, herself, had never made an official complaint about Pead's treatment of her.

What, then, was all the fuss about?

Yet Twist needed something more. She asked Hiley what she knew about exam procedures in schools, to which she replied, "...Nothing really..."

Most investigators at this point would either have asked her to clarify what she meant by that comment to elicit just what she did know or they would have dropped that line of questioning immediately.

But Twist is not a professional investigator.

Note how she ploughs on regardless of Hiley's answers, and note her leading question:

Twist: It has been alleged that a number of pupils were given special treatment in relation to their exams, i.e. some were allowed to take them at different times. Do you know if these arrangements were contrary to those allowed for in the procedures?

Hiley: No. I only know about other exam arrangements that were made through conversations with Maryn. For example, that Cassandra Trimmings was able to sit her exams outside of the exam time. **I know that Brian was very involved with Cassandra and she was very positive about him.**

Notice how Hiley answered the original question in the negative. That should have been the end of it. But no, she sees an opportunity to try to further damage Pead's reputation by discussing Cassandra Trimmings.

It should be noted that this is mere hearsay. She has absolutely no knowledge of which pupils sat which exams, yet she states on the record that she has engaged in conversations with Murray about these alleged events.

Later this same day, Colin Hill denied that Cassandra Trimmings or any other student ever received 'favourable treatment' and he provided photocopies of the exam results. Cassandra Trimmings did not even sit the Maths exam which Murray – and Hiley – claimed she had received favourable treatment for.

Why then did Twist not recall Hiley and tell her that Trimmings had not actually sat the exam?

Why did Twist not ask Hiley why she had not asked Murray to provide evidence of this 'favourable treatment'?

The pattern has emerged throughout – allegations were flying about from Murray. The weak and unprofessional female members of staff were accepting these allegations at face value without ever asking her to provide evidence. Hiley – who wasn't even a member of the OLCVS staff – just swallowed whatever information Murray threw at her.

Notice, too, how Twist failed to ask Hiley exactly what she meant by the term "...I know that Brian was very involved with Cassandra and she was very positive about him..."

Of course Pead was very involved with his pupils – all of them. As Duane Maddison later pointed out, certain pupils needed more of Pead's time because they had more complex needs. Pead's job description included the necessity for him to "...be responsible for [...] the welfare and social development of pupils including child protection..." (Refer to chapter 3, clause 8).

And of course Cassandra would be positive about her Head teacher, who was offering her support and an education and trying to ensure that she believed in herself in spite of her deprived upbringing. Pead never made judgments about any of his pupils – some of them came from appalling backgrounds and his sole remit was to try to provide them with the best possible start in life. He knew he was not their parent – he never tried to be. But he did want to help them on their journey through life. Which is more than the self-proclaimed Christian and 'deeply spiritual' Anya Hiley did. She had a propensity to keep cancelling appointments to meet with the 'rougher' male pupils.

Amazingly, she never seemed to cancel appointments with the 'attractive' female pupils. Her record of interviews with pupils will confirm this.

The next part of the Hiley interview simply defies belief.

Twist: Did you have any concerns about the time Brian spent with Cassandra Trimmings?

Hiley: Yes, I was concerned. Cassandra was a vulnerable young person. I don't know if she had an assigned social worker; I know that she had an abusive boyfriend and lived with her grandmother. I'm not aware if the grandmother had concerns about Brian. I know that Cassandra's boyfriend had accused her of sleeping with Brian. Cassandra had told me that this wasn't true.

This passage from the interview is extremely damaging to both Hiley and Twist.

Hiley admits here that she does not know much about Cassandra Trimmings' background – yet this was a part of her role. Pead had assessed Hiley to be ineffective and somewhat lazy. She was certainly not thorough and Pead did not like that. She had acquired all this information from Murray.

Hiley makes a contentious statement: "...I'm not aware if the grandmother had concerns about Brian..."

Why would Cassandra's grandmother have concerns? They spoke at frequent intervals on the telephone about Cassandra's welfare – this fact is corroborated by Duane Maddison in his interview. Furthermore, Mrs Trimmings would often come into the OLCVS – also corroborated by Duane Maddison and Colin Hill – to discuss her grand-daughter's progress and emotional wellbeing.

What purpose – other than being a malicious comment – does this serve? Hiley, the self-proclaimed Christian, appears to have fallen from grace.

What is deeply disturbing is that Hiley admits to having had a conversation with Cassandra and asked her whether she was sleeping with Brian Pead. This is appalling. It is an abuse of her power as a Connexions Advisor and it also shows that Hiley was up to no good.

Twist asked a further leading question about Pead's language and tone of some conversations with female pupils. Hiley's reply? "...I never witnessed any conversations in which his language and tone with female pupils was inappropriate. Brian had a playful and jokey approach with students. **I didn't think this was great.**"

Clearly, then, Hiley is more than confused. She states that she never witnessed any inappropriate conversations. On the other hand, she was worried that Pead might be grooming young women. These two statements simply do not correlate in this context.

Hiley also shows her woeful inexperience of the pupils at the OLCVS when she says that she didn't think it was great that Pead was playful and jokey. It was precisely his ability to relate to these deprived youngsters that led Nadia Al-Khudhairy to call the OLCVS "...the best pupil referral unit in London..."

When asked to describe Pead's relationship with staff, Hiley said that he seemed "...quite hands off..." and that he "...didn't do a lot of teaching..."

This is a quite remarkable statement for her to have made. It proves she was not a credible witness. For the first three months of the OLCVS, Pead was the **only** teacher. As supply teachers came on board, Pead still continued to teach Personal and Social Health Education (PSHE) as well as fulfilling his duties as a Head teacher. And when Fraser Hall, the Maths teacher, went on an extended holiday, Pead took over the teaching of Maths until Hall's return. These facts were corroborated by every member of staff, even by Murray herself!

Hiley's statement proves that she did not really know what was going on at the OLCVS other than whatever Murray was feeding her with. Hiley also seems to forget that she claimed that she witnessed Pead engaging in long one-to-one conversations with female pupils at times when he was, in fact, teaching.

When asked if Pead treated male and female staff the same, Hiley said that he didn't have "...the same emotional interaction with male staff as he did with female staff..."

Twist did not seek to uncover precisely what Hiley meant by her ambiguous comment. Yet Twist did not concern herself with that – she could, quite literally, twist that ambiguous statement to cast Pead in a bad light to the uneducated and gullible.

The interview took place on 25 January 2007. Hiley did not receive a copy of the interview notes to sign off until 12 June 2007 – Pead's 54th birthday!

On the papers that the authors obtained from Lambeth using a Freedom of Information Act request, Hiley had scribbled all over each of the six pages of notes.

Normal protocol would suggest that Hiley would then send back these notes to Lambeth, who would re-type them according to Hiley's annotations and then send them back to Hiley to sign off.

This process was not achieved. The entire case against Pead was, therefore, unlawful.

The question also has to be asked – why did Hiley not receive her statement to sign **until six months after her interview?**

Again, this is an abuse of process.

barry gilhooly interview

assistant director, inclusion division

If the Lambeth documents are a true record of the events of 25 January 2007, there was a mere ten minute break between Anya Hiley's interview and Barry Gilhooly's interview. All of the personnel were the same. The meeting room was the same.

An analysis of the Gilhooly interview makes for interesting reading: it lasted only an hour. The Hiley interview had taken 80 minutes, and she wasn't even a member of staff at the OLCVS. Gilhooly was Pead's line manager and a reasonable person would expect that the Gilhooly interview would have taken a lot longer, not least because their working relationship had been over a period of 18 months.

Another surprising statistic is that 91% of questions that Twist asked Gilhooly were closed questions. Six per cent were leading questions.

Twist asked Gilhooly when he first became aware that Pead used more than one name. Gilhooly replied: "...During the contract process. I became aware that Brian Johnson also used the name Brian Pead officially. Due to personal reasons he preferred to be known as Brian Johnson. So Brian Pead was used for official documents e.g. contracts and payslips. In the capacity of his role at the Centre he would be known as Brian Johnson..."

Twist: Were CRB checks carried out for both names?

Gilhooly: Yes, as confirmed by Human Resources.

Gilhooly's reply is accurate. Yet it completely contradicts the statement of Rosa Vaz, who worked in the Human Resource department at Lambeth. Vaz had claimed that Pead was always known as Pead at the OLCVS.

Gilhooly claimed that he met Pead every three weeks – but this was a lie. Pead documented every meeting that he had but his office had, of course, been ransacked, so Gilhooly could have said anything and Pead would not have been able to disprove it. As Gilhooly knew.

Twist, who has already just interviewed Anya Hiley who stated on the record that she had never had any complaint from either a member of staff or a pupil about Brian Pead, asks Gilhooly about the email Hiley sent to him in June 2006.

Twist: Can you discuss Anya's concerns about Brian raised in her email?

Gilhooly: She was not comfortable with his manner. Brian said that Ellie and Anya had colluded in their complaints about him and that they had some kind of agenda towards him. I thought this didn't match with my view of Brian being an open person. I spoke to Brian about these two complaints. **There were no complaints from students and there seemed to be a happy feel about the Centre.** Regarding Jenny Foster, **I had no doubt that if she had any problems with Brian she would have raised a complaint against him.** At the end of the Summer term 2006, I received Anya's complaint that she felt uncomfortable with Brian but there was no evidence and I told her that I would talk to Brian about it. I did talk to Brian about Anya's complaint but did not mention her name although he guessed it was her that made the complaint but I did not confirm or deny this to him.

The emphases are the authors'. Gilhooly also confirms that there were no complaints about Pead from pupils. He also says that he has no doubts that if Jenny Foster had any complaints about Pead – as Murray claimed in her 8-page document – that she would have raised these issues with Brian Pead. But she did not. This therefore makes Murray's complaint on behalf of Foster completely redundant.

Twist then turns her attention to what she called a 'high turnover of staff'.

Twist: It is suggested that there has been a high turnover of staff at the Centre. Do you know the reasons why staff left the Centre?

Gilhooly: Jenny Foster didn't mention she had any issues with Brian; I knew she was anxious about the security of her role. I knew Ellie Whitmore was unhappy with Brian **after** he had dismissed her. **After** Annabel Field left the Centre I heard that she had had issues with Brian. **The Local Authority couldn't offer long term contracts to Centre staff so it wasn't a surprise that people would leave for more secure positions.** I only became aware of Maryn's issues with Brian **after** she made her complaint which was **after** he had dismissed her on my advice for racism and for the sexual grooming of young, white girls.

This is an important extract from Gilhooly. He explains that the Local Authority was unable or unwilling to offer long-term contracts and that this was a significant contributory factor in some staff leaving. Gilhooly also explains that Whitmore was unhappy **after** she left. He fails to explain – and Twist never asks – how he came to learn that Annabel Field was allegedly unhappy with Pead.

But the most significant element of this extract is that Gilhooly makes Twist aware that Pead had told him about Murray's racism and grooming. At this point, it would have been judicious for Twist to ask Gilhooly to explain this in great detail, but she never asks that important question and Gilhooly does not elaborate.

Thus, the entire process was unlawfully proceeded with, when any genuine investigator would have stopped it there and then.

Twist: How would you describe Brian's management style?

Gilhooly: Initially Brian was very thoughtful and inclusive with the way he involved staff. As things developed, it seemed that Brian focused on discussion too much and not on leadership enough. He seemed to have a good rapport with staff.

Thoughtful and inclusive – this militates against what Murray, Whitmore, Foster and Field said. Derek Langan, Colin Hill and Duane Maddison all described Pead as 'an excellent leader', but Gilhooly appears to have overlooked this. Perhaps this was because he hardly ever visited the OLCVS. Yet Gilhooly comments that Pead had a good rapport with staff.

How, then, did Murray's claims gain credence in Twist's investigation? It is already clear that they had no merit, yet Twist pursues her quarry relentlessly and with no conscience.

Twist asked Gilhooly: "...Did you ever receive any complaints about Pead from either students or staff?..." and Gilhooly is unequivocal: "...No..."

When asked if Gilhooly noticed any differences between Pead's treatment of male and female staff, he replied, "...No..."

When asked if Gilhooly had ever witnessed any conversations between female students and Pead that were inappropriate, Gilhooly replied, "...No..."

Crucially, Gilhooly informed Twist that **there were no private areas in the OLCVS** where Pead could have taken pupils. This completely rebuts Murray and Hiley's allegations that Pead engaged in one-to-one meetings with female pupils in private areas. Additionally, Gilhooly told Twist that he had attended two or three staff meetings and that he had not witnessed any problems with Pead's management style.

Crucially, Gilhooly also stated that Pead had discussed staff contracts with him. Gilhooly said that he visited the Centre "...a couple of times..." to discuss staff contracts and that due process would have to be followed. This clearly militates what Murray claimed – that Pead had offered her a permanent contract. He didn't even have a permanent contract, so he would hardly have offered her one! Gilhooly said that "...Brian's interim position would have to be made substantive before anyone else's..."

When asked whether Gilhooly thought that Pead was using the Centre to run a life-coaching business, Gilhooly replied emphatically, "...No..."

Thus, in that hour-long interview, Gilhooly had completely refuted Murray's complaints against Pead.

Alarmingly, Gilhooly did not sign his copy of the statement until 25 June 2007 – six months after the interview!

Even more alarmingly, Twist – despite having had Gilhooly refute Murray's allegations – continued in her irrational pursuit of an innocent man.

sandra roach interview

p.a. to brian pead

It would seem that Cathy Twist was at least paying lip service to the idea that she was diligent in her investigation because she had only a half-hour break for lunch if the Lambeth documents are to be believed.

Twist and White met Sandra Roach in Meeting Room 8 – it had been requisitioned for the day. Karina O'Neill was once again the note taker.

The interview lasted for one hour – the same as Gilhooly's. Roach had to answer 45 questions and 89% were closed. Thirteen per cent were leading questions.

Sandra Roach explained that she had come to the OLCVS via the Protocol teaching agency in April 2006.

When asked about the 'high staff turnover', Roach said that Annabel Field had left to pursue a career in acting and that Fraser Hall had returned to New Zealand because of family commitments.

She never met Jenny Foster or Ellie Whitmore and felt that she was unable to comment on their departures.

Sandra Roach described her working relationship with Brian Pead as "...very good..." She said that his management style was different from what she was used to, but that she liked it as it was mature and he allowed staff a lot of leeway. This contradicted Murray's claim that Pead was a controlling autocrat.

Roach said that Brian Pead was always known at the Centre as Brian Johnson – this again rebutted Murray's assertion that Pead had used three names whilst at the Centre.

Twist: Allegations have been made that Brian may have given favourable treatment to female students and female staff. Are you aware of any situations where this may have been the case? Did you witness this happening?

Roach: No, I have never seen this at all. I had been a Teaching Assistant in Brian's classes in Maths and PSHE. I felt that the students respected him. I didn't witness anything untoward. In the PSHE classes Brian talked about safe sex to the class because it was on the curriculum and nothing was said that I would perceive as inappropriate. Brian answered students' questions using suitable language for that age group.

Twist: Did you ever receive any complaints from students or other colleagues concerning Brian?

Roach: No, never.

Thus Twist has now asked that same question of Hiley, Gilhooly and Roach and always received the same answer: that no complaints had ever been made against Pead by pupils or staff members.

When Twist asked if Roach knew of any pupils who had received favourable treatment in their exams, she replied that she had invigilated several exams and that she was unaware of this happening.

Roach also added that she was never aware of any inappropriate conversations having taken place between Brian Pead and female students.

This corroborated what Hiley and Gilhooly had said earlier that morning in their interviews.

When asked how Roach saw Pead's relationships with staff, she said that they were good and that he treated both male and female staff the same. This corroborated Gilhooly's statement. Yet Hiley – who worked two floors above the OLCVS and was hardly ever in the building – claimed she had seen different treatment of male and female staff.

Roach said that at no time did she ever make any complaints about Pead and nor had she received any such complaints from staff.

Twist asked Roach if she had detected a change in the working relationship between Pead and Murray. She said that she had and she cited an instance whereby Murray had been delegated a task of sending confidential letters out to parents. Murray had wanted to go to the pub to do this, but Roach had suggested that this would be wholly inappropriate. Pead overheard this part of their conversation and told Murray that under no circumstances should she take private and confidential letters off site to the pub to put them in envelopes.

This is one example of where Pead began to doubt that Murray was a credible Head of Department at St. Augustine's School in Ealing. Pead had worked in schools since 1982 and in all that time had never heard of a member of staff taking private letters to the pub to be put into envelopes.

In respect of contracts, Roach said that Pead had emailed Gilhooly about her contract and had copied her into the email. This is yet further evidence that Pead involved Gilhooly and Human Resources in all of his dealings over contracts.

When asked if she had anything further to add, Roach said, "...I was shocked and surprised by Murray's allegations. I found Brian to be very professional to staff and students alike. I would give Brian 100% support on this..."

Not getting the answer she wanted, Twist then continued to trawl for information:

Twist: Did you have any concerns about his other use of names?

Roach: Anyone can use whatever name they wish, providing it is not for fraudulent purposes. Brian has a therapeutic approach to students and I don't think he ever put pressure on students. Now that he is not at the Centre, some students are looking for the support that they had from him and me. The students are missing Brian, as are the staff.

Sandra Roach had given Brian Pead an excellent appraisal of his time at the OLCVS.

She was sent her statement to amend on 13 June 2007 – six months after she had been interviewed.

duane maddison interview

student well-being officer, olcvs

Within ten minutes of Sandra Roach leaving Meeting Room 8, Duane Maddison was interviewed. It lasted only 55 minutes – yet he had worked with Brian Pead from the very first day in September 2005. He was asked 32 questions and 84% were closed questions, with 19% being leading questions.

Mary White was in attendance – how much were Lambeth paying for her services? Notes were taken by Karina O'Neill. The meeting commenced at 1.45pm and finished at 2.40pm.

As previously outlined, Brian Pead had the highest regard for Duane Maddison, both as a colleague and as a man. A detailed account of the man and his work can be found on the website <www.amennoir.weebly.com>

Maddison informed Twist that he had been employed on a fixed, one-term contract and that he had previously worked as a learning mentor in a primary school. Unlike Jenny Foster – who also had only primary school experience – Maddison had actually worked with youth groups and teenagers in Lambeth and other boroughs.

After having explained his role at the Centre, Maddison was asked about the high staff turnover that Twist was keen to ask every interviewee. Like all the others before him, Maddison gave sound reasons for the departure of certain members of staff and he cited the fact that one reason was to do with contracts and the length of contracts. He said that it had taken two school terms for him to be paid correctly. Thus he has confirmed that Lambeth, and not Pead, were responsible for not issuing contracts at the OLCVS.

Pead recalled in an earlier discussion with John Callow that he felt that Lambeth Council and the line management of the OLCVS might not wish to continue with the project, because it was possible that, by not issuing contracts and in the event of the closure of the OLCVS, this might negate an obligation on the part of Lambeth to make staff redundancy payments.

When asked to describe his relationship with Brian Pead he said that it had been challenging at first (as most relationships are) and added that the OLCVS was short of staff and they had to work with a large number of students. "...Initially I worked more as a Teaching Assistant. I had numerous conversations with Brian regarding the challenges of my role. Brian understood my role and was aware of the shortage of staff and the challenges that we all faced. Brian gave support..."

Twist: How would you describe Brian's management style?

Maddison: There were different elements of it and these were beneficial. For example, the personal development aspect was beneficial for the staff. Brian allowed staff to opt out of this aspect. His style was structured to personal and professional development. With the personal development we looked at working with young people and our communication with pupils and how we received pupils.

Here Duane Maddison has shown that Pead's management style was multi-faceted yet beneficial. Maddison points out that Pead allowed staff to opt out of any aspect of personal development that they felt uncomfortable with – this is diametrically opposed to Murray's description of Pead (after she was dismissed by him) in which she described him as an autocrat.

Maddison also stresses that Pead focussed on communication between the staff and young people.

Twist: Did you think this was an appropriate style?

Maddison: We didn't spend a lot of time on this. I think it depends on your view of personal development and professional development.

Maddison had told Twist that "...with the personal development we looked at working with young people and our communication with pupils and how we received pupils..."

This followed the guidance of the United Nations charter for young people, the UK Government's guidelines for emotional well-being and also Lambeth's own guidelines.

That Maddison corroborated that Pead was, in fact, following the National guidelines in respect of supporting pupils and staff must have contributed to the fact that Twist did not call Maddison as a witness to the Disciplinary Hearing. **Not calling him as a witness obviously made the entire process unfair and unlawful.**

When asked by Twist what name Brian Pead used at the school, Duane replied, "...Brian Johnson... and no other names."

This is unequivocal. Pead had asserted that he had never used any other name at the OLCVS. Colin Hill had corroborated this. Derek Langan had also. Now Maddison was providing further evidence that no other names had been used. Yet Murray claimed he had used three names, and this was 'verified' by Whitmore and Hiley, yet no evidence had been provided by them.

When asked whether Brian Pead had favoured certain pupils, Maddison replied: "...Specific female students did get more attention from Brian **and these were** students who were going through immense difficulties at home and who were very vulnerable teenagers..."

Thus Maddison had provided Twist with an extremely logical reason for Pead to have some lengthy conversations with certain pupils – they were going through difficulties at home and were extremely vulnerable. Given this knowledge, why wouldn't Pead be engaging in conversations with them to support them? He would have been failing in his job had he not supported them.

Maddison also cited the case of Cassandra Trimmings, who was being mistreated by her boyfriend. He also said that Pead had supported the girl on the phone as well as in the Centre. There is nothing unusual with this, yet Twist sought to make this support from Pead into something nasty and perverted when it was nothing of the sort.

When asked whether there had been any problems with exam procedures, Maddison replied that he had invigilated some exams, monitored the rooms to make sure no one was talking and that he accompanied students to the toilets if needed. All of this is normal practice in any school in the land.

When asked specifically whether any pupils had received preferential treatment by Pead in taking their exams, Maddison replied, "...I was not aware of this..."

Why, then, did Twist not mention this in her '...thorough report...'?

Twist then asked Maddison whether he ever witnessed any conversations between female students and Brian Pead that were, in his opinion, inappropriate in terms of language and tone.

Maddison's reply is staggering: **"...No. I was around the conversations that Brian and students had and I was happy about the topics of conversation. I didn't see anything untoward..."**

This is an amazing statement. Maddison – a highly experienced learning mentor and educational workshop provider – said that he had seen nothing untoward and that he was with Pead when many of the conversations had taken place!

And Twist failed to include this in her 'thorough report'.

When asked to describe Pead's relationships with staff, Maddison provides yet another revelation: "...It seemed that Brian got on well with everybody..."

Why did this not get mentioned in Twist's report? And if Maddison had thought that Brian got on well with everybody – which is a quality learned through working for almost 40 years – why did Murray and Whitmore state otherwise?

And why was this obvious contradiction not more fully explored in Twist's 'investigation'?

When Twist asked Maddison whether he felt if Pead treated male and female staff in the same way, he said, "...I'm not sure that the treatment was different. I couldn't see this..."

When asked by Twist whether any of his colleagues had complained to him about Pead and his style of management, Maddison said, "No."

Thus there was not a single complaint to anybody about Pead's management style until **after** he had to dismiss Murray because of her inappropriate treatment of children.

When asked about the 'Mental Health Check' worksheets which Murray complained forcibly about (but not until after her dismissal), Maddison said that they were fine. He added that he had had an opportunity to give feedback on management and that he had made his disagreements known to Brian in an open forum and that Brian's response had been fine.

Yet Murray and her cronies had claimed Pead could not take criticism – something that no other member of staff corroborated and all of Pead's counselling peers and supervisors would not agree with.

Twist – in an attempt to trawl for any information that she could dismiss Pead for – asked Maddison about his contract. He said, "...Brian clearly told me that my current post is an interim one and would need to be advertised before being made permanent..."

This clearly militates against what Murray claimed, that Pead had told her that her contract was "...in the post..." Why would he say one thing to Murray and a completely different thing to Maddison?

When asked whether he had anything else to add, Maddison said that it was difficult in the Centre without Brian and that the students were suffering as there had been a lack of continuity. He added that the pupils did not know why Brian had left and were not even sure if he would be returning. (This is typical of an organisation with something to hide. Keep people in the dark. Spread confusion and doubt amongst them so that they lose focus and particularly so that they do not ask searching questions.)

But perhaps the most intriguing aspect of Maddison's entire statement is that **it was not signed by him until 18 June 2007 – six months after he had been interviewed!** This statement was never made available to Pead either before he himself was interviewed or at any other stage of the process.

Why had it taken Lambeth six months to get a copy of Maddison's interview to him for his signature?

And – more importantly – why had Lambeth, under the unethical Twist, commenced Hearings against Pead **before** they had all of the evidence in front of them and signed off by all of the people who had been interviewed?

This is a clear abuse of process. It is illogical and improper to start Disciplinary Hearings against someone before all of the available evidence is before the investigating officer. Thus Twist commenced a hearing against Pead when Maddison's account had not even been signed. And no pupil account had ever been sought. Nor, for that matter, was any parent ever asked to submit to an interview.

Maddison had been asked 32 questions in 55 minutes. 84% of questions had been closed and 19% had been leading – that is, 1 in 5 questions had been leading.

But if all of these transgressions gave cause for great concern, the interview with Eloise Whitmore and her responses was even more worrying.

Whitmore's interview provides incontrovertible evidence of not just a poorly-conducted investigation by Cathy Twist and others, but a cover-up of immense proportions which had sinister overtones to it.

eloise whitmore interview

Whitmore was interviewed on Monday 5 February 2007 in the 7th floor meeting room at International House in Brixton. In attendance were Cathy Twist, the ubiquitous Mary White, Eloise Whitmore and Karina O'Neill, who took notes.

Having established her name and position, Whitmore then explained that Gilhooly had given her a one-year contract from 5 September 2005 to 31 August 2006.

This is a remarkable piece of evidence. The school administration officer (school secretary) had been given a one-year contract whereas the Head of Centre had only been given a one-term contract. This unfavourable approach to the issuing of contracts was to prove one of the most unedifying aspects of Gilhooly's line management of the OLCVS.

Whitmore also made a *faux pas* when she added that her contract was "...subject to a satisfactory probation period..."

When Pead had had cause to fail her initial probationary period, she called in her union – the GMB – and during a meeting with her union representative present, she claimed that she had not known that the post was conditional on the successful passing of a probationary period. It is clear from the evidence before the authors that Whitmore is a person who has no problem with telling lies – the authors invite a law suit from Miss Whitmore.

When asked by Twist why there had been a 'high turnover of staff' at the OLCVS, Whitmore said that she had not known any reasons why staff left, since she had been the first to leave. She also said that she had kept in touch with Jenny Foster and that the latter had left because the role really wasn't what she was looking for. Thus Pead could not be held responsible for this, since he had not interviewed Foster for the role – Gilhooly had.

When asked by Twist to describe her relationship with Brian Pead, Whitmore said that she had not been told about her probation period. This completely undermined and contradicted her earlier statement in which she said that her contract was conditional upon her passing her first probationary period.

Yet Twist failed to bring this to Whitmore's attention. Her investigation was far from 'fair and thorough'.

Whitmore was asked to describe how her attitude changed towards her line manager and she revealed that she had kept a diary about Pead's behaviour.

However, a genuine investigator would simply have asked her to produce the diary in order to substantiate her own allegations against Pead, but she did not produce this alleged diary and Twist never asked her to produce it. This exactly mirrored what Murray had also claimed: that she had kept a diary about Pead. She never produced it and she was never asked to produce it by Twist. Furthermore, if this diary ever existed – which the authors strongly believe did not exist – then it ought to have been disclosed to Brian Pead. He had the right to see it. He asked Twist to produce a copy for him, but she failed to comply with his reasonable request.

Twist then asked Whitmore to describe what the first probation meeting established. This had nothing whatsoever to do with Murray's allegations. Whitmore had been dismissed on 19 January 2006 – more than a year previously – and she had been called on by Twist to "dish the dirt".

Whitmore's presence had no relevance whatsoever to the proceedings, but it did provide her with a platform to air her one-sided and narrow perspective. This was precisely what Twist wanted – to provide an open forum and to trawl for any information on which to build a case against Pead.

Whitmore was asked a total of 36 questions in her two-hour interview and an astonishing 34% of questions were open – the average in all of the interviews was just 19%.

When asked by Twist whether Brian Pead ever saw counselling clients in the Centre, Whitmore said, "...No, not that I was aware of..."

Murray, of course, had claimed in her 8-page document that he had been working in a paid capacity as a life coach and counsellor whilst at the OLCVS.

Then Whitmore spoke about Pead's alleged favourable treatment towards young female pupils. She claimed that he had shown favourable treatment to the female pupils. She claimed that "...Cassandra Trimmings, Chloe Gordon and Gemma Mandry were very young and vulnerable female students who had one-to-ones with Brian..."

She failed to add that Duane Maddison or Cassandra's grand-mother were often present during these 'one-to-one' interviews.

Whitmore – given an open platform on which to vent her anger at being dismissed for being incapable of holding down the post as school secretary – claimed that Pead had never made cups of tea for male pupils or had one-to-ones with them. This point has been disproved elsewhere in this book.

When asked about the language and tone of Pead's conversations with female pupils, notice how the maleficent Whitmore responds:

> "...I felt uncomfortable with the way he spoke to female students. He discussed students' private lives. I found it strange and was uncomfortable with this. I felt it was inappropriate and that Brian crossed the boundaries with his counselling and prying into their private lives. It was further than a Head teacher should have gone..."

At no point does Whitmore state why she felt uncomfortable. However, she has also lied again. She claimed earlier that she had been marginalised by Pead and forced to work on the second floor of the Centre which housed computers and printers. If, therefore, she had been marginalised, how would she be able to comment on the tone and language of Pead's conversations with students – male or female?

If, on the other hand, she had been a party to these conversations in Pead's office, then it shows that she lied about being marginalised. Either way, she had demonstrably lied.

Whitmore continued her vitriolic onslaught against Pead.

Twist: Did Brian make inappropriate comments to staff?

Whitmore: Yes. **I heard him ask Maryn if she wanted to go walking in the woods with him.**

The conspiratorial Murray, Hiley and Whitmore had obviously not rehearsed their lies well enough – Murray had claimed that Pead had asked her **in private** to go walking in the woods.

Murray claimed that it had been in private in order to dispose of the fact that any genuine investigator would ask if anyone was present when Pead allegedly made this invitation.

Whitmore, on the other hand, was always a hostage to the truth, and she claimed that she had been present when Pead made this invitation.

One – or both of them – was lying. Pead asserts that he never made this invitation to any single member of staff but to the entire staff in a meeting that was minuted.

Twist, however, failed to notice this discrepancy in the testimonies of Murray and Whitmore. What, after all, did the truth matter? Twist had her own agenda.

It is said that a liar has to have a good memory. Whitmore's memory failed her within seconds. When asked by Twist if all staff had one-to-one meetings with Pead she replied, "...No... supply teachers didn't..."

The very next statement she made was "...Maryn had one-to-one meetings with Brian..."

Maryn Murray was – on her own admission – a supply teacher. Whitmore, who allegedly kept a diary, obviously failed to consult it to ascertain the facts.

Whitmore claimed:

> "...I think he is dangerous. He has issues with power and women. He told the staff that he had been adopted and never met his mother. He was paranoid about control and power..."

Pead had never said that he had been adopted. He was never adopted. Presumably Whitmore had referred to her 'diary' – if she had, then she inputted the wrong data. But this was nothing new. Whitmore was simply out of her depth. A bullshitter, she had been found out. How strange that Whitmore should describe Pead in this way, yet no members of staff had ever received complaints about him, no pupils had ever complained about him and no parents had ever complained. Furthermore, Pead's counselling peers had an entirely different view of him from Whitmore and Murray.

Whitmore's final comments are worth recording. Twist asked "...Do you think that Brian Pead should hold senior management positions or positions relating to young people?...", Whitmore could not resist releasing all her bile and viciousness in her response:

> "...No. He messed with my head when I worked at the Centre. It definitely changed me after my time there. He gave out hand-outs to staff regarding counselling and proverbs and he would ask for our responses to these in staff meetings. He asked Duane, Jenny and I to write down notes on the way that he had supported us..."

The gullible Whitmore failed to understand that Pead's management was partly to ensure that people **would** change in order to meet the considerable challenges that the pupils presented. Pead had assessed Whitmore to be insensitive, inflexible and immature and he would assert that her responses and behaviour simply demonstrate that his assertion about her was correct and that he was right to dismiss her (having consulted with HR first).

Whitmore annotated the notes transcribed from her interview. In the margin, she added some **six months later** that "...I do not think he should be a manager, he should not be working in Lambeth and he should not be working with children..."

The Lambeth record shows that "...Copies given of diary notes, staff meeting minutes, probation report and counselling hand-outs..."

If this is to be regarded as a true record of what was said and done at the meeting, why did Twist fail to provide Pead with a copy of all the hand-outs – especially the alleged diary that Whitmore claimed to have completed each day?

Were it even true that Whitmore kept a detailed diary on Pead's movements each day, then no wonder he had recourse to dismiss her for being ineffective in her role. She was so busy maintaining the diary that she failed to complete the tasks she was actually paid to do.

gilhooly re-interviewed

Barry Gilhooly was re-interviewed on Monday 5 February 2007 from 2pm to 4.10pm in the 7th floor meeting room of International House.

Twist and White were present and the note-taker was Karina O'Neill.

In his first interview on 25 January, Gilhooly had been somewhat complimentary towards Pead. However, Twist had not received any concrete evidence of wrong-doing by Pead, so she had to ensure that his line manager would be able to assist her in her mission to rid Lambeth of Pead's services.

A reading of the transcript of this interview provides interesting reading. He was asked 32 questions. The length of the interview was 75 minutes. This means that in total Brian Pead's line manager was interviewed for a total of 105 minutes – yet Eloise Whitmore had been interviewed for 120 minutes and she had worked only four months at the Centre.

Annabel Field had been interviewed for 100 minutes – and she had only worked at the OLCVS for four months.

Anya Hiley – who didn't even work at the OLCVS – had been interviewed for 80 minutes.

Twist used this second interview to discuss child protection issues with Gilhooly. By taking this line of questioning, she had, in effect, proved that she had lied to an employment tribunal in stating that the case against Pead had not included any child protection issues which was the reason she gave for not calling any pupils or parents. This was, of course, nonsense.

Murray and Hiley had claimed that Pead was grooming young female pupils. This is, in itself, a child protection issue. Lambeth failed in its duty of care towards pupils and their parents or carers.

Gilhooly demonstrated his inept management when he commented on child protection issues:

"...The Centre was not specifically set up for vulnerable pupils. There were initial meetings with Di Burton and Claudia Deiter and a number of staff with Brian where this might have been discussed. I became aware after the Autumn term that a number of pupils had vulnerability issues. The second half of the Spring term saw a focus on curriculum planning. Brian asked if he could take on extra teaching staff and I said yes. Perhaps I was naive about the needs of the pupils. Brian said that pupils had a need for emotional development. In May or June I was worried that Brian was focusing too much on the therapeutic emotional development of students. Brian had a plan for the second year of the school for this but I asked him to rewrite this plan..."

This lengthy response from Gilhooly demonstrates his woeful inadequacies.

Brian Pead had informed Gilhooly from the very start that the pupils who had arrived at the OLCVS were extremely vulnerable in a number of ways. Gilhooly's claim that the Centre was not set up for vulnerable pupils shows a naivety that an Assistant Director of Education should not have. That Gilhooly claims that he had been "...worried..." that Pead's focus was on a therapeutic model for the OLCVS was patent nonsense, as Duane Maddison, Colin Hill and Derek Langan had pointed out. The emphasis was always on teaching and learning, but the pupils' emotional difficulties presented barriers to learning. These barriers had to be removed before learning took place. An Assistant Director of Education ought to have known this.

Twist asked Gilhooly if he held regular management meetings with Pead:

Gilhooly: Yes.

Twist: Do you have any notes from these meetings?

Gilhooly: No. I didn't always take notes of our meetings.

Again, this shows Gilhooly's weakness as a manager and as an Assistant Director. He also lied. He and Pead rarely met. Pead asserts that Gilhooly was often unavailable. This can be confirmed by Beverley Williams, Gilhooly's PA.

Furthermore, the question has to be asked "If Gilhooly didn't **always** take notes at the meetings, this must mean that he took notes at **some** of the meetings. Why did Twist not ask for these notes?"

What transpired next in the interview is extremely worrying for all Lambeth taxpayers and all parents and pupils in Lambeth schools.

Twist: Did Pead consult you before dismissing Murray?

Gilhooly: No, I was shocked at his decision.

Gilhooly had patently lied. Pead **had** consulted with him about Murray's racism and grooming of young girls and Gilhooly had suggested that Pead call the teaching agency and ask them to call Murray and tell her not to return to the OLCVS.

This meeting had been documented and notes taken. It was logged on Pead's office computer and a hard copy printed off.

Gilhooly then ordered that Pead's office be ransacked once he had been suspended.

Twist then asked Gilhooly one of the most banal questions it is possible to ask: "...Did you renew Pead's contract after complaints by Hiley and Whitmore? To which Gilhooly replied, "...Yes, it was renewed in July 2006..."

Twist fails to ask why it was renewed and merely moves on to a completely different question. Yet, had she enquired why Pead's contract had been renewed, she would have learnt that it was because he was a valuable member of staff. How had he descended so rapidly from a valuable member of staff to someone involved in such allegations? The catalyst, of course, had been his dismissal of Murray.

Twist then discusses an email that Pead had sent to Rosa Vaz in Human Resources on 5 November 2006 that he had copied Gilhooly into. This email was about his being bullied by Murray, especially in relation to her wanting a contract.

Twist: How did you react to this email?

Gilhooly: I talked to Rosa about this and she said it was not appropriate for them to investigate the matter. She said that Brian should investigate as he was the Centre manager. Brian said that Maryn was in collusion with Ellie and she wouldn't meet with Brian to discuss issues. This email did trigger concerns for me and I met with Maryn soon after and asked her to put her complaint in writing. **I thought he wasn't being bullied but it was people reacting to him.** The timing of events overtook any action to this email as Maryn made her complaint soon afterwards. Brian had mentioned that he would request a FOI request to get a copy of the complaint about him that was emailed to Phyllis. **This was Anya's complaint: I advised Brian not to go ahead with this as if he did so it would raise awareness even further.**

This response from Gilhooly is difficult to believe on several levels. Firstly, he is wrong to say that Rosa Vaz said it was not appropriate for Lambeth to investigate Pead's bullying complaints. Lambeth Council owed him a duty of care and they were negligent in failing to investigate an official complaint. The subject heading of this email had been entitled "*Bullying: Official Complaint*". There was no room for ambiguity.

Gilhooly was wrong to assume that Pead – just because he was manager – could not be bullied. There was demonstrable collusion between Murray and Hiley and this can be seen in the witness statements.

Pead did, indeed, tell Gilhooly that he would action a Freedom of Information request to obtain a copy of the Anya Hiley email sent by her on June 2006 – this situation should never have arisen because Pead should automatically have been given a copy of the email since he was named in it. Again, Lambeth failed in its duty of care towards Pead.

Why would Gilhooly advise Pead not to go ahead with the FOI request? Why did he not want this to "...raise awareness even further?..."

What was Gilhooly hiding?

When asked by Twist if he had anything to add, Gilhooly ended the interview with a cryptic response:

> "...Yes. There are two aspects to this issue. There is the supervision of Brian by me and there is the nature of the complaints that have been made. I am concerned about the balance of the investigation report. I am concerned about the shortcomings of the management of Brian. It leaves out the fact that the Centre has had success and no complaints have been raised from students or parents. There is the issue of Brian's management style. It is easy to be critical after the event and my role has to be seen in the context of my other roles. I had lots of conversations with Brian about the provision of the centre and his focus on therapy. That was his style but the delivery of the Centre was not about this..."

On the face of it, this response by Gilhooly is a masterful approach to saving his own skin. He is saying that he was not responsible for what happened at the OLCVS because he was a busy man. In any event, he tries to claim, he had had lots of conversations with Pead - but he did not. Nor did he ever provide the dates and times of all these alleged meetings, nor any notes.

Yet Gilhooly appears to have had a pang of conscience when he says that the investigation report was not balanced and that it had not included anything about the success of the Unit and the fact that there had never been any complaints from pupils or parents. He fails to add that there had never been a single complaint about his management of the Unit until after Murray had been dismissed for racism and sexual grooming of young white girls.

Why would he omit such crucial information?

76

deadline

Lambeth's self-imposed deadline for the completion of disciplinary hearings was 13 weeks from the first complaint. The deadline of 9 March 2007 was fast approaching.

"...The world is a dangerous place, not because of those who do evil, but because of those who look on and do nothing..."

Albert Einstein

field of nightmares

Annabel Field was interviewed on Friday 23 February 2007 in Room 1 on the Second Floor of International House in Brixton.

In attendance was Twist and the corrupt Mary White, the Human Resources Consultant.

Annabel Field did not take anyone with her for support.

The meeting commenced at 1pm and finished at 2.40. She was thus interviewed for an hour and forty minutes – far longer than Duane Maddison, for example, who worked with Pead for 18 months, whilst Field only worked for a matter of four months. And far longer than Gilhooly's interview lasted. Yet Gilhooly was Pead's line manager throughout the 18-month period that Pead was running the OLCVS.

Field confirmed her name and position and that she was employed through an agency called Teachweb. **Had she been CRB checked?** She also stated that she was interviewed by Pead for the role in November 2005 and that she started working at the Centre in January 2006. She says that she left the Centre in May 2006.

When asked why she left the OLCVS, she said – quite properly – that she wanted to focus on her acting rather than teaching and moved away to Bath in order to do so. However, Twist cited Field as another example of Pead's mismanagement and blamed Pead for her moving away. Yet Field's response clearly proves that it was **her** decision to leave the OLCVS and not Pead's fault in any way.

When Twist asked Field if she knew of any reasons for the 'high turnover of staff' at the OLCVS, Field answered that she had no idea. She also added that she knew Jenny Foster wanted to move back into primary teaching. Again, Twist laid the blame for Foster's departure at Pead's door, but Field provided a sound – and true – reason for Foster leaving.

However, Field's relationship with the truth then became strained. She made a number of allegations against Brian Pead (after having been brain-washed by Murray) that had no bearing on the truth whatsoever.

The authors reproduce much of her testimony in this chapter because it raises far more questions than it answers and it also demonstrates that Field lied.

When asked how she would describe her relationship with Brian, she replied:

> "...Mixed. At first, I did a couple of example lessons for Brian and he was very positive about my teaching. At the start of my job Brian gave me a card saying that I was clever and other positive things. I thought it was over the top

for someone I'd just met. Brian had an open and relaxed relationship. Over time Brian became too intrusive, I found it too much. Brian pushed his personal questions too far. Our relationship became quite fiery. I once told Brian that he was a head-fuck. Brian was manipulative but I stood up for myself. Brian had unprofessional and unnecessary conversations with me...”

This card – first mentioned in Murray's report – was never produced as evidence. It was part of Murray's fantasy – she claimed she had been sent poems by Pead and this was part of her attempt to destroy him.

Field displays her inability to be decisive in this reply. She claims that Pead was open and relaxed and then that he was a 'head-fuck'.

Yet she seems to have completely forgotten her email to him of 17 April 2006 in which she thanks Pead for his support and says that her experience at the OLCVS was her best in London.

Why did Twist not ask Field about this email, since she was in possession of it?

Field continues her tissue of lies:

“...It's difficult to define Brian's behaviour. I couldn't understand what his motives were for his personal style. He seemed to be trying to solve peoples' problems and using his counselling techniques often with both staff and students. I thought this was too much. Even though I was employed at the Centre through an agency I gave Brian three weeks' notice that I was going to leave the Centre. At this time Brian emailed me saying that he had so many questions to ask me about why I was leaving...”

This alleged email has never been produced either.

“...Towards the end I wasn't enjoying work a lot. Brian once told me that he knew what the problem was with me but that he wasn't going to tell me and that I would have to find out the answers for myself. I thought he should have just told me what the answers were. I told Brian that he shouldn't have said this to me and that I didn't want to be having these sorts of conversations with him. Brian replied that I was very frustrating to have these types of conversations with. I thought that Brian was having these counselling types of conversations with female students. I was concerned about what effect he might be having on the young people at the Centre. For example, I saw Brian and a female student, Ashleigh Mills, having in-depth conversations. Ashleigh had been given a work experience opportunity in the Centre office where these conversations would take place. Brian also talked with Ashleigh and her aunty. I thought he was trying to counsel both of them. I didn't overhear any of the 1-to-1 conversations that Brian had with Ashleigh or any other students...”

Field is clearly confused here. She claimed earlier that she "...stood up to him..." and yet now claims that she was having a large number of conversations with him which made her feel uncomfortable. Why, then – had this even been true – did she simply not just walk out of the office? Why did she not report him? Why did these conversations not get mentioned in staff meetings? Why did Annabel Field not ask Marion Richards – the English consultant – to speak with Brian about it? Why did Field not ask to speak with Brian's line manager, Barry Gilhooly, about these alleged conversations? Why did she not speak with Lambeth Human Resources? Or to her agency, Teachweb? Or to her parents or sisters? Or her friend Alicia Harris, who had introduced her to the OLCVS?

And why, then, did she send – unsolicited – such a praiseworthy email to him in April 2006?

Why would she be concerned about the conversations he had with pupils and/ or their relatives? It was his job to have such conversations.

And why did Twist fail to mention in her 'unbiased' report that the vast majority of conversations Pead had had with Ashleigh Mills was with a relative present – usually her aunt?

Further examples of Field's brain-washing by Murray are cited here: "...I was shocked by Maryn's experience with Brian. Maryn was so professional. Brian would switch his behaviour, at first he is over praising of your work then this becomes less so..."

That this statement is a fabrication is obvious: Annabel Field had left the OLCVS **before** any problems with Murray arose. How would she, therefore, be able to comment on Brian's relationship with Murray? And why are the words she has chosen to use to describe that relationship an exact match of the words used by Murray in her 8-page report? The actress had learnt her lines well.

Twist then asked Field: "...How would you describe Brian's management style?..."

Field replied:

> "...Brian suggested that I didn't need to have 1-to-1 meetings with him but that we should have chats instead. Brian was not so supportive on the finer details of my work. I had a lot of work to do for a supply teacher and I felt that Brian did not make sure that I had enough support..."

According to his peers and to his supervisors, Brian Pead is a master of understanding people and being able to spot any inconsistencies in their 'story'. All of his counselling clients have established long-term relationships with him and say that they stay with him over a long period of time because of his 'real-ness'. He doesn't use bullshit. He 'says it as it is'.

He had initially liked Annabel Field but found that she would often 'fall to pieces' when under stress. She was also easily led and it was known to him that she formed an unhealthy alliance with Anya Hiley and Maryn Murray: "Show me a person's friends and I will show you the person."

Brian Pead bears no ill-will towards Annabel Field, despite all of her lies. He bears no ill-will in spite of the fact that she claimed here that he had offered her no support, despite writing in April 2006 (just three weeks before she left): "...I have really enjoyed working at the school and it's definately (sic) been my most positive teaching experience in London. Thank you for all your support to me!"

This is a clear contradiction. An investigating officer should have been aware of this and then ought to have questioned her about this discrepancy. In any event, it renders Field's statement invalid. She has clearly lied – or, if we are being kind – she has evidently been unclear about her feelings.

Brian Pead agrees that they did have the odd chat – the kind of chat staff members have in every school or office throughout the world. Field states in that email that "...As predicted after our chat this has been a very reflective holiday for me!"

This comment of Field's seems to indicate that Pead had told her that once she had gone away on holiday, she would have had an opportunity to reflect on whether to teach or act. There is no mention by Field of any improper conduct by Pead in these 'chats'.

The email that Field sent in April 2006 indicates her state of mind: "...To cut a long story short the gist of it is that I'm moving out of London in the next couple of weeks. I know that this is not ideal in terms of the exam groups and I'm sorry for that. I did intend to stay on but to be honest, the chance has suddenly come up this weekend to move to Bath and I feel that I have to take it as soon as possible in an effort to quosh (sic) my recent restless state!

I am sorry to make things difficult for you guys - I do feel bad but hey I'm sure there is someone ready and waiting to take on the job without having crazy burning ambitions to act at the same time!"

It would appear that Field has some guilt about leaving the OLCVS just before the students were due to take their English GCSE examinations. This guilt would, of course, be assuaged in her own 'restless mind' by laying the blame at Pead's door for her departure.

Field then ends the email on a positive note: "...I'll see you tomorrow and I'll certainly aim to get the English work as organised as possible over the next week or so..."

It is interesting to note that Field fails to mention in her statement to Twist that it was Pead himself – a former English teacher – and Marion Richards, the English

consultant to Lambeth, who sorted out the files of work that were necessary for the pupils to pass their GCSE in English. Richards felt that Annabel Field was a good-enough teacher but extremely weak on completing tasks and delivering what she promised. This turned out to be the case – she left the OLCVS before the end of term and immediately prior to the pupils taking their exam so that she could chase her dream of becoming an actress at the age of 26. After appearing in the Horse Dealer's Daughter in 2006, she then appeared as the Narrator in 'Christopher and the Christmas Tree' later that year. In 2007 she was the female lead in 'The Jabberwocky' and Amy in 'Building Planets', a Fat Cats Production. Her final part came in 2007 as the female lead in another Fat Cats Production. Then her career as an actress seems to have abruptly ended.
Source: http://www.total-talent.com/uk/view.php?uid=94717

Field continued her assessment of Brian Pead: "...Brian didn't always seem to know what he was doing..." This comment was also made by Maryn Murray, who wasn't even a qualified teacher. Annabel Field had two years' experience and was working as a Supply Teacher at the time. Yet they felt they had the necessary qualifications to make such comments against a man who had taught in all sectors of education, who had won prizes for Excellence in Teaching, who had been awarded 7 out of 7 'Excellent' grades by OfSTED and who had taught since 1982.

Field then introduced a whole new complaint against Pead: "...I thought Brian may have been looking for case studies for his psychology work. I don't know what his motives were for his line of questioning. I had mentioned his behaviour to friends and family of mine and they had told me that it sounded as if Brian fancied me..."

This is a remarkable comment from Field. She seems to have overlooked the most obvious questions: if Pead really did have this kind of conversation with you that you did not like, why did you continue to have them? Why didn't you report him? Why did you continue to converse with him if you felt that he 'fancied' you? Did you, in fact, fancy him? Were you jealous that he attended the play in which you acted with a woman of the same age as you? And why did you wait until more than **nine months** after you left to make these allegations? Was it because you had a close relationship with Murray? Was it because you had read her 8-page report prior to being interviewed?

Despite already having been told that Field left the OLCVS to pursue a career in acting, Mary White continues to probe her reasons for leaving and asks a leading question designed to get only one answer: "...Did Brian's behaviour influence your decision to leave the Centre?"

Field starts to realise what answer she **ought** to be giving: "...I did want to move into an acting job but I also didn't want to be around Brian anymore. Sometimes I would leave work in tears after a conversation with Brian..."

This is an amazing statement for Field to make. It is completely opposite to her email to Pead. If she really didn't want to be around him anymore, why did she tell him she had had such a great time working in the OLCVS?

Twist sought to probe yet further: "...What did you understand Maryn Murray's post to be?"

Field replied: "...Maryn was the deputy head teacher. But I know that she didn't have a contract for this role as she was promised by Brian..."

Any investigator would then be obligated to ask, "How did you know this?" but this question was never asked and Field's comment was left hanging in the air.

Twist then asked about Brian Pead's professional conduct towards students and staff: "...Allegations have been made that he may have given favourable treatment to female students and female staff. Are you aware of any situations where this may have been the case? Did you witness this happening?..."

Field replied: "...I was not aware of any preferential treatment towards staff. I know that Brian didn't have long 1-to-1s with any male staff. He did have long 1-to-1s with female staff; Sandra, Maryn and myself..."

The confused Field claims she does not know of any preferential treatment towards staff. Then, mysteriously, she plucks a statement from the ether: that Pead did not have one-to-one conversations with male staff. All of the male staff: Colin Hill, Duane Maddison and Derek Langan stated that they **had** had one-to-one meetings in accordance with good management practice. It has to be asked: where did this comment originate? Read on for the answer.

According to Field, "...Brian Pead also had in-depth conversations with female students. These were held in the office or in otherwise empty classrooms. For what it's worth, these students were young and blonde..."

This is an astonishing comment from Field, yet it actually supports Pead's case against Lambeth. Field states that Pead conversed with students in the office. Everything that happened in this office was visible to everybody in the Centre, since it had a glass frontage and glass doors.

However, Field shoots herself in the foot when she claims that Pead met with pupils in empty classrooms because there were no empty classrooms in the Centre. There was full occupancy of the Centre and this can be borne out by an examination of the booking schedule of the OLCVS. The booking schedule was the responsibility of Sherine Thompson. Why was she not called as a witness? Why was she not asked to provide a copy of the booking schedule?

On her own admission, Field was a part-time teacher, working only two (and later three) days a week. How remarkable, therefore, that she should have been able to see all of these alleged conversations.

Field claims that all of the conversations were with female pupils who were "young and blonde". Given that pupils are young in any event, that pejorative adjective can be discounted. However, in her testimony Murray claimed that Pead had had conversations with Gemma Mandry and Kerrie Hamilton – neither of whom was blonde – and Cassandra Trimmings, who was also not blonde but later dyed her hair blonde.

Field – the woman who sent an email thanking Brian for his support and then claiming she didn't receive any – claims that Mandry and Hamilton were blonde. She is clearly not the most reliable of witnesses.

Twist then asked Field: "...Did you ever receive any complaints from students or other colleagues concerning Brian?..."

Field answered: "...Not written complaints but verbal. Melissa Whitrod, a student, complained to me that Brian was picking on her. I didn't hear any complaints from staff although Maryn had mentioned her personal type of conversations with Brian.

In all schools, every teacher will have heard the phrase "You're picking on me." This is usually when pupils do not get their own way. Brian Pead never had discipline problems in his career as a teacher because he knew how to handle all types of pupils. Just like Alex Ferguson or Harry Redknapp in football, where they know that one player might respond to an arm around the shoulder, another might need a verbal 'kick-up-the-arse'; it is ridiculous to treat all of the players the same. However, they all expect to be treated fairly – which is a completely different thing. This is how Pead managed pupils. He was, at all times, fair. He never shouted at pupils or staff. He knows that once you shout, you have lost control.

Twist continued her interview with Field: "...It has been alleged that the language and tone of some of Brian's conversations with female students was inappropriate. Did you witness any conversations between female students and Brian that in your opinion was inappropriate in terms of language and tone?

Field replied firmly, "...No, I didn't overhear any conversations between Brian and female students. I did wonder why Brian and students would go into a private room to have a 1-to-1. I felt uneasy about this..."

Field clearly states that she had not overheard a single one-to-one conversation between Pead and pupils. Why, then, would she feel "uneasy" about them? And she failed to establish the location of this alleged 'private room'. All of the rooms were captured on CCTV. None of the rooms was 'private'. Even Barry Gilhooly had said that there were no private rooms in the Centre.

Twist then asked Field about the alleged masturbation in the theatre in which she had acted: "...It has been alleged that Brian behaved inappropriately in a public place. Can you please comment on this and how you felt about it?..."

Field's answer is reproduced in full, save for corrections in spelling and punctuation:

"...I invited all of the Centre staff to a play that I was performing in at the White Bear Pub, Kennington. Brian was the only colleague who attended the play and he was there with a woman whom I had not met before. She seemed to be in her late 20s or early 30s and sounded as if she was foreign. I only said a quick hello to Brian and his companion before the performance.

On the night Brian and his companion attended the play, they sat next to a cast member's wife. After the performance this cast member's wife told me that she had seen Brian and his companion fondling each other during the performance and that at one point Brian's companion had her hand down his pants. The theatre was small with three rows of seats for the audience and it was not very dark. There may have been 20 or so audience members that night.

Brian and his companion were seated in the back row. I was talking with this cast member and his wife after the performance because I was planning on introducing this cast member to Brian regarding some possible acting work for him at the Centre as Brian had mentioned he was interested in an acting project at the Centre.

After his wife had told me about Brian's behaviour during the performance I felt too embarrassed to introduce my friend to Brian and did not do so. I did not mention Brian's behaviour to Brian afterwards. **I think my cast member's wife knew that Brian was my boss and the Head Teacher of the Centre, as her husband may have pointed Brian out to her before the performance...** "

The emphasis is the authors'. The entire passage is full of inconsistencies and flaws. The main ones are listed here:

1. No dates are provided for this performance .
2. The cast member is not named
3. The wife is not named
4. The entire passage is based on the words "I think..." and "may have"

Annabel Field lied here. The authors invite a lawsuit for libel. This incident never happened. Again, she has tried to be far too clever. The theatre was not very dark – this is true. Therefore, why did no actors and other audience members not see anything? Pead is a little over six feet tall and did not sit in the back row as claimed because he likes to stretch his legs out. Friends will testify that he always sits either in the front row or in an aisle seat so that he can stretch out. Furthermore, Field claimed that there were three rows of seats in the theatre, but there were only two rows.

Twist failed to robustly test this 'evidence'. John Callow read this passage with incredulity. He would have pulled it apart and robustly interrogated Field's version of events. How did the unnamed cast member know that Pead was Annabel's boss? She stated that she met Pead and his companion outside of the theatre before the play started and only for a very brief period of time. Therefore, at what point did this alleged cast member know that Pead was her boss? Pead was never introduced to anybody either before or after the performance.

And how did the alleged 'fondling' become 'sexual acts' as described by Twist? And how did the 'hands in the pants' become 'masturbation' as alleged by Twist?

The whole event never occurred. The authors have contacted the theatre and the pub and all concerned state that **this event never happened.**

When asked by Twist to describe Pead's relationships with staff, Field replied "...Friendly, relaxed..." This is a bizarre response, given her earlier allegations that he was a "head-fuck". This is just another example of her statement being full of contradictions.

Continuing to trawl for information, Twist then turned her attention to Pead's behaviour in meetings and how he organised and ran them, asking Field: "...Allegations have been made concerning the way that Brian conducted staff meetings and individual meetings. Was there a timetable of meetings, agendas and minutes for meetings?

Notice that for each question, Twist makes a leading statement first before asking the question. This has been carefully designed by Twist to obtain a certain answer. She is not being impartial at all – she is merely looking to obtain an answer which will lead her to her objective: that of dismissing Pead.

Field claimed that there was no timetable of meetings and that there was usually one staff meeting once a week.

When asked by Twist, "...Who was responsible for organising and leading meetings?" Field responded with "...Brian would ask someone to take staff meetings if he couldn't be there. Agenda were given out on the day of the meeting. There was always an opener for staff meetings, for example, a thought for the day..."

Twist: Did any of your colleagues complain to you about the nature or content of these meetings or the way in which they were treated?

Field: No.

This answer clearly shows that Murray, Hiley and Whitmore had all lied in their statements because they all said they had complained to Annabel Field about Pead and that she had complained to them about him.

Twist had interviewed Murray, Hiley and Field **prior** to interviewing Field. Twist therefore knew that Field's answer was either (a) a lie or that (b) the others had lied.

In any event, what an investigating officer **has** an obligation to do is to investigate: in this instance, she should have asked Field why the others had incriminated her by saying they had all complained to her.

But Twist did nothing, whilst claiming that the investigation was 'thorough and fair'.

It was nothing of the sort.

Twist then asked Field to comment on Brian Pead's management style. Field replied:

> "...I ended up feeling suffocated by him. I was worried that he would control students through his counselling style. I think he tried to get into people's heads using his counselling skills. I think he thought of himself as some sort of guru. He wants to make it look like he has all the answers. I had concerns about the students as they were vulnerable and didn't have the support networks at home to deal with him. I don't know if he had motives with students of a sexual nature..."

This is an incredible statement from Field, given that she sent that email of 17 April 2006 thanking him for his support and saying that working at the OLCVS had been her best experience of a London school.

This reply also demonstrates that she knows nothing about Pead. As a qualified counsellor, he has a particular style and he has always maintained this style since he first qualified. At no point does he ever feel that he has 'all the answers'. His counselling approach is to let his clients know that they are the best person to comment on their lives and that his role is to support, guide and 'handhold' them through a process.

It is extreme to move from thinking a person with counselling skills should have sexual motives.

Under 'Section 5: Contract Issues', Twist asked Field: "...Allegations have been raised in relation to some staff contracts and agreements on pay and conditions. Did any of these concerns apply to you? Are you aware of any of your colleagues who may have had difficulties with their contract or pay?"

Note the leading question again.

Field replied: "...No. I was originally working two days a week then increased that to four or five days a week. I was employed through an agency. I knew that Maryn was never provided with a contract as she was promised by Brian..."

According to Murray, she had been 'promised' a contract **after** Field had left the OLCVS. Field could not have known, therefore, that Murray had been promised a contract unless she heard it directly from Murray herself – thus breaking the conditions of non-contact with other witnesses, or she had read it in Murray's report – and thus had been led into making that comment. Whichever, the entire statement and hearing was farcical.

When asked by Twist whether she had anything else to add, Field said, "...It was a difficult experience working with Brian. I'm angry at the way that he treated Maryn. **But reading Maryn's statement made me realise that Brian had bullied me.** I didn't feel that he was quite trustworthy.

I didn't think that I had any concrete evidence to make a formal complaint about Brian. My conversations with Brian did upset me. In the end I didn't want to be near Brian anymore. I was wary of him..."

When asked by Twist if she thought that Brian was an appropriate person to be in a management role, Field replied curtly, "...No..."

If she had really had a difficult experience with Brian Pead, why did she send her email of 17 April 2006? She then says that her entire perception of Pead changed **after** she had read Murray's report. This clearly shows that Twist was wrong to send that report to witnesses before interviewing them. This was a breach of the Duty of Care that Lambeth owed Pead.

The authors are in possession of a transcript which is allegedly a true copy of the interview between Twist and Field. This transcript was not signed by Field until 17 June 2007 – some four months **after** the interview had taken place.

The transcript has a codicil added by Field "...Please note that I am signing on the assumption that you have received the attached notes..."

The attached notes are reproduced in full:

"...Additional Notes to be attached to Annabel Field's Notes for Disciplinary Investigation Interview. June 2007

Please note the following points with regard to my Notes.

- It is important for me to add here that the notes from the Interview do not have all of the questions that I was asked. These questions provide the context for my answers.

- I did not say all of my answers without the interjection of smaller questions. For example, on page 5, I was specifically asked to state how old I thought Brian Johnson's companion was and how I could describe her. This applies to many of the questions and as I said, I feel it is important to be aware of this.
- It does not state in the notes but I did say at the start of the interview that I didn't find the process easy. This was not only because I found it a bit upsetting to go over things but also because I did not have many concrete examples - it was not clear cut.
- Not all of the context in the notes is provided. For example, I was reluctant to give the name of the person who introduced me to Brian as I didn't want her to have to be involved.
- Please see a couple of alterations in the margins of the notes.

Thank you

The Additional Notes are signed by Annabel Field.

The Additional Notes by Annabel Field are not dated. This is highly irregular. Any serious investigator would insist that these notes were dated. Neither were these notes date-stamped upon receipt by Lambeth.

It is clear that the transcript of the interview with Annabel Field has been doctored. Shades of Hillsborough. To her credit, Field mentions this to Twist.

The emphasis in the above Additional Notes is the authors'. It seems that Field has had something of a change of heart. Something appears to be bothering her. Things have been left out of her transcript. Her conscience finally returns to her.

It is appalling that Field should be asked how old Brian's companion to the theatre was and to describe her. This has absolutely nothing to do with the allegations against him. What if he had taken his grand-daughter? Or daughter?

Field also states that she had no concrete examples. Everything in her statement has been based on a feeling – after reading the 8-page report from a person who had been dismissed for grooming female pupils. Murray hid her lustful thoughts and actions well. She was clearly a better actress than Field.

Apart from being a trawling expedition, why would Twist need to know who introduced Field to the school? It had nothing to do with the investigation. Field was being manipulated by Twist, yet failed to notice it. Twist was merely trawling for information. It was not the first time she had been fishing in this way. It would not be the last.

78

deadline passed

The 13-week deadline that Lambeth guaranteed its employees for dealing with disciplinary hearings passed on 9 March 2007.

medical review

Having been unlawfully suspended and isolated from colleagues and pupils, Brian Pead went to see his doctor – Doctor Martin of the Barnard Medical Centre in Sidcup - and was officially signed off from work with Stress Reaction on 8 February 2007.

Gilhooly sought to have Pead re-examined by a Dr John Sterland, an occupational physician employed by the Norwich Union. Pead was forced to attend the meeting on 2 April 2007.

A copy of Sterland's letter to Rosa Vaz at Human Resources was obtained using the Freedom of Information Act. It is reproduced here:

> "...I saw this Head of Centre of two years at management request for his first sickness absence review.
>
> Background: As you know, he has been off work for six weeks with a given diagnosis of "stress reaction". We discussed risk factors for stress. There are no personal factors apparent. He told me that his workload was moderate; he has good relationships with colleagues and a clear idea of his duties. However, he told me that he felt unsupported from the beginning of his job, and in the last few months has also had support issues, along the following lines:
>
> 1 He had difficult access to rooms in the original building.
>
> 2 There were difficulties with legacy staff contracts.
>
> 3 There were difficulties with his own contract when it came up for renewal in 2006.
>
> 4 When the Centre changed premises there was little consultation.
>
> 5 He felt unsupported over a complaint issue, which he felt was not investigated fully, and which seemed to escalate fairly rapidly.
>
> 6 He felt unsupported when a second complaint was made against him and he was suspended before he had any further details, and was told to avoid further contact with work, which has increased his anxiety as he is unable to collect information.
>
> 7 He feels unsupported over his own complaint that others had been acting against him.

8 He feels unsupported over lack of choice of dates for hearings, which also seem to take many weeks to arrange.

He attended his GP, and has been receiving certificates. As you know, he has been attending weekly counselling. He has not been receiving medication, and has not been referred to a specialist. He reported good coping, assertiveness, and time management skills. There are no personal risk factors apparent. He is otherwise well.

Present situation: He has some continuing symptoms of anxiety. He can perform day-to-day activities normally.

Specific questions: He is not fit for his own work at present. He can attend for an investigation meeting, but has been unable to assemble his case or seek representation yet. However, he could return to his duties after discussion, if appropriate adjustments can be made.

I have the following suggestions for his return:

1 Phased return to work starting at three days per week for two weeks then four days per week for two weeks more before full-time.

2 Attention to apparent organisational risk factors for stress, especially support issues.

3 General stress adjustments of continuing to ensure adequate support and supervision, tolerable workload, clear duties and responsibilities.

4 Self-control and self-esteem building measures of positive criticism and praise for achievements.

Further plans: I have not asked for a GP/specialist report, and we do not need to see him again except at your request.

Thank you for asking us to see this employee. Please let us know if we can help further.

Yours sincerely,

Dr John Sterland MBBS, DOccMed, AFOM Occupational Physician

It is evident from Sterland's letter to Lambeth that he has placed great responsibility upon Lambeth Council to address Brian Pead's complaints that he had not been supported by Gilhooly and ultimately Lambeth Council itself, who owed him a duty of care. It had been an extremely well-crafted letter inasmuch that it adequately served two masters – Pead and Lambeth Council. Sterland had to take into account the fact that Lambeth Council had hired him to meet with Pead and offer a diagnosis. He who pays the piper calls the tune. However, Sterland had also to pay regard to the duty of care that he himself owed to Pead – several doctors have been successfully sued on the basis of a poor or inadequate diagnosis. It is clear that Sterland's letter steered a fine line between serving his paymasters and the duty of care that he owed to his patient.

What is significant in this letter, however, is not the mere fact that Sterland had confirmed what Pead's own GP had stated – that he was suffering from stress reaction – but also that he had been unsupported and not allowed access to his office to gather up evidence that he would need to undermine the allegations against him.

Sterland also makes note of the fact that Lambeth were not making Pead aware of Hearing dates with sufficient notice.

Perhaps the most significant aspect of Sterland's letter is that the physician had recommended a phased return to work for Pead. He also stressed that it was important that Lambeth pay attention to organisational risk factors to stress, especially support issues. It should be remembered that Gilhooly was always busy, rarely visited the centre and holidayed frequently in Goa.

Lambeth paid total disregard to this letter because they forced Pead to attend a Medical Outcome Meeting on 2 April 2007 whilst he was then suffering from influenza. He telephoned Rosa Vaz to inform them that he was too unwell to travel to Brixton, but Gilhooly and Vaz insisted on his attendance.

It should be remembered that Pead at this time had still not been able to gain entry to his office and that certain people Twist was intent on interviewing had not yet been seen. Lambeth's self-imposed 13-week period for Disciplinary Procedures had long since passed. The Council was keeping as much distance between the suspension and the Hearings as they could.

Murray, on the other hand, was still in employment and still had contact with young females, despite having been dismissed by Pead and despite Gilhooly having full knowledge of Murray's propensity to groom girls. Gilhooly had placed her in Norwood School for Girls – had the parents, staff and pupils been informed that she had been sacked as the direct result of racism and the sexual grooming of girls?

It seems apparent that another reason Lambeth had for dismissing Pead was that they could avoid the cost of a phased return to work. Yet Lambeth had itself created the situation that meant that Pead was signed off from work.

replaced - 1

Brian Pead was replaced on 2 April 2007 as Head of the OLCVS. He had not been dismissed. He was legally 'under suspension'. His investigatory hearing was still on-going.

Yet Lambeth simply replaced him.

On 11 January 2008, Greg Sorrell conducted an OfSTED inspection on the OLCVS. The report states:

> "...In July 2007, the Open Learning Initiative for Vocational Education (OLIVE) changed its name from The Open Learning Centre for Vocational Studies (OLCVS). It is located within a self-managing and multi-purpose use community centre attached to a local secondary school. Two terms ago, after a period of management difficulties the executive headteacher and her seconded team took over the centre. **Since April 2007, the centre has been led and managed by the executive headteacher** and the leadership team of a local secondary special school. This arrangement is due to end officially in April 2008. A new assistant headteacher has recently been appointed..."

gilhooly's response

On 5 April 2007, Gilhooly wrote to Pead about the Medical Outcome meeting held on 2 April.

Pead had requested Minutes of the meeting – Gilhooly failed to include a set of Minutes with his letter.

Gilhooly – described by several Head teachers in Lambeth as a 'bully' – threatened Pead with the following statement:

> "...I need to advise you that where attendance continues to be unsatisfactory, this may be referred to a formal sickness review panel hearing. One outcome of this hearing could be dismissal..."

Lambeth had unlawfully suspended Brian Pead. He had been made ill by Lambeth's tactics. Now that he was unwell, they were threatening to dismiss him for being unwell!

Yet he had already been replaced by Gilhooly three days earlier.

alex passman

Pead conducted some brief research and made contact with a solicitor, Alex Passman, who was practising in employment law and who lived in Plymouth.

They met at Paddington Station in London.

"...Lecturer wins prestigious national award for Law Clinic

Date: 26 June 2012

Summary

An employment lawyer who helps law students take their first steps in the legal profession has received a prestigious national award.

Further detail

Alex Passman, an associate lecturer at Plymouth University, was presented with the Law Society's JLD Pro Bono Award during the 2012 LawWorks Pro Bono Awards ceremony.

The accolade came in recognition of his work with students through the South West Employment Rights Centre (SWERC), part of the Plymouth Law School's Law Clinic, which offers free advice to people who cannot afford to pay for legal action against their employers.

Alex, who was a student at Plymouth University from 2002-05 and returned to the city to run his own practice after completing his legal qualifications, said: "This award is great reward for the University, not just myself, and brings the work we are doing into the national spotlight. The work of SWERC has so many benefits, for the students involved and the clients we help, and we are looking to expand its offering in the future."

The SWERC, based in the University's Cookworthy Building, was established in 2001 and works with third-year law students to give free advice to people wanting to make a claim against their employers.

They work in association with Citizens Advice Bureaux across the region and while some cases are dealt with quickly, others can see the students and centre tutors having to formulate complex arguments for the courts.

Alex said: "A couple of years ago, one of our students took on a case and ended up winning the client around £22,000 in compensation. Another student was personally commended by the case judge for the arguments they had put forward, and the way they had done so. This kind of experience is invaluable for students as when they go on to complete their qualification, they can say they have already represented clients and come up against barristers in a courtroom situation."

The awards were judged by a panel including former attorney general Baroness Scotland, Law Society president John Wotton and legal journalist Joshua Rozenberg. For the JLD award, the judging panel also included the JLD chair Hekim Hannan. The ceremony was hosted by the Law Society in London last week.

Professor Simon Payne, Head of the Plymouth Law School and one of the founders of SWERC, said: "Studying law at Plymouth is not only about understanding the intricacies of the law and legal system, but also gaining experience of advising and representing real clients with real legal problems. The Law Clinic provides this opportunity for students and, while SWERC is the longest established part, it now includes representation for victims of domestic violence, support for elderly clients and investigation of miscarriages of justice. Alex has done a great job leading SWERC and deserves congratulations for this national recognition of his work..."

Sources: http://www.plymouth.ac.uk/pages/view.asp?page=39103
            http://www.plymouth.ac.uk/pages/view.asp?page=34181
            www.innocencenetwork.org.uk

Over a coffee (Pead had tea), Passman informed the Head teacher that the Murray report was nonsense, that it lacked supporting evidence and was mere hearsay. They discussed the fact that it would be relatively easy for Pead to defend these allegations because the pupils and parents would be able to corroborate his version of events.

They also agreed that Passman would represent Pead at his initial investigatory hearing.

Passman did, in fact, represent Pead at that first hearing. What he heard there worried him immensely. Recognising that Pead was innocent of all charges, Twist at first refused to allow Passman's presence. Pead insisted – as did Passman – that he had every right to be legally represented. Passman was allowed to stay, which was just as well since Pead would have left the room had Passman been forced to leave.

The meeting took place on Thursday 19 April 2007 in Meeting Room 8 on the second floor of International House in Brixton. It commenced at 1.35pm and concluded at 5pm.

In attendance were Cathy Twist, Assistant Director, Standards Division; Mary White, Human Resources Consultant; Brian Pead, Head of Centre, OLCVS; Alex Passman, supporting Pead; and Karina O'Neill, note taker.

Twist introduced those in attendance to one another. She explained that the purpose of the meeting was to investigate allegations of gross misconduct that had been made against Brian Pead.

Twist claimed that the meeting was in accordance with the Council's Disciplinary Procedure and that, following the investigation, if it was found that there was a case to answer it would be taken to a Disciplinary Hearing which Pead would be required to attend.

Twist claimed that the matter should not be discussed by Pead with anyone, including witnesses, other than his Advisor/Union representative at this stage.

She told Pead that he would need to sign and date a copy of the notes of this meeting. (He was never sent a copy of notes from any of his four interviews.)

Mary White took up the baton and said that the allegations include the following:

1.   Irregularities in not following procedures when students taking exams;

2.   Inconsistency in the treatment of particular students;

3.   Inappropriate language to a student;

4.   Not adhering to Council Recruitment and Selection procedures;

5.   Unfair treatment of staff members;

6.   Causing distress for members of staff through inappropriate management style;

7.   Bringing the Council into disrepute whilst attending a play.

The original five allegations had now grown to seven. This list was yet to grow significantly under the management of Twist.

Pead immediately went on the offensive: "...I would like it noted that my G.P. has stated categorically that I shouldn't be here today and that it will be impossible for me to answer these allegations fairly without access to copies of Minutes and having had discussions with those interviewed. I was also suspended without being told the reasons why..."

It is evident that there was already an abuse of process because he had not been provided with copies of transcripts of interviews with witnesses. Thus he was working blind.

White retorted: "...You had a meeting in December 2006 with Barry Gilhooly to discuss your suspension and you were then sent a letter on 12 December 2006 outlining the reasons for your suspension. I can confirm with those who met with you on 8 December 2006 what you were told. However, Cathy Twist and I were not at that meeting and are therefore unable to comment..."

This is nonsense. Pead was never told of the reasons for his suspension (see the letter dated 8 December 2006 in chapter 45). White claimed that neither she nor Twist was at that meeting between Pead, Gilhooly and Vaz and, of course, they were not. Therefore it was incumbent upon them to have detailed notes of that meeting. The word 'meeting' suggests that all parties were willingly engaged in it. They were not, because in effect Pead was frogmarched out of the building by Gilhooly and Vaz - hardly a 'meeting'. White has shown that she and Twist were in breach of the duty of care that Lambeth owed Pead.

Alex Passman joined in the opening exchanges: "Can I just confirm that this meeting is to allow Brian to give his version of events and if the investigation is taken further, then Brian will be given copies of the notes of all of the other meetings?"

White claimed that Pead would be given copies ten days before a Disciplinary Panel hearing.

Pead ensured that he entered a copy of Nadia Al-Khudhairy's email into the hearing. The transcript notes that the authors have obtained show that he handed the email praising him and his methods to Mary White and that she organised copies for all parties present. This was a significant act on the part of Pead because he knew that this evidence from Al-Khudhairy was completely contradictory to Murray and her cronies including Hiley, Whitmore and Field.

Pead also knew that it meant that Twist had been given contradictory evidence – and that legally, this was a crucial move on his part. Twist was thus obliged to interview Al-Khudhairy, but she failed to do so. She was also both legally and morally obliged to re-interview Murray and others and ask them how Al-Khudhairy had come to write such a praiseworthy email of Brian Pead and his running of the Unit when their testimony was so different. But Twist failed to take these basic steps in her 'full and thorough' investigation.

The hearing did not go well as Lambeth attempted to throw as much mud at Pead as possible in an attempt to 'make it stick' and to discredit him. The act of discrediting Pead was of paramount importance to Lambeth and the police.

As they left the building in Canterbury Crescent, Lambeth, the Head teacher and the lawyer de-briefed in a nearby coffee house.

Passman told Pead that he was being set up, and that Lambeth would find him guilty on all counts. Twist didn't allow any of Passman's rebuttals to the allegations and Passman said that this was absolute nonsense. He added that there was something incredibly strange about this case. He also mentioned that local authorities are taken to court on a daily basis and Pead wondered how many millions of pounds are squandered by each local authority on an annual basis because of inept management and consequential law suits arising out of that mismanagement.

Yet this was not just a case of inept management. This was a case of racism, of child abuse, of corruption and a cover-up of Hillsborough proportions.

"...Each person has inside a basic decency and goodness.
If he listens to it and acts on it, he is giving a great deal of what
the world needs most.
It is not complicated but takes courage.
It takes courage for a person to listen to his own goodness and act on it..."

Pablo Casals

beverley williams

p.a. to barry gilhooly

According to Brian Pead, Beverley Williams is an extremely decent woman. She happens to be black.

He had only met her briefly on two occasions when he had applied for the position as Head of the OLCVS. Without saying too much to one another, they somehow discussed the spiritual side of life and they found that they shared a common philosophical approach to life.

They had also shared one or two brief telephone conversations whenever Pead called Gilhooly's office and there was something about Williams that Pead admired – she had a certain wisdom and dignity about her, rather like Doreen Lawrence. Brian Pead is particularly drawn to such people. He loved her soul.

As he was leaving International House after a long and stressful day, she came up to him in a long corridor of the building and walked alongside him as he went to find the lift. Matching him stride for stride, she said, "Don't stop to talk ... just carry on walking with me. What Lambeth are doing to you is disgraceful...it's not right. Good luck."

And, as he stopped outside the lift, she gave him a brown manila envelope, smiled at him and turned and walked away in the opposite direction.

Aware that there would be CCTV in the lift, he held on to the envelope until he had left the building. In fact, he didn't open it until he arrived home.

It was a framed line drawing that Beverley herself had created. It was of a black woman in profile with corn-row hair and it had been entitled *Peace*. It was also signed by Beverley.

Naturally, this moment of beauty deeply touched Brian and he felt more able to cope in the face of such extreme hostility that Lambeth Council was showing him.

investigation meeting – day two

Brian Pead was signed off work from the doctor on the grounds of stress due to these unfounded allegations.

However, Lambeth breached his rights and insisted that he attend another investigatory meeting the following day – Friday 20 April 2007 – at International House. Alex Passman was not in attendance. He felt he could offer Brian no help – that the outcome was a foregone conclusion based on what he had already heard.

This meeting lasted from 2.20pm until 4.50pm. This was another tactic used by Twist and White – try to wear down your opponent, especially when he is outnumbered. Pead was not at all well, yet was bombarded by questions from Twist and White.

Twist led the hearing. She was trawling for more and more information. Pead referred her to Lambeth documents and manuals, but he knew he was really wasting his time. As an experienced manager and counsellor, Pead could tell that Twist was merely seeking information which she could manipulate to fit any allegations against him. When an investigator asks a question and then that question is replied to and then a new question is asked without reference to the previous answer, a wise person knows that the hearing is fixed with only one purpose in mind. This was how the meeting went. A Twist question, a Pead answer, a new Twist question. No reference to Pead's answer. An investigator conducting an unbiased investigation will always listen to an individual's response and then base his/ her next question on that response. But not Twist. Or White. They were a carbon copy of one another.

Pead asked Twist, "...Have staff been issued with copies of the allegations?" because he knew that if Twist replied in the affirmative, the entire process would be sunk. If, on the other hand, she declined to answer, that would also prove that the process was corrupt since Pead was entitled to know this important fact. Twist's reply? "...This interview is not about staff talking with one another..."

This is a nonsensical response by Twist because it is clear that she has gone onto the defensive. She is also denying Pead his basic constitutional rights.

Mary White, however, said, "...You will be given copies of staff statements and notes of interviews if this case goes any further. **The staff members already interviewed were sent copies of the allegations...**"

This was further proof that the entire process was corrupt and an abuse of power. This case cost Lambeth thousands of pounds of taxpayers' money and this book will ensure that questions are asked of Lambeth Council.

The transcript shows that Twist bombards Pead with question after question about his running of the Centre. He should not even have been there according to his doctor.

As an Assistant Director of Standards, Twist was keen on steering the meeting to a discussion of Pead's therapeutic style of management and learning. She wanted to try to dismiss him on the basis of a lack of teaching and learning – but Colin Hill's statement of 25 January 2007 refuted her allegations that teaching and learning suffered under Pead. It was quite the reverse – all of the pupils left with at least one qualification.

Twist: I haven't heard about appraisals, quality of teaching and improving outcomes for pupils. I have heard you talk about creating an empathetic environment for pupils. Do you think the balance was right between providing an empathetic environment and a learning environment and students receiving a good level of education?

Pead: I think the balance was spot on. The questions I've been asked to answer have focused on the therapeutic side of the Centre. I feel I haven't had an adequate opportunity to talk about the teaching and learning.

Pead's response is vitally important. It shows that Twist conducted hearings based on biased and leading questioning. He states quite forcefully that he has not been given an opportunity to discuss his version of events. Twist's narrow line of questioning was designed to prevent Pead from giving a full response to her questions.

Twist: I have asked about the content of meetings, not about the therapeutic aspect of the school. Did your management style and approach build a cohesive team?

Pead: I object to the term 'therapeutic environment'; it was a learning environment. There is evidence of successful student results. The emphasis was on the teaching and learning. I was working on a huge plan to get all of the asylum seekers and refugee students accredited. Students were taking exams in their mother tongue. The main emphasis was on the teaching and learning. I worked very hard to get appropriate staff to deliver the teaching and learning. Part of the issues we had in getting students through exams was based on the way we got students to engage. We devised a system to look after the emotional needs of students in order to get the teaching and learning outcomes. We had to deal with pupils' emotional issues to get them to engage in learning. I was getting the right team I wanted before I was unlawfully suspended.

[A break here at 3.25pm, resumed at 3.40pm.]

Pead: In relation to students, I built very good relationships with Marion Richards, the English consultant, and Mus Bagum of the Ethnic Minorities Achievement Team. We had regular meetings to improve student progress. Tutorials were taking place, led by Duane, we had Circle Time; pupils were told that if they missed just one session a week they would be missing out on 25% of their education. We focused on the teaching and not on the counselling. The Every Child Matters booklet published by Lambeth refers to the importance of the mental health of young people. It was important to get this right.

Twist also tried to claim that the Centre had a high turnover of staff, but it did not. Pead stated that "...The Institute of Directors' website provides evidence that 75% of staff in an organisation's first year will be lost. Staff expectations are sometimes not met. Some people left for personal reasons. It was not unusual to me..."

Twist did not like being given hard facts that refuted her assertions. Neither did she like being told that there no hard facts to support the wild allegations against Pead. When she asked, "...It has been alleged that you gave favourable treatment to female staff. Are you aware of any situations where this may have been the case?..." Pead replied, "...Not in my opinion. Nothing was bought to my attention to support this spurious allegation..."

This, of course, is the crucial statement for Pead to have made. At no time had **any** of the allegations in Murray's report been brought to his attention. The entire investigation should have ended there. No allegations came to light until **after** Murray had been dismissed for child abuse.

Determined to pin something – anything – on Pead, Twist tried another angle: "...It has been claimed that you booked counselling sessions on the school phone on several occasions..."

Pead replied, "...I completely refute that allegation. I kept my volunteer counselling work separate from my OLCVS job. Furthermore, there was a telephone log of all incoming and outgoing calls kept in the office. Where is the record of these alleged calls?

Twist was unable to provide evidence that these calls had ever taken place. Had she been genuinely investigating to establish the truth, the truth was there for her to establish but she failed in her duty of care to Pead.

Twist continued in her attack: "...It is alleged that you gave Annabel Field a card when she first started at the Centre telling her that she was clever and being very positive about her. Why did you give her this card?"

Pead responded with "...I never gave her a card. It's good management to be positive to one's staff. I certainly have no knowledge of any card. Where is this card?"

Twist could not produce the card.

Twist said, "...It is claimed that you asked Annabel many intrusive questions about her personal life. Why did you need this information?..."

Pead answered, "...I don't acknowledge any personal conversations with Annabel at the beginning. Marion Richards had mentioned to me that Annabel had considerable emotional problems at that time. Annabel asked me if she could speak with me privately about being torn between teaching and acting and being heavily in debt. Why don't you interview Marion Richards and ask her what her opinion of Annabel was?..."

Twist did not call Marion Richards as a witness, despite her working in the same building as Richards.

Twist: Can you comment on the alleged personal conversation with Annabel where you said that she should be having that conversation with her boyfriend?

Pead: I never said anything about a boyfriend. To my knowledge she didn't even have a boyfriend. Marion Richards was concerned about Annabel's emotional well-being and her teaching performance. I had to make a decision about Annabel; about keeping her in employment. I had to weigh the situation up. The conversation was personal around her debt issues and her issues around acting and/ or teaching. A good manager needs to know if there are serious issues which are impacting upon a staff member's ability to perform. In my view, I was being a good manager and trying to offer whatever support Annabel told me she needed. Any conversations were driven by Annabel and not by me. There was nothing personal as in sexual in any of our conversations. It was personal in the sense that she was heavily in debt and not happy being a teacher. If I have a teacher who is not happy teaching I should know about it because it might impact upon the quality of teaching and learning that takes place. I object to the suggestion that I ever bullied Annabel. At no point did she ever say to me or anyone else in an official capacity that she felt that I was bullying her. It's sheer nonsense. It didn't happen. I will want to question Annabel Field. Make sure she is called as a witness and I will challenge her on this. Besides, why didn't she make a complaint? This has all allegedly come through Murray after I was

242

forced to dismiss her and you know the reasons why I dismissed her. I can't believe you're giving this nonsense any credence.

Twist: Referring to the nature of your conversations with Annabel, it is claimed that you had an intrusive style and that Annabel felt you were gaining statements from her that she was uncomfortable with.

Pead: Who claimed this? Murray? After I had to dismiss her for racism and grooming young girls? Annabel came to me to ask for a specific meeting. I asked her if she was sure she wanted to have this conversation with me. She said yes and started crying about the debt she was in and because she had an inner feeling of unfulfilment due to not acting. How come this is alleged **after** Murray has gone? I refute that my questions were probing at all. The use of the words 'intrusive' and 'probing' are words used by Anya Hiley in her email - I want to point this out. The words used here are exactly the same as used by Anya in her email in June 2006. This was an email to her line manager about me and my "probing questions" and my meetings with "vulnerable young women". She mentioned that she didn't want anything done about her email, she just wanted it brought to people's attention. She was very good friends with Murray. The conclusion is that Murray and Anya Hiley have colluded together in these allegations. I made this explicit to Barry (Gilhooly) at the time of the allegations. I made this allegation based on written evidence and third party evidence from a person who is an expert in relationships in the work place. You need to be aware of the relationship between Hiley and Murray, because if I had to dismiss Murray for grooming young white girls, what is Hiley up to? They're as thick as thieves.

Twist did not like this response from Pead because it meant that she was now obligated to investigate the collusion. She did not investigate this. Notice how Twist fails to discuss the racism and the grooming.

Instead, Twist tried to trip Pead up:

Twist: Returning to Annabel.

Pead: Are you aware of the email from April 2006?

Twist: That is not for us to comment on.

This is a disgraceful answer from Twist. It **was** her duty to comment on that email. That email – written by Field of her own volition (which she makes clear) – completely vindicated Pead from the allegations he was facing. Twist knew this, but deliberately chose to ignore it.

Pead: I have a copy of an email from Annabel which I've sent to you previously. This email refers to the conversation I had with Annabel which is mentioned in the allegation. Annabel had had an opportunity to reflect on our conversation. In that I asked her questions to help her decide things on her own, about whether to continue as a teacher or to leave teaching and try acting. Annabel was of no use to the pupils if her heart and mind were elsewhere. My primary concern was the teaching and learning and having the best and most-focussed teachers in front of the pupils.

Note here how Twist – despite again being given a copy of the email of 17 April 2006 in which Field thanks Pead for his support – fails to call a halt to the meeting in order to read the email thoroughly and digest its contents and then ask questions about why it was so markedly different from the allegations of Murray.

Twist then asked Pead about his visiting the play at the White Bear Theatre in which Annabel Field played the part of Lizzy Price, the Horse Dealer's Daughter.

Twist: Can you tell us about the alleged incident at the play you attended in Kennington that Annabel invited you to?

Pead: I'm glad you referred to it as an 'alleged' incident, because that is all it was. The facts of the matter are that Annabel invited all members of staff to the play and I did attend with a female friend, not that that is any business of yours or Lambeth's. Those are the facts. The rest is complete rubbish. The theatre was small, in the back of a pub in Kennington. There were only two rows of seats. Any sexual activity would have been known by anybody including the audience and the actors. It would be impossible to do any of those things without everybody seeing. I have been back to the pub where the play was held and talked to bar staff there and none of them recall any such incident. I am getting written evidence of this from the bar staff. At no point was I ever introduced to anybody so I don't know how Annabel's friend knew I was her boss. Have you been to the theatre and seen for yourself that it could not have happened? Have you called Michael Kingsbury, the theatre's producer?

Pead informs Twist that this incident didn't happen. He asks her whether she has been to the theatre to see if it was at all possible. She didn't respond to this question for obvious reasons. Had she actually gone the mile or so to the theatre from her office, she would have found that had any sexual act been committed in that theatre, it would have been impossible for others not to have seen it.

This was yet another significant mistake by Twist. The Court of Appeal in the Roldan case stated that it was an employers' duty to visit an environment in which allegations had been made to see for themselves whether it was realistic to believe the allegations.

In the Roldan case previously mentioned, Lord Justices Etherton and Elias make reference to Section 98(4) of the Employment Rights Act which focuses on the need for an employer to act reasonably in all the circumstances. In the case A v B [2003] IRLR 405 the EAT (Elias J presiding) it was held that the relevant circumstances include the gravity of the charge and their potential effect upon the employee. **So it is particularly important that employers take seriously their responsibilities to conduct a fair investigation where, as on the facts of that case, the employee's reputation or ability to work in his or her chosen field of employment is potentially apposite.**

The emphasis is the authors'. Justices Etherton and Elias put forward the view that it is of vital importance in cases such as Pead found himself in that an employer – in this case, Lambeth – takes seriously their responsibilities to conduct a fair investigation, especially where the employee's reputation or ability to work are called into question. Twist was not acting responsibly.

Twist: You did go to the play with a female friend?

Pead: It's no business of yours or Lambeth's, but yes, and I have a statement from that friend. Mary White made copies of a printed copy of an email from my female friend. As stated in the email my friend says that the allegation is false. This friend has returned to live in Turkey but I met her when she was in London studying business management, English and Literature.

Mary White asked a valid and important question: "...Would it be possible to get her contact details in Turkey in case we need to contact your friend?"

Pead: Yes. I absolutely deny the incident. It would appear that this incident in the theatre was cleverly used so that the woman apparently knew that I was Annabel's boss. This was obviously included in the report to support the allegation that I had brought the name of Lambeth Council into disrepute.

Commentary: In asking whether she could be furnished with the contact details of Ipek Yÿlmaz, Mary White inadvertently added a further nail into Lambeth's coffin. Yÿlmaz was **never** contacted by either White or Twist. It is obvious that she ought to have been contacted since she was a key witness.

Notice how Brian Pead informs Twist that he is aware of the game that Lambeth have been playing by adding ludicrous allegations which were included to try to damage Pead's reputation.

Twist told Pead, "...We will meet again next Wednesday, 25 April, 2.00pm. After that meeting there may be a period of further interviews with others and we may need to speak to you again. We will then write a report on the investigation..."

Pead cleverly asked "...Will any further interviews still be a part of the **investigation** process?" Mary White replied: "...Yes..."

Pead asked this question to establish whether the process would be conducted properly. It would have been right and proper for some witnesses to have been interviewed again – **but none were** except for Gilhooly – and it would have been right and proper for Pead to have been interviewed again in response to those second interviews so that he had the right of reply.

85

the farce continues

The meeting scheduled for Wednesday, 25 April did not take place due to Pead obtaining a certificate from his doctor that he was suffering from extreme stress at the absurdity of the allegations and the hostility shown towards him by Twist and White in particular and Lambeth Council in general.

The final investigatory meeting took place on Wednesday 16 May 2007 at 2.20pm in Meeting Room 8 on the second floor of International House in Brixton. Mary White chose to explain to Pead that "...we are currently undertaking an investigation and will then decide on whether or not to take it to a hearing..."

Pead replied, "...I am aware that this is an investigation meeting..." He wanted to ensure that the meeting would come under this term, since he knew that it had not been conducted properly at all.

Twist went straight onto the offensive: "...Do you think there is any validity in the allegation that you gave extra time to specific female students?"

Pead: I don't think there is any validity in this statement whatsoever.

Twist: Did you give extra time to particular female students? Also did any female students complain about you giving extra time to other students?

Pead: No.

Twist: It is alleged that you gave extra time to some girls.

Pead: I don't agree with this, that I gave preferential treatment to some pupils. I find it disturbing that labels have been given to pupils by Murray and her cronies such as Hiley, Whitmore and Field, such as 'attractive'. I have shown this allegation document to other professionals and they agree with me. Don't you find this disturbing as well? You ought to! I gather that Murray was trying to identify a group of particular students.

Twist: There is a perception that Murray is claiming that you spent extra time with a particular group of students.

Pead: I certainly spent more time with certain girls than others and I spent more time with certain boys than other boys. Every teacher and Head teacher does. Show me one who doesn't.

Of course Pead would spend more time with certain students than others. The mother of Ashleigh Mills had recently been sectioned under the Mental Health Act. It is obvious that he would have had to spend considerable time with this pupil in order to help her overcome her considerable difficulties – she had also come to the OLCVS later than other pupils and so had to 'catch up'. Pead did such a good job with Ashleigh that she obtained a 'C' grade in English at GCSE level. He is proud of this achievement to this day and makes no apology for spending time in meetings with her to help her succeed.

Head teachers – by the very nature of their job – often spend more time with certain pupils than others. In fact, the average Head spends more time with 'naughty' pupils than 'good' pupils – yet do all the 'good' pupils complain that they are being neglected in 'favour' of the 'naughty' ones?

Twist: Was your time allocated according to need?

Pead: Absolutely.

Twist: It is alleged that some female members of staff were praised by you and made much of at the beginning of their role and when something went wrong your attitude towards them changed and you became less positive towards them.

Pead: Which members of staff?

Twist: The specific members of staff mentioned in the allegations. We'll keep discussing this in terms of individual staff. Referring to Murray, it is alleged that you were very positive towards her at the beginning of her role, that you gave her a poem and your life coaching business card and that you asked her to go walking in the woods with you.

Pead: That I gave her my home phone number and asked her to go walking on her first day at the Centre - I completely refute these allegations. I didn't give her my home number. If you assume that these two things are true, why would a woman keep coming back to work after this experience? She's with an agency and the agency could find her work in any one of hundreds of schools, so, if she really felt uncomfortable, why would she (a) never mention any of this until after she was sacked for grooming young girls and racism and (b) why wouldn't she simply find another school? Besides, she claimed she had a £38,000 contract offered to her by St. Augustine's. If she felt uncomfortable at the OLCVS or with me specifically, why on earth didn't she just take it and go back there?

Note how Pead rounds on Twist and specifically asks her why a woman would keep attending the Centre if she felt unsafe and uncomfortable. After all, by her own admission, Murray was a supply teacher, and could easily have chosen to go to another school, but she did not make that choice.

Note also how Twist fails to answer the question, and thus breaches the Duty of Care that she owes Brian Pead.

Twist: My question is not about that. Did you invite Murray to go walking?

Pead: No. I gave **all** my staff my mobile number because the OLCVS had no phoneline. I invited **all** the staff to go walking; it would have been as many staff who were there at the time e.g. Eloise, Duane, Fraser and Maryn. All this was Minuted – where are the Minutes that will prove I offered **all** the staff to visit Scadbury Park? Why haven't you obtained **all** the Minutes of **all** the meetings we had as a staff? This is a misnomer. It was not walking with me. I was at the time the Chairman of The Friends of Scadbury Park. This group wanted to publicise itself and it offered guided group walks around the woods. The invitation was not to come walking specifically with **me** in the woods. Murray claimed that she had a boyfriend and I said, "Oh good!" and to bring him along as the group also had working parties in the woods that he could help on. Like everything else in Murray's document, the invitation has been taken out of context. I can provide an itinerary for the group, The Friends of the Woods, for Scadbury Park.

Twist failed to contact the Friends of Scadbury Park to establish the veracity of Pead's statement. Pead points out that the invitation had been taken out of context, like so many other comments.

Note how Twist refuses to let this point go, even though she has been challenged to seek the facts.

Twist: To clarify, on Murray's first day at the Centre, you didn't give her your home phone number or invite her to go walking? Later on, did you give her your home phone number and invite her to go on a guided walk? Did you give her your life coaching business card?

Note how Twist questions Pead – there are five separate parts to these questions and her questions also contradict each other.

Pead: No, I didn't give her a Steve Goodfellow life coaching business card. I never offered her life coaching. Murray doesn't understand how professional life coaching works. No professional life coach would ever give their business card to someone unless there was a mutual understanding of a life coaching need. I had a case of life coaching business cards in my bag with me at the Centre. I never gave her one. Why would I give her a card with my home number on it when I had given her my mobile number separately as I did with all staff because they had no way of initially contacting me otherwise, and because the Centre did not have a phone line at that time. By the way, if I gave her a business card, where is it? You haven't shown me one.

Twist continued to harass Pead with her line of questioning, which bore no relation to common sense, given Pead's responses. Note how Pead asks Twist to produce a copy of the business card that Murray claimed he gave her. If he had given her a card, surely she would have kept it. She claimed that she kept a diary on Pead from her first day at the Centre, so it is likely that she would have kept a card.

Twist: Did you ever invite Murray to dinner and drinks and give her a poem?

Pead: Certainly not. I never invited her out for dinner and drinks at any point. I didn't give her a poem. Why would a woman keep going back to an environment where her male boss was – as she claims - making her feel uncomfortable? Why wouldn't her boyfriend (whom no-one ever met incidentally) tell her to leave that job? If I ever gave her a poem it would have been a poem I gave to all staff. The implication is that I gave her an intimate poem, but I didn't give her a poem. There were poems in circulation around the Centre in the complex as there were people around the building who were quite spiritual and liked to share motivational poems. We had poems in staff meetings. I never gave her a poem individually. She is a fantasist. Sherine Thompson, the manager of the Old Library Community Centre, would often bring poems to me and other staff at the OLCVS. I never gave Murray a poem without ever having given the same to others. Check this out with Sherine Thompson. I want her called as an independent, third party witness. Ask her to bring copies of all poems that she circulated around the Centre. I want to see these poems.

Pead continued to rebut Twist's ineffectual questions and showed the lack of 'investigation' – he asked Twist why Murray would continue to work at the OLCVS if she felt uncomfortable from the very first day. He also asked Twist why Murray had never mentioned any of this to anybody until after she had been dismissed for child abuse.

Twist failed to answer these questions.

She did, however, ask Pead a series of questions based entirely on Murray's allegations. Pead rebutted all of these allegations. Twist ought, therefore, to have dropped all charges at this stage – it was a clear case of two people with different versions of the same events.

Notice in this next section how Twist deliberately introduces the word 'attractive' – used by Murray in relation to pupils – in relation to female staff members.

Twist: Can you comment on the allegations that you had one-to-one conversations with attractive female staff members?

Pead: Hiley and Murray – whom I had to dismiss for child abuse - both state that they support one another in their complaints. Who were these 'attractive' members of staff supposed to have been? Who can say what I would find attractive? This is nonsense.

Notice how Pead ensures that Twist knows the reasons why he dismissed Murray. Note also how Twist does not even respond to the serious statement that Pead has made. Twist had a legal obligation to report Murray to the Independent Safeguarding Authority and to the Local Authority Designated Officer (LADO). She failed to do this in a clear example of negligence.

Twist: There are allegations that a number of female staff felt uncomfortable with your management style e.g. Jenny Foster, Ellie Whitmore, Annabel Field, Anya Hiley, Maryn Murray. Why do you think that some women might have felt uncomfortable about your management style?

Pead: I have already showed you the email from Annabel saying thank you to me etc. Anya Hiley was not a member of my staff. She's clearly got issues. Why did none of these women ever complain through official channels?

Twist: Why might these women have felt uncomfortable with your style? There are more than two women who have stated that they felt uncomfortable with your style.

Pead: It's not three or four women, it's an alleged three or four women by Murray. If it actually turns out to be three or four then what on earth were all of those women doing not complaining to anybody except to Murray (allegedly) and what was she doing holding onto this information and not doing anything about it until after her dismissal? Where is the proof that these women felt uncomfortable? You have given me no proof whatsoever apart from the alleged statements of women who have clearly colluded on their statements. That is not evidence. At most, it's hearsay and that's worth nothing. Anybody can say anything about another person. You need proof and you haven't shown me any **proof**.

Note how Twist fails to address Pead's trenchant questioning. She merely continues her inadequate line of questioning.

Twist: There is no reason you can think of as to why these women would be uncomfortable with your style?

Pead: If I'm working in a team and somebody doesn't approve of something, it's normal behaviour to make this known. It would be a remarkable occurrence that all of these women wouldn't say anything until after Murray is dismissed for child abuse and then they are all sent her 8-page report by you before you interview them. That is an abuse of process. The only reason these women would say anything against me now is that they have colluded and that this is a set-up!

Pead leaves Twist in no doubt that he believes that the females colluded and that this entire process is a 'set-up'. Note that Twist fails to ask: "In what way do you believe they colluded?" and "Why do you believe that this is a set-up?" Any genuine investigator would ask these important questions, if only to protect their own back against such allegations being made public at a later date. But Twist merely ignores all of these comments and relentlessly pursues her quarry.

Twist: These women may have felt uncomfortable voicing their concerns to you as a male, an older male and in charge of them. As their boss, might there have been anything you did that made them feel this way?

Pead: Nothing at all because they've made it all up. To reiterate, they could've mentioned their concerns to me or anybody in Human Resources, to Barry Gilhooly and staff at the Old Library. Whichever management style you adopt, you're always going to find someone who doesn't like it.

Clearly any of these female staff could have complained about Pead a year earlier, when these allegations were said to have occurred. Had they been frightened of discussing these allegations directly with Pead, why didn't they ask boyfriends/ husbands to get involved, or fathers? It is interesting to note that all of the female staff mentioned were single women in the age range 25-45.

The 'investigation' by Twist took on a different and darker aspect when she commented to Pead, "....Later on, when your overtures were declined, the relationships between you and female staff changed..."

Pead was incensed at this pejorative use of language and he said that he was amazed at her use of the word 'overtures'. He stated quite categorically that he was not interested in making overtures to anybody.

Then Pead introduced another important element into the meeting when he said, "...Nadia Al-Khudhairy and her team had been CRB checked via the psychiatry department at King's College..." He added that he had spoken with Dr Patricia

Conrod at the College and had assurances that all of her staff had been CRB checked.

What then occurs in the meeting is of huge significance. Twist attempts another of her long-winded questions. Under 'Charge 5, Contract Issues', she asked Pead:

Twist: It is alleged that you promised Murray a permanent contract as Deputy Head of Centre and on the basis of the agreement you made with her, she resigned from a permanent contract at her previous school. Was this in accordance with Lambeth Council recruitment procedures and why did you do this?

Pead: I didn't do this. I'm beginning to doubt the validity of the contract that was offered to Murray in Ealing.

This response by Brian Pead is of tremendous significance. He had long doubted this alleged permanent contract that Murray claimed she had been offered by St. Augustine's School in Ealing.

It is important to note that Twist – who was charged with conducting a full and thorough investigation – fails to ask Pead precisely why he doubted this contract. There was no attempt by Twist to obtain a copy of this contract, yet it would have been easy for her to obtain a copy. She failed in her duty as an investigating officer and she failed in the duty of care that was owed to Pead.

Twist: Did you offer Maryn a permanent contract as Deputy Head Teacher of the Centre?

Pead: No, it was not my place to promise a contract. Why would Murray want to leave a permanent contract at another school when she was uncomfortable working at the Centre? No, I didn't promise her a permanent position as Deputy Head Teacher but I said this was what could be achieved. I got advice from Rosa Vaz and Barry Gilhooly on this at every step of the way. I did everything to the best of my ability with assistance from either Barry or Human Resources in respect of contracts. I don't think a permanent contract was possible. And where are the copies of all the emails between me and HR and me and Barry that will prove that I consulted at all stages with them? Why haven't I been provided with this basic information? And where is a copy of this alleged contract that Murray claims she had been offered by St. Augustine's?

Notice how Pead poses an important question – why would Murray leave a permanent contract at St. Augustine's School in Ealing to try for a contract at the OLCVS where she claims she was uncomfortable working from the very first day? If it were true that she felt uncomfortable at the OLCVS and had a firm offer of a permanent contract at St. Augustine's in Ealing, any reasonable person would leave the OLCVS and take up the offer of the contract. But Murray was not a reasonable person, and she wanted to remain at the OLCVS for ulterior purposes.

Note how neither Twist nor White considers Pead's questions, yet they were both morally and legally obliged to investigate this line of questioning.

Note how neither Twist nor White responds to Pead's request for basic information.

Twist: What was your reason for terminating her contract?

Pead: There were a number of reasons. At 4.45pm it is very difficult for me to make a list like this. Overall, Murray did not perform the duties of a Deputy Head teacher. Her management of other staff, relationships with students and me - she was in charge of the procedural side of the school - she simply didn't do this. Furthermore, she had been racist to young black male students and she had bribed a young white female (Gemma Mandry) to go with her to her gym, and she also asked Ashleigh Mills round her flat and to go shopping with her at the weekend. She was grooming young, white girls and I got statements about this. Sandra Roach was present at all times. I reported all of this to Barry Gilhooly – he has done nothing about it so far. What are you going to do about it? Why hasn't she been reported to the ISA? Why hasn't she been arrested and interviewed by the police? And why has Lambeth reinstated her?

Pead pulled no punches here. He leaves Twist and White in no doubt of the reasons he dismissed Murray and that it had been reported to Gilhooly. He also said that she had not been reported to the Independent Safeguarding Authority **and he wanted to know why she had been reinstated at Lambeth, putting more children at risk.**

Notice how Twist fails to respond to Pead at all, and how White merely asks yet another pointless question:

White: Did you set targets for improvements for Murray and professional development?

When asked if he had anything to add, Pead replied: "...I would like you to accept this as part of my response. I feel that I haven't had an adequate opportunity to present in this forum, my full statement. I want to present a written response to the allegations; I haven't had enough time to present my full case. Neither you nor Barry has reported Murray – why not? ..."

Pead gave Mary White his 32-page typed document which responded to Murray's allegations in full. Several friends – especially John Callow – had read Pead's response. Copies were made and Twist signed the front sheet only to give Pead as a receipt. She did not record the number of pages on the receipt, so it was a worthless piece of paper. This was yet another example of her unprofessional and inept handling of the case.

Just before the meeting ended at 5pm, White added: "...Just to let you know that if this investigation goes to a hearing you will have more time to present your case..."

This was improper and an abuse of process. Pead had every right to have had all of his case heard by Twist and White during the investigatory meetings, but they did not allow him to do so.

Pead's response was firm: "...This is just phase one. There will be plenty more evidence from me. I am considering taking libel action against Murray and Hiley. There is another potential case against Murray regarding the lady included in the allegation relating to the trip to the theatre.

Brian Pead had left Twist and White in no doubt about his anger in respect of this case and the improper way they were dealing with it. Note how White responds:

White: We are still completing the investigation. We may have to question others again. When we have finished the investigation, Cathy Twist will process all of the information we have gathered and decide if it should go to a panel hearing. You can have a representative with you at the hearing who can be a colleague or a Trade Union representative but not a solicitor. The procedure for the hearing is set out in the procedures I have sent you.

White lies here. Pead was entitled to have a solicitor present.

Pead: The statement I have given you is just a first draft. It is a response at phase one.

Notice White's response – another lie:

White: You are not supposed to share the allegation document widely.

Pead: I'm able to use my professional judgment about who I show the allegations to. Everyone I've shown it to already thinks it's complete nonsense and no-one can believe that you're taking Murray's allegations seriously.

White has lied to Pead – she cannot control who he does or doesn't show Murray's report to. In fact, he showed it to teaching and counselling colleagues, he showed it to his daughter and to his many friends.

White then asked for two important pieces of information and evidence: she wanted the address of Ipek Yÿlmaz in Turkey and **she asked Pead for a copy of his Steve Goodfellow business card.**

It was obvious that Twist and White had not got a copy of this business card – despite four female members of staff claiming that he had given them one. Had they all disposed of it? Had they all by some strange quirk of fate mysteriously lost the card they alleged they were given? No, the reason she wanted this card was to photocopy it and present it as part of Murray's evidence **against** Pead. He had already asked for a copy of the card from Twist and White – but they were unable to provide him with a copy.

Thus the investigatory interviews were concluded.

But the case itself was far from over. This had been the most significant of the meetings for reasons that will become clear in the following chapters.

twisted process

Brian Pead's final investigatory meeting had taken place on 16 May 2007. Twist and White had interviewed Murray, Hiley, Whitmore and Field – who all made similar complaints, not because they actually happened but because they all colluded – and they had also interviewed Sandra Roach, Colin Hill, Duane Maddison and Derek Langan.

They had also interviewed Barry Gilhooly (Pead's line manager), Rosa Vaz (Human Resources) and Alicia Reynolds (Human Resources).

And, of course, they had interviewed Pead.

To the uninitiated, this might appear – and it was certainly designed to appear – as though it were a thorough investigation.

But it was not. In a thorough investigation, the following would also have been called: Fraser Hall (a young Maths teacher from New Zealand), Ermina/Paul Waters (ICT consultant to Lambeth), Sherine Thompson (Head of the West Norwood Community Centre), Alphonso Augustus Harris (Lambeth Detached Youth Worker), Alicia Harris – no relation to Alphonso – from West Norwood Library, Denise Campbell-Downie (head of the Redfearn Centre in Vauxhall), Cassandra Trimmings (female pupil), Mrs Trimmings, (Cassandra's grand-mother), Rickkardo Crawford-Burrows (male pupil), Mrs Crawford-Burrows (Rickkardo's mother), Cathy Sesinyi (black, female pupil), Mr Sesinyi (Cathy's father), Kerrie Hamilton (dark-haired female pupil), Kerrie Hamilton's parents, Ashleigh Mills (blonde, female pupil), Ashleigh Mills' aunt and mother, Melissa Whitrod (dark-haired female pupil), Glenice Lake (Anya Hiley's line manager), Chris Ashton (Barry Gilhooly's line manager), Chloe Gordon (blonde, female pupil), Chloe Gordon's parents, Gemma Mandry (dark-haired female pupil), Gemma Mandry's parents, Talya Cuthbert (dark-haired female pupil), Mrs Cuthbert (Talya's mother), Shelaine Clarke-Kyaw-Zayya (dark-haired female pupil who Brian gave the job of creating artwork for the noticeboards to), Mauro Brito, Jose Mario Pontes Centeio and Miguel Neves (the three black Brazilian male pupils who accused Murray of racism and bullying - proven), Diego Costa (Brazilian male pupil who sought Brian's counsel on a number of personal issues), Emmanuel Ello (a French-speaking black African male from the Ivory Coast), Glauce Biagio (a 25 year old Brazilian whom Pead asked to help out with the Portuguese pupils) and others.

It should be noted that Pead enjoyed many conversations with the three Brazilian students and Emmanuel Ello based on football and boxing, interests which they all shared. Ello was from the Ivory Coast, as was Didier Drogba, the Chelsea FC striker. Furthermore, there was also the 2006 World Cup in Germany going on at the time, so this was a major topic of discussion, particularly as the Ivory Coast suffered two narrow 2-1 defeats to Argentina and Holland before finally beating Serbia and Montenegro 3-2. Ello was devastated that his team had failed to qualify for the latter stages of the World Cup.

There was considerable evidence that various witnesses alluded to, yet was not produced in order to verify their statements.

This evidence included the telephone log books of calls into and out of the Centre (once a phone line had been added). Pead initiated this professional procedure. Foster, Murray and Whitmore had all stated that calls came in to the Centre for a Steve Goodfellow – yet no evidence of these calls was ever produced.

Murray set great store by the fact that Marion Richards had received an email from Pead under the name of Steve Goodfellow – this alleged email never materialised.

Murray also claimed that Pead handed her a business card in the name of Steve Goodfellow on her first day in the centre – yet she was unable to produce it. Furthermore, Field, Whitmore and Hiley also made a similar claim – yet were unable to produce a copy of the business card. Is it feasible that all four would mislay these cards?

Annabel Field claimed that Pead had given her a card on her first day in which he was alleged to have told her what a wonderful teacher she was – this card never materialised.

Lambeth were unable to produce copies of Pead's CRB checks in which they claimed he had failed to declare the name of Steve Goodfellow. [Pead, however, **was** able to produce a CRB certificate which included the Goodfellow name.]

Murray mentioned staff meetings – yet not a single copy of Minutes of these meetings was ever produced.

Pead – of course – was unable to produce certain copies of Minutes because his office had been ransacked. However, he had typed out some Minutes on his home computer, so some records were still available to him. Twist never asked him to produce these.

Murray tried to make capital out of the fact that Pead had once said that he had managed people since the age of 18. His Curriculum Vitae would demonstrate the truth of this – yet Twist never asked him for a copy of his CV.

The email that Anya Hiley sent to her line manager – which was then escalated to Phyllis Dunipace, then the Director of Education in Lambeth – was never produced by Twist. Pead was forced to initiate a Freedom of Information Act request for its production.

Full copies of the OLCVS examination records were never produced – though Twist tried to mislead the Panel and a subsequent Employment Tribunal by producing some of the records.

Murray claimed when giving her evidence that she had felt uneasy about Pead from her first day and thus kept a log of everything he did and said.

This log was never produced.

No CCTV tapes were ever produced. These would have shown Pead's movements in the Old Library Centre and the Redfearn Centre.

Murray had claimed – quite rightly as it happens – that Pead had offered Ashleigh Mills (whom Murray had described as 'very attractive') an admin post in the office. Pead – and Colin Hill – stated that this exam was part of the ASDAN group of vocational exams. Twist failed to produce copies of the exam results.

Murray claimed that she had heard Whitmore crying in the ladies' toilets. How could this have been, since all the toilets in the Centre were single occupancy? Unless she had gone into the same single occupancy toilet with Whitmore, it would have been impossible to hear anybody crying. The reality is that this never happened. Murray claimed that she had logged everything – so where were the written records of these events? No dates or times were ever recorded against any single allegation.

Murray claimed that Whitmore often worked late – this was erroneous. The CCTV records would have proved this to be false. And how would Murray have known – given that she always left on time?

Murray claimed that she had been Head of the ICT Department for five years at St. Augustine's School in Ealing. Murray also claimed that she had been offered a full-time contract by St. Augustine's School in Ealing. Where was the evidence to support this statement?

This was basic information that Twist out to have had at her fingertips. Having made that claim, Twist was then obligated to seek evidence to establish the veracity of Murray's claim. She did not.

Not only did Twist fail to visit the White Bear Theatre, but she also failed to obtain the names of the alleged cast member and his wife who were supposed to have witnessed sexual activity between Pead and his female companion. Yet - had this been a fair and thorough investigation - Twist ought to have obtained witness statements from these people. She failed to do so.

Murray claimed that Annabel Field had sent staff a card to be displayed on the staff noticeboard. This card has never been produced.

Murray claimed – falsely – that Hiley was 'very involved' with the OLCVS pupils. No evidence was produced to support this wild assertion. Yet, as a Connexions advisor, it would have been easy for Hiley to have been asked to produce this evidence. Twist did not ask her to.

Murray claimed that Hiley filed various concerns about Pead – why were these 'various concerns' not produced as evidence?

Murray claimed that Pead had frequently texted her to ask Colin Hill or Duane Maddison to take 'circle time'. These 'frequent' texts were never produced at the hearings.

Murray claimed that current staff had made complaints about Pead but "...since they are still working there, I do not wish to document these without their permission..." No evidence was adduced to support these spurious claims of Murray's.

Murray claimed that Pead had an all-day meeting with her – yet failed to produce Minutes of this meeting or even state the time and date.

Murray claimed that Pead had produced a flowchart telling which members of staff could speak with which other members of staff. Clearly nonsense, this flowchart was never produced.

Murray claimed that staff often worked late in the OLCVS. This was impossible. At the Old Library Centre in West Norwood, the classrooms had to be emptied as soon as the lessons were over because the rooms were being used by other community groups. At the Redfearn Centre in Vauxhall, the terms of the lease agreement were that the building had to be vacated by 5pm because other groups needed to use the building. It would have been impossible for staff to 'work late'. Twist did not ask to see the lease agreements at either building.

Murray mentioned the school nurse, Ruth, but she was not called as a witness.

Murray claimed that agenda for meetings were not handed to staff until immediately prior to the meeting. No computer files were ever adduced to prove that Pead would produce agenda sheets for staff days before a meeting, so that they could add any items to be discussed. Computer files could not be produced because they had been wiped from his computer when his office was ransacked.

Although Murray claimed "...I always took notes of meetings to have a record of what was requested of me..." no such notes were ever produced.

The Court of Appeal has also recommended in cases such as Pead's that the Investigating Officer should visit locations which have a bearing on the case.

It is approximately 2.7 kilometres from Canterbury Crescent, Brixton – the site of International House - to the White Bear Theatre.

Twist failed to make that short journey in the interest of justice.

Furthermore, Twist also failed to visit the Old Library Centre in West Norwood to establish the layout of the building, to establish that it had CCTV throughout the building and to establish that all of the doors had anti-slamming devices on them, yet Whitmore - who failed her probationary period and was paid £8,000 for so doing – claimed in her statement that Brian Pead had slammed doors in her face. This would have been impossible. Twist clearly failed in her duty as an investigating officer.

But the biggest question of all still burned: why were Twist and Lambeth going to such extraordinary lengths to find anything with which they could dismiss a man who was doing an excellent job?

What possible motives could they have had for such a strategy?

pead's rebuttal

On 16 May 2007, Pead gave Twist and White a 32-page document which clearly rebutted all of Murray's wild and spurious allegations. He even supported his statements with evidence.

In the 22,568 word document, Pead asked many questions about Murray, Twist and White in this document. There were so many questions that any decent investigator conducting a genuine investigation would have been forced to drop all charges and allow Pead back into the job he loved and, by all the accounts of others, was doing extremely well.

The main statements he made and the questions he asked in that document are reproduced here:

Where is the logbook of all incoming and outgoing calls at the OLCVS?

Why did Brian Pead have to make an official Freedom of Information Act request to obtain the information that Hiley had libellously written about him to others?

Why did Twist and White not visit the Old Library Centre in West Norwood to check that there were anti-slamming devices on all doors – thus negating Whitmore's lies that Pead slammed doors in her face?

Why did Twist and White not visit the White Bear Theatre?

Why did Twist and White not visit the Redfearn Centre in Vauxhall?

Why did Twist not obtain full records of all exams undertaken – and not undertaken – by pupils at the OLCVS?

Why were no students interviewed?

Why were no parents/ carers interviewed?

Why were no other third parties interviewed?

Why was Pead's office ransacked **before** he was finally allowed access to it?

Why were all his files removed?

Why was Duane Maddison not invited to the Disciplinary Hearing?

Why was Annabel Field not invited to the Disciplinary Hearing?

Why was Nadia Al-Khudhairy not invited to the Disciplinary Hearing?

Why did Lambeth suspend Pead without providing him with a reason?

Why did Lambeth interview staff **after** they had been sent copies of Murray's spurious allegations?

Why did Lambeth ensure that the entire process lasted **fifteen months**?

Why did Twist and White accept Hiley's evidence when she didn't even work at the OLCVS and she worked two floors above the OLCVS?

Why did Twist not even interview Nadia Al-Khudhairy?

Why did Twist not make contact with Dr Patricia Conrod, creator of the Preventure Programme?

Why did Twist fail to call as witnesses Pead's counselling peers, tutors and supervisors?

Why did Twist fail to make contact with Amanda Glass, Pead's supervisor at Whitefield School in Barnet?

Why did Twist appear to fail to note that all of these allegations against Pead were made by a child-abusing female teacher **after** she had been dismissed from the school?

Why did Twist fail to call Ipek Yÿlmaz as a witness?

Why did Twist fail to establish the name of the cast member in the Horse Dealer's Daughter who allegedly told Annabel Field of sexual misconduct in the theatre?

Why did Twist fail to interview him?

Why did Twist fail to obtain a copy of the Steve Goodfellow business card from Murray, Hiley, Whitmore and Field – who all claimed they had been given one by Pead?

Why did Twist not produce any Minutes of staff meetings at the OLCVS?

Why did Pead never receive his interview statement to sign before it progressed to a Disciplinary Hearing?

Why did Pead never receive the interview statements of his colleagues at any time throughout the Investigatory process?

Why did Twist keep hold of witness statements by Field and others for up to **six months** before sending them off for signature?

Why did Twist unlawfully alter Annabel Field's statement?

Why did Twist unlawfully alter Duane Maddison's statement?

Why did Twist not ask herself why Murray would keep returning to the OLCVS if she felt 'uncomfortable' with Pead from the first day?

Why did Twist not ask herself why Murray would keep returning to the OLCVS if she felt 'uncomfortable' in her second week by being asked out by Pead for a meal and drinks?

How did Twist investigate the truth of Murray's claims in their entirety?

Did Lambeth check Murray's identities and were they all CRB checked?

Had Lambeth ever investigated Murray's claim that she was offered a Head of Department post at St. Augustine's School in Ealing?

Why did Twist and White not seek professional advice from psychologists in respect of Murray's use of the terms 'not so attractive', 'attractive' and 'very attractive' when describing pupils?

Why was Murray operating under multiple identities? She did not come to the OLCVS using her birth name.

Why would Murray keep a 'dossier' on her manager from the day she joined?

Why did Lambeth fail to report Murray to the Independent Safeguarding Authority?

Why did Twist fail to report Murray to the police for her grooming of female pupils?

Why did Twist fail to report Murray to the police for her racism towards black pupils?

Why did Twist fail to report Murray to the police for her harassment of black pupils?

Why did Twist fail to report Murray to the police for her harassment of Brian Pead?

Why did Phyllis Dunipace, Executive Director of Education for Lambeth resign from her post?

Why would Lambeth deliberately destroy evidence and remove all files and documents from Pead's office immediately after his unlawful suspension?

fixed term contract meeting

Despite being unwell and despite Lambeth dragging their heels over the investigation into Murray's allegations, Gilhooly forced Pead to attend yet another meeting. The meetings were coming thick and fast. They were designed to keep Pead busy. He knew too much about Murray and her behaviour at the OLCVS and that she had been re-employed by Lambeth despite the Council being in possession of facts that she was guilty of racism and child abuse.

The meeting was held on 18 May 2007 at Hopton House in Streatham. This was just two days after his final Investigatory Meeting. He was still officially off work through illness.

Rosa Vaz was also in attendance.

Gilhooly presented Pead with another *fait accompli*. His contract was not being renewed. Thus Lambeth were dismissing him **before** the outcome of an investigation. A Freedom of Information Act request has shown that Pead did not receive a letter about this meeting until 31 May 2007 – some two weeks after the meeting. There can be no valid excuse for this.

In this letter, Gilhooly made reference to the fact that Pead's contract would not be extended due to three reasons:

"...A monitoring visit by Lambeth Advisors on 6th March 2007 (copy attached).

• The OfSTED inspection of a similar provision in Southwark which was placed in Special Measures.

• The need for a close link with a secondary school (through the leadership and management of an Executive Headteacher) in order to significantly improve the curriculum offer for students and widen staff development opportunities..."

This letter was staggering on a number of counts.

Firstly, the monitoring visit by Lambeth Advisors on 6 March 2007 had no relevance to Pead. He had been suspended in December 2006 and Colin Hill was Acting Head.

There was no copy of this visit attached as Gilhooly's letter claimed.

The OfSTED inspection of a similar provision in Southwark which was placed in Special Measures also had no relevance to Pead - his Unit had been described as the best Unit in London. Southwark is also in London.

The need to develop the curriculum was something that Pead was always bringing to Gilhooly's attention. The letter indicated that the OLCVS would come under the management of an Executive headteacher.

However, the letter was dated 30 May 2007. **Pead had already been replaced in April 2007.**

Lambeth were attempting to 'cover their tracks', but the chronology let them down. They had already replaced the successful Head of the OLCVS with an Executive Head teacher and **then** cited that as a reason in a letter dated one month after their unlawful action.

The letter also stated that "...You have the right to appeal against this decision..." and, of course, Pead did appeal but his complaint went unanswered by Lambeth.

Gilhooly's letter informed Pead that he was under three months' notice and that the notice period ended on 31 August 2007.

Lambeth were going to extraordinary lengths to dismiss Pead. On the face of it, they could have found logical reasons not to extend his contract (as they tried in this letter). However, having had his contract terminated, why then did Twist continue to pursue Pead and attempt to blacken his name? Why not just let him leave and seek employment elsewhere? What had he uncovered at the OLCVS that meant that he and his reputation had to be destroyed?

interview with rosa vaz, human resources

On 4 June 2007, Twist interviewed Rosa Vaz, the Schools' Human Resources officer whom had attended the Eloise Whitmore meeting in which her GMB Union representative, Robin Irwin, had accused Pead of trying to sack her because she was of child-bearing age. Mary White was also in attendance, as was Karina O'Neill, the note taker.

The meeting took place in Meeting Room 1 on the second floor of International House in Brixton.

The purpose of the meeting was to investigate the allegations that had been made against Brian Pead.

Note the date: the 4 June was a full **six months** after his unlawful suspension. Lambeth Council was dragging its feet. The Court of Appeal had shown that six months was an extraordinary length of time in which to address the issues. Lambeth Council was 'buying time' which usually indicates two main tactical advantages to them: (i) cause as much disruption to Pead's life as possible and keep him 'on tenterhooks' about his future and (ii) provide as much distance as possible between the suspension and the Hearing so that paperwork can be lost, people can be moved on and memories will fade.

But note the date. Brian Pead has already (a) been replaced and (b) been informed by Gilhooly and Vaz that his contract would not be renewed after it expired on 31 August 2007. Yet here they were, just a month before the expiration of his contract still going through the motions of a 'fair and thorough' investigatory meeting. Twist was clearly continuing to trawl for **any** information that she could justify her dismissal of Pead with.

In this interview, Rosa Vaz – who worked closely with Gilhooly - demonstrably lied. When asked by Twist, "What name was the Head of Centre known by?" Vaz replied, "Brian Pead."

This was clearly false. Even the malevolent Murray had stated in her report that Pead was known by Brian Johnson at the Centre. All of the pupils and parents knew him by this name. All the official Lambeth reports issued by consultants in ICT, maths and English used the name Brian Johnson. Pead even received a P60 income tax form in the name of Brian Johnson. And all emails to Lambeth HR and Gilhooly and anyone else he needed to contact in his role as Head of Centre were from the email address brian.pead89@hotmail.co.uk

Vaz therefore lied. There is substantial documentation in the public domain that shows that she lied. She is guilty of perverting the course of justice.

Having initiated a Freedom of Information request, Lambeth Council provided to Brian Pead a document entitled *Lambeth Payroll Services*. This document was an Employee Engagement Notification (LPS1). This document has a specific serial number (112772). It is made out in the name of Brian Johnson and clearly states that his birth name is Brian Pead.

This document was signed by Carol Palmer, who would later form part of a Panel to conduct Pead's Disciplinary Hearing.

This document would have been available to Twist. It is proof that Rosa Vaz lied and perverted the course of justice. It is also further proof that Twist conducted an unlawful hearing.

Cathy Twist's questioning was extremely basic. The question "What name was the Head of Centre known by?" is a question of stunning paucity of intelligence. She ought to have made the question clearer – she ought to have said, "What name was the Head of Centre known by to pupils, parents, colleagues, Lambeth consultants and HR?"

But her inept questioning was designed with one purpose in mind – to remove Pead from office, whilst simultaneously discrediting him.

Rosa Vaz continued her web of lies when asked:

White: Pead claims that he discussed with you and Barry Gilhooly at the beginning of his placement that he wished to use the name Brian Johnson. Did you agree with Pead that he could be known as Brian Johnson for his work at the OLCVS?

Vaz: No, because Pead did not have any official documentation under the name of Brian Johnson. All of our correspondence with Pead was under the name of Brian Pead only. We had to use the name Brian Pead for work purposes, i.e. for payroll. We agreed that we would call him Brian Pead and not Brian Johnson. We agreed that he could use Brian Johnson for other purposes but for work purposes he would use Brian Pead.

This is incontrovertible evidence of perjury. Rosa Vaz was in possession of knowledge that she herself had emailed Pead on numerous occasions when he used the name of Brian Johnson. She had attended the Eloise Whitmore farcical hearing when Pead was, of course, referred to as Johnson.

But Twist showed herself to be inept in her questioning. Of course Pead was known by that name on the payroll, since his salary was paid directly into his bank account of that name. A wise investigator – if one is actually investigating properly and not merely 'going through the motions' – would have asked: "If you say that all of Lambeth HR correspondence with Brian Pead was under that name, can you please provide examples?" and, of course, Twist failed to ask that simple – yet obvious – question. This was just another example of how Twist was seen to be doing an investigator's job but she was, in fact, doing nothing of the sort.

But Twist has, by this time, already interviewed Gilhooly, Pead's line manager on three occasions prior to her interview with Vaz. She has been told by members of staff – even Murray herself – that Pead had only ever used the name of 'Johnson' in the Centre for his own personal reasons. Yet Vaz has been tasked with providing some evidence – lies, in fact – that would give her a reason to dismiss Pead.

However, the Rosa Vaz interview did provide Pead with some useful evidence that other people interviewed by Twist had also lied and perjured themselves.

When asked by Twist, "...Did Brian Pead seek advice from you on staff contracts?..." Vaz replied, "...Yes, Alicia [Reynolds] was involved in this..."

Yet, in a later interview, Pead's line manager, Barry Gilhooly, claimed that Pead had never consulted Lambeth HR about staff contracts and that he had made promises to Murray that her contract was "in the post".

Thus Rosa Vaz contradicted Gilhooly's evidence. At least one of them was lying. In fact, both were, as will be explained later.

Vaz, for the moment, was asked whether she had witnessed Pead using a "...personal and intrusive style..." and she replied that she had not.

She was then asked whether she thought Pead's manner was appropriate, and replied, "Yes."

Worryingly, Vaz was asked whether all OLCVS staff were CRB checked. Her reply is staggering: "...Yes, all contract staff were CRB checked..."

To the uninitiated, her reply is of little consequence and it appears to establish a degree of comfort in the mind of the reader. However, what her reply **actually** said was that people worked in the Centre who were not on a contract and therefore **they had not been CRB checked by Lambeth HR.**

This is a staggering admission by a Schools' Human Resources Officer. Yet the degree of ineptitude worsens.

Vaz admitted that "...We [Lambeth HR] wouldn't know if agency staff were CRB checked or not..."

It is a Local Authority's statutory duty to conduct CRB checks wherever necessary. It is clearly necessary for a Local Authority to conduct such checks on people working in any form of school and having contact with children. Cathy Twist – as an Assistant Director of Education – would have known this. It is a fundamental principle underpinning her role.

Yet she did not question Vaz further, save to ask her leading questions which would elicit a response from Vaz that would lay the responsibility for CRB checks on all third parties at Pead's door. It was **not** his responsibility; it was Lambeth's.

Maryn Murray was never CRB checked. She had 'escaped the system' and worked in the school and bullied male pupils and was racist towards male pupils and bribed young girls and wanted them to visit her flat **and Lambeth HR had failed to ensure that she had been CRB checked.**

In the presence of Sandra Roach, Gilhooly and Pead had discussed Murray's racism, bullying and sexual misconduct. This had been recorded on Pead's work computer and on paper records.

These had all been unlawfully removed from Pead's office whilst he was under suspension.

90

replaced - 2

Brian Pead's 'eyes-and-ears' in the form of the dependable Sandra Roach ensured that he came into possession of a document that proved that Lambeth had been acting unlawfully in his case.

A letter from the Open Learning Centre for Vocational Studies dated 7 June 2007 to Parents and Carers begins with:

> "...My name is Ginni Bealing and I am the new Executive Headteacher at the Open Learning Centre..."

This means, of course, that Pead had been replaced as Head whilst he was still officially only under suspension and whilst the 'thorough and fair' investigation and disciplinary meetings were still on-going. He had, in fact, been replaced by Bealing in April, but this was her first official letter to parents. At no point had the parents or carers and the pupils (or the staff) been told of the reasons why Pead was no longer at the Unit.

Such is the arrogance of Lambeth.

third interview with barry gilhooly, assistant director

Gilhooly was interviewed for the third time on Monday 11 June 2007 in Meeting Room 8 on the second floor of International House in Brixton. Mary White, a Human Resources Consultant, was also in attendance, as was Karina O'Neill, the note taker. The Lambeth records show that the interview commenced at 11.30am and finished at noon.

At this point in the chronology, both Twist and Gilhooly know that Pead has already been replaced at the OLCVS. They also know that Murray has been reinstated. They also know that Murray had been racist and that she had been inappropriate around young girls.

Twist's first question was: "What name was Brian Pead employed under?" to which Gilhooly replied, "Brian Johnson. All of the Human Resource forms were under Brian Pead **but I agreed that he could be known as Brian Johnson at work...**"

It can be seen that Gilhooly has completely undermined Vaz's testimony of a week previously. Their statements are diametrically opposed to one another. Vaz claimed that Pead was known as Brian Pead at work, while Gilhooly claimed that he was known as Brian Johnson at work.

The 'thorough and efficient' Twist failed to ask Gilhooly about this contradiction. She also failed to re-interview Vaz, which any self-respecting investigator would do in the circumstances. The set of investigatory hearings and disciplinary hearings failed, therefore, to meet the Burchell Test. The length of time that this 'investigation' was taking had already breached Lambeth's own policies with regard to the efficient disposal of the proceedings.

There were a number of irrelevant questions that filled most of the thirty-minute interview between Twist and Gilhooly.

Only one other question – out of the 32 questions asked in the interview - had any relevance to the proceedings at all. Most responses by Gilhooly were simple "Yes" or "No" responses due to the large number of closed questions (91%) that Twist asked. An investigator who is genuinely determined to get to the bottom of a problem will obviously ask *some* closed questions, but these are usually at the beginning of an interview merely to 'set the scene'.

But Twist asked a much higher proportion of closed questions throughout all of the interviews she conducted.

She asked yet another closed question:

Twist: Did Brian Pead take advice from you regarding the termination of Maryn Murray's contract before he terminated her contract?

Gilhooly: No, not before. Pead told me his perception of the situation with Murray e.g. that she was undermining him. I advised him to discuss the issues with Murray. He presented Murray with some options. After he told me that he had met her I thought that he hadn't consulted with her properly as he had presented her with an ultimatum. The first I heard about her termination was when Murray phoned me to tell me about it. [...] **There had already been so many changes at the Centre that I didn't want to lose her and she was good at her job..."**

The emphasis is the authors'.

This was Gilhooly's longest answer to any of the 32 questions he was asked. He has committed perjury. He has lied to an investigation officer who is going to decide the entire future career prospects of Brian Pead. He is protecting Murray – why?

He claims that the first he knew that Murray had been dismissed by Pead was when she called him. He did not produce evidence of that telephone call.

Nor did he provide – and nor was Pead asked to provide – evidence of Pead's call to him about dismissing Murray.

This lack of *bona fide* evidence was to prove a theme in Pead's life for a number of years afterwards. This tactic of making wholly unsubstantiated allegations against him without the slightest shred of evidence against him was also to occur for a number of years afterwards.

But how did a supply teacher gain such ready access to an Assistant Director of Education at Lambeth HQ? Whenever Brian Pead called Gilhooly's office, Beverley Williams – Gilhooly's PA - would often claim that he was 'busy' or 'out of the office' and all the other excuses that managers ask their PAs to make on their behalf.

How, then, did Murray always gain instant access to a man in such an elevated position within the Lambeth hierarchy? It would be extremely rare for an ordinary supply teacher to always gain such immediate access to an Assistant Director of Education unless that supply teacher had some form of complex relationship with that person. The authors believe that Murray had Gilhooly's private mobile number because there is no other way that she would have always gained instant access to him. The efficient Beverley Williams would have screened the calls to him and calls from a supply teacher would simply not get through. Yet Murray's calls regarding her contract got through to Gilhooly. It is simply not feasible that a man in Gilhooly's position would be discussing contracts with supply teachers. Had he allowed himself to be put in this position, he would have been inundated with similar discussions throughout his working week.

Then Gilhooly claims that Murray called him with regard to her being asked not to return to the Centre. Again, supply teachers are asked not to return to schools every day of the school year. The reasons they are asked not to return are manifold. It is not always because of sexual impropriety. Sometimes it can simply be down to the fact of how a teacher dresses or because they have a nose-ring, for example, and they refuse to take it out.

Yet here we have a situation in which Gilhooly had been in discussions with Pead about Murray's racism and sexual impropriety and yet he **takes calls from the deviant teacher.**

Why on earth would Gilhooly put himself in such a vulnerable position? What did Murray know about Gilhooly that meant that he would take her calls at any time of day or night? Or that he would take her calls at all? By taking calls from a supply teacher who had been dismissed for racism and sexual impropriety, Gilhooly was putting himself at enormous risk. Why would he take those risks, especially when he had such an excellent and professional PA to distance him from such people and such calls?

Pead had consulted with Gilhooly about the evidence that he had collated against Murray in respect of her racist and bullying demeanour towards young black male pupils.

Pead had also consulted with Gilhooly about the fact that Murray had offered Gemma Mandry a bribe to go to the gym with her. And Pead had told Gilhooly that Murray had asked Ashleigh Mills to go to her flat and to go shopping together.

Sandra Roach corroborates that Gilhooly knew about the reasons for Murray's dismissal and that Pead had consulted Gilhooly **before** Pead called the teaching agency which employed Murray.

But what is simply staggering is Gilhooly's final sentence: "...I didn't want to lose her and she was good at her job..." These words were uttered by a man who had been informed about Murray's wrong-doing and inappropriate behaviour towards children. This information had been recorded on Pead's work computer and stored as hard copy in a locked filing cabinet.

Upon Pead's suspension, Gilhooly gave instructions for the removal of all evidence of that conversation around Murray's behaviour.

Evidence the authors have secured from a large number of pupils and third party staff who came into daily contact with Pead provides incontrovertible proof that Murray was **not** good at her job and that she had made inappropriate advances to young female pupils.

Gilhooly was supporting her. The transsexual Ermina – or Paul – Waters aligned herself with Murray. Anya Hiley made false allegations against Pead, claiming she had witnessed "...many hour-long conversations..." he had had with "...attractive young white girls..." from her lofty perch on the third floor of the Old Library Centre in West Norwood.

Gilhooly, Murray, Waters and Hiley. Were these people involved in a paedophile ring? The perceptive and intuitive Pead needed to be gotten rid of and he needed to be discredited. The wrongdoing of Murray et al had to be thrown on to Pead as a smokescreen in order to deflect people's attention away from their wrong-doing.

There can be no other reasonable and logical explanation for the fact that Gilhooly – a frequent visitor to the paedophile haven of Goa (that is the Indian Government's description of the island and not the authors') – would claim that he did not want to lose Murray from the staff, when he was in possession of incontrovertible evidence that she was a bully, a racist and demonstrated paedophilic tendencies towards young, white, (unattractive/ attractive/ very attractive) girls.

Was the reason that Gilhooly wished to retain the services of Murray because she was a conduit between him and young girls?

Was the reason that Gilhooly actually reinstated Murray and allowed her to work in Lambeth schools alongside Ermina/ Mina/ Paul Waters so that they could operate as 'partners-in-crime' around young girls ... the company of which Waters had craved ever since he was a little boy in a "...male-dominated household...' as he told the BBC?

Was the reason that Gilhooly reinstated Murray in an all-girls school just a ten-minute walk from Hiley's office (and therefore on Hiley's 'patch' as a Connexions personal advisor) so that he could ensure continued access to vulnerable young girls? What other reason can there be for Gilhooly placing her at Norwood School for Girls when he was already in possession of *bona fide* evidence of her wrong-doing?

At no point in the thirty-minute interview did Twist ever ask Gilhooly about Murray's bullying or racist behaviour or inappropriate sexual conduct towards young white female pupils, **yet she was aware of these facts**.

Why would this be the case? If an investigator was truly seeking to establish the facts, why would these important questions around child abuse not have been asked?

And why did Twist never ask Gilhooly what he thought about the fact that Murray had compiled the 8-page document on Pead until **after** he had dismissed her?

And why did Twist never ask Gilhooly about the fact that Murray did not report the alleged 'masturbation in the theatre' incident until **eight months** after it was alleged to have occurred and, furthermore, until **after** she had been dismissed?

There is strong evidence to suggest that Murray was ingratiating herself with young, white girls for the benefit of herself and others.

There is even stronger evidence to suggest that Brian Pead had discovered these unlawful activities and that he had to be silenced.

At any cost.

signing off interview statements

It is usual protocol for an interviewee to receive notes from a meeting such as this within a working week, then annotate them and have a final draft ready for signing off as an official document within a fortnight of the interview.

However, this did not happen with any interviewee. The minimum period was **four months** and the most common length of time between an interview and final copy was **six months**. This breaches employment law and all common sense.

But note the pattern with regard to Gilhooly's interviews:

Date of Interview	Notes signed off
25 January 2007	25 June 2007
5 February 2007	25 June 2007
11 June 2007	28 June 2007

This is, of course, highly irregular. This means that Gilhooly had access to all of the notes at the same time, so that he could ensure that he had not made any mistakes.

It should also be recorded that Gilhooly did not annotate any of the notes that Lambeth sent him. This would be unusual.

interview with alicia reynolds, human resources

Also on the 11 June 2007 between 12:05 and 12.30pm a meeting took place in Meeting Room 8 between Twist and Alicia Reynolds who, as Senior Human Resources Officer, worked alongside Rosa Vaz in the Schools' Human Resources Department at International House.

The precise time of this meeting is significant. Twist's interviewing of Brian Pead's Line Manager, Barry Gilhooly, had taken place between 11.30 and midday.

According to Lambeth records, Twist then initiated another meeting just five minutes after Gilhooly departed the room, if he did depart the room.

No investigator who was seriously investigating such a matter would book back-to-back meetings. A thorough investigator would allow sufficient time between meetings to make notes, to discuss the meeting with colleagues and to come up with further questions or note inconsistencies between the accounts of different witnesses.

Twist did not undertake these basic safeguards.

In this interview, Reynolds confirms that Brian Pead was known at the OLCVS as Brian Johnson. This is in direct contradiction to Rosa Vaz's statement – yet the two women worked alongside one another in the same office.

Reynolds also confirms that the names of Brian Pead and Brian Johnson **were** CRB checked. So much for Murray's wild assertion.

Reynolds further confirms that Pead would contact HR to discuss any concerns he had with regard to Human Resources. This militates against what Gilhooly claimed.

Reynolds also said that Murray had called her about a contract. Her contact details had been given to Murray by Pead himself. If he was not using HR as he claimed and working unilaterally – as Gilhooly claimed – why would he have given Murray the contact details of Alicia Reynolds so that she could discuss the awarding of contracts directly with HR?

Gilhooly had claimed that Brian Pead was not adhering to Lambeth's policies and procedures around advertising staff posts and the recruitment of staff.

Yet Reynolds stated that Pead would "...email us regarding issues of contracts, **after confirming them with Barry Gilhooly.** [...] I have a copy of an email from Brian regarding staff contracts...**"

This emphasis is the authors'. Reynolds makes two vitally important and significant points here.

Firstly, she states that Pead was in the habit of discussing staff contracts with Gilhooly and that Pead would confirm things with his line manager in the first instance. Given Pead's propensity to confirm such matters with Gilhooly, is it at all realistic to assume that Pead did **not** – as Gilhooly claimed – contact him with regard to dismissing Murray for inappropriate sexual behaviour, racism and bullying?

Secondly, Reynolds has evidence of emails that Pead sent to her (and to Rosa Vaz) with regard to staff contracts. The Minutes of the interview record that Alicia Reynolds handed copies of emails between Pead and her and Pead and Vaz in respect of his seeking advice with regard to the issuing of staff contracts and advertising posts.

These emails have never been seen. Since they proved that Pead had been telling the truth all along – and since they proved that Gilhooly had lied – they went missing.

The ultimate responsibility for the safekeeping of all documents relating to the investigation is, of course, Cathy Twist's. The fact that they mysteriously went missing lies at her door.

However, what is even more disturbing is the fact that – once Twist had been made aware of evidence that (a) proved that Brian Pead had been telling the truth all along, that (b) Gilhooly had been lying in his interview and that (c) Rosa Vaz had also lied in her interview – Twist did not make copies of these emails and store them off-site and that Twist failed to re-interview Alicia Reynolds or seek further copies from her.

With the paper copies having mysteriously gone missing – which they apparently had done so – a thorough and proficient investigator would simply have contacted Reynolds and asked her to print them off her computer again.

But Twist failed to take these basic steps.

Alicia Reynolds also states that the names of Brian Pead and Brian Johnson were CRB checked and that Lambeth "...were satisfied with his references..."

She also states that "...When we became aware of his use of the name Steve Goodfellow we had all three names checked on List 99..."

"...A List 99 check is a check against information held under Section 142 of the Education Act 2002. The list is maintained by the Department for Children, Schools and Families (DCSF) and contains the details of those who are banned or restricted from working in **an education setting.**

Local authorities, schools, and further education institutions must check the List before confirming a person's appointment in order to ensure that they do not appoint someone whose employment is banned or restricted. A List 99 check is carried out as part of the Enhanced Disclosure process; however, obtaining a List 99 check separately may enable an applicant to start work before the Enhanced Disclosure is completed.

There are a variety of guidelines, rules and regulations for the acceptance/ appropriateness/ eligibility of a List 99 check. These are specific to different organisations within the education sector and vary depending on the post being applied for and the reasons for the List 99 entry.

If you have any doubts whether a List 99 check is appropriate/ acceptable for your applicant/s, we would advise you to check with the relevant educational organisation, prior to ordering from us.

A list 99 check (a prerequisite for those wishing to work in an Education setting) does not include a check against the ISA Children's Barred List, which contains information about people barred or restricted from working with children in **any** setting. This can only be obtained as part of the Enhanced Disclosure process.

So, a separate List 99 check, depending on the result, may enable an applicant to start work while the Enhanced Disclosure is being processed (subject of course to all other relevant references and pre-employment checks being completed)..."
Source: <http://www.criminalrecordchecks.co.uk/list-99-checks.htm>

Vetting and Barring Scheme (Previously known as list 99 checks)

The Independent Safeguarding Authority (ISA) assesses every person who wants to work, or volunteer, with children or vulnerable adults. The check is completed using information previously found in:

-        the Protection of Vulnerable Adults (PoVA) list

-        the Protection of Children Act (PoCA) list

-        List 99 (a list of people considered unsuitable for work with children, held by the Department for Children, Schools and Families).

This information is assessed to decide whether to give the individual concerned ISA registration, or put them on one of the ISA Barred Lists. It is not a replacement for a CRB, but can be done whilst waiting for a CRB check to come through.

The records are constantly updated as fresh information is gathered. If new data indicates that an individual might pose a risk to vulnerable people, they will be put on one of the ISA Barred Lists immediately.

If your employee has an enhanced CRB Disclosure, it is not necessary to have them checked against the ISA as this would have already been carried out within the CRB process.

Source: <http://www.parenta.com/list99-checks/>

This raises, of course, a number of human rights and civil liberties issues, not least because a person could be added to a list barring them from working with children or vulnerable adults when they ought not to be on that list at all because, for example, they have committed no crimes and have been erroneously added to the list **without being informed that they are on the list**.

In total, Reynolds had been asked 31 questions in 25 minutes. A huge 93.5% of the questions were closed. These figures demonstrate Twist's mindset – she restricted her questioning to such a high proportion of closed questions because she was not interested in justice but rather she sought to obtain specific information that she could later manipulate against Pead.

disciplinary

Having completed all of the interviews that she saw fit to conduct and having gathered all of the evidence together, Twist decided that the allegations were such that this should proceed to a full disciplinary hearing.

There was no evidence, of course. The interviews had been conducted in such a way that an average of 81% of all the questions asked by Twist were closed. No pupils or parents and carers had been interviewed. No third party had been interviewed. Not all of Pead's staff had been interviewed – Fraser Hall, for example, was a glaring omission from Twist's list of interviewees.

The purpose of this exercise was to keep Brian Pead busy. By dismissing Maryn Murray for racism and the sexual grooming of young girls, he had inadvertently broken the chain of command that allowed her to work in schools without CRB checks and without qualified teacher status.

Pead had to be marginalised and isolated. Lambeth worked hard to turn people against him and to discredit him.

Meanwhile, the South African racist and pervert was continuing to work in Lambeth schools. She was working in Norwood School for Girls.

disciplinary hearing - day 1

The first day of the Disciplinary Hearing took place on Monday 23 July 2007 – more than **seven months** after his unlawful suspension. It was held in Room 2 of the Professional Development Centre at International House in Brixton. The hearing commenced at 9.45am – which meant, of course, that Pead would have to leave his house by 7.30am in order to ensure his timely arrival.

This meeting was costing the Lambeth taxpayer thousands of pounds. Lambeth lined up several high fee earners. Cathy Twist was in attendance with Mary White. Judith Hare, a Lambeth Advisor, was Chairwoman of the Disciplinary Panel. She was supported by Carol Palmer from Human Resources, Paul Barraclough, an Education Advisor and Brian Netto, head of the Ethnic Minorities Achievement Team (EMAT). Rene Katisa was the note taker.

Hare asked Pead if he required representation and his reply was that he had already had representation in the form of Alex Passman, but he had been denied by Lambeth. Pead knew that this was an abuse of process, but, as his late father often told him, "Give them enough rope and they will hang themselves."

Pead explained that he had asked John Callow – a good friend – to be in attendance, but Lambeth denied his presence, too.

Lambeth refused all of Pead's requests for representation. Of course, they did this because they did not want this farce being made public. They wanted to isolate Pead and control him.

Hare then asked Pead if he admitted or denied the allegations against him and he said that he denied them all.

Management in the form of Twist read out her report. It was the most biased and one-dimensional report that it was possible to produce. After this report was read out, Hare again asked Pead if he was happy to continue without representation. He said he was not at all happy, but that he would continue. He knew the entire proceedings were a farce and that – in his opinion – it was best to deal with them and move on.

Twist's first witness was Maryn Murray, whom Twist said "...now works as a consultant at Norwood School for Girls..."

This was an unbelievable comment for her to make. In earlier chapters, it has been shown that Twist was aware that Pead had dismissed Murray for racism and sexual impropriety and here was Twist almost boasting that Murray had been re-employed by Lambeth and was now working in an all-girls' school.

Murray, of course, was given the stage by Twist to simply reiterate all that had been written in the 8-page report against Pead.

But Twist had underestimated Murray's hubris. Having been given the stage, Murray allowed herself to run away with herself. When speaking about the Chloe Gordon "low-cut top" incident, she said "...I think Chloe said that she felt uncomfortable about the conversation..."

This was designed to create a feeling of antipathy towards Pead, but in fact it ensured – in that one single comment – that Twist had not conducted a fair and thorough investigation and that the matter was a Child Protection matter. This meant that Chloe Gordon should have been interviewed, along with her parents. The fact that they were not interviewed renders the entire proceedings null and void.

Then Murray attempted to make matters even worse for Pead: "...Sometimes female students, vulnerable female students would stay very late into the evening and he would take them in separate private areas..."

Clearly nonsense, all of the other members of staff had said that there were no private areas in the Centre. Even Barry Gilhooly had confirmed this.

At this point, had the Panel consisted of genuine members rather than corrupt officials who had been lined up to deliver a guilty verdict, one of the panel members would have asked her to provide firm details. What were the names of these girls? How late would they stay? Where were the private areas? How did you know this if you went home on time?

Twist asked Murray to explain to the Panel about Pead's unfair treatment of female pupils.

Murray: He allowed two female students to write their exams early which was against exam regulations. I had been an exam invigilator for 5 years in my previous school and was fully aware of the exam conditions and policies very well.

In her hubris, Murray laid claim to having been an exam invigilator for five years at St. Augustine's Priory School in Ealing. Why, then, had she not mentioned this before when asked the same question by Twist of 19 January 2007?

Even more worryingly, why did no Panel member ask her to substantiate her claim?

But it has already been shown elsewhere in this book that one of the students named by Murray as having received 'preferential treatment' had not, in fact, even sat the exam! This was corroborated by Colin Hill, who produced robust and incontrovertible evidence that she had not sat the exam.

Twist knew this. Twist had interviewed Hill herself. Why, then, did she not stop Murray in her flow and ask her to provide evidence?

Murray's entire testimony to the Panel was fabricated. At no point was she asked to provide evidence of her assertions.

Then the Chairperson, Judith Hare, asked Murray what guidelines there were in dealing with such vulnerable pupils. Murray claimed that there were none. Yet in her interviews in January and indeed in her 8-page submission to Lambeth, she stated that Pead had produced reams and reams of materials about psychology and approaches on how to deal with difficult and emotionally-damaged pupils.

Yet not a single Panel member picked Murray up on this issue.

Pead knew his fate.

Then Carol Palmer asked Murray about a definition of harassment. She was leading Murray down a path, and Murray was happy to follow. It was clear to Pead – who sat impassively observing this farce – that Lambeth wanted to find him guilty of harassment.

Not one Panel member challenged Murray about a single statement that she made. All they did was simply ask her further questions which were designed to show Pead in a negative light. Murray, of course, was happy to do this. She was now on the Lambeth payroll as a consultant.

She left at 2.55pm. With two natural breaks, Murray had been given a platform for her vitriolic comments for four-and-a-half hours.

Twist's next witness was Rosa Vaz, who confirmed that no member of staff had ever raised a complaint against Pead before he dismissed Murray.

Twist asked Vaz: "...Were you aware that Pead was carrying out Life Coaching work at the Centre?" to which Vaz replied, "...No..."

Not one Panel member asked Twist to provide evidence of this allegation. Brian Pead had never carried out such work at the Centre, yet Twist introduced the allegation here as if it were fact. The fools on the Panel merely soaked it all up.

Twist asked Vaz if she had received an email from Pead on 6 May 2006 concerning advice on contracts. She agreed that he had emailed her asking about contracts. This completely undermines Twist's assertion that Pead did not consult Lambeth in respect of contracts.

When Twist had finished with Vaz (she was only asked sixteen questions – all of which were closed), Pead asked just one:

Pead: Did you receive a copy of the allegations made about me before your interview?

Vaz: Barry received all the allegations and I was involved in the decision for suspension. So, yes, I would have seen them before my interview.

This had been an important question as far as Brian Pead was concerned. He was not concerned about the little details of Murray's contract – that was all smoke and mirrors. What he was interested in was an abuse of process, and Vaz had admitted that she had been sent a copy of all of the allegations before a decision was taken to suspend Pead.

At 15:55, Barry Gilhooly entered the room.

Twist asked Gilhooly when he first heard about the allegations. Gilhooly claimed that he had first received a telephone call from Murray then had a written document in November 2006.

Gilhooly claimed to have had concerns about Pead's management style. Yet he was never asked to produce evidence of these concerns. He was never asked why – if he had really had such concerns – he had awarded Pead a substantial pay increase and had claimed that he was a valuable member of staff. Gilhooly's claims to the Panel did not accord with the evidence.

When asked by Twist about the email that Anya Hiley had sent, Gilhooly also claimed that he had met with her, her line manager and the entire head of the Connexions service. Gilhooly failed to mention this in **three** previous statements. He was 'laying it on thick'. Note how he fails to provide names or dates and times of these alleged meetings.

Gilhooly also confirmed that both the Old Library Centre in West Norwood and the Redfearn Centre in Vauxhall were open plan so that he did not have any worries about the safety of children. Why then did no Panel member think to ask why this was even an issue?

Gilhooly was asked about Murray's contract and said that Pead had, in fact, always consulted with him about a possible contract for Murray.

When asked if he had been aware that Murray's contract had been terminated, Gilhooly lied. He said he had never been consulted about it.

Twist then asked Gilhooly an incorrect question: "...Were you aware that Pead had made special arrangements for two female students to take their GCSE exams?" to which Gilhooly replied, "...No..."

Twist had the knack of making a false statement sound as if it were a fact. Two students had not been given special arrangements.

When asked by Twist if he was aware if Pead had shown favourable treatment towards pupils, Gilhooly replied, "...No..."

Pead then had an opportunity to question his line manager: "...Did you not question the veracity of these allegations after I had dismissed Murray on your instructions after she had been racist and grooming young white girls?"

Gilhooly replied, "...I was taken aback by the allegations. I told her that we would have to follow the policy and the next stage was to test out the allegations..."

Of course that is the next stage in any similar scenario – the allegations must be robustly examined. But this was not done. Lambeth merely accepted Murray's word on every allegation. Even when Pead provided robust evidence that he had not been masturbated in the theatre, no-one at Lambeth thought to question the veracity of the other allegations. Lambeth merely lined up any idiot – and there were plenty of them on the Lambeth payroll – who could be wheeled out to say anything their paymasters wanted them to say.

In the previously mentioned Roldan case, Justices Etherton and Elias stated that "...Section 98(4) of the Employment Rights Act focuses on the need for an employer to act reasonably in all the circumstances. In A v B [2003] IRLR 405 the Employment Appeals Tribunal [EAT] (Elias J presiding) held that the relevant circumstances include the gravity of the charge and their potential effect upon the employee. So it is particularly important that employers take seriously their responsibilities to conduct a fair investigation where, as on the facts of that case, the employee's reputation or ability to work in his or her chosen field of employment is potentially apposite. In A v B the EAT said this:

"Serious allegations of criminal misbehaviour, at least where disputed, must always be the subject of the most careful investigation..."

The emphasis is the authors'. It is evident that Pead had been subjected to serious allegations of criminal behaviour and yet he had not received anything like a "...most careful investigation..." This Disciplinary Panel was yet a further example of corrupt Lambeth Council officials masquerading as honest officials.

Judith Hare asked Gilhooly a telling question: "...Had you received Murray's allegations by the time her contract was terminated?" to which Gilhooly replied, "...No..."

Not a single Panel member picked up on this damaging answer.

The meeting concluded at 5pm. It had been a full day. Pead had a two-hour journey home. This was all part of Lambeth's policy – keep him busy and keep his head turned away from the truth about Murray's grooming and racism and towards these unfounded and spurious allegations.

96

disciplinary hearing – day 2

hiley farcical

Tuesday 24 July 2007, 10:00

Room 2, Professional Development Centre Suite, International House

In attendance: Cathy Twist – Assistant Director, Standards Division
Mary White, Human Resources Consultant
Judith Hare, Advisors Team Leader (Chair)
Carol Palmer – Principal Human Resources Manager
Paul Barraclough – Education Advisor
Brian Netto – Head of Ethnic Minorities Achievement Team
(EMAT)
Rene Katisa – Note taker

The full transcript of this Disciplinary Hearing can be found online at
www.lambethchildabuseandcoverup.com

For any decent manager who possesses qualities of honesty and integrity, it makes for uncomfortable reading.

Anya Hiley, the unmarried close confidante of the Machiavellian Murray, was a Connexions Advisor and had significant access to the private contact details of children. We saw in chapter 7 that Hiley's remit was to "...Work with a caseload of young people who require intensive, individual support, befriending and mentoring. Maintain contact with young people forming caseload, and monitor the progress of all young people referred to the Connexions service. Keep accurate records of all contacts..."

This post gave Hiley significant access to young girls. She had to have 'intensive' relationships with the young people she was supposed to be mentoring. The authors allege that Hiley was working with Murray to groom young girls for her own pleasure and also that of others higher up in the 'food chain'.

Some of Hiley's testimony to the hearing is reproduced below. Note her use of language and how similar it is to Murray's:

Hiley: He made some uncanny observations about me. [...] At that stage I was intrigued how he could see things about me...

Maryn Murray had also observed that Pead was able to 'read' her.

Then Hiley goes on to tell the Disciplinary Panel about her and Annabel Field, whose friendly and supportive email to Pead can be found in chapter 18.

Twist: Can you describe Annabel Field's relationship with Brian Pead?

Hiley: Only through what Annabel told me. I didn't see them together that much. She said that she felt uncomfortable. Pead asked her loads of personal questions that she wished she hadn't answered and divulged. He drew her into those conversations and it sounded like they had some heated debates about his inconsistencies on the treatment of students. From my experience, too, he would not take criticism and didn't like being challenged.

The question has to be asked: "Why did Annabel Field never report these allegations herself to anybody?" She might have spoken with Pead's Line Manager. She might have spoken with Marion Richards, the English consultant to Lambeth. She, in fact, did neither.

And – if she was so concerned about her conversations with Pead – why did she allow herself, at the age of 25, to become involved in them? And why did she not put this in her email to Brian Pead on 17 April 2006, some **fourteen months** before this Disciplinary Hearing?

But another question has also to be asked: how did Anya Hiley, who worked two floors above Pead, acquire all of this information?

She tells the panel that she discussed Brian Pead with Annabel Field. This is mere hearsay. Anybody can say anything about anyone else ... but what is needed is robust evidence. No such evidence against Pead existed.

The main question to be asked, of course, is why did Twist not call Annabel Field as a witness?

The answer, of course, is that had Twist called Field as a witness, she knew that Brian Pead's robust questioning would have exposed her lies and those of her accomplices.

Justices Etherton and Elias in their Judgment in the Roldan case state that "...It is common experience that if part of a story begins to unravel, other aspects may do so also. Doubts begin to emerge and the interpretation of actions changes..."

Pead had shown Twist significant doubts in Murray's allegations, yet Twist had taken this farce all the way to a Disciplinary Hearing and failed to call Annabel Field.

The next part of the Disciplinary Hearing transcript makes for further disturbing reading.

Twist: You raised concerns to your line manager about Brian Pead. Can you describe what these were?

Hiley: My concerns were in relation to how uncomfortable he made me feel on a personal level. His manner and how he was intrusive, analytical and controlling. His treatment of students and I thought that if that was how he made me feel as an adult how he would be making the students feel. Also, his one-to-ones with young women and I noticed that they followed a pattern.

Hiley's description of Pead, of course, matches precisely with Murray's description of him. She doesn't, however, provide examples of his alleged intrusiveness, analysis or controlling behaviour which, in any event, is wholly unsupported with substantial evidence from psychologists and counsellors who know Pead.

The farcical interview of Hiley continues:

Twist: Can you describe Brian Pead's pattern with these young women?

[This was a rare open question from Twist.]

Hiley: Blonde, pretty, vulnerable and with a lot of problems. He would use life coaching as a reason for spending time with these students and I was concerned especially as how he made me feel uncomfortable.

Twist: In your interview on the 25 January 2007, you said that "...he may be grooming women..." What did you mean by that?

Hiley: His favourable treatment of women and from my encounter with him, is what I believed was the first stage.

At no point did Twist ever ask Hiley to name these alleged "pretty" girls that Pead was supposed to be grooming.

At no point did Twist interview these pupils.

At no point were they called as witnesses.

The case against Pead was entirely based on hearsay from a woman who had been dismissed for sexual misconduct and who was her best friend.

And Murray was supported by Gilhooly and Ermina/ Paul Waters.

From her comments, it is clear that Anya Hiley has lied. She alleges all this activity was going on and yet she worked two floors above Pead and she was also often out of the building on visits within the community.

Justices Etherton and Elias in their Judgment in the Roldan case stated [at 53] that "...the employers ought at least to have tested the evidence (against Roldan)..." In that particular case, an inexperienced health care assistant made complaints against nurse Roldan based on the geography of a nursing room. Justices Etherton and Elias – sitting in the High Court of Justice (Civil Division) in the Strand – set down that it was proper for an investigating officer to have visited the nursing room in question. In the Roldan case, the investigating officer failed to take this basic step. In this particular case, Twist and Hare failed to visit the White Bear Theatre, the Old Library in West Norwood and the Redfearn Centre. Justices Etherton and Elias found in favour of Roldan.

Anya Hiley did confirm, however, that Brian Pead was called Brian Johnson at the Centre, thus proving that Rosa Vaz had lied in **her** statement.

Further examples of lies or - at the very least – misinformation followed:

Twist: Did you know of any inconsistencies of Pead's treatment of students with regards to rewards and sanctions?

Hiley: To the students he liked. Another student Cassandra Trimmings was allowed to sit her exam at another time than everyone else. Cassandra was a young woman who fitted that pattern, she was vulnerable and he seemed to have an extensive knowledge of her background. I was concerned about the amount of time that Pead spent with her. One day Cassandra's boyfriend came into the school demanding to see Brian, because he was convinced that Brian was sleeping with the student.

That this entire Disciplinary Hearing was nothing more than mere pretence is in no doubt. As the Head of the Centre, part of Brian Pead's role was to gather as much information about each student as possible, so that he could better understand them and serve their needs. He devised a database which contained all this information on every pupil – regardless of gender, race or any other factor.

Here Hiley attempts to cast aspersions on Pead by stating that Cassandra Trimmings was a vulnerable pupil. Of course she was. Almost all of the pupils at the OLCVS were vulnerable. Two had terminated pregnancies whilst being under the lawful age for sex. One young man was a 'rent boy' in London. This information was known to Social Services. Others had serious psychological issues. They were all outside of mainstream education – of course they were vulnerable. And of course Pead, as Head of Centre, would have an "...extensive knowledge..." of each pupil's background. That was his job. There was nothing strange in that.

And then Hiley maliciously introduces the scenario of Cassandra's boyfriend who did, indeed, come into the OLCVS, 'wanting it out' with Pead. It was obvious to Pead as they spoke that the boy was controlling and jealous in the extreme. The discussion ended without any problems.

However, the question needs to be asked: "How did Anya Hiley, working two floors above Pead, come by this information, particularly when the boy came in on a day when Hiley wasn't working in the building but out on calls in the community?"

As a postscript to that event, the boyfriend later kidnapped Cassandra in a hotel room and refused to let her go until the situation was resolved by the police. This information was conveniently omitted by Hiley.

Some of Pead's discussions with Cassandra involved the controlling boyfriend, but other private information will remain exactly that – private.

Twist: Why do you think that Cassandra's boyfriend came into the school?

Hiley: Cassandra must have talked a lot about Pead to her boyfriend. The boyfriend would have been jealous and wondered why she was talking about her teacher so much and whether they were having a relationship. I remember it was mentioned that Cassandra's boyfriend came to school a few times.

Thus Hiley – who made false allegations about Pead and who said she was made uncomfortable by his 'analytical' approach - appears to have analysed the event between Cassandra and her boyfriend rather extensively. Hiley claimed that the boyfriend had visited the OLCVS "...on a number of occasions..." Not only is this untrue – he visited only once – she provides no dates for the alleged visits. She makes a number of assumptions, none of which Twist asks her to justify.

Twist: Did you ever see the boyfriend?

Hiley: No I didn't. Cassandra was positive about Pead and how he was very supportive of her. There was no suggestion that they were sleeping together, but it says a lot about the intensity of the relationship for her boyfriend to come to the school and I also think it says a lot about his boundaries with students.

This reply from Hiley makes for interesting reading. She actually confirms that Cassandra had said that Brian Pead was extremely supportive of her. This would rather match what Annabel Field had also put in writing: the fact that she felt supported by Brian. It would match what Sandra Roach said about him. And Colin Hill. And Derek Langan. And Fraser Hall. And Duane Maddison. And, in earlier chapters, his counselling peers also noted how he had supported them, and one even noted that he "...is the best example of how to be..."

Thus there is much evidence in the public domain which proves that Brian Pead is a very supportive person and that this is usually in the form of emotional support. Only the pernicious Hiley and malevolent Murray – and to some extent the dismissed Eloise Whitmore – seemed to think differently.

Hiley had been asked if she had ever seen 'the boyfriend' in the OLCVS and she said that she hadn't. How, then – other than from hearsay which is inadmissible evidence in this situation – could she have come by this (false) information?

Twist: You've mentioned the blonde, pretty girls but can you tell us what was the ethnic mix of the OLCVS?

Hiley: There were around 60 students in 2 groups. There was a big ethnic mix of students.

Note here how Twist uses the term "...blonde, pretty girls..." in order to ensure that this terminology is made known to all those present and to anyone reading the transcript. Her investigation was not thorough and it was not fair.

Note, too, that Hiley is imprecise. As a Connexions Advisor to the school, she would have had precise information about the numbers of pupils attending the OLCVS and would have records about the ethnic origin of pupils since this is information that both Lambeth Council and Connexions collects. Had Hiley thoroughly prepared for the interview, she would have ensured that she would have had this information to hand. Hiley was neither thorough nor professional. Her language is that of the average eight year old: "...There was a big ethnic mix..."

Twist: Can you tell us the names or initials of the girls that followed the pattern you mentioned before?

Hiley: There were 3 or 4 girls including Cassandra and another girl beginning with G who wasn't blonde but Pead favoured her.

Hiley claimed that she had witnessed numerous hour-long meetings between Pead and "...pretty, blonde girls...", yet she is unable to even name them when called upon to do so. She is also imprecise about the number of girls. She can't even recall the name of pupil 'G'. [This would be Gemma Mandry.]

Yet, this seeming paragon of religious virtue informed the panel that she can read a person's mind and his emotions, when she claimed "...he favoured G..." How would she know this? Did her ever tell her that? The answer is no.

Thus, this person who worked two floors above Pead, can only be making an assumption based on the small number of times that she saw Pead and Mandry interact. Pead did not favour any pupil. He had a close working connection with **all** of his students, just as he had done for more than 25 years in teaching, **without a single incident against his name.**

Twist: As a visitor, did you feel and see his treatment of these students was different to the other students?

Hiley: Yes, this is what I observed and saw.

The futility of Twist's question – when asked in isolation – is quite staggering. At no point did she ask Hiley to explain exactly what she felt or saw. At no point did she ask Hiley how she came to these decisions when she worked two floors above Pead and the students. At no point did Twist ask Hiley for any evidential proof. Hiley based her account, it would seem, purely on her feelings and, of course, her numerous 'playground' discussions with Murray. At no point did Twist ask Hiley about her relationship with Murray – heaven forbid that that topic should be discussed in a disciplinary hearing set up to establish the 'truth'.

Why would Twist avoid such questions if she were to be thorough and professional?

However, it was not only Twist who was unprofessional and asked leading questions.

Carol Palmer, Principal Human Resources Manager at Lambeth, took up the baton and continued running with the farce that was masquerading as a *bona fide* Disciplinary Hearing. The reality was that it was anything but.

Palmer: You mentioned the grooming of female students and young women. Can you explain that a bit more?

Hiley: That was the worst case scenario.

Palmer: Did you share your concerns with the deputy head?

Hiley: I knew she was struggling in her job and with her working relationship with Brian. We had become friends and I may have verbalised my concerns to her but not in so many words.

Carol Palmer displays an appalling lack of professionalism in this extract. This was not mere naivety on her part, but a cunning way to introduce something as fact (grooming) that was simply not fact at all.

That Palmer allows Hiley to answer the question with a bland "...That was the worst case scenario..." is as unprofessional as one could get.

The answer by Hiley says absolutely nothing. What was the worst case scenario? She was asked to explain about possible grooming of young women and fails to answer the question at all.

Hiley then goes on to say that she had, in fact, discussed the case with Maryn Murray, the woman who was, in fact, grooming young girls at the OLCVS and Hiley, of course, aligned herself with Murray. Little wonder, then, that Hiley should attempt to throw mud at Brian Pead.

And little wonder that it was only Hiley and Murray who 'saw' this potential grooming, and Hiley worked two storeys above the OLCVS. One has to ask how she managed to see all of this alleged activity when she was supposed to be getting on with her own job, two floors above. There is little doubt that Hiley and Murray – both of whom make mention of 'pretty' or 'attractive' girls – colluded on the allegations against the innocent Brian Pead.

Then Brian Netto – Head of the EMAT team which integrated the refugee and asylum seekers into the OLCVS through Mus Bagum – asks a question:

Netto: You said you raised your concerns and wrote an email to your line manager. Why didn't you pursue it?

Hiley: As you all heard, there was no concrete evidence. I couldn't quantify it as they were my concerns. I was being very watchful of his behaviour with students and young women and I raised concerns when I heard that he used other names. At that point I couldn't underpin those concerns. That's when I emailed my manager and this was then escalated to Barry. I had a meeting with Barry and the outcome was because I had no concrete evidence there couldn't be an investigation. Barry said that he appreciated my concerns. It was explained to me that nothing further could happen. This happened summer 2006. The concerns I've expressed were my original concerns.

Hiley states on the record that she "...had concerns about Brian Pead..." but that there was "...no concrete evidence..." and that therefore there could not be an investigation. She also states that she went behind Pead's back and met with Barry Gilhooly who told her that without any evidence, nothing could be done. Gilhooly had claimed that two other people had been present at this meeting – Glenice Lake, Hiley's line manager, and the unnamed Head of the Connexions service. If this were true, why does Hiley fail to mention it here to the Panel? Why did Hiley omit it from her original statement of 25 January 2007?

Is it not strange that Hiley should be 'watchful' of his behaviour when she should have been getting on with her own job? Is it not strange that she then embarked upon a process of obtaining 'evidence' to prove her strange feelings around Pead, when no-one else had these feelings about it? And is it not strange that the unmarried Hiley should embark upon a campaign of harassment against Pead and collude with Murray in an effort to remove Pead from his post and have Murray installed as Head of Centre?

Neither did Hiley produce any documentary evidence of these alleged abuses, meetings or other assignations. This was all in her mind. No-one on the Panel asked her to produce any evidence, even though she referred to "...gathering evidence..."

Since Hiley and Murray had full access to all the contact details of all the students at the OLCVS, what were their motives?

At 11:15, Hiley left the room and there was a 15-minute break.

eloise whitmore - 2

Eloise Whitmore – who had failed her first probationary period and had been removed from her post by Rosa Vaz – was then called as a witness by Twist at 11.30am. To suggest that the Disciplinary Hearing was fair would be implausible.

Yet Whitmore served a purpose. Too stupid to even see it, she had been lined up as just another duck in a row to throw as much mud as she could at Pead in the hope that some of it would stick. What she failed to understand – due, in Pead's opinion, to her appalling lack of self-awareness – was that when mud is thrown, it often says more about the person throwing it than it does about the person at whom it is aimed.

Whitmore claimed that "...Gemma was 14 and vulnerable...and Pead made her cups of tea, especially if she was late..."

Whitmore was referring to Gemma Mandry. She would often arrive late and in a state of heightened emotional distress, so Pead wisely made her a cup of tea and talked to her about her state of mind before placing her with all the other students. This type of behaviour by Pead was highly praised by Nadia Al-Khudhairy, a research psychologist and counsellor with King's College, London.

It is probably more sensible – when deciding whether Al-Khudhairy or Whitmore would make the more credible witness – to lean towards the educated, intelligent, sensitive and articulate Al-Khudhairy rather than the uneducated, boorish, insensitive and inarticulate Whitmore, as Pead has described her. And Whitmore had a strong propensity to lie. Furthermore, she stated on the record that she had been sent a copy of Maryn Murray's 8-page report **before** she had even been interviewed!

In fact, **all** of the Lambeth witnesses were sent a copy prior to being interviewed in an appalling abuse of process.

The pugnacious Whitmore, when asked why she had never made her alleged concerns public prior to this Disciplinary Hearing, replied, "...I was going to do it after my second probationary meeting..."

It took her five attempts and two hours to type a one-page letter and she **was** going to report her concerns, but never got round to it until **after she had been dismissed**. The pattern with Murray is unmistakable – save for the corrupt Twist who did apparently miss the link.

Brian Pead then asked Whitmore a classic sucker-punch question. Whitmore had claimed to Twist and now to the Panel, that working for Pead had left her

"...distraught... unable to function ... unable to leave the house... depressed..." so Pead merely asked: "...Did you consult your doctor?" Whitmore, of course, said "...No..."

Whitmore also stated on the record that this job was an entirely new career for her. This corroborated what Pead knew – that she was simply not up to the task. He had been right to fail her during her first probationary period.

The Eloise Whitmore interview had lasted for an hour and 35 minutes. It added nothing material to the proceedings but at least it provided her with a platform to vent her very nasty feelings. Lambeth had paid her the sum of £8,000 prior to her interview. She had earnt £84.21 per minute to vent her anger at Brian Pead and create as much damage as she possibly could. It seems like a significant sum of money, but in the process she sold whatever was left of her soul.

Yet the main question remains: why did Lambeth Council pay £8,000 of taxpayers' money to her when she failed her probationary period? Thousands of people all over the UK (and, indeed, the world) fail their probationary period. They do not get handsomely rewarded. Whitmore received a significant sum of money for being inept at her job. But why had Gilhooly – if he really wanted the OLCVS to be a success – put her there in the first place? Even a cursory glance of her CV would have shown an experienced manager that she was not capable of holding down the job as school administration officer. In fact, her CV showed that she rarely held down **any** job, always moving from job to job and rarely staying longer than six months in any one place. Friends of Pead often mentioned to him that "...no-one in their right mind would have put her in that post if they wanted the venture to be successful..."

It seemed inconceivable, therefore, that Gilhooly had not only put her in that post, but he had given her a one-year contract which even the Head of Centre did not have. Clearly Gilhooly had an ulterior motive in placing her there. Then, just before Pead failed her probationary period, Gilhooly sent in Maryn Murray, who was an unqualified teacher from South Africa who had not been CRB checked by Lambeth.

At this stage, Gilhooly had placed an inexperienced and unqualified school secretary in the OLCVS, an unqualified teacher to teach ICT, and a Connexions personal advisor who clearly had no understanding of the needs of the pupils at the OLCVS. What on earth was motivating Gilhooly in placing these pieces on the chess board that was the OLCVS? Why did he need these pieces in position at any cost? What game was he playing?

colin hill

After a thirty-minute break for lunch, the Panel interviewed Colin Hill.

Lambeth had an assortment of people whom they wheeled out every half-an-hour or so – all with one common purpose: to 'officially' rid the OLCVS of Brian Pead, who had already been replaced. Colin Hill had been Acting Head of the OLCVS between Pead's suspension in December 2006 and April 2007, when Ginni Bealing took over as the new Head teacher.

Colin Hill – a year or two older than Pead – was extremely favourable towards him. This was no accident. It was common knowledge that the two men shared many similar philosophical attitudes with regards to teaching and Lambeth needed to keep up the pretence that this was a *bona fide* Disciplinary Hearing when the intelligentsia knew that it was nothing of the sort. But the Murrays and the Hileys and the Whitmores believed in the process because it deflected attention away from themselves and their inadequacies.

"...My name is Colin Hill and I took on the role of Acting Deputy Head and prior to that I was English and Media teacher at OLCVS. I was Acting Deputy Head from November 2006 and also an exam officer..."

When asked by Twist to describe Pead's management style, Hill replied: "...He made decisions, he was direct and authoritative. We had regular reviews on his management style; every matter was discussed at staff meetings. Brian always asked staff to give feedback on his management style and this was a regular feature. He wanted us to be part of a collective..."

The late Bill Shankly was more than just a football manager. He was a socialist with a keen understanding of human nature. In his autobiography *Shankly* (Arthur Barker, 1976) he wrote: "...The socialism I believe in is not really politics. It is a way of living. It is humanity. I believe the only way to live and be truly successful is by collective effort, with everyone working for each other, everyone helping each other, and everyone having a share of the rewards at the end of the day. [...] It's the way I see football and the way I see life..."

The young Brian Pead – aged around ten or eleven – had heard the voice of the Liverpool manager and become mesmerised by its power and vision. He sought to create an Anfield at the OLCVS in the image of the great Scot. Colin Hill had recognised Pead's passion and humanity.

In his response to Twist, Colin Hill is quite adamant that there were regular reviews of Pead's management style, that the staff was asked to comment on it and that every matter was discussed at staff meetings.

Why, then, did Eloise Whitmore not raise any of her concerns about Pead at these meetings? Why didn't Murray? Why didn't Annabel Field mention that Pead bullied her and made her cry?

No such concerns ever came out until **after** Murray was dismissed and then Hiley and Whitmore joined in the collusion. At one point Annabel Field was also part of the triumvirate, but she regained her locus of control and found her integrity once more. Integrity was something that Hiley, Whitmore and Murray did not possess, as is evident from their interview statements.

Twist then asks Hill: "...Were you aware of mental health checks that Brian Pead asked staff to complete?..." to which Hill replied: "...I don't remember them as that. Brian felt strongly that it was relevant for staff to have good mental health for staff and students, that there should be an integral awareness of the mental, emotional and physical and this should be part of the ethos of the OLCVS..."

By asking the question as she did – a leading question (one of many throughout the 'investigation') – Twist called Pead's workshops for his staff with regard to their own mental health when working with such difficult pupils "...mental health checks..."

Colin Hill recalls that that was not his view of the workshops. He goes on to say that Brian Pead felt strongly about the 'whole pupil' – in other words, he felt it was the responsibility of the OLCVS to take care of the pupils' academic, emotional and physical needs.

But Pead was not promoting these views in isolation. Twist attempted to infer throughout the proceedings that Pead was a maverick madman with an agenda all of his own. Whilst he has the ability to be – and is - his own man, he does nothing without first investigating and then thinking about things. Research forms part of his way of life, and it informs him.

He had long been a student of the wellbeing of pupils and had felt over a period of many years that most schools fail their pupils on many levels but in particular in meeting the emotional needs of pupils. These pupils then leave school and take those emotional problems with them into society at large. Teenage pregnancies are ever-rising. Knife crimes are ever rising. Unemployment is ever rising. Crime in general is rising. He would often talk to friends about the fact that the Government ought to invest in decent talking therapies within schools in order to ameliorate emotional problems amongst the young and then – hopefully –reduce crime and anti-social behaviour once the pupils leave school and join the 'real world' of work and mortgages and families. Indeed, Colin Hill shared many of Pead's views on education.

The United Nations Convention on the Rights of the Child (UNCRC) was something that Pead was aware of. As a boy he was sexually abused and he had long been passionate about improving the lot of survivors of abuse. He had three grand-children of his own at this stage in his life and the rights of his grand-daughters and grand-son were also a passion of his.

Article 12 of the UNCRC states that Governments should ensure that children have the right to express freely their views and to take account of children's views. Children have the right to be heard in any legal or administrative matters that affect them.

Although Pead subscribed to this view, it was not his own view *per se*. He was not the maverick that Twist was portraying him to be.

Article 39 of the UNCRC states that Governments should help restore a child's health, self-respect and dignity after abuse or neglect. Many of the pupils at the OLCVS suffered from abusive relationships in all their forms. Almost all of the pupils suffered from low self-esteem. As Nadia Al-Khudhairy pointed out, Brian Pead was doing an excellent job in repairing the lives of many of the pupils.

Article 29 of the UNCRC states that Education should develop each child's personality, talents and abilities to their fullest potential, as well as develop respect for parents, other members of human society and the environment.

This is precisely what Brian Pead was doing at the OLCVS – as witnessed by the pupils, parents, Alphonso Harris, the Lambeth Detached Youth Worker, by Beverley Williams, (Barry Gilhooly's PA), and by Nadia Al-Khudhairy.

In fact, the only people who felt that Pead was not doing this were the triumvirate of Murray, Hiley and Whitmore.

Lambeth published its own version of the Department of Children and Families Service in 2008 called the *Social and Emotional Aspects of Learning* (SEAL). Although not published at the time Brian Pead was under unlawful suspension, he and other Head Teachers were well aware of its impending publication because notices about it were circulated periodically to them. This is an important document in relation to the charges against Brian Pead inasmuch that he was charged with focussing more on the emotional development of pupils than the academic. But it also shows that his programme of Continuous Professional Development that he put together for the benefit of his staff was exactly the thing he should have done according to the United Nations, to the UK Government and to Lambeth Education. But not to Twist.

The SEAL document provides examples of what a well-run school or pupil referral unit might look like. It provides a set of criteria which a Head teacher or local authority might use in order to see how far a school or PRU meets those criteria. A brief examination of these criteria is relevant at this point.

At A4.7 of the SEAL document, 'The effectiveness with which the school promotes community cohesion', the document states: "...All staff are aware of their own emotional needs and the impact they have on learning & teaching..."

As a therapist, and as a manager of people since the age of 18, Brian Pead was able to identify the strengths and weaknesses of the personnel in his team, and use this information to inform him when constructing a programme of continuous professional development. Murray was always resistant to this area of her working life and often made negative comments about this.

The barriers that she erected to defend herself were some of the most powerful that Brian Pead had ever encountered in his life. The reason she erected such seemingly impregnable barriers was that she was hiding the secret of her penchant for young, white, 'attractive' and 'very attractive' females.

At A4.7 of SEAL, the document states that "...Resources are available to help ALL staff acquire the skills, knowledge and understanding about SEAL. Protocols are provided for adults offering guidance and support to pupils so that it is consistent with SEAL..."

Brian Pead had ensured that such protocols were in place.

The role of a counsellor usually embodies knowledge of a wide range of approaches to deal with human distress. Indeed, Pead was studying for a Diploma in Humanistic Integrative Counselling, and thus the course of study was specifically tailored to introduce all students to a wide range of therapeutic approaches. At A4.7 of SEAL, the document states: "...Staff have a knowledge and understanding of SEAL and are aware of the significance of modelling these skills (e.g. solution-focused approach, conflict resolution, and assertive strategies)..." Pead had a very good working knowledge of these approaches – and several others – and was thus working within the guidelines set down by the Department of Children and Family Services and Lambeth Education Authority.

This Disciplinary Hearing made no sense whatsoever, since Brian Pead was assiduously following the national and local guidelines.

Furthermore, at A4.7 of SEAL, the document states that in a well-managed school or PRU working within the emotional wellbeing guidelines, "...All members of staff have knowledge of the social and emotional aspects of learning and model, coach and promote it throughout the school day..."

Brian Pead had ensured that this occurred, though Murray was extremely resistant.

At A4.7 of SEAL, the document states "...Staff skills, knowledge and understanding are continually being updated through CPD and group and individual reflection..."

Brian Pead was castigated by Twist, who cited that his interventions were "...intrusive...", whereas, in fact, they were not intrusive at all, but a necessary part of the work being undertaken at the Pupil Referral Unit.

At A4.7 of SEAL, the document states: "...Staff have high levels of understanding of the social and emotional aspects of learning and appropriate pedagogical approaches to promoting SEAL..."

Brian Pead, in order to meet this outcome, authored a programme of continuous professional development (CPD).

This Government-published document states on page 7 that: "...the key issue is that schools have a direct influence on the emotional health of their pupils and staff; and that this, in turn, has an impact on academic and other achievement..."

Academic achievement at the OLCVS surpassed all expectations when taking into consideration the baseline level of ability of the pupils taking the examinations and socio-economic factors. Brian Pead had based his role upon concepts promulgated by the Government itself.

The National Curriculum and the OfSTED Framework for inspecting schools (2003) place clear requirements on schools to take account of and promote Emotional Health and Wellbeing. The National Curriculum states: "...The personal development of pupils, spiritually, morally, socially and culturally, plays a significant part in their ability to learn and to achieve. Development in both areas is essential to raising standards of attainment for all pupils..."

Sources:
<Promoting Emotional Health and Wellbeing, Crown Copyright, 2004, page 9>
<Promoting Mental Health and Wellbeing in Lambeth, Lambeth Mental Health Promotion Strategy 2005-2008, published 20 June 2005>

Thus Pead was running the OLCVS according to published standards. Cathy Twist was an Assistant Director in the Standards division of Lambeth Education. She knew that there was never a case against Pead, but she had to maintain the illusion.

She quizzes Colin Hill again.

Twist: Were you aware of how staff felt about the mental health checks, staff feeling uncomfortable or that they were inappropriate?

Note here that Twist – despite being told by Hill that he did not view the workshops about mental health as 'mental health checks' – continues to call them that. This is yet another example of her unprofessionalism and that she had only one outcome in mind: to rid Lambeth of Pead. He knew too much.

Hill: Some members of staff really flourished and didn't think that the questions were too personal. One or two staff members including Maryn felt disconcerted about what their expectations were and whether they should be considering this as part of their personal and professional development. Brian reminded us that it was important for staff to be mentally healthy to do their work. He said that "it would be ill-advised not to take part" and that if staff weren't developed then we wouldn't have the right tools to do our jobs..."

Colin Hill represented Brian Pead extremely well at this point in his interview with Twist.

Twist then asked Hill to describe his relationship with Brian Pead. Hill replied that Pead "...was approachable, respectful, and he kept my personal concerns private, which I appreciated. We had an equal relationship man to man, and as a manager he was supportive..."

Here is yet another member of Pead's staff who states on the record that Brian Pead is a supportive manager. Hill also describes other qualities of being approachable, respectful and confidential. Hill describes the relationship as being 'equal'.

Twist asked Hill whether he had any one-to-one meetings with Pead.

Hill replied, "...Yes, we had weekly meetings. Sometimes we met every two weeks at our request. If it was too busy then we would have to reschedule. I found them to be very supportive..."

Again, Hill uses the word 'supported'. He doesn't say that Pead was 'intrusive'. Indeed, he had already praised Pead's ability to remain discreet. And Hill describes the amount of flexibility in his work. This militates against Murray's description of Pead as an inflexible and controlling autocrat.

When asked by Twist about Pead using the name of Steve Goodfellow (which he never did at the OLCVS) and whether this caused any problems for him, Hill replied: "...No, I didn't [have any concerns] because my partner is a psychotherapist and it's common practice to use a different name..."

This is a point which Pead had made all along. Had Twist conducted a thorough and fair investigation, she would have established that it is common practice amongst therapists to use different names, but Twist was attempting to make political capital out of Pead's lawful use of names.

When asked to describe Murray, Hill said she had a "...strident approach..." and that she would often wag her finger at staff and pupils whenever she spoke to them. She often adopted a 'lecturing' tone when speaking with peers, as if she was the only one who knew anything.

When asked whether Pead treated male and female staff differently, Hill replied, "...Differently, yes, due to their personality and their needs. It wasn't unfair. With Fraser Hall, they would share jokes and they had a man-to-man relationship. Duane was a self-guarded guy but they had an equal respect for each other and certainly this was the same with me. Brian was praiseworthy of all staff and he was very discreet about certain personal concerns and problems that I had and he kept those private..."

Colin Hill was an experienced teacher. He makes it quite clear here that Brian Pead was managing the OLCVS and the staff very well.

Twist asked Hill about Pead's treatment of pupils and whether he showed favouritism to any pupils. Colin Hill – now Acting Head and therefore a possible dangerous witness to Pead (since it was in his interests if Pead were dismissed) – said that Pead did show favourable treatment to female pupils but they **were never private as there were no private areas in the Old Library**. He added: "...Even in Brian's office there was still an open environment..."

Hill continued to explain further, "...As for the female students, there was no imbalance of favourable treatment. There were a few young women who were at risk and Brian spent a considerable amount of time counselling them. He would talk to them about their difficult lives. Some students were difficult and that was because of their difficult lives outside school. One young person, Melissa Whitrod, was having difficulties with her mum and perhaps she was treated differently because he would talk to her about it..."

Thus a teacher with more than 30 years' experience stated that Brian Pead had **not** shown undue favouritism towards young female pupils. How remarkable, then, that a woman working two floors above the OLCVS should say that he did. How remarkable that a school secretary who took two hours to type a one-page letter should say that he did (after he dismissed her) and how remarkable that an unqualified teacher who was sexually grooming young, white girls should say that Pead was guilty of favouritism. No evidence existed other than the hearsay of three women who colluded.

Twist was determined to find reasons – **any** reasons – to dismiss Brian Pead. She turned her attention to the counselling that took place at the OLCVS.

Twist: You mentioned a counsellor-client relationship. Can you elaborate on the terminology?

Hill: Because of the new centre in Vauxhall, the school had evolved. As the numbers of students grew, Brian's approach of informal counselling was the main focus. Duane was also counselling young people as part of his role. Brian's role as Headteacher was kept separately from his counsellor role.

Colin Hill could not be more truthful in his comments. He said that the number of pupils grew significantly. Many were refugees and asylum seekers, two of whom had witnessed the murder of their parents in Angola.

Significantly, Hill states on the record that Brian Pead **kept his role as Head Teacher separate from his counsellor role**, thus establishing that Pead's boundaries were clearly in place. All of his counselling supervisors outside of the school also commented on his ability to maintain excellent boundaries.

Twist, however, was not receiving the answers from Colin Hill that she wanted. She asked another leading question. Instead of asking an open question such as "What was your feeling about the Centre's approach?", she instead asked:

Twist: Was it your feeling that the Centre's approach was based around psychotherapy?

The reply from Hill is significant to this case.

Hill said that the Centre's approach was **not** based around psychotherapy. He cited an example that the good teaching and learning would substantiate his claim. He also said that the OLCVS had a good time table, and good exam results. "...The principles of mental, physical, emotional and spiritual went hand in hand. Staff agreed that you couldn't learn if you were damaged..."

Hill's reply shows that Brian Pead was running the Centre completely in accordance with best practice as promulgated by the United Nations, the UK Government and Lambeth Council.

In her role as an Assistant Director, it should be noted that Twist ought to have had knowledge of the expectations of the UK Government and especially, of course, of Lambeth's own strategic policies around pupil and staff well-being.

Colin Hill – despite unfair and leading questions from Twist which were designed to have only one outcome in mind – continued to praise Brian Pead and his methods of working, his ethos for the OLCVS and his management of staff. He also said that Pead **was** consistent in his handling of pupils. He did, however, cite two examples where he felt that Pead had unfairly managed incidents with two male pupils. Yet this would occur in every school in the world. A Head Teacher has to have the ability to see the "bigger picture" of what he or she is trying to achieve at the school or pupil referral unit. Naturally, it falls upon the Head to try to communicate his or her vision to his or her staff. There is no school in the world where every member of staff "sings from the same songsheet" and there is no school in the world where every member of staff thinks that the Head's treatment of every pupil is always fair. There will always be differences of opinion. Brian Pead handled the two male pupils cited by Hill for reasons that would (a) benefit the OLCVS and (b) benefit the pupils themselves.

Hill had already mentioned that Brian Pead was aware of certain human weaknesses surrounding Hill's personal life. That information will remain private between the two men. However, the authors can show that it was these weaknesses in Hill's character that meant, according to Pead, that he was unable to always see the bigger picture. He would often become bogged down in the tiniest of details and fail to take a "helicopter" view of a situation. Pead, on the other hand, usually saw the detail **and** took the helicopter view of a situation, which is why he was the Head.

However, Pead knew that for all his idiosyncrasies, Hill was an enthusiastic teacher and he brought a certain unique energy to the OLCVS. He was also, Pead thought, a very human soul and Pead liked this and respected this about Hill, who – like Pead - always wanted the best for the pupils at the OLCVS. Occasionally Hill's over-exuberance would cause him problems and he occasionally rubbed staff and pupils up the wrong way because of this, but Pead knew that he could manage this and he also knew that Hill was a valuable addition to the OLCVS.

Brian Netto held down a responsible position within Lambeth EMAT team. Note now his use of the following question:

Netto: Did one student arrive too late for an exam?

Hill: Yes, I think she was 20 minutes late.

And Netto leaves his questioning there! He doesn't ask for the name of the student who allegedly arrived late. He doesn't ask for evidence. He doesn't ask for the time she arrived, or the time when the exam was timetabled to start. He doesn't ask which exam it was supposed to be.

Yet, more importantly, he fails to ask the next question "Is being 20 minutes late actually **too** late?" because it isn't. Pupils throughout the land will arrive late for exams for a large number of reasons. Some of those reasons will be false and some will be genuine, such as transport or road conditions which are no fault of their own.

As discussed previously, all examination boards make allowances for the fact that some pupils might arrive late to an exam. The pupil in question was late, but it did not infringe any of the exam board's regulations. Everything that occurred was within the rules. Both Brian Pead and Colin Hill ensured that the obligations of the OLCVS as an exam Centre were complied with and it was awarded its Centre and an Identification number: 10923.

Yet Netto failed to ask whether the late arrival of the pupil infringed any specific exam board rule.

This is just one example where a question was asked by either Twist or another Panel member in which a particular answer was sought and that, once an answer had been obtained – however inaccurate – the topic under discussion was left and a separate topic discussed. This is clearly an improper way to conduct an investigation, especially one of such importance to Brian Pead, or any other employee faced with losing their job.

derek langan

As the OLCVS grew rapidly at the Redfearn Centre in Vauxhall, Derek Langan was given to Pead to manage. There were no discussions – this was yet another *fait accompli* by Gilhooly that Pead had to deal with on an almost weekly basis.

Pead found Langan, from Ireland, to be an 'old school' type of teacher. He had been brought in to teach the pupils who had English as an Additional Language (EAL). Although old school and quite proper, Pead felt that Langan had more than a touch of Irish humour about him and, on occasions, a twinkle in his eye. He was hard-working, thoughtful and extremely approachable.

Langan also supported Pead's version of events. Murray and Twist attempted to make great capital out of the fact that the staff – in accordance with national guidelines – were offered workshops in which they could learn more about themselves and how to work with such disadvantaged and, in some cases, disturbed pupils. This was good management by Pead and Langan stated on the record that Pead never forced this on his staff – they were given the right to withdraw from any specific meetings to do with their own mental health or the mental health of pupils. However, the only person who withdrew was Murray. Every other member of staff attended the sessions because they saw the value of developing themselves and they saw it as it was intended – continuous personal and professional development.

But not Murray. She labelled it 'intrusive' because she was hiding a secret.

Langan also stressed that Pead was thoroughly professional in his running of the Centre and that in one-to-one meetings he was always focussed and professional. Only Murray presented a different picture. But then again, only Murray was hiding a dark, deep secret of child abuse, racism and bullying.

And Pead could see right through her.

Langan also said that he was sent a copy of all of Murray's allegations to him **before** he had ever been interviewed by Twist. This is clearly a breach of protocol and renders the entire process unlawful and unfair.

When asked by Twist about the alleged high turnover of staff, Langan stated firmly that Annabel Field had left the pupil referral unit because she had an acting contract in Bath, and that Fraser Hall left as he had always planned to do to return to New Zealand.

When asked by Twist whether Pead had used any name other than Brian Johnson at the Centre, Langan replied, "No."

Every member of staff had thus confirmed that Pead had never used any other name at the Centre than Brian Johnson. Except the triumvirate of Murray, Whitmore and Hiley.

When asked if Pead had shown favourable treatment to female pupils, Langan said, "...No, I didn't witness any of this conduct. Brian was an outgoing man who liked to talk. He certainly talked to the students a lot. I don't have a recollection of Brian talking to particular students more than others..."

Thus Twist had been provided with evidence which completely rebutted Murray's spurious allegations. She never used this information in her final report.

When asked about exams, Langan said that all students took exams at the correct times. Here was a very experienced man who had considerable experience in educational settings of pupils taking exams and he was fully aware of what constituted good practice.

Twist never used this information in her final report.

When Twist asked him whether he had received any complaints from pupils or colleagues about Pead, he said, "...No. Maryn made one comment that there were too many meetings..."

Thus Langan, like Hill and Maddison before him, had confirmed that no complaints had been made against Pead by either pupils or colleagues.

Until this 8-page document allegedly authored by Murray.

When asked by Twist if he had witnessed any conversations between Pead and female students that were inappropriate, Langan replied, "...No..."

That is an unequivocal statement.

Twist asked Langan about Pead's relationships with staff. Langan said that Pead was extrovert, cheerful and direct.

This not being what Twist wanted to hear, she tried baiting another hook: "...Were both male and female staff treated in the same way?" to which Langan replied, "...Yes. Most of the staff had lunch together every day and these were friendly and jovial times..."

Again, Langan's honest and truthful answers were not what Twist wanted to hear. This man was de-constructing her case against Pead brick by brick. Twist tried again.

"...Did you ever make complaints about Brian Johnson and did you ever receive any complaints from staff about him...?"

To which the laconic Langan replied, "...No..."

Thus the picture presented by Murray, Hiley and Whitmore of a bullying and insensitive manager was being erased by this truthful testimony from Langan, who presented a picture of relative harmony and jovial times. No pupils or staff members had complained about him. Staff comings and goings were all reasonably explained. All pupils sat their exams in accordance with regulations. Pead never favoured females. He never had inappropriate conversations with them.

How, then, did Murray come to author such a pernicious document? Why was Twist still willing to believe its contents when all the evidence was showing that it was nothing more than a tissue of lies?

With regard to complaints made by Murray about staff agenda, Langan also rebutted her allegations saying that agenda were usually given out in advance. He also spoke about the two types of meetings that staff had with Pead – one-to-one personal development meetings and the whole-staff meetings.

But perhaps the most interesting part of Derek Langan's interview with Twist was with regard to how Pead ran the unit and his management style. This section from the interview is reproduced here:

Twist: Did you think it was appropriate for Brian to set up the school as a therapeutic community?

Langan: That's my term 'therapeutic' and it meant that the school needed to be psychologically aware of the students' needs. There were not many problems with the EAL students who mostly had good family lives. I would discuss with Brian how I reacted with pupils. One student, Gemma, could provoke others and she had a past where her mother had been beaten by her father. I mentioned at a meeting that things should be let go with students and Brian seemed okay with this. He had a great understanding of students' problems. He tried to get one student, Rickkardo, some psychiatric help. It seemed that Brian knew about psychiatric organisations. The Centre did have an emphasis on academic performance and there was success with this.

Twist had asked yet another leading question – she displayed a propensity for this line of enquiry.

Langan explains that the word 'therapeutic' was a word that he had chosen to use – it was not necessarily an accurate description of how Pead ran the Unit.

Langan also states quite categorically that Pead understood the students' problems. This was his job. How else could he understand their diverse problems unless he had meetings with them, sometimes individually? And all those meetings were either in the company of Sandra Roach, Duane Maddison, parents or guardians or occasionally on his own. But, as Hill and others pointed out, there were no **private areas** in the building.

Derek Langan also stated that no colleague had ever complained to him about the nature or content of meetings. Thus another of Murray's spurious allegations had been swept aside.

Twist then continues to fish for anything she can level at Pead. At no point had Pead's use of time ever formed part of the case against Pead, but that didn't worry the inquisitor:

Twist: Did you think it was an appropriate use of time to conduct meetings in Brian's style?

Langan: The problems of some students called for psychological skills and from what I saw students benefited from this. Sandra Roach benefited from Brian's style as he wanted to broaden her role and added administration to it. His psychotherapeutic approach with Sandra was successful. It made her feel useful and helped her feel more interested in her role.

Twist then asks Langan about staff contracts. He told her that he had no problem with his contract but that Murray had approached him about hers. Thus Murray had approached every single member of staff about her contract, Barry Gilhooly and even Lambeth Human Resources. She had tried to bully Pead into awarding her a permanent contract when he had no power to do so.

She went to extraordinary lengths to secure a contract and caused great disruption in the Unit, and manipulated weak people like Hiley and Whitmore and Field into creating spurious allegations against her line manager.

Why, then, did she simply not return to St. Augustine's in Ealing where – she claimed – there was a £38,000 Head of ICT contract sitting on the table awaiting her signature?

What was keeping her at the OLCVS?

100

sandra roach

Sandra Roach was interviewed by Twist. She was fully supportive of Pead and said that his management style was appropriate for staff and students.

When asked whether Pead's use of multiple names was of concern to her, Sandra Roach replied, "...No. He only ever used the name Brian Johnson at the Centre. People can call themselves what they like as long as it's not fraudulent..." which is, of course, the right answer.

Cathy Twist brought up the issue of the alleged unfair treatment of pupils at the OLCVS and asked Roach whether she knew of any inconsistencies that Brian Pead had with the treatment of students in terms of sanctions and rewards. Roach said that she was not aware of any such inconsistencies.

This corroborated what Twist had been told by Derek Langan and in part by Colin Hill and Duane Maddison.

She also explained that Brian Pead had not allowed a trip to the cinema to take place because a risk assessment exercise had not taken place beforehand. This is good management on the part of Pead.

Sandra Roach also stated on the record that she, too, had received a copy of all of the allegations against Pead **prior to having been interviewed**.

Sandra Roach also stated that the focus of the OLCVS was on the teaching and learning, but Twist did not want to hear this. Yet Colin Hill, Derek Langan and Duane Maddison all commented on this fact.

Twist did not want to hear any praise towards Pead. She was merely trawling for any form of evidence to blacken his name.

More tellingly, Roach told Twist that she had been present when black male pupils had complained about racism and bullying and when young white female pupils had complained of being groomed.

She was not asked further questions.

Twist did not want to hear this information – she was determined to bury it.

What were her motives in wanting this buried?

jenny foster

After an hour-long interval, the Disciplinary Panel then interviewed Jenny Foster, who arrived at 5.35pm. Lambeth were determined to ensure that Brian Pead endured long days in Brixton before his journey home. Their policy of keeping him focussed on these allegations and hearings to ensure that he did not focus on Murray and her criminal activities was clearly working.

Brian Pead felt that he had a good working relationship with Foster. She was clearly a hardworking person who wanted to give of her best, but she did find the secondary-aged pupils somewhat challenging. Brian always attempted to support her, but found that she was not always open to learning about new ways of doing things. In truth, he felt that she was out of her depth. This was not her fault. She had worked her entire career in the primary sector, and Gilhooly had put her in the OLCVS without any specific training or understanding of the psychology needed to deal with secondary aged pupils. But these were not just any secondary-aged pupils – they were hugely disadvantaged and mostly disaffected and they had been rejected by the very system that was supposed to cater for their needs.

Brian Pead felt that Jenny Foster was abused by Gilhooly in the sense that he had put her into an environment on a temporary contract and provided her with no training whatsoever around how to deal with such difficult pupils and then how to deal with her emotions when dealing with such pupils. The process is two-fold. Pead felt that it was abusive for Gilhooly to give Jenny Foster a temporary contract which meant that she had no personal security of tenure. Thus, he had impacted upon her home life. He then failed to provide her with adequate training. Which impacted on her professional life. He then failed to take account of the impact such difficult pupils would have on her emotional and spiritual life. All of which Brian Pead found to be abusive towards her.

Yet Foster blamed Pead for all of this. She had not been able to distance herself from what was happening to her, and the easy target for her anger and dissatisfaction was, of course, her line manager.

Yet, in her interview with Twist on 25 January 2007, Foster had said that Pead had mentioned that he discussed delays with contracts with Barry Gilhooly. She added that when she discussed her contract with Pead he said Barry was dealing with the contract. Even at the time of her leaving the OLCVS, her contract had not been confirmed. This was not Pead's responsibility. The onus was on Gilhooly and Lambeth HR. They were negligent in their duties, but it was Pead who was the fall-guy for staff dissatisfaction.

Foster added that at one time she and Maddison had expired contracts and did not know if they were supposed to continue working at the Centre. She said, "...There was a need for contracts to be renewed and confirmed and I don't know why no one else saw this as an urgent need..."

Yet Pead had seen this as an urgent priority. Just after Foster had left the OLCVS, citing her contract as one of the reasons for her leaving, Pead sent the email of 7 May 2006 to Gilhooly, requesting that the line manager address the problem with staff contracts.

Jenny Foster also told the Panel that she had been called at home by Mary White about Murray's allegations against Pead. This is a significant breach of protocol. Lambeth management were contacting staff at their home to inform them about allegations made against Pead. They failed to inform Pead's staff that he had been forced to dismiss Murray because of her inappropriateness around children.

Jenny Foster claimed that pupils who voiced their concerns would speak to her about Brian Pead and complain that he was treating them differently. She provides no names. She provides no concrete examples. Twist asks her for none. Yet Foster had ample opportunity to address the alleged concerns in staff meetings – yet she never did.

Furthermore, Foster said that all students received one-to-one mentoring meetings with staff. Pead had over sixty pupils. Time constraints meant that he was not able to interview all of the pupils himself. So he devised a system whereby he allocated an equal number of pupils to each member of staff. He also ensured that the 'easier' pupils would be mentored by Jenny Foster and the much more difficult pupils by him. This is simply good management.

The reason Jenny Foster became somewhat antagonistic towards Pead was that Gilhooly and Murray had carefully crafted an 8-page document in which it appeared that Pead disliked Foster, who then felt the need to retaliate.

When questioned by the panel, Foster admitted that she was employed by Gilhooly and not by Pead, that she left the OLCVS because there were problems with staff contracts and because she was not performing her role as a mentor. Instead of realising that these issues were, in fact, caused by Gilhooly's weak and ineffective management, she merely blamed Pead.

When Jenny Foster left the room, it was 6.30pm. Lambeth had kept Pead in the building from 9.30am. This was their way of trying to tire him out. Give him so much information in a day that he would become muddled and overwhelmed by it all.

The Hearing was adjourned until Friday 27th at 9.30am.

the missing witness

Cathy Twist had failed to call a key witness – Annabel Field. What possible reason could there be for Twist not calling Annabel Field? There is no logical reason, save for what will now be explained.

In fact, Field **had** to be called as a witness in order to ensure a fair Hearing. She was, in fact, a key witness – known as a Witness as to Fact.

According to Murray's report, Annabel Field had been told by an unnamed cast member's unnamed wife that Brian Pead had engaged in sexual acts (plural) whilst attending the White Bear Theatre and that his (young) female companion had masturbated him during the play.

Thus Annabel Field was a key witness. However, her importance did not just lie with the allegations of sexual impropriety in the theatre.

Murray claimed that Field had told her that Pead had "mind-fucked" her, bullied her and that he was intrusive.

Yet Field's email of 17 April 2006 shows that none of these allegations can be true. In that email, **Annabel Field thanked Brian for his support and says that her experience at the OLCVS was her best experience in a London school.** This would accord with the comment of Nadia Al-Khudhairy that the PRU managed by Brian Pead was "...the best in London..."

Annabel Field thus had to be called as a witness so that she could be interviewed by the corrupt Twist and cross-examined by Brian Pead. Yet she was not called.

The reason she was not called as a witness was that Annabel Field's testimony would have sunk the entire farcical proceedings and it would have blown away the smoke and mirrors.

Brian Pead had **not** been masturbated in the theatre. He had **not** engaged in any sexual acts. He had **not** bullied Annabel Field (or any other member of staff for that matter). He had **not** "mind-fucked" her. He had **not** been intrusive.

Annabel Field would have confirmed that Murray's allegations were a tissue of lies. And once those lies had been exposed, it naturally calls into question every other allegation.

By not calling Field, Twist and Lambeth did not give Pead a fair hearing. In the Roldan case, Justices Etherton and Elias stated [at 13] that:

> "...A careful and conscientious investigation of the facts is necessary and the investigator charged with carrying out the inquiries should focus **no less on any potential evidence that may exculpate or least point towards the innocence of the employee as he/ she should on the evidence directed towards proving the charges against him...**"

The emphasis is the authors'. The Justices state clearly that it is the duty of an investigator to acknowledge all of the evidence in a case against an employee – even evidence that will absolve the employee from any blame. Throughout this book, the authors have drawn the reader's attention to many examples of robust and incontrovertible evidence of Pead's innocence, yet Twist had deliberately ignored this evidence. Clearly she felt that she could run the investigation outside of the law.

Furthermore, the proceedings were taking a considerable length of time to be concluded – far too long if the Court of Appeal is to be followed.

And at this time, Maryn Murray – the racist bully towards young black males and the inappropriate teacher towards young, white females – was left free to work in Lambeth schools and to have access to hundreds of children. All of this was known to Lambeth, to Cathy Twist, to Barry Gilhooly and to Ermina Waters, the father-of-four transsexual.

Yet Lambeth did nothing. Their sole intent was to remove the dangerous Brian Pead. He was never a danger to children – he was a danger to the corrupt individuals in the system who were disguising their abuse of children.

This pattern of making false allegations against Pead, providing no hard evidence, defaming him at every possible opportunity, removing all of his evidence, attempting to undermine his credibility as a researcher, failing to call Witnesses as to Fact who would have proved his innocence and holding 'kangaroo courts' or hearings against him was to follow him for another five years.

103

second missing witness

A second missing witness was Duane Maddison. Why would Twist not want to wheel him out in front of the Panel? After all, in the interest of justice, he ought to have been put before the panel just like any other witness. Indeed, he had a fundamental human right to be interviewed by the Panel. And Pead had a fundamental right to have him interviewed by the Panel. But the rights of the ordinary individual are not taken into consideration by Lambeth Council.

But – like Annabel Field – Maddison was not put before the Panel by Twist because she knew that if he had been present, her entire case against Pead would have been sunk.

Maddison had told Twist that the 'high turnover' of staff was due to contracts and that this was not Pead's fault, but Gilhooly's and Lambeth's.

He told Twist that he liked Pead's management style and had felt supported.

He also said that the personal development work for staff was beneficial to staff and pupils.

Maddison also told Twist that Pead had never used any other names.

He told Twist that no students received favourable treatment in their exams.

Crucially, he told Twist that he had often been present when Brian Pead had the alleged 'one-to-one' private conversations with female pupils.

He said that he had not noticed that female staff were treated differently from male staff.

He said that he had never received complaints about Brian Pead from staff or pupils.

He also told Twist that the OLCVS staff and pupils and parents had not been told why Brian had been suspended.

In short, his entire testimony rebutted all of Murray's spurious assertions.

This was why Twist failed to call this witness in her 'fair and thorough' investigation.

disciplinary hearing – day 3

Friday, 27 July 2007 10:00am

The meeting room had changed to Room 567 in the Professional Development Centre at International House. Twist was in attendance, along with Mary White, Judith Hare, Carol Palmer, Paul Barraclough and Brian Netto. The note-taker was now Rene Katisa.

The order of the day was that Brian Pead could ask questions about Management's presentation. This was followed by the panel asking questions on Management's presentation. Pead was then given an opportunity to make his presentation to the panel and invite any witnesses that he may like to give evidence. Management could then ask Pead questions in regards to his presentation. Then both parties would be asked to summarise.

This was the game that Lambeth was playing. They had no other intention than to dismiss Pead. He was far too dangerous. He knew too much. Yet Lambeth had to go through the motions so that, to the outside world, it would look as though they were conducting a thorough and fair investigation. To the Whitmores and the Murrays and the Hileys, and even to the Fosters, to the Langans and to the Hills, the investigation appeared to have been conducted properly.

Pead had, by now, discussed this case with several of his friends, including those he worked with inside of counselling. He also told his counselling supervisor and he told Jenny Sandelson and Lynne Kaye, the two female Directors of the Centre for Personal and Professional Development.

It was clear that the onus was on Lambeth to prove their case. There was much evidence in existence which showed that Pead had been 'set up' after dismissing the child-abusing Murray. Lambeth needed to keep Pead quiet and the best and easiest way to do this was to throw the system at him – hold meeting after meeting, throw more allegations at him and hope that he would forget the original complaints against Murray: that it would be lost in the smokescreen that they had created.

Annabel Field was not the only witness Lambeth failed to call. Duane Maddison was not called as a witness either. Either one of these witnesses would have shattered the illusion that masqueraded as a hearing. Pead had established excellent working relationships with several Lambeth consultants, managers of community centres, cleaners and caretakers, but Lambeth failed to call as witnesses the Head of the Redfearn Centre itself (Denise Campbell-Downie), the Head of the Old Library Centre in West Norwood (Sherine Thompson), the Lambeth English Consultant (Marion Richards), the Lambeth Future Schools consultant, the Lambeth

Mathematics consultant (Michael Hall) and the consultant representing Refugees and Asylum Seekers (Mus Bagum).

Importantly, the ICT consultant, Paul Waters, masquerading as Ermina Waters, was also not called. Was this because Waters had aligned herself with Murray?

Pead presented his own case to the Panel. He knew that the entire case was an abuse of process from the very moment all of the witnesses that Lambeth **did** interview were sent a copy of Murray's complaints against Pead. From that very moment, the entire proceedings were flawed. This was the equivalent of a Jury in a Crown Court being sent all of the Prosecution's case against a Defendant before the trial commences, so that – without ever hearing the Defendant's version of events – they would be forced to think unfavourably towards him and be biased against him.

In some strange parallels, this *modus operandi* would also be used against Pead in **five** separate criminal trials which are highlighted in the following book in this true-crime series, 'For Whom the Bell Tolled'.

Immediately prior to this hearing, Pead had taken the advice of Alex Passman, who advised him to take out a formal Grievance Procedure against Lambeth for the improper way that they had conducted this entire process.

At this hearing, Pead gave sound, reasonable explanations for everything that had occurred at the OLCVS. He explained, for example, about the fact that the Centre had more female students than male students and that, therefore, he was also bound to have had more conversations with female pupils than male pupils. He explained – and brought along proof – that late entrants into exams are specifically catered for and that neither he, nor Colin Hill, the Examinations Officer, had broken any rules.

He was open and transparent. The late Frederick Gerald Pead had taught the young Brian well, saying that "...If you give them enough rope, they will hang themselves..."

Brian Pead therefore let Lambeth hang themselves, knowing that his day would come when their corruption and cover-up of child abuse would be made public.

Pead patiently explained about the integrity of his personal boundaries. He explained that Rickkardo Crawford-Burrows had not only been entered for his English exam (something Murray strenuously claimed did not happen), but he was entered a full year earlier than his chronological age normally allowed for. In all the smoke that pervaded this case, so many insignificant details had been magnified and so many significant details had been overlooked or even 'lost' when Pead's office was ransacked. Brian Pead provided unequivocal evidence that Crawford-Burrows had been entered – and passed – the exam. Twist, and Lambeth, had been keen to perpetuate the myth that he had not.

Pead informed the Panel that he had never worked as a Life Coach or run a counselling service whilst in the employ of Lambeth Council. He also asked for evidence that he **had** undertaken these activities. None was forthcoming.

Pead then informed the Panel about Murray's racist bullying and sexual grooming of young white children.

Cathy Twist claimed that she had never heard of this information before.

If this is true, why, then, did she not ask for his report? Why, then, did she not stop the proceedings with immediate effect and instigate a thorough investigation? Why, then, did she continue to harass and persecute Brian Pead?

The reason is that she **did** have prior knowledge of Pead's complaints. He had provided Gilhooly with this information and Gilhooly would have been required to share that with his colleagues, one of whom was Cathy Twist. Of course she knew of Pead's investigation against Murray. This was a cover-up of huge proportions. Slowly and inexorably, the noose was tightening around Pead's neck.

Twist attempted to belittle Pead when she asked – in front of the Panel – whether Pead knew the BACP guidelines on Trust and Working with Young People.

"...15. Working with young people requires specific ethical awareness and competence. The practitioner is required to consider and assess the balance between young people's dependence on adults and carers and their progressive development towards acting independently. Working with children and young people requires careful consideration of issues concerning their capacity to give consent to receiving any service independently of someone with parental responsibilities and the management of confidences disclosed by clients..."
Source:
<http://www.bacp.co.uk/ethical_framework/ETHICAL%20FRAMEWORK%20(BSL%20VERSION)/ Keepingtrust.php>

Of course Pead knew about these guidelines. The BACP ethical guidelines underpin all responsible counselling training in the UK. Twist was once again attempting to make capital out of something that had no relevance. Derek Langan, Duane Maddison, Colin Hill and Sandra Roach had all commented on Pead's tight boundaries. Furthermore, Nadia Al-Khudhairy had described the OLCVS as the "...best pupil referral unit in London..." Had Pead's boundaries been weak, she would not have made such a bold statement.

In a Hearing that was nothing short of a fishing expedition about the Grievance Procedure that Pead had initiated, Carol Palmer then asked Pead to tell her "...all about the grievance procedure so that we can deal with it now..."

Pead knew that this simply did not make sense. The Panel was, itself, eroding the boundaries that should exist. It was attempting to deal with a Grievance Procedure **inside** a Disciplinary Hearing. Pead refused to discuss his forthcoming Grievance Procedure.

A significant piece of evidence finally found its way into the proceedings. It had long been suggested that Anya Hiley had, in effect, started all this off by sending her line manager an email in which she stated that she "felt funny" around Brian Pead.

She then met behind Pead's back with his line manager, Barry Gilhooly and neither Hiley nor Gilhooly informed Pead of this meeting.

Even to the uninitiated, it is obvious that that email was a critical piece of evidence. Yet it had not to date featured in the proceedings – despite Pead having been suspended some seven months previously. He had previously asked for this email to be sent to him, but he had to initiate a Freedom of Information Act request in order to obtain it.

Twist asked Pead if he minded a copy of the email being shown to the Panel. He said he did not mind, but he raised the issue that management had not provided a copy beforehand. No apology was forthcoming.

Cathy Twist continued to question Pead about wholly irrelevant issues.

Pead commented to Twist that he would co-operate only minimally with this farcical procedure, that his defence against allegations had not been sent out to all the witnesses prior to their being interviewed (as had Murray's) and that evidence that had been admitted by Twist was not *bona fide* evidence and that *bona fide* evidence submitted by Pead had not been admitted. A gross miscarriage of justice was taking place and he brought it to Twist's attention and to the Panel's attention.

They, of course, did nothing.

Pead also informed the Panel that he had consistently been denied access to his office until 19 July 2007 – some seven months after his suspension. By the time he did enter his office, it had been stripped bare of everything, save a desk and chair.

Pead also demonstrated that witnesses Hiley, Murray and Whitmore and – to a lesser degree, Field – had all been in contact with one another prior to the hearing and compared notes and statements. Pead challenged Twist to obtain the mobile phone records of these witnesses to prove that collusion had taken place, but she failed to obtain these. Thus, she was not only condoning the collusion, but she perverted the natural course of justice.

Pead informed the Panel that despite allegations of long conversations with students, not a single student, parent or carer had been called for interview.

Witnesses were coached by management and allowed to mingle with one another whilst waiting to be interviewed.

He went on: "...To clarify a general comment, I need to make reference to an allegation. Management did not pursue a certain line of question in regards to charges. Annabel Field alleges that I was being masturbated in a theatre whilst attending a show. Management did not write to the theatre director to ask if this incident had occurred. I have written to the theatre director and his response will be in my grievance..."

Pead actually misrepresented Annabel Field here because it was **not** her who said that Pead had been masturbated in the theatre, but Murray who said that Field had said it had occurred.

Pead therefore told the Panel that management had been lax in its 'investigation'. The Panel members did nothing.

Then Pead followed his earlier comments about the mismanagement of the entire process with these incisive comments: "...The panel is forced to consider the veracity of these allegations made by management. One has to consider the motives of someone to add something like that..."

He continued to fire with both barrels at the weak and inept Panel members: "...In Annabel Field's email, sent in April 2006, she says that she had a wonderful experience at the OLCVS and this was not included in management's presentation. One would have expected Twist to submit this to make a balanced judgement..."

Pead – a student of observing people – noted that not a single Panel member made notes whilst he was speaking. He knew that his volley against Lambeth was like pissing in the wind. These were highly-paid Lambeth robots with substantial pensions as a reward for corrupt practices – they were not going to rock the boat.

Brian Pead went on to say exactly what his associate, solicitor Alex Passman, had told him to say. He added that all the charges 1-4 were based on hearsay and that there was no evidence whatsoever to substantiate the allegations.

Judith Hare claimed that she would discount this because "...this grievance is against the process and not against the charges..."

She had, in one short statement, attempted to turn this disciplinary Hearing into a Grievance Procedure hearing.

Cathy Twist was asking all the questions in yet another abuse of process. She had led the initial 'investigation', then the Disciplinary Hearing and now – according to Hare – she was leading a Grievance Procedure hearing. This is corruption at its worst.

Twist used this hearing to continue to trawl for information. She kept bombarding Brian Pead with wholly irrelevant questions designed to trip him up and ensure that she could have something – anything – which she could use against him in order to dismiss him from his post.

Twist's propensity for trawling for information was not new. It is a tactic she had used before and since Pead's case.

The case of *James Walker* v *Lambeth Council* was reported in the London Evening Standard on 6 December 2011 – almost five years after Pead was suspended.

Under the headline "Headmaster gets £100,000 over 'cancer sacking', Anna Davis, Education Correspondent, wrote:

> "...A former London head has been awarded more than £100,000 in compensation for being unfairly sacked after he returned to work following chemo-therapy treatment.
>
> James Walker, 55, who was head of Henry Fawcett School in Kennington, agreed to the out-of-court settlement. He said he was "relieved" that his family can "move on with their lives".
>
> His wife Becca said they had gone through three years of stress, adding: "They have taken away James's career, what he worked all his life for.
>
> "I just want to get things back to how they were before. It's not about the money, it's about clearing James's name and being vindicated."
>
> Mr Walker had just returned to the Henry Fawcett School in Kennington after six months of cancer treatment in 2008 when **he was accused of bullying by another member of staff.**
>
> The father of two said the allegation was part of a **"witch-hunt"** by Lambeth council, which runs the school, which left him feeling "depressed and suicidal". He said: "Once it was clear I wasn't leaving [the job] **they spent a huge amount of time finding anything they could pin on me.** They put in this bullying allegation which was not believed by the court. **It's inhumane how they treated me.**
>
> **He was suspended from the school,** where Jack Straw's son Will was once a governor, in November 2008.

An employment tribunal in Croydon upheld his claim of unfair dismissal against the council. The tribunal found **the council had cleared his office, destroyed his files, insisted on draconian suspension conditions and failed to adopt impartiality.** A disability claim that he was discriminated against because of his illness was not upheld.

Employment judge Lindsay Hall-Smith said the tribunal was "**struck by the level of hostility" the council showed** towards Mr Walker. A council spokesman said it was "sorry that Mr Walker was found to have been treated unfairly. The education of pupils has always been an overriding priority and when allegations are brought to our attention we must respond." **Mr Walker said no action has been taken against the people responsible for damaging his career...**"

The emphases are the authors'. Note the extraordinary parallels between the two cases:

- both Heads were accused of bullying members of staff
- both men describe a witch-hunt against them
- both men describe how Lambeth spent huge amounts of money and time finding anything they could pin on them
- both men describe inhumane treatment meted out to them by Lambeth Council
- both men were suspended
- both men had their offices cleared
- both men had files destroyed
- both men were subjected to draconian suspension conditions
- both investigations failed to adopt impartiality
- both men complained of Lambeth's hostility towards them
- no-one has ever been held accountable within Lambeth

But the two cases have further disturbing parallels. James Walker was, like Pead, an astute individual. He had also identified serious weaknesses within Lambeth. And, once he made his line manager – also Barry Gilhooly – aware of the problems, the allegations were turned against him.

In evidence presented to the court by James Walker, the Tribunal heard that two teachers had told the council's whistle-blowing department shortly after the suspension, that Mrs Bermingham – a key witness in the case - was 'fabricating her claims', but this evidence was not acted upon by Phyllis Dunipace, the Executive Director for Children Services at the time.

This is an exact copy of what happened to Pead. He presented to the Investigatory Hearing and to a Disciplinary Hearing evidence – incontrovertible evidence – that Murray and others had fabricated their claims. Twist did nothing. Hare did nothing. Gilhooly did nothing. Palmer did nothing. Dunipace did nothing.

They had all been given evidence that Murray and others had fabricated evidence. They had all been given evidence that Murray was sexually interested in young, white females.

No-one did anything to bring her to account.

In fact, they even reinstated Murray and allowed her further access to thousands of children.

In the case of *Walker* v *Lambeth*, the court heard that by February 2009 Ms Dunipace wanted to remove Mr Walker from his post and had commissioned a strategy to bring about an end to his employment with the council. This is an exact echo of what happened to Pead.

In yet another echo of the Walker case, Mr Walker said: "...The tactics used by Lambeth felt like they were designed to make me give up and walk away but I was determined to fight this unjust set of actions..."

Again, this mirrored the Pead case. Lambeth took months before arranging a Disciplinary Hearing. They produced more than 600 pages against him, which could, realistically, have been reduced to no more than 50 pages and they organised a raft of witnesses which had no relevance to the allegations before him.

reasons for the cover-up revealed

Twist's ruthless interrogation of Pead did not finish until 17:05. There was a ten-minute break and then the Panel had an opportunity in which to ask questions of management's role in the entire process.

It is clear that the 'investigation' was quintessentially flawed: independent third parties were not called as witnesses, the provenance of documentary evidence had not been robustly established and pupils (who had allegedly been the subject of 'inappropriate conversations' with Brian Pead) were never called as witnesses. Nor were their parents or guardians.

Thus the Panel had ample opportunity to seek justice and truth. It played at doing so.

Brian Netto asked why all the witnesses had been sent Murray's vindictive report prior to them being interviewed. This was answered by Mary White, the 'independent' consultant to Lambeth. (The reason she was independent was that – in the event of adverse publicity – Lambeth Council would be able to distance itself from her and she would become 'the fall guy'. In reality, she wasn't independent at all – Lambeth were paying her handsomely for her time).

White blatantly lied, saying, "...The procedure does not say that this shouldn't happen..."

She was trying to hide behind 'the procedure'. She failed to say that she knew it would be prejudicial to Brian Pead.

She explained to the Panel that she had telephoned a number of witnesses to ask whether they would be willing to attend a hearing and, once they had accepted, the allegations were sent out 5 days before the interview date. However, she did not send out "...the allegations..." – she sent out Murray's entire 8-page document. This was, of course, wholly unnecessary and extremely prejudicial.

Mary White then explains how they handled Annabel Field, who did not attend as a witness: "...We sent hers out earlier, twelve days before her interview because she did not live in London and wanted us to send them to an address where she could collect them from when she was next in London..."

The authors of this book have **never** seen a signed copy of any interview between Lambeth and Annabel Field. They have seen an unsigned witness statement purporting to have been an interview with Annabel Field in which she claimed that "...I didn't know I had been bullied by Brian until I read Maryn Murray's report..."

This from a 26 year old actress.

And in the witness statement purporting to be from Annabel Field, she makes no mention of the alleged masturbation in the theatre, only that she was supporting Murray's allegations in respect of his treatment of her.

It is clearly a bogus document.

Brian Netto – like his peers on the Panel – was only, of course, going through the motions in an attempt (and not a very good attempt) to appear as if the Panel members were taking Pead's complaints about mismanagement of the process seriously. They were not.

Here is yet another example of Netto's weak and ineffective questioning:

Netto: Why did Mr Pead only have access to his office on 19 July 2007?

White: If we refer to the letter sent on the 8th December, this is in Section 11 of the presentation pack, Paragraph 5; it states that "If you need to make contact with your colleagues or any other employee, you must first contact Barry Gilhooly." We did clarify this again with Brian on 20 April 2007, when he came for his interview that he needed to make contact with Barry or Rosa. He did raise it and he was reminded that he could have access.

This is, of course, a non-answer. Brian Pead asked for access to his office immediately after his suspension on Friday 8 December 2006. He called Barry Gilhooly on the following Monday (11 December) and asked to be allowed to visit the OLCVS and obtain evidence that he needed to be able to address the allegations against him. **This basic human right was denied to him by Gilhooly.**

Pead being Pead, he then called Rosa Vaz. She also denied him this basic right.

On Wednesday 13 December 2006, Sandra Roach called Pead to tell him that his office was being ransacked and that all evidence was being removed from his office.

Compare this with the *James Walker* v *Lambeth Council* case some two years later, in which exactly the same thing had happened when James Walker – who, like Pead, fought for his students – had had his office ransacked. Both Head teachers were line managed by Barry Gilhooly.

Brian Netto failed to ask the most obvious question following Mary White's reply. When she said that she clarified the point about him obtaining entry to his office, she gives the date of 20 April 2007. Had Netto been genuinely interested in seeking justice, he would have asked the most obvious question to White: "Why did you wait until 20 April 2007 to ask Mr Pead if he had had access to his office when this was a full four months **after** he had been suspended by Lambeth?"

He also failed to ask Mary White or Cathy Twist why Pead was not allowed immediate access to his office so that he might better be able to defend himself but, of course, he was merely enacting a pretence at questioning management's handling of the case.

Netto continues his questioning of Mary White:

Netto: Had Brian Pead asked for access?

White: Not specifically to us, I told him to refer to Rosa and Barry.

Which is precisely what Pead did, of course, after having spoken with his friend, John Callow, who had conducted a disciplinary investigation and several breaches of the BT disciplinary code of practice in his time as a manager with British Telecom.

Carol Palmer then takes up the baton:

Palmer: So to your knowledge he hadn't asked for access?

White: He just made a comment that he wanted access and we reminded him of whom to contact. No-one has denied him access.

This was, of course, a lie. Yet, whether or not it was a lie, matters little. What both Netto and Palmer have done is fail to ask the obvious question: "Why did Lambeth not grant Brian Pead his basic human right to defend himself and allow him immediate access upon his suspension to his office, files and computer?"

This question was never asked.

The Panel's Brian Netto then asked White why no pupils or parents had been interviewed. Her reply is simply staggering:

White: They would have had to ask Social Services and that would have taken it to a new level. Cathy Twist was asked to investigate by Graham Griffin so that it was a disciplinary and not a Child Protection case or issue.

This is also a lie and a non-answer. Let us imagine, for a moment, that it was Pead and not Murray who **was** guilty of grooming young women, of having inappropriate contact with young women, of favouring female students over male students, then these **would have been child protection issues.**

The real reason Lambeth did not conduct a Child Protection case against Pead was because it feared what he knew about Murray and Hiley and Waters and Gilhooly becoming public.

What is even more disturbing in this transcript is that Netto never asks whether Mary White felt that pupils **should** have been interviewed in order to ensure a fair hearing. He never asks this fundamental question. The pupils mentioned in Murray's twisted report were all aged between 14 and 16 – and thus clearly quite capable of being interviewed. Indeed, several of them had been interviewed by the police in their personal lives outside of the school, so being interviewed by 'kindly' Lambeth officials would have been a walk in the park for them!

Murray claimed that Brian Pead and Rickkardo Crawford-Burrows disliked one another. Had this been the case, wouldn't Rickkardo have **wanted** to have been interviewed so that he would be able to make matters worse for his former Head Teacher?

Murray claimed that Melissa Whitrod had 'stood up' to Pead and that they disliked each other intensely. Again, this was a fabrication. Wouldn't **she** have wanted to grasp an opportunity to "drop her former teacher in it"?

Kerrie Hamilton – the dark-haired pupil described in Annabel Field's unsigned statement as a blonde – was allegedly spending hours and hours of her time with Pead. Wouldn't she have wanted to make things worse for him if she had genuinely felt violated?

And so it goes on.

Not a single pupil was ever interviewed. The reasons for this are three-fold:

(i)   the pupils liked and respected Brian and he liked and respected them
(ii)   they would have shown that Murray had fabricated her entire report
(iii) this would have been made public by the pupils and parents because of the allegations of child abuse

Netto fails to dig deeper with regard to the fact that no pupils were ever questioned. Instead, Paul Barraclough (a Primary Advisor sitting in on a Secondary school Disciplinary Hearing) merely asks:

Barraclough: And parents?

To which Mary White responds: "...We didn't invite them because we felt that if we invited the parents whilst investigating, the allegations may have not been founded, we would risk publicising unfounded allegations..."

Language experts and psychologists would find this response extremely telling. Her use of the phrase "...the allegations may have not been founded..." is an indication of her mind-set: "We are going to find Pead guilty."

The grammatical construction of the phrase is highly unusual: "...may have not been..." In this particular setting, a more usual grammatical construction would have been "...the allegations might have been unfounded..." but White uses the past tense, as if she already knows that the allegations **will** be founded. Which is, of course, precisely what she does know.

White also provides an indication of Lambeth's underlying motives: that had parents been involved, "...we would risk publicising unfounded allegations..."

This might appear at first glance to be an indication that Lambeth were considering Pead's feelings. The authors discount that because of the harsh way in which they treated Brian Pead (and James Walker in a separate case).

Lambeth knew that if they invited pupils or parents, the story would have broken to the press. Brian Pead was a well-liked and well-respected Head teacher who had created a pupil referral unit out of nothing. He had broadened the curriculum, given disadvantaged pupils a belief in themselves and he had also been told by a wholly independent third party – Nadia Al-Khudhairy - that his Unit was the "...best in London..."

Gilhooly had been told that Murray was a danger to children and, by implication and association, so was Anya Hiley and Paul/ Ermina Waters. Gilhooly had been given incontrovertible evidence of Murray's racism, bullying and her offering bribes to, and grooming of, young females.

This evidence had been removed from Pead's office. He was suspended because he was a danger to Lambeth. He knew far too much about Murray's motives. And he knew that Murray had aligned herself with Hiley because the unmarried Hiley had full access to the private and confidential details of all the pupils. Of course Pead was a very dangerous man – not to pupils, but rather to Lambeth.

There is a saying that "The best form of defence is attack" and that is precisely what happened to Pead. Lambeth turned all of his *bona fide* complaints against Murray on to him. The only accusation they did not throw at him was one of racism because they knew that they could not possibly make that stick because he had enjoyed numerous conversations with black and Asian members of the West Norwood and Vauxhall communities and he is one of the least racist people that most people have ever encountered. Like Martin Luther King, Jr, he is not interested in the colour of a person's skin but by the content of their character.

The Hearing ended at 5.35pm, which meant that questions about management's handling of the entire proceedings had lasted a mere 30 minutes. It had been a farce and pretence all along.

The Disciplinary Hearing was adjourned until Monday 30 July 2007 at 9.30am.

a busy weekend

Brian Pead had been busy over the weekend speaking with Alex Passman the solicitor in Plymouth who had been providing assistance to Pead on a *pro bono* basis. Passman had seen how Lambeth had been mismanaging this case and was also aware of the fact that the authority was dragging its feet and buying as much time as it could. It was now almost eight months since Pead had been unlawfully suspended.

Passman told Pead over the weekend of 28 and 29th July 2007 that he must produce a list of complaints to the Panel on the Monday. Passman suggested that Pead make a list of each and every complaint and then provide supporting evidence to corroborate each complaint.

Passman and Pead discussed the headings of each complaint which included the integrity of the allegations, improper procedure, leading questions, collusion and hearsay evidence.

Pead, of course, had significant experience of this type of report in his job as a Head Teacher and as a Managing Director of Einsteinonline.co.uk.

final day of hearing

The next disciplinary hearing meeting was held in Room 2 in the Professional Development Centre Suite at International House in Brixton on 30 July 2007.

Lambeth's line-up included Cathy Twist, Mary White, Judith Hare, Carol Palmer, Paul Barraclough, Brian Netto and Rene Katisa was the note taker.

For the defence, just Brian Pead.

The meeting commenced at 9.30am.

For the uninitiated, this is another tactic employed by those in authority: seek to outnumber the opposition, particularly when you are in the wrong. It is a psychological tool used to try to intimidate one's opponent and to try to get them thinking, "There's more of them than there is of me, so they must be right" and so on.

The purpose of the meeting was outlined by Judith Hare: "...Good morning and thank you for attending today. The order of the day is Management will make their summary, followed by Mr Pead's summary. The panel will then discuss and make their decision. The panel's decision will be sent to you in writing within the next 5 working days..."

That was the intended outline for the meeting. In reality, it did not follow that pattern.

The meeting was, once again, led by the ubiquitous Cathy Twist. Her pernicious demeanour permeated every minute of every meeting.

Twist started by reading out a long list of all the things that she had done to "...conduct a full and thorough investigation..." when the evidence showed that she had not done so. She read out a list of those whom she had interviewed. However, as any half-decent solicitor or barrister will tell you, it is not what the prosecution put in as evidence that matters, but what they leave out.

Twist noted – as she was duty bound to do – that Duane Maddison and Annabel Field had not attended the hearings. No reasons were given.

The reason they did not attend is that they were not invited by Lambeth to attend and the onus was on Lambeth to invite them to attend. This was not Pead's responsibility. Pead and Maddison enjoyed a healthy working relationship and both men had immense respect for one another. Pead, as part of his role, noted the strengths and weaknesses of each member of his team and he had noticed something in Maddison that delighted him. Duane Maddison was a listener. He kept his own

counsel. He displayed a maturity beyond his years. He established a rapport with students based on mutual respect. Pead instinctively felt that here was a counsellor in the making. Duane Maddison is now a qualified counsellor.
Source: <www.amennoir.weebly.com>

Thus Twist knew that calling Maddison as a witness would sink her case without trace, since Maddison would speak highly of Pead and of his methods and contradict all of the allegations against him.

Similarly with Annabel Field. She was not invited to attend because the crucial email that she had sent on 17 April 2006 in which she stated of her own volition that she had had the best teaching experience in London at the OLCVS and in which she thanked Brian for all his support provided a further volley into Twist's unlawful case against Pead. And she would have been grilled by Pead over the alleged masturbation in the theatre.

Twist also failed to call the English consultant, the Maths consultant and the ICT consultant. She failed to call staff working in the Community Centres at West Norwood and Vauxhall.

Twist provided a list of all those she **did** interview as if this would impress Pead or any other reader of her document. It might impress primary school aged children, but it would not be sufficient to impress intelligent adults.

Twist claimed that she had met with Murray on 19 January 2007 – almost **seven weeks** after Pead's unlawful suspension. This proves that Pead did not receive the allegations against him until after 19 January 2007 – something which Twist had previously denied.

It is simply not lawful to suspend a person without providing them with a reason and certainly not giving them any reasons until seven weeks after the suspension.

Hitler's Fascist state had been defeated in 1945 – it was, apparently, still alive and well in 21st century Lambeth.

In the meeting with Murray on 19 January 2007, an unnamed "...HR Advisor..." was present. Why was this person not named if the investigation was "thorough and fair"? (The authors have since found out that this Advisor was Mary White. What they also have established is that Murray was accompanied by a person claiming to be Murray's sister, Gerlize de Villiers, a lawyer. Why would Twist allow Murray to be accompanied by a lawyer and not Pead?)

Twist then hangs herself: "...Once we'd heard the allegations that she had made, we deemed it necessary to investigate..."

Thus – in Twist's own words – Pead had been suspended **before** Lambeth had even known of Murray's allegations. He had, of course, been suspended on 8 December

2006 and Twist states on the public record that she – and therefore Lambeth – did not know of Murray's allegations until 19 January 2007.

Why, then, suspend Pead? How can an employer suspend someone **before they even know that any allegations have been made?**

The reason is that Gilhooly had been told by Pead that Murray was a racist and a bully and a child abuser in respect of young girls. Gilhooly was in possession of this information **and Pead had to be removed at any cost.**

His office had to be ransacked and evidence destroyed.

And this was not done in order to protect "the good name of Lambeth". This was done in order to protect certain people who were abusing children **and who were working for Lambeth.** Pead knew this. And Pead had to be removed from office as swiftly as possible, all his evidence destroyed and his name and reputation blackened.

Twist claimed that the witnesses **had** to be sent a copy of Murray's report "...in the interest of natural justice..."

This is complete nonsense. As discussed elsewhere in this book, it is not natural justice to send a person whom you are calling as a witness an 8-page report (all of which was fabricated) before you interview that witness. This is prejudicial in the extreme.

Twist also tried to justify her sending the report out to witnesses prior to her interviewing them on the grounds that the case was "...complex..."

Twist continued her diatribe against Pead: "...Brian Pead was given the chance to respond to the charges. We invited staff to the hearings to give evidence and have included other documents that he requested we added. However, he had not invited any witnesses..."

As Alex Passman had pointed out, it was not Pead's responsibility to call witnesses. Charges had been put to him and it was management's responsibility to call witnesses. However, Twist only called witnesses who had an axe to grind, or who could be easily manipulated.

She continued: "...He alleges that he was suspended without being given a reason for suspension. However on the letter dated 8/12/2006, it states that he was suspended because of an investigation into gross misconduct. The letter dated 12/12/2006, gave details of the investigation and allegations of gross misconduct..."

Her hubris knew no bounds. Neither did her stupidity. She had already informed the Panel that she did not meet with Maryn Murray until 19 January 2007. How then could she say that Pead had been suspended because of an investigation into gross misconduct when she hadn't even met with Murray to find out what Murray's allegations were? After all, the allegations may just have fallen into the 'misconduct' category rather than 'gross misconduct'. But no, Twist is adamant that Pead knew the allegations against him by 12 December 2006. He could not have known.

The letters of 8 and 12 December were generic 'catch-all' letters. Gilhooly had to find a reason to suspend Pead because of what Pead had told him about Murray. It didn't matter that they had no legal basis upon which to suspend Pead – that could be sorted out later. Gilhooly had to suspend Pead in order to ransack his office and remove vital evidence of Murray's child abuse.

Twist continued to run through the charges against Pead. Charge 1 was that concerns were raised over the appropriateness of Brian Pead's management style.

Twist claimed that Pead, as Head of Centre, crossed professional boundaries with staff members. Both Eloise Whitmore and Maryn Murray said that he was overly intrusive and overly personal.

This is hardly surprising. Both had been sacked by Pead – Whitmore for failing her probationary period and Murray for racism, bullying and grooming young female pupils.

Of course they were going to say negative things about Pead.

However, no other staff complained of this alleged treatment. And given that Pead held weekly meetings with all of his staff, why had neither Whitmore nor Murray seen fit to add this alleged mistreatment to the meeting agenda?

And then Twist demonstrably lies to the Panel: "...Colin Hill said that he had a therapeutic and psychotherapeutic approach in staff meetings..."

Consider here, again, an extract from Twist's interview with Colin Hill:

Twist: Was it your feeling that the Centre's approach was based around psychotherapy?

The reply from Hill is significant to this case.

Hill – whose wife is a qualified psychotherapist - said that the Centre's approach was **not** based around psychotherapy. He cited an example that the good teaching and learning would substantiate his claim. He also said that the OLCVS had a good time table, and good exam results. The principles of mental, physical, emotional and spiritual went hand in hand. Staff agreed that you couldn't learn if you were damaged.

Thus Twist had lied. She had presented a statement as fact (that Pead ran the OLCVS along psychotherapeutic lines) when it was not fact at all. Furthermore, she fails to cite the email from Nadia Al-Khudhairy in which she praises Pead's running of the Centre for the way he had focussed on the academic **as well as** the emotional needs of the pupils.

And it should be remembered that Pead was following national and local authority guidelines in respect of meeting the emotional needs of his pupils and his staff.

Yet Twist had to justify her one-sided investigation.

She added that "...Annabel Field said that she was given a lot of work by Brian, that he was intrusive in his questioning and coaxed her into saying things. Her family told her that it sounded like he fancied her..."

That Annabel Field's family said such things was completely new information. However, Twist was unable to provide evidence to prove this assertion. She also failed to inform the Panel that Pead had received an email from Field on 17 April 2006 in which she thanked him for his support. Why would she send such an email if he had been intrusive in his question and "...coaxed her into saying things..." Annabel Field was a 25 year old woman with a mind of her own. Twist fails to inform the Panel that Field did not attend an interview, even though Pead had asked her to attend and even though Twist should have insisted on her attendance, or discounted her alleged evidence. No signed statement by Field is in existence.

Twist continued to misinform the Panel when she stated that "...Brian Pead also alleges that there were three incidents of Maryn Murray's conduct. However he failed to mention these three allegations in the three interviews we had with him and also failed to produce any written evidence..."

This is a complete fabrication. Pead had provided his line manager, Barry Gilhooly with sufficient evidence, both oral and written. And Pead had always had Sandra Roach with him when pupils made statements against Murray, but Roach was never questioned about these incidents, despite management knowing she had been present when Pead interviewed the pupils.

In the event, it matters little because, having now been given the information, Twist was duty bound to investigate the claims and she failed to do so. The question has to be asked: "Why would Twist so deliberately and pointedly not conduct an investigation into racism and child abuse by Maryn Murray and was Twist a party to the abuse?"

charge 1

The charges are reproduced in part below (a full copy can be found on the website accompanying this book), with commentary by the authors introduced at each salient point:

Charge 1 - Concerns were raised over the appropriateness of Brian Pead's management style.

"...As Head of Centre, Pead crossed professional boundaries with staff members. Maryn Murray said that she was given two personal poems and was invited out for dinner, and was offered life coaching by Brian Pead..."

Twist was told that **all** members of staff were given poems as part of a team-building exercise. Why did Twist not ask all the other staff whether they had been given the poems?

Where is the proof that Murray was invited out to dinner by Pead? There is none because it never happened. But even if it had happened, so what? There is no proof either way, so, in the circumstances, the allegation should have been erased. But Twist held on to it like a drowning woman clinging to any semblance of safety. Twist was out of her depth, but she was supported by Lambeth and she was covering up significant abuse by Murray.

Brian Pead maintained that he never offered Murray life coaching. She was always saying that she never had any money – even the cunning Gilhooly states this about Murray – so why would Pead offer to life coach her when she couldn't even pay?

But the most significant reason he would never have offered to life coach her was because **she was resistant to learning about herself**. No life coach worth the name – charlatans excepted, of course – would offer to life coach someone who was resistant to self-improvement and who was so well defended.

Again, Twist had misrepresented the truth and she has merely taken the view of Murray without considering alternative evidence.

Twist continued: "...Maryn Murray also said that staff had to fill out questionnaires as part of a mental health framework. Jenny Foster said that these questionnaires had no relevance..."

It has been shown in previous chapters that Brian Pead was following guidelines, both national and local, in taking responsibility for the mental health of his staff since they were working on a daily basis with extremely challenging pupils.

However, the most important aspect of Twist's fabricated report is that **Jenny Foster had left the OLCVS by the time Brian handed out the Mental Health Check questionnaires.** Twist – who constantly alleged that she had conducted a thorough investigation - obviously forgot to check the chronology of events. This questionnaire was not handed out until the OLCVS moved to Vauxhall, by which time Jenny Foster had moved back to the primary level of education, which she was far more suited to.

Twist: "...Although Miss Whitmore had carried out an appeal for unfair dismissal and won, her statements have given us an insight into Brian Pead's management style..."

This is a significant misrepresentation. It has been designed to force the reader to think that Whitmore took her appeal to an Employment Tribunal in a court. She did not. Lambeth merely offered her an out-of-court settlement in the sum of £8,000 which the inept Whitmore greedily seized. She had, in effect, won the Lottery, since she was being paid £8,000 because she couldn't type, she couldn't spell, she had no clear work patterns and she would invent whatever it was necessary to invent to get her own way.

That Twist should even consider relying on the 'evidence' of a woman who failed her probationary period and claimed that she had never been told she was on probation says much about Twist.

Twist: "...Anya Hiley said that she found Brian Pead to be probing, analytical, intrusive and inappropriate and she didn't like the way he would look at her. In June 2006, she sent an email to her line manager with her concerns of Pead..."

Again, Twist is let down by the chronology. On her own admission, Hiley agreed that she interacted with Pead in September and October 2005, but that after that she didn't want to continue to meet him. (Pead said this was because he felt she wasn't doing enough to support his pupils and that he would ask her why this was. His view is that she did not like being taken to task.)

Twist claims that Hiley sent an email to her line manager claiming concerns about Pead in June 2006. Why would Hiley wait so long before sending an email? Why would she "sit" on her feelings for eight months before sending an email?

Pead asserts – and there is some evidence to support his assertion – that by June 2006, Hiley and Murray were "thick as thieves" and that Murray desperately wanted the position as Head of Centre. By this time, Murray was already showing signs of being racist, but Pead had not been able to gather sufficient evidence. (This did not occur until October 2006).

Murray and Hiley would meet outside of work. Both were unmarried. Both spent a lot of their time in the company of young girls at the Centre. Both did not get on well with the boys at the OLCVS, especially the 'rougher' boys who could not be controlled by them.

Part of Hiley's job was to offer 'careers advice' to the pupils at the OLCVS. Pead's pupils complained to him that she was 'useless'. One or two of the quieter girls said that she was 'nice'. However, the boys – and in particular the black pupils – started to complain that she would cancel their appointments at short notice and that when they tried to book another appointment, she would claim that she was busy and that it would be weeks before she could see them. It is evident that Hiley was accusing Pead of all the things **she** was doing. She spent far more time in the company of the female pupils, she was bullying towards the black males and she was also racist towards them. Pead felt that it was inappropriate for her to be a Connexions Advisor.

Twist: "...Brian Pead said that he had an open style of management, that staff were part of the decision-making process and that he led by consensus. From what we've been told, his influence as Head of Centre had a lot of impact. Out of the five female staff felt distressed by his behaviour, two had been dismissed and by October 2006, there was only one female member of staff. As a person in position as Head of Centre, I'm led to believe that Pead abused his power of position..."

This is a clever piece of data manipulation by Twist. There were not five female staff who allegedly felt distressed by Pead. Two females were dismissed: Whitmore for failing to pass her probationary period and Murray for abusive behaviour towards children. They cannot, therefore, realistically claim to have been distressed. Annabel Field is one of the alleged five, yet she sent an email to Brian thanking him for his support. Jenny Foster left because she wanted to return to the primary sector and that leaves only Anya Hiley – who was not even an employee of the OLCVS. She worked two floors above the OLCVS and she hadn't made a single complaint about Pead for 8 months and not until she became great friends with the fabulist Murray.

Twist has manipulated the evidence to make it appear that Pead had been mismanaging these five women.

Why, then, had this never become an issue in Pead's entire career? He had worked with women from the age of fifteen, when he was a Saturday boy at MacFisheries. He was now 53. Thus, in a career spanning almost 40 years, he had not had a single complaint against him. Until Murray.

Sandra Roach spoke of him supporting her. Annabel Field spoke of him supporting her. Male staff spoke of him supporting them. Pupils spoke of him supporting them. Caretakers and cleaners spoke of him being always friendly and engaging in decent conversations.

Only Murray thought differently.

charge 2

Starting with a definition of harassment from the Council's policy, Twist then reads out Charge 2:

> "...Harassment is a form of direct discrimination. It is defined as behaviour which is objectionable and offensive to the victims and which might threaten their job security or create an intimidating and hostile working environment which may hinder the victim in his or her work performance.
>
> Harassment can comprise of demeaning or threatening remarks or actions associated with a person's gender, sexuality, race, or other personal characteristics, the effects of which may be to cause humiliation, offence or distress. In order to constitute harassment the behaviour must be both unreciprocated and unwelcome...

We have heard that Pead spoke differently to the female members of staff. Maryn Murray said that she was distressed and was reduced to tears when she was being questioned by the Panel. [Twist then lists a number of alleged examples of how Pead caused distress to Murray] In conclusion, it is evident that Pead crossed professional boundaries which caused distress to Murray. The Panel in coming to a decision need to consider the style, nature, professionalism and inappropriate behaviour of Pead and whether his behaviour falls below that of an adult in a position of authority as of the Head of the Centre..."

Even those people not familiar with the psychology of human behaviour will know of the phenomenon commonly referred to as "crocodile tears". Murray was good at this.

Twist concludes – by considering only the evidence from Murray and her associates – that Pead had crossed professional boundaries. This was never picked up by Duane Maddison, Annabel Field, Nadia Al-Khudhairy, Colin Hill, Derek Langan and many others. Why did Twist not even mention these in her report to the Panel "...in the natural interest of justice..."?

The Lambeth document entitled 'Bullying and Harassment' provides specific action that will be taken. Once the informal stage has passed, a complaint will move to the formal stage.

If we assume that this is the case with Murray's complaints, then the following action is necessary if Lambeth are to follow their own policies and procedures:

BULLYING AND HARASSMENT POLICY

4.   ACTION

4.2. Formal steps

4.2.1. Where an employee decides to raise the issue formally, or where informal steps have failed to resolve the issue, then there will be a need for the allegation to be formally investigated; such an investigation shall be conducted on a similar basis to the conduct of a disciplinary Investigation. All investigations are conducted confidentially although evidence obtained during the course of an investigation may be required for any disciplinary proceedings and all employees will be advised of this..."

It is evident that Murray had made a formal complaint **after** she was dismissed, but it is also evident that Field, Whitmore, Hiley and Foster **never** made formal complaints. No written accounts of their alleged complaints have ever been produced. To hold an investigation, therefore, into complaints about a person (in this case, Brian Pead) where there has been no official complaint made and documented in writing is an entirely unlawful process.

4.22. The employee should raise any formal complaint with their line manager/supervisor. In circumstances where this is inappropriate then it should be raised with that manager's manager. In very exceptional circumstances where this is inappropriate, then the complainant may wish to raise the complaint in the first instance with the Directorate/Business Unit lead officer for personnel.

If we are to accept that Hiley, Field, Whitmore and Foster made formal written complaints about Pead, they would have had to have done this through his Line Manager, Barry Gilhooly. When interviewed by Twist, Gilhooly – the regular visitor to Goa – did not once make mention that he had ever conducted formal or informal interviews about complaints made by these women against Pead. In fact, he said that he had never received a single complaint against Pead from either a member of staff or a pupil.

4.2.3. Where, arising from that investigation, disciplinary charges are forthcoming then the individuals concerned will be dealt with in accordance with the disciplinary procedure.

4.2.4. It may be necessary in serious cases either to suspend the alleged harasser or to arrange for them to be moved pending the outcome of an investigation/ disciplinary process. The complainant should not normally be moved, and certainly not without their agreement.

4.2.5. There is a commitment to the speedy resolution of complaints, but it is recognised that this does require the co-operation of the complainant. Normally all cases should be investigated and concluded **within 13 weeks of the complaint being made**. However, it is anticipated in non-complex cases that matters should be dealt with more speedily.

Note that in the worst-case scenario, Lambeth's policy states that complaints will be investigated and concluded within 13 weeks of the complaint being made. Murray made her complaints 'official' on 19 January 2007 – this information came from Twist herself. Thus, the 13-week maximum limit to conclude the investigation would give a date of Friday 20 April 2007.

This 'investigation' was certainly not concluded by then. Most witnesses had not even been interviewed by that date. Brian Pead was not interviewed until 19 April 2007 – just a day before Lambeth's self-imposed deadline for such disciplinary matters expired.

Given that Lambeth's own policy stated firmly that the 13-week limit was its aim, why had important witnesses not been interviewed? Why was Lambeth Council buying time? What did it need to distance itself from?

charge 3

Twist then reads out Charge 3, that Brian Pead harassed Annabel Field:

> "...Annabel Field was not able to attend the hearing but was available for interview. She described her relationship with Brian Pead as mixed from the beginning. She described him as intrusive and manipulative and found his behaviour inappropriate. She said their relationship became fiery and she found it difficult to define Pead's behaviour. He added the email sent to him by Annabel Field and this is now a tabled document. The panel will need to look at this evidence but also compare this to the interview notes of AF. In conclusion, Pead did cross professional boundaries which resulted in the harassment of Annabel Field between the period of January and May 2006. In deciding, the panel will need to consider whether his style and nature of conversations with Field was appropriate for a Head of OLCVS and whether his behaviour falls below that of an adult in a position of authority as the head of the Centre..."

This is one of the most worrying charges in the entire report by Twist and it is particularly damning of the Panel members (who had all been seconded on to the Panel because they would deliver a 'guilty' verdict.)

No reason is given to the Panel for the non-appearance of Annabel Field. Not a single Panel member bothers to ask why.

Twist refers to a 'statement' from Annabel Field – this had not been supplied to Brian Pead at any stage of the proceedings. This renders the entire charge unlawful and inappropriate.

Twist was then forced to mention the email from Annabel Field to Pead of 17 April 2006 in which she says that working at the OLCVS was her best experience in London.

This email completely contradicts the allegations that Twist has just read out.

Not a single Panel member stopped her at this point and pointed out the obvious discrepancy. They allowed her to continue to weave her fabric of lies.

Pead should have been given the opportunity as to whether he would allow a statement from Field to be admissible evidence. Given her non-appearance at any stage of the proceedings, he would not have allowed the alleged statement (which he had never seen) to form part of the proceedings.

It should also be noted here that Twist omits any mention whatsoever of the alleged masturbation in the theatre. This is for obvious reasons. Had she mentioned it here, the Panel would have been forced to address it and ask – did this happen or not? And, of course, when they learnt that it could not possibly have happened, they would have had to call into question all of Murray's other allegations. Twist therefore malevolently omitted the incident altogether.

charge 4

Twist reads out Charge 4 – that Pead harassed Eloise Whitmore. Strangely, Whitmore had never accused Pead of this before – not even when she had been dismissed by him, but suddenly she came out of the woodwork to make allegations which were a carbon copy of those made by Murray! Perhaps she smelt a possible opportunity for another cash hand-out by Lambeth Council.

> "...Ellie Whitmore described Pead as overly friendly and that he had an intrusive personal style. She described how supportive he was at the beginning, when OLCVS had opened and then how things changed in October 2005. He became more formal, made jokes about her, made light of her going shopping with her mum and also would refuse her having lunch with other staff members. Her job description was changed and revised and he often referred to her as his PA and Secretary. She said that he was rigid, controlling and bullying. This issue was also dealt with in the employment tribunal but also gives us an insight into his management style. She said at the beginning he was flexible and sociable but when things changed she began keeping a diary of his behaviour towards her. He told her that he was concerned with her attitude and that she was not performing contractually. Jenny Foster said that Ellie was side-lined and was treated awfully by Pead. Ellie said that she left the OLCVS feeling de-skilled and without confidence. In deciding, the panel will need to consider whether his style and nature of Pead and treatment of Ellie was appropriate for a Head of OLCVS and whether his behaviour falls below that of an adult in a position of authority as the Head of the Centre..."

Eloise Whitmore did not produce a single piece of evidence to prove any of her allegations. Her entire statement was nothing but fabrication and hearsay evidence. As Sandra Roach pointed out, "anyone can say anything about anyone, but can they prove it?"

Twist claims that Whitmore kept a diary of Pead's alleged behaviour towards her. **Why was this diary never adduced as evidence?** This might have gone some way to 'proving' her allegations, but she did not produce it.

Twist also mentions that Whitmore had left the OLCVS feeling "...de-skilled and without confidence..." When this was first reported to Pead by Twist, she also claimed that Whitmore was now "...too afraid to leave the house..." and that she was "...suffering from severe depression..." as the result of Pead's bullying of her. He challenged Twist (and Whitmore) to produce doctor's certificates to prove that this was the case. Pead knew this to be a likely fabrication, since both Murray and Hiley had said that they were still associating with her outside of work. Presumably this was not coffee and a slice of cake at Whitmore's house.

Furthermore, Twist lied in respect of the Employment Tribunal. Whitmore's appeal against dismissal never went to an Employment Tribunal - she was paid in an out-of-court settlement.

Why would Twist lie so much and so often?

What did she have to gain by lying?

charge 5

Twist went on to read out Charge 5 that Brian Pead harassed Anya Hiley.

"...Anya Hiley said that Pead was overly friendly initially and did cross boundaries. She started working as a Connexions Personal Advisor in September 2005 to August 2006. Whilst at the OLCVS site in Norwood, she said that Pead was enthusiastic and insightful. However, she felt that he was not genuine and his extensive flattery was inappropriate and made her feel uncomfortable. She also commented that if she felt uncomfortable around him, how would he make vulnerable young people feel? She said that Pead gave a Life Coaching business card to one of her clients, a heavily pregnant young female. She found that his questions were inappropriate and was concerned that he was grooming young women. She brought her concerns to her line manager when she found out that he was using another name. In conclusion, Anya Hiley was subjected to harassment whilst striving to forge professional relationships and give support to students between September 2005 and August 2006. In deciding, the panel will need to consider whether Pead's style and nature of conversations with Anya Hiley was appropriate for a Head of OLCVS and whether his behaviour falls below that of an adult in a position of authority as Head of the Centre..."

There is no evidence to corroborate Hiley's assertions whatsoever and considerable evidence from staff at the West Norwood community centre that Brian was doing an excellent job and that staff and pupils respected him. Twist makes no reference to the fact that there is no solid evidence. Nor does she state that Hiley worked on the top floor of the Old Library and that the OLCVS was on the ground floor. If Hiley was doing her job properly, how did she manage to see all that she alleged was going on?

According to Pead, he did give a heavily pregnant late teenager/ early twenties young woman a Life Coaching card because (a) at that time the OLCVS did not even have a phone of its own and, more importantly, (b) Hiley was not in her office and the young woman was in a state of distress because she was unable to contact Hiley. With a child and heavily pregnant, she told Pead that she had no place to live. Brian Pead said that he would have offered his card (with his home number on it so that she call him in an emergency) to anybody in a similar situation, including a male. He has worked with the homeless at Crisis for Christmas.

Why was this information not given to the Panel? Why, indeed, was the young woman not called as a witness if Twist really was conducting a full and thorough investigation? After all, Hiley claimed that this woman was a client of hers, so she would have had her contact details.

If Hiley had found Pead's questions inappropriate, why did she not report this for **eight months** and why did she not report it at all until after Murray had been dismissed?

Why would Hiley even think that his conversations with some very challenging and often disturbed pupils – male and female – would be grooming? The authors allege that this is because of projective identification – that **she** had these feelings and had projected them into Pead as if they were **his** feelings and not her own. After all, Hiley and Murray were "as thick as thieves" and both had full access to the contact details of many vulnerable young people.

Twist states that Hiley brought her concerns to her line manager when she found out that he was using another name. How did Hiley come by this information? She was not even employed by the OLCVS. She could only have come across this information through Murray herself.

Twist claims that Pead harassed Hiley. How can he possibly have done? According to Hiley's own testimony, she ceased all relations with him and they had no contact. By definition, it is not possible to harass someone with whom you have no contact.

charge 6

Twist then turned to Charge 6— that Brian Pead used inappropriate language towards young female pupils.

> "...In considering this allegation, the panel will have to give due regard to the interpretation of the phrase "inappropriate" style of language. For this investigation, it relates to the nature of conversations and conduct with female students. Murray described in detail that incident [of the low-cut top] and thought that the conversation was inappropriate for the Head of Centre to have with a female student. Pead said that he chose to participate in the conversation with Chloe Gordon..."

In conjunction with Duane Maddison, Brian had put on a Fashion Week in which pupils learnt about exploitation through fashion. When Chloe Gordon seemed perplexed about having to wear a low-cut top at her hairdressing job, Pead said he saw this as an excellent opportunity in which to teach Chloe, aged 14, about how fashion can exploit people – especially young women. Pead discussed this with Maddison too. It is the sort of conversation, Pead asserts, that any concerned parent might have with their daughter. The conversation had been entirely initiated by Chloe Gordon and Pead had simply and effectively dealt with the issue.

But why was Chloe Gordon herself not called as a witness, or her parents?

This is the very basic requirement of such an allegation.

Twist continues with Charge 6:

> "...Maryn Murray said that she also had concerns about Pead's intentions and motives for his personal conversations with Ashleigh Mills about her home life. She said that this made her feel uncomfortable. Colin Hill was concerned about the parameters of these conversations with students. Colin Hill appeared to be ambivalent when he came to the hearing last week compared to his interview earlier on this year..."

Had there really been concerns, why was Ashleigh Mills not called as a witness? Why was her aunt not called? Ashleigh Mills' mother had been sectioned under the Mental Health Act and that, as a direct consequence of this, Ashleigh was looked after by her aunt. This is not an ideal situation for any pupil. Furthermore, Ashleigh had started at the Centre several weeks after it had first opened its doors and she therefore missed a lot of the coursework that she needed in order to take her GCSEs.

It is reprehensible that Twist did not investigate all of these facts. A simple invitation to Ashleigh and her aunt would have provided completely satisfactory reasons for Pead's discussions with Ashleigh Mills – they needed to discuss her work, how she could catch up and they naturally needed to discuss her emotional life since the impact upon Ashleigh of her mother being sectioned was considerable. Ashleigh was an intelligent and sensitive 15 year old pupil at the time and Pead was doing everything he could to offer her stability and ensure that she was well prepared for her GCSEs.

Why did Twist not investigate this? Why did she completely take Murray's view, when the facts would have shown a completely different story?

These are not mere 'worrying lapses'. This is perverting the natural course of justice.

> "...The panel in deciding will need to consider whether Brian Pead's style and nature of conversations with students was appropriate for a Head of the OLCVS and whether his behaviour falls below that of an adult in a position of authority as Head of the Centre with a large proportion of vulnerable young people..."

It is precisely because of the nature of the pupils and their vulnerability that Pead was forced to engage at times in some lengthy conversations. It would have been insensitive of him to try to deal with Ashleigh Mills' problems in, for example, just ten or twenty minutes. At no point had Ashleigh herself ever stated that she did not want these conversations – in fact, she usually initiated them with a comment about her home life and she welcomed the conversations, often with her aunt in attendance.

Twist apparently failed to understand that this was Murray's thinking – at no point did Ashleigh Mills or her mother or aunt ever make any complaints against Pead.

Twist informed the Panel that **Murray** "...felt uncomfortable..." when Pead engaged in lengthy conversations with female students. This raises two main issues: (i) she makes no reference to the sometimes lengthy conversations he had to undertake with male pupils and (ii) it is Brian Pead's assertion that Murray "felt uncomfortable" because she was jealous – she wanted lengthy contact with female pupils. He cites her sexual grooming of Gemma Mandry and Ashleigh Mills as evidence to support this assertion.

In respect of male pupils, Pead engaged in some lengthy conversations with two in particular. Both pupils will have to remain anonymous for reasons of confidentiality.

Pupil A was a Brazilian male who struggled with his sexuality, as many teenagers do. He was a particularly sensitive young man who was also anorexic. He was, at times, suicidal. It is inconceivable that Pead, with all his counselling training, would **not** have had lengthy conversations with such a pupil. However, Murray – of course – failed to note these conversations with this young man of 15. Twist failed to call him as a witness.

Pupil B was a rent boy and this fact was known to Social Services. He was a 'Looked After Child' by Lambeth and lived in a children's home. He would go AWOL from time to time and sell his body in London. He was 16. It is inconceivable that Pead would not have had lengthy conversations with this young man, too.

And he had lengthy conversations with the three Portuguese-Brazilian males who had complained about Murray's bullying and racism.

Yet none of this information made its way into the investigation which the deluded Twist continued to claim was both "...thorough and fair..."

charge 7

Twist continued with Charge 7 and read section 7 of the Lambeth Staff Code of Practice: Working for yourself and Others –

"...We heard that Brian Pead solicited work during his work hours at the OLCVS. He failed to notify the council that he was taking on paid and unpaid work even though he did sign a declaration of interest form.

Rosa Vaz and Barry Gilhooly have said that Pead did not state he had taken on paid and unpaid work and did not inform them in writing. Maryn Murray, Anya Hiley and Annabel Field all received business cards for his Life Coaching Work. This was an abuse of his power.

Anya Hiley also described an incident where Brian Pead gave his card out to a German woman whilst they were in a café having a work meeting. The Panel will need to take this evidence into account and decide on an appropriate response to this charge..."

At no point had Pead ever taken on paid work whilst in the employ of Lambeth Council. Thus Twist lied to the Panel.

Furthermore, he had not taken on any unpaid work either, since his counselling placements were not work, but formed part of his education which the OLCVS benefitted from and which Gilhooly – on his own admission - had agreed to.

Pead did not hand out his business card to Murray, Hiley or Field. In fact, there is no evidence from Field to suggest that he did.

If Pead **did** hand a card to a German woman in a café, the question has to be asked, "So what?" The card had on it his contact details and the OLCVS at that time did not even have a telephone. The German woman was a part-time art teacher and photographer and Pead asked her to contact him with regard to the possibility of her teaching art and photography at the OLCVS. This was not a man 'touting for life coaching work' but a man seeking to exploit every opportunity he had to introduce people into the OLCVS who could benefit his pupils, since several had requested that photography be added to the curriculum.

Another example of Brian taking every possible opportunity to benefit his pupils was when he volunteered at Crisis at Christmas in December 2005. He met a 25 year old woman - according to Murray's categorisation that would make her a 'young woman' – and he noticed that she spoke Portuguese.

Glauce Biagio takes up the story:

"...Brian noticed that I spoke Portuguese and asked me if I would be able to help out Portuguese-speaking pupils at OLCVS, since he said there were problems with providing a rounded education due to language difficulties.

I agreed to work at the OLCVS because I could see Brian's passion for, and commitment to, the job and for helping the students. I started working at the OLCVS in January 2006 and stayed until June 2006. I want to say that in all those months I was made to feel welcome, to feel part of the team and that my work (and myself) was valued.

At all times, Brian acted in a professional way with me. I noticed a lot of growth amongst all the students, not just the Portuguese-speaking ones.

I was impressed with Brian's professional attitude to the job, his staff and the students..."

The email was sent to Brian Pead by Glauce Biagio on 7 February 2007 at 14:00:25 via Hotmail.

Since this woman was in the age range that Murray claimed Pead was intrusive to and since she was a 'very attractive' Portuguese-Brazilian, why was she not called as a witness?

The reason is that she would have been a dangerous witness for the unprofessional Twist to call ... she was extremely close [in a professional way] to the three black Portuguese-speaking boys who complained and provided evidence of Murray's racism and bullying. Little wonder, then, that Glauce Biagio was not called.

charge 8

Twist read out Charge 8 –

> "...that on the 27 February 2006, Brian Pead did not comply with Lambeth's recruitment policy when he offered a post to Maryn Murray. We have heard from witnesses that Pead offered Murray a permanent contract from April 2006. The contract never appeared and she was always being told that it was in the post. Murray said that she was concerned when the contract didn't appear as she had resigned from a post as Head of Department at St. Augustine's School in Ealing..."

The evidence does not support Murray or Twist. On 7 May 2006 – a month **after** Pead was alleged to have offered Murray a contract – he wrote to his line manager about his concerns in respect of staff contracts not being issued by Gilhooly and Lambeth. He wrote: "...I feel sure that you will agree that this is an unacceptable situation which we now need to resolve. We have spoken in the past about the posts being advertised, and staff applying for their own jobs. I have met with Duane and Maryn, and they fully understand the process that must take place..."

This is clear evidence that Pead had **not** offered Murray a contract and furthermore that he had met with Duane Maddison and Maryn Murray and fully explained the process of jobs having to be advertised formally. Pead would have recorded these meetings – in fact, Murray viewed Pead as 'obsessive' with regard to his meticulous habit of recording Minutes of meetings, printing them off, showing them to other staff, asking for their comments, possibly re-typing the Minutes and then finally signing them off once all parties involved had agreed that the Minutes were a true record. This is not 'obsessiveness' as Murray claimed, but rather good management and business practice. Pead kept a record of his meetings with Maddison and Murray but these were unlawfully removed from his office when Twist gave orders for it to be ransacked.

The email Pead sent to his Line Manager is incontrovertible evidence that Pead **had** not offered a contract to Murray outside of Lambeth's policies and procedures.

Furthermore, Twist is confused – once again – in terms of chronology. She informed the Panel that Pead had offered Murray a contract on 27 February 2006 and then that he offered her a contract in April 2006. Both dates cannot be true. The truth is that Pead did **not** offer Murray a contract. He did enter into discussions with her around a contract being awarded, which is not the same thing at all.

Twist continued to misinform the Panel when she said:

"...In conclusion, on the 27 February 2006, Brian Pead offered Maryn Murray a post of Deputy Head. On the strength of this, she resigned from her post at St Augustine's School in Ealing. This constitutes gross misconduct and the Panel will need to consider all the evidence and decide on an appropriate response to this charge..."

Note the name of St. Augustine's School in Ealing.

charge 9

Determined to find Brian Pead guilty of something – anything – Twist moves forward to Charge 9:

> "...in the investigation interview with Pead on 19 April 2006, he told us that Nadia Al-Khudhairy, a student from King's College London undertook a 3-week research project at the OLCVS in the Autumn Term of 2006 and commended his approach..."

It should be remembered that when he was unlawfully suspended, Brian Pead was charged with just five 'offences' – none of which was identified: they were all just generic terms. These five original charges grew month on month to **fifteen** separate charges. This is clearly unlawful. Alex Passman – who has been instrumental in the University of Plymouth's Innocence Project <http://www.plymouth.ac.uk> - told Pead that "...the goalposts keep moving..." as further charges were added once Pead had rebutted the original five charges.

Twist continued:

> "...Barry Gilhooly said that he never knew anything about this project and did not authorise it. Rosa Vaz also said that she was not made aware of the project. Brian Pead could not confirm CRB checks had been carried out on Nadia and her team and therefore was putting young people at risk. Colin Hill said that the project was about Addictive Personalities and that Nadia had recently come back to the school to finish off the project. This offence constitutes gross misconduct and the Panel will need to take all the evidence into account and decide on an appropriate response to this charge..."

Of all the allegations against Pead, this was one of the most outrageous for a number of reasons. Neither Gilhooly nor Vaz needed to know anything about the project. Vaz worked in the Human Resources department at Lambeth and thus had no need whatsoever to know about this project. It fell outside of her remit, as Twist would know. Yet this charge and Twist's handling of it exemplifies her inappropriate and unlawful handling of the entire case. She had a propensity to throw names around as if trying to add weight to her allegations. The fact that she said "Colin Hill said the project was about Addictive Personalities" has no significance whatsoever.

But the most worrying aspect of this charge is that it was not Pead's responsibility to ensure that Nadia Al-Khudhairy and her team of three were CRB checked. Pead had, in fact, spoken with Dr Patricia Conrod, the creator of the Preventure Programme about the project and she ensured Pead that **all of her staff had been CRB checked** by King's College in order to be allowed onto the programme. Of course they would have been. Furthermore, they were subjected to **enhanced checks** which are, as their name suggests, more detailed searches into the backgrounds of personnel. Pead asked her to send him a letter on King's College notepaper confirming that the researchers had been CRB checked. Dr Conrod sent this letter and Pead filed it away. It was removed from Pead's office when it was ransacked in December 2006.

All Twist had to do was make a single telephone call to Dr Conrod at King's College and get copies of the team's CRB checks faxed over to her or put in the post.

That she failed to make the call to Conrod is a breach of the Duty of Care that she owed Brian Pead and Twist is guilty of negligence since it is clearly negligent not to have made this call, just as it was negligent of her not to have visited the White Bear Theatre, little more than a mile away from Brixton.

In May 2012, Nadia Al-Khudhairy provided further evidence to the authors that all members of her team had been subjected to enhanced CRB checks. Pead, therefore, could never have been guilty of the offence and Twist knew this.

charge 10

Twist also knew that Pead could not be guilty of Charge 10 or any other charge:

> "...Charge 10— From the investigation interviews, it's clear that Brian Pead used two other names and staff found this to be unnecessary as why he would have three names. [...] Pead denies touting for business; however giving out business cards and taking phone calls for Steve Goodfellow shows that he was doing his Life Coaching business whilst he was working for Lambeth..."

Twist had conducted a fishing expedition when interviewing Pead – she had not conducted a professional investigation. To suggest to the Panel – as she does here – that a man handing out cards is proof of his conducting a life coaching business whilst working for Lambeth is nonsense. It proves nothing of the sort. In fact, it corroborates Pead's claim that he had to hand out cards to certain people so that they could contact him because the OLCVS had no telephone number.

No evidence was ever adduced to show that calls were taken in the name of Steve Goodfellow at the OLCVS. In fact, the reverse is true. If Pead gave out his 'Steve Goodfellow' card in order to provide people with his mobile number so that he could be contacted regarding school matters at the time the OLCVS had no number, why would he continue to hand these cards out once the OLCVS did, finally, obtain a number? He would not have had a need to continue to hand out cards **unless he was operating a life coaching business from the OLCVS.** He had no time to do such a thing and he had no inclination. But the key to this allegation is Murray herself – "...I don't know if Brian was running his business from school..."

Thus Twist was trying to convince the Panel that Pead was guilty of an offence when even the person making the allegations – Maryn Murray – did not even know if Pead was running a life coaching business from his office.

Furthermore, the business cards that Pead handed out to about four or five people clearly have the website www.stevegoodfellow.com printed on them. All Twist had to do was log on to that website. She no doubt did. She would have found that the website had not even been created – it did not exist. This was proof that Pead was not running a life coaching business under that name (or any other name).

Twist's propensity to pervert the course of justice knew no bounds. She continued to lie to the Panel:

> "...Brian Pead was the name on all his documents including his email and Barry Gilhooly stated that he allowed him to be known as Brian Johnson..."

Brian Pead was **not** the name on all his documents including his email. For example, the email Annabel Field sent to him on 17 April 2006 was sent to brian.johnson89@hotmail.co.uk – this is irrefutable proof that Twist lied. On 10 October 2006, Pead emailed Alicia Reynolds – which Reynolds confirmed – using the same email address. This demonstrates that Pead had been using that email address for some months. In fact, he used it throughout his entire tenure at the OLCVS (1 August 2005 – 8 December 2006).

The devious and lying Twist told the Panel:

> "...This offence constitutes gross misconduct and the Panel will need to take all the evidence into account and decide on an appropriate response to this charge..."

charge 11

Twist continued to mislead the Panel:

"...Charge 11 - The panel has heard evidence from three female staff, who say that at the beginning of their time at the OLCVS, Pead would ask personal questions and was intrusive. Derek Langan said that several meetings were in line with a mental health check; Pead had a psychoanalytical approach that made staff uncomfortable and if he was in his position he would be more careful. [...] Anya Hiley said his behaviour was inappropriate and in the worst case might be grooming young women. In conclusion, this constitutes gross misconduct and the panel will need to take all the evidence into account and decide on an appropriate response to this charge..."

Twist not only perverts the natural course of justice, but she also abuses her power in using the process to throw as much mud at Pead as she could. Pead has never groomed young women or young men for that matter. To suggest this here is wholly unprofessional and inappropriate and slanderous. Derek Langan had said no such thing to Twist about meetings being in line with a mental health check.

Twist continues her tirade against Pead, knowing that she is lying to, and misleading, the Panel.

charge 12

"...Charge 12— Throughout the investigation and hearing, you've heard from witnesses who said that Brian Pead gave favourable treatment to some female students between November 2005 and November 2006. Murray cites a number of incidents including how two female students, Cassandra Trimmings and Kerrie Hamilton were allowed to take exams without following exam regulations. Brian Pead admitted offering an admin post to a female student and also had a number of conversations with student Ashleigh Mills about her personal life and her relationship with another student. Murray thought that Ashleigh Mills was uncomfortable with the conversations and Pead said that he would also have 2, 5 or 20 minute conversations with her and at times asking her whether she would like to talk and Ashleigh saying 'No.'..."

This extract is yet another example of how Cathy Twist carefully selected sentences from people's statements and wove them into 'proof' that Pead had committed these offences. Only one female student was allowed to sit an exam late and this was in line with the Exam Board's regulations.

That Pead offered Ashleigh Mills an admin post at the OLCVS is not in dispute. Even Murray – in her statement of 19 January 2007 – states: "...Brian had mentioned to Ashleigh an opportunity to do a vocational course which would involve doing administration work at the Centre. **I thought this would be a good opportunity for Ashleigh...**"

Thus Murray herself told Twist that Ashleigh Mills had been offered an admin post at the Centre because it would be a vocational course (and she could obtain a certificate).

Yet Twist never presented a full and balanced account, omitting this vital piece of information.

Murray also made the following comments about Pead's conversations with Ashleigh Mills: "...**Their conversations were not in complete privacy as the Centre is open plan...**

This piece of evidence had never been reported to the Panel. Pead had told Twist that the Centre was open plan and that there were numerous staff always around who worked for the West Norwood Community Centre. Of course Pead occasionally withdrew female – and male – pupils from lessons so that he could have conversations with them about matters which were sensitive to the pupil concerned. But at all times, Pead and the student were always in sight of other adults and always captured on the CCTV that operated in the Centre.

Murray added: "...I didn't want to listen in on their conversations but what I did hear related to Ashleigh's home life and later about her relationship with another male student..."

It is clear that Pead would have spoken about Ashleigh's home life, since her mother had been sectioned and she was living with her aunt. It is also clear – and acceptable – that Pead would have spoken with her about her 'relationship' with another male student, since he wanted to avoid unnecessary frictions between students. These conversations formed part of Pead's role as head of the OLCVS. He was merely doing his job, and doing it very well, since the OLCVS was rated "...the best PRU in London..." by Nadia Al-Khudhairy of King's College.

Twist informed the Panel that:

> "...Murray also cites a conversation that Pead had with student Chloe Gordon about a low-cut work top and Maryn Murray intervened in this conversation because she thought it was inappropriate..."

Murray may well have cited this conversation. However, it did not happen in the way in which Murray described. She had delusions of grandeur and always felt that she knew better than anyone else, even though her CV did not support this. She was not even a fully qualified teacher, something Twist would have known about.

But – as has been mentioned previously – Twist failed to call the key witness, Chloe Gordon, who would have given her a completely different version of events. Gordon trusted Pead and he trusted and respected her. They enjoyed a positive and professional teacher-student relationship.

Twist continued:

> "...Murray said that she does not recall male students being given the same amount of time or being shown favourable treatment..."

Murray did not recall this? Hadn't she earlier claimed that she had been keeping a dossier on Pead from her first day at the Centre because he had asked her to go for a walk in the woods? Why didn't she consult this alleged dossier?

charge 13

"...Annabel Field said she wanted to enter a student Rickkardo Crawford-Burrows for an exam and Pead disagreed and refused to enter the student and would subsequently move him down..."

Rickkardo Crawford-Burrows did sit the exam. A year early.

"...Cassandra Trimmings, Chloe Gordon and Gemma Mandry were all vulnerable students who were given favourable treatment by Brian Pead..."

Where is the evidence that these female pupils received "...favourable treatment..."? This is just a wild assertion by Murray and then perpetuated by Twist with no proof whatsoever to substantiate it.

"...Anya Hiley was concerned about the amount of time that Pead was spending with particular students. All students had tutorials and he had the more emotional students. He denies giving preferential treatment to students and that they had been referred by other staff and chosen to meet him according to their need. One has to ask how he identified their needs. He said girls talked more than boys and so they would have longer conversations. The Panel in considering this charge will need to consider that although these incidents are minor; the cumulative effect of these is very serious and as such constitutes gross misconduct..."

Although Twist says "...One has to ask how Pead had identified their needs..." at no point did she ever actually ask this question of him or other staff. The more emotionally vulnerable and 'needy' pupils were often easy to recognise. Jenny Foster, for example, did not like tutorials with the more difficult boys. As a good manager, Pead ensured that either he or Duane Maddison would have tutorials with these boys, since both men were well equipped to deal with these often boisterous young men. Yet Twist makes no mention of these sound management principles.

It is common knowledge within counselling that female clients access the talking therapies in much larger numbers than male clients do. Pead offers no apologies for the fact that more female students sought his help than male students. Obviously, more sensitive issues around pregnancy or the possibility of pregnancies do not really loom as large in the lives of young men as they do in the lives of young women.

For reasons of confidentiality one pupil cannot be named, but she had several discussions with Brian about an ectopic pregnancy that she had endured. This requires significant sensitivity since it involves a wide range of feelings, not least that of bereavement. No other member of staff was as suitably qualified to undertake this type of conversation.

charge 14

Twist added:

> "...Charge 14 - Duane Madison described an incident where Pead went outside with a student to have a cigarette after DM had already refused the student's request. When DM questioned Pead about this, he said that he was talking to the student because she had told him that he was being beaten up by her boyfriend. However this was not followed up by Pead with child protection or with her parents. The evidence shows that as Head of the OLCVS Pead's application of rules were not consistent with students at the OLCVS..."

This is a complete misrepresentation of the facts. Brian Pead does not smoke. He would not allow the students to smoke but knew he could not police what they did in their private lives outside of the OLCVS. On one occasion, Brian did go outside the OLCVS to talk with a pupil about her being beaten by her boyfriend and they discussed intervention by the police and social services. Once Pead had the information he needed, he checked this with the girl's mother on the telephone, who corroborated the girl's story.

Twist then gives her findings to the Panel, which came as no surprise to Pead, John Callow or Alex Passman:

> "...My overall conclusion is that after due consideration charges against Mr Pead have been proven. In my view he has behaved reprehensibly.

> He terminated two contracts and another teacher said that she was shocked when Murray left because she was the only female staff member left by October 2005. Pead tried to create a therapeutic community where he acted as the counsellor and leader. His behaviour was detrimental to the female staff.

> He also used three names and did not legally disclose this information to Lambeth Council and he also used council time to further his life coaching business.

> For charges 1 - 12 constitute gross misconduct under the council's disciplinary code and are very serious offences and as such it is for the panel to consider an appropriate response. Charges 13 and 14 constitute the other misconduct under the Council's Disciplinary Code. The Panel need to be mindful of the fact that the charges made against Brian Pead do not need to be proven beyond reasonable doubt but on balance of probability..."

The more observant reader will note that Brian Pead had previously been charged with fifteen separate counts. This had grown exponentially from the original five counts. However, Twist only mentions **fourteen** counts - this being that count fifteen, the alleged masturbation in the theatre was mysteriously dropped immediately prior to the Panel hearing. It stands to reason that if one count is dropped, the reasons would have to be provided to a Panel considering all of the charges. Had Twist, of course, informed the Panel that count 15 had to be dropped because it was untrue, and could easily be proven to be untrue, then all of the other charges would have to be dropped too, since the veracity of them would automatically have to be called into question.

Thus Twist deliberately misled the Panel.

Brian Pead called for a natural break. Judith Hare suggested a fifteen-minute break. The pretence that was masquerading as a Hearing resumed at 11:55.

pead's grievances against abuse of process

Pead summarised his complaints against the process. He provided a full and frank report about Twist perverting the course of justice.

Pead's complaints are reproduced below so that there can be no doubt that Lambeth had been provided with full knowledge that the proceedings were unfair and unlawful and that he had been forced to dismiss Maryn Murray because of her racism towards black pupils and her sexual grooming of young female pupils:

Presented by Brian Pead

30 July 2007

1. Bullying

My bullying complaint made prior to these allegations was not followed through by my Line Manager and Human Resources.

Prior to Murray's allegations against Pead – after her dismissal – he had informed Gilhooly that Murray was bullying him, as well as black male pupils. Gilhooly and Rosa Vaz did nothing to address these formal complaints. Gilhooly had even claimed, "...You can't be bullied, you're the manager..."

2. Management's request to Miss Murray

Management requested Maryn Murray to submit a list of allegations after her employment was terminated, despite the fact that I had already complained of her bullying towards me. Why is management giving any credence whatsoever to a document created by a person who has been dismissed for racism and bullying towards young black males and for the sexual grooming of young white female pupils? Why hasn't Barry Gilhooly reported Murray?

3. Integrity of allegations

A very serious allegation - forming part of my reason for being suspended - had been entirely fabricated by Miss Murray. The fact that Miss Murray should include the notion of my being masturbated in a theatre in full view of all the actors, actresses and audience (of 20) provides sufficient doubt with regard to the integrity of the other allegations. The inclusion of this allegation - along with terms separating students into 'attractive' and 'non-attractive' groups - also provides an indication of the disturbed emotional state of Miss Murray.

Lambeth were given substantial indication that Murray was a very disturbed individual who was a danger to female pupils. Lambeth did nothing to either address this problem with Murray or report her to the safeguarding authorities or the police.

4. Improper procedure - prejudicial methodology

A copy of all of Miss Murray's allegations was provided in advance to witnesses by management, before the witnesses were interviewed about the allegations. Management's claim that they sent out copies of the allegations prior to interviews because of the nature and breadth of the allegations is more reason not to prejudice the witnesses in advance. My rights have not been considered during this investigation.

Again, Brian Pead leaves Lambeth officials in no doubt that there has been an improper and unfair procedure. He also informs Lambeth that his rights have been breached.

5. Improper procedure - leading questions

The witness interview notes show that witnesses were provided with leading statements of an allegation prior to questions being asked of them. This is not acceptable practice during an investigation. Furthermore, this line of questioning has also taken place throughout this Disciplinary Hearing.

Alex Passman, as a qualified solicitor, knew very well that Cathy Twist's questioning was far from impartial. She would make a negative statement about Pead and then ask a question around that negative statement.

6. Collusion

During these proceedings the questioning has demonstrated that collusion in these allegations has taken place.

Eloise Whitmore, Maryn Murray and Anya Hiley all actually said that they had spoken to one another whilst the proceedings were on-going and before they were individually interviewed. This is, of course, improper. There was significant evidence of collusion – Lambeth did nothing to investigate this obvious collusion.

7. Improper content – hearsay

The witness statements, and cross-examination, have been based on hearsay and not factual information.

Alex Passman was astounded and appalled that Lambeth Council would spend hundreds of thousands of pounds of taxpayers' money on an investigation founded entirely on hearsay. There was no proof of any allegation other than Murray corroborating what Hiley said, Hiley backing Whitmore and all of them backing one another. This is not evidence, but mere hearsay and no-one can be found guilty on mere hearsay. Whitmore had been paid £8,000 in an out-of-court settlement even though she was unable to do the job for which Gilhooly had hired her, and Murray and Hiley had aligned themselves with one another. Of course they would all support one another's statements. Lambeth failed to investigate.

8. Improper Conduct by Management - misleading information and interpretation

The Panel was informed of me supposedly 'working' as a counsellor, during my suspension and sickness. This was 'Training with supervision' in a voluntary placement that was an integral part of my course requirement to become a qualified counsellor. My Line Manager was aware of my undertaking a course leading to a diploma in counselling. At no time did he point out to me that this had to be declared in writing, despite me informing him of the added value that this course would bring to the role, not least because of the Extended Services offered by the placement school.

It is recognised by ACAS and the Health and Safety Executive that activities not forming part of the activity or behaviour of that which caused the stress can be an aid to recovery.

It was assumed without evidence by management in their investigation that I was 'touting' for work as a Life Coach in a private business, which I do not have. My cards were printed in preparation for future use. With the benefit of hindsight, handing out these cards may have been naive on my part, but it was in order to provide a telephone number for contacting me in regard to matters arising in my role at Lambeth. Several witnesses spoke of a lack of resources at the commencement of the OLCVS. Not one witness mentioned that cards were given out after December 2005, save for the client of Miss Hiley's. It is illogical to assume that a Life Coach would 'tout for business' from a heavily pregnant, unemployed teenager seeking housing. This illustrates that I only ever handed out cards for the purposes of contact.

Pead drew attention to the disinformation and interpretation of events by Lambeth officials, particularly Cathy Twist.

9. Management Failure - lack of supporting evidence; gaps in methodology

A lot of time was spent around management exploring the fact of responsibility for an exam allegedly being taken outside of the regulation time. This was denied by Colin Hill, the exam officer, who - although reporting to me in my role - was, in fact, responsible for ensuring that the exams were carried out in the required manner, which he - and others - has stated they were. Management failed in its duty to provide a timetable for the exams in 2006 to ensure the veracity of Miss Murray's allegations.

Basic investigatory procedures were not followed by Cathy Twist. One of Murray's allegations was that Brian Pead had not allowed Rickkardo Crawford-Burrows to sit an examination. She cited the reason for this as being that Pead disliked Crawford-Burrows. The fact that Pead liked him a good deal is, in fact, neither here nor there. The issue is simple: did Crawford-Burrows actually sit the exam or not? The answer is that he did sit the exam. Where is the evidence? The evidence is provided in the list of exams that each pupil sat. This list **cannot** be falsified: it is put together by the Examination Board.

Pead informed Twist that Crawford-Burrows had not only sat the exam, but that he had been entered a year early for it, at the age of 14. Yet Twist did not see that this fired a warning salvo into the credibility she gave Murray's 8-page report.

Twist had incontrovertible evidence that Murray had lied about the exam. She had incontrovertible evidence that the masturbation in the theatre had never occurred. Yet she still pursued Pead.

10. Improper Conduct by Management - misleading information and interpretation

The Panel has been misled on some important relevant facts, inasmuch as these facts have been omitted from Management's investigation, report and comments during this Hearing. These include:

(1)   Witness statements that contradict the charges, although in the witness statement notes, are not included to provide balance in the report to the Panel.

(2)   The opening paragraph of the report entitled 'Background' did not inform the Panel as to how the project was required to be run in reality. It only refers to how it was intended to be run. This is a major factor in the way in which students' needs - both personal and educational - were subsequently required to be met.

(3)   All of the named students in Miss Murray's allegations were over the age of 14 and could be called without Social Services being involved. Yet their age was given as a reason by Management for them not being called as witnesses.

(4)   That at least 6 members of my staff were not interviewed or called as witnesses by management. The inclusion of these staff in the investigation was relevant in order to provide a fair balance in the findings to this Panel.

(5)   That not one member of Lambeth Council with whom I had significant contact was called by Management to provide a fair and balanced perspective

of events at the OLCVS on a daily basis. These employees include staff at the Old Library Centre, staff at the Redfearn Centre, and Lambeth Consultants.

(6)   That not a single member of any third party organisation associated with the OLCVS was called by Management to provide a fair and balanced perspective.

(7)   That no student was interviewed.

(8)   That no parent or carer was interviewed.

(9)   That additional allegations were added to the report to the Panel, over and above those for which I was suspended pending this Disciplinary Hearing.

This is a comprehensive list of complaints against Lambeth and Cathy Twist. Any single one of these complaints renders the entire investigation unfair and therefore unlawful. In cases such as this, the Court of Appeal stated that "...a careful and conscientious investigation of the facts is necessary..." Twist had not been careful and she certainly had not been conscientious. Her investigation was subsequently flawed.

11. Harassment

Management has constantly contacted me while I was suspended, instructed me to attend meetings whilst suffering from influenza, and being registered sick through my doctor due to the stress of being previously bullied, which was exacerbated by the lack of support from my Line Manager and Human Resources. I have also been harassed whilst at home.

It is clear that Brian Pead was not only subjected to an unfair and unlawful set of hearings – which lasted over a period of some eight months – but that he was constantly being harassed by Lambeth even when he was off work sick.

This tactic of trying to wear down the opposition was one that Twist and Gilhooly employed in the James Walker case, too.

Finally:

This summary is part of why I have resolved to take action (outside of Lambeth) against Lambeth for the treatment towards me.

Given the unreasonable circumstances and the treatment I have had to endure, I have no option but to seek relief from the incessant pressure upon my character and integrity.

It is evident that Brian Pead was under a great deal of stress at this point. This was exacerbated by Lambeth's failure to address the issue with Maryn Murray, who was abusing young female pupils **with the full knowledge of Barry Gilhooly,** his line manager.

He knew that, as he uttered each word of complaint, his words were falling on deaf ears. He knew that the whole process was a sham. And he knew that the sham was a cover for more serious issues of child abuse by Maryn Murray and others at Lambeth.

Hare told Pead that the decision would be made by the Panel – a Panel that had not challenged a single statement made by Twist.

Carol Palmer told Pead that he would receive a decision from the panel in writing within five working days and if this was to take longer then he would be notified and given the reasons why. She confirmed his address.

At 12:15 the Hearing was adjourned for the Panel to discuss. Management and Pead left the room.

Pead was already resigned to his fate.

outcome letter

It was expected that Brian Pead would be dismissed by Lambeth. Everything had pointed to this from the day he was suspended. But Pead is nothing if not a fighter and he fought hard and played fair. He knew he was up against the vast monolith that is Lambeth Council, but he had been up against the Premier League and the Football Association and won.

But victory against Lambeth was not his at this time. The entire course of natural justice had been perverted by Twist and White. The catalogue of perverse actions by these two was long and significant.

On 31 July 2007, Judith Hare, Chair of the Disciplinary Panel, sent Pead a letter entitled *Disciplinary Hearing – Outcome*.

The date of this letter is significant. It was authored **only one day** after the final day of the Hearing.

It might as well have been dated 8 December 2006, since Pead's fate had already been sealed on that day.

The letter is reproduced here in its entirety. Hare claimed that Pead had entered into evidence an email from Annabel Field. She does not add that he also entered evidence from Ipek Yȳlmaz, his companion to the theatre. Thus the letter contained serious errors.

The corruption and cover-up is of staggering proportions.

Re: Disciplinary Hearing - Outcome

I am writing to convey to you the decision resulting from the above hearing that was held over 4 days: 23, 24, 27 and 30 July 2007. You attended the hearing without representation although the panel enquired on several occasions whether or not you wanted further opportunity to gain representation. You advised the panel that trade union representation was not required at this time.

The panel heard evidence from management's witnesses: Jenny Foster - Learning Mentor; Barry Gilhooly - Assistant Director Inclusion; Anya Hiley - Connexions Advisor; Colin Hill - Teacher; Derek Langan - Teacher; Maryn Murray - former Teacher; Sandra Roach - Teaching Assistant; Rosa Vaz - Principal Human Relations Officer; Ellie Whitmore - former SAO. You did not present any witnesses or documentation (other than the tabled email from Ms Field - dated 17 April 2006) in defence of your case. The panel took into consideration the written and verbal submissions you provided.

After careful consideration of all the information presented by both parties, the panel found as follows:

A. GROSS MISCONDUCT

1. Charge 1: Harassment, bullying and victimisation of any employee (Section A2 of the Council's Disciplinary Rules)

That during the period November 2005 to November 2006 you caused distress to members of staff through an inappropriate style of management.

PROVEN

Reasons: Charge 1

The panel heard from you that you had an open style of management and that no concerns about your management style were raised by members of your team. However, the panel considered that frequent one-to-one meetings and the content of your conversations with some staff were at times inappropriate and that they were generally uncomfortable with your approach to them.

It will be seen that Hare has made reference to the fact that no staff had ever complained through the official channels. The frequent one-to-one meetings were weekly. Colin Hill had told the Panel that the meetings would be cancelled if a member of staff had a particularly heavy workload that week. Duane Maddison told the Panel that he had learned a great deal from these meetings.

Note the Panel fails to name any individuals who found the meetings 'inappropriate'.

2. Charge 2: Harassment, bullying and victimisation of any employee (Section A2 of the Council's Disciplinary Rules)

That during the period November 2005 to November 2006 you harassed Maryn Murray, teacher at the Open Learning Centre for Vocational Studies. The harassment took the form of crossing professional boundaries in deploying an overly intrusive personal style.

PROVEN
Reason: Charge 2

The panel focussed on more recent incidences and found that you created a hostile and intimidating environment for some staff. The panel were of the view that some witnesses were able to clearly demonstrate that they had experienced various forms of harassment by you and that your actions and comments were unacceptable to them.

Again, no specific names are mentioned. It is clear from the evidence in Brian Pead's possession – which the authors have had sight of – that the only members of staff who complained about his management were Maryn Murray (dismissed because of proven racism, bullying and child abuse); Eloise Whitmore (dismissed by Rosa Vaz for failing her probation period); Anya Hiley (who was never an employee of Pead's).

That Hare, White and Twist should put their names to this shameful Outcome Report demonstrates the high level of corruption and arrogance that exists within Lambeth Council.

3.   Charge 3: Harassment, bullying and victimisation of any employee (Section A2 of the Council's Disciplinary Rules)

That during the period January 2006 to May 2006 you harassed Annabel Field, teacher at the Open Learning Centre for Vocational Studies. The harassment took the form of crossing professional boundaries in deploying an overly intrusive personal style.

NOT PROVEN

Reasons: No reasons were given.

In any report like this, reasons have to be given for finding an employee guilty of an offence or not guilty. But not Hare – she lived by her own set of rules. She felt protected by Lambeth.

4.   Charge 4: Harassment, bullying and victimisation of any employee (Section A2 of the Council's Disciplinary Rules)

That during the period September 2005 to January 2006 you harassed Ellie Whitmore, Administrative Officer at the Open Learning Centre for Vocational Studies. The harassment took the form of crossing professional boundaries in deploying an overly intrusive personal style.

PROVEN

Reason: Charge 4

The panel focussed on more recent incidences and found that you created a hostile and intimidating environment for some staff. The panel were of the view that some witnesses were able to clearly demonstrate that they had experienced various forms of harassment by you and that your actions and comments were unacceptable to them.

Eloise Whitmore was actually sacked by Lambeth because she failed her first probationary report. It once took her two hours and five attempts to type a letter which was just one side of A4 in length. She had also claimed that Brian Pead slammed doors in her face when all the doors in the building had anti-slamming devices fitted. Whitmore had once accused Pead of dismissing her because she was of child-bearing age. She was paid £8,000 of tax-payers' money by Lambeth Council in an out-of-court settlement.

5.   Charge 5: Harassment, bullying and victimisation of any employee (Section A2 of the Council's Disciplinary Rules)

That during the period September 2005 to August 2006 you harassed Anya Hiley, Connexions Personal Advisor who was based at the Old Library. The harassment took the form of crossing professional boundaries in deploying an overly intrusive personal style.

PROVEN

Reason: Charge 5

The panel focussed on more recent incidences and found that you created a hostile and intimidating environment for some staff. The panel were of the view that the some witnesses were able to clearly demonstrate that they had experienced various forms of harassment by you and that your actions and comments were unacceptable to them.

Anya Hiley was never employed by Pead. On her own admission, she never spoke to him after October 2005, so the dates used by Hare, Twist and White are erroneous. The unmarried Anya Hiley became extremely friendly with Murray and had access to sensitive personal details of vulnerable teenagers. She described Pead as particularly 'insightful'. Little wonder, then, that she should claim that Pead 'harassed' her.

6.   Charge 6: Serious breach of the Staff Code of Conduct (Section A16 of the Council's Disciplinary Rules)

That you spoke inappropriately to a female student Chloe Gordon at the Open Learning Centre for Vocational Studies in that you told Chloe Gordon that she would get more tips if she wore her low cut uniform top for her part-time job.

NOT PROVEN

Reasons: No reasons were provided.

This unproven charge is incredible. Brian Pead actually admitted that he **had** had a conversation with Chloe Gordon about her low-cut work top. This conversation had been initiated by the pupil.

This charge had merely been included for its salacious properties. Of course Pead had not breached any code of conduct, but it had been included here to make the readers of this rubbish think that Pead was some form of pervert.

The reality is that it was Murray who was the proven pervert. She was assisted by Hiley and then reinstated by Gilhooly, Twist and Waters.

7.   Charge 7: Serious breach of the Staff Code of Conduct (Section A16 of the Council's Disciplinary Rules)

That you did not inform the Council in writing that you were undertaking unpaid work as a Volunteer for the Community Drug Agency in Surrey and paid work as a Life Coach during your employment with Lambeth Council.

PROVEN

Reasons: Charge 7

The Staff Code of Conduct clearly states that employees must notify the Council in writing before undertaking any other employment and must declare any voluntary or unpaid work. You received a copy of this form when you commenced employment with the Council, but clearly failed to notify your employers of the same.

Brian Pead had never worked as a paid life coach whilst in Lambeth's employ. Furthermore, there was no evidence of this. Lambeth failed to produce any evidence to support their wild allegation.

Brian Pead had informed Human Resources and Gilhooly about his unpaid volunteering as a counsellor at a Barnet school. He produced evidence to support these assertions at the investigatory meeting, but it was ignored by Twist and then Hare.

Twist failed to produce a copy of the alleged form that she claims was signed by Pead. It does not exist.

8.   Charge 8: Serious breach of the Council's Financial Regulations, rules and codes of Practice. (Section A18 of the Council's Disciplinary Rules)

That on 27 February 2007 you did not comply with the Council's Recruitment Policy and Procedures in that you offered Maryn Murray a contract as substantive deputy headteacher at the Open Learning Centre for Vocational Studies with effect from April 2006 without following the appropriate procedures.

PROVEN

Charge 8

The panel were satisfied that you had offered Ms Murray a permanent Deputy Headteacher post at the OLCVS without complying with the Council's Recruitment Policy and Procedures. This was evidenced in the email which you sent to Human Resources requesting that Ms Murray is the Deputy Head Teacher and should receive financial remuneration in acknowledgement.

Hare had obviously failed to take account of Pead's email to his line manager, Barry Gilhooly, dated 7 May 2006 in which he wrote "...We have spoken in the past about the posts being advertised, and staff applying for their own jobs. I have met with Duane and Maryn, and they fully understand the process that must take place..."

The language in Pead's email clearly shows that a contract is NOT in place for Murray and that a process must take place. The use of this tense is such that the contract cannot possibly have been issued or that the appropriate procedures had not been adhered to.

9.   Charge 9: Serious breach of the Council's Financial Regulations, rules and codes of practice. (Section AI8 of the Council's Disciplinary Rules)

That during the Autumn Term 2006 you allowed Nadia Al-Khudhairy a researcher from King's College to undertake a 3-week research project at the Open Learning Centre for Vocational Studies without ensuring that she had a current enhanced CRB Disclosure and without informing your Line Manager.

PROVEN

Reasons: Charge 9

The panel considered that your reported conversation with an employee at King's College as to whether or not Ms Al-Khudhairy had a current enhanced CRB disclosure was unacceptable practice, because you neither had the authority to assign Ms Al-Khudhairy in the first instance nor had sight of the CRB disclosure or written assurance that the CRB had been cleared.

It is worth noting the charge. Pead had been accused of some form of financial irregularity – yet this charge has nothing to do with finance and so it cannot be proven.

However, neither was Pead guilty of a breach of failing to see the enhanced CRB forms for Al-Khudhairy and her team. He had been assured by Dr Patricia Conrod that her entire team had all been subjected to enhanced disclosure checks. He asked her to send him a letter on King's College notepaper confirming this, which she did.

This evidence was removed from Pead's office when it was ransacked immediately after his unlawful suspension.

In a meeting with Al-Khudhairy in May 2012, she again confirmed that she had, in fact, been checked – as had her two colleagues. Pead, therefore, was never guilty of this charge.

10. Charge 10: Serious breach of the Council's Financial Regulations, rules and codes of Practice. (Section A18 of the Council's Disciplinary Rules)

That when you commenced employment you failed to disclose to Lambeth Council that you used the name Steve Goodfellow on the CRB Disclosure Application form that you completed for Lambeth Council.

PROVEN

Reasons: Charge 10

The panel were therefore satisfied that you were known by and had used the name Steve Goodfellow prior to your appointment with Lambeth, based on your own admission and on documentary evidence contained in the CRB disclosure form for your employment with Kingston-Upon-Thames. It was clear to the panel that you have had experience of completing CRB forms for various posts prior to your employment with Lambeth Council. Further that you were requested to provide details of any other names used at any time during your lifetime and the dates during which the names were used but failed to do so.

Pead did not fail to disclose this name. He had mentioned it to Lambeth in October 2006 and at the time he completed his first CRB form with Lambeth, he was not using that name. All of these demonstrable facts were explained by Pead – and evidence provided to support his assertions – but first Twist, then Hare, drove a coach and horses through the natural course of justice by completely ignoring the facts.

What is even more worrying is that this is, again, factually incorrect. **Pead has never been employed by Kingston-on-Thames** and his CV will demonstrate this fact. Therefore, Hare is seeking to rely on a fact which is not a fact at all – again, this shows sloppy and unprofessional work. Pead cannot, therefore, be guilty of this offence.

11. Charge 11: Misconduct in relation to other members of staff.

That you were inconsistent in your treatment of staff during the period November 2005 to November 2006.

PROVEN

Reasons: Charge 11

The panel were sufficiently satisfied that there was an inconsistency in the way you treated female staff from male staff members at the OLCVS. The panel noted that under your leadership most of the female staff left the OLCVS. The panel also heard evidence from some female members of staff that your overly intrusive style crossed professional boundaries. Male staff at the centre seemed to be unaffected by your actions.

This 'charge' is not a charge at all. It merely replicates the alleged charges against Murray, Hiley, Foster and Field.

It is also nonsense because no member of staff ever made a single complaint against Pead. Annabel Field had thanked Pead and Sandra Roach, for example, was extremely praiseworthy of Pead, so he cannot have been guilty of inconsistent treatment of female staff.

The question has also to be asked: how had Pead never received such a charge in more than 30 years of management? And why did his class of 17 females (he was the only male) on his counselling course all praise him for his 'sensitivity and support'?

12.   Charge 12: Misconduct in relation to students

That you were inconsistent in your treatment of students in that you gave favourable treatment to female students during the period November 2005 to November 2006.

PROVEN

Reasons: The panel found that on your own admission, you did have more one-to-one conversations with female than male pupils. The panel considered that in your role as Head of the OLCVS, it was important to lead by example and to ensure equitable treatment of all pupils at the centre.

Pead did admit to having more one-to-one conversations with female students simply because **there were more female than male students at the OLCVS**. Furthermore, females are more likely to engage in counselling and other talking therapies than are males.

To have found an employee guilty of such an 'offence' is palpable nonsense.

B.   OTHER MISCONDUCT

13.   Charge 13: Negligence in the Performance of your duties. (Section 82 of the Council's Disciplinary Rules)

That in June 2006 you made special arrangements for 2 students to take their mathematics examination and were negligent in the performance of your professional duties in that you did not comply with the procedures for public examinations issued by Joint Council for Qualifications - instructions for conducting examinations.

NOT PROVEN

Reasons: No reasons were provided for Pead not being guilty of this alleged offence.

That this allegation had not been dropped at a much earlier stage was deliberate. Pead had provided evidence to show that the students had not even sat the exams. This ridiculous charge had been added simply to add greater credibility to the alleged case against Pead.

Yet this charge serves another, more cunning, purpose. To the lay person, or outsider reading this afresh, it looks as though the entire process was fair because the lay person will look at it and say, "Well, he must have been guilty of the other charges and it must have been a fair and thorough investigation because they have clearly looked into a lot of different things and even found him not guilty on some charges."

Thus this charge performs a smoke-and-mirrors function.

14.   Charge 14: Negligence in the Performance of your duties. (Section 132 of the Council's Disciplinary Rules)

That you were negligent in the performance of your duties in that you failed to ensure the consistent application of rules for students at the Open Learning Centre for Vocational Studies in that you went outside with a 14 year old student so that she could smoke resulting in negligence in performance of your duties as Head of the Open Learning Centre for Vocational Studies.

NOT PROVEN

Reasons: No reasons were provided.

Had the entire process been thorough and fair, why was this pupil not interviewed?

Again, see commentary on charge 13.

Charge 15 – bringing the Council into disrepute following an allegation of masturbation in a theatre – had been mysteriously dropped. Why? And why was no reference made to it in this final report?

The reason is that this was clearly a lie. And given that it was a lie, it then called into question the entire charges against Brian Pead.

Judith Hare then gave an account of the Panel's views of Pead's grievances about the entire process. Her comments below are reproduced in their entirety, with the authors' commentary:

Grievance

At the stage of proceedings when management had the opportunity to question you on your presentation, you informed the panel that you have raised a grievance that had a bearing on the disciplinary hearing panel's decision making process. The panel asked you to make specific reference to your grievances as they relate to the disciplinary hearing proceedings. These were as follows:

1. The witnesses were sent a copy of Ms Murray's allegation prior to being interviewed.

2. Documents provided by you were not included in management's presentation of the case.

3. That you were denied access to the office up to July 2007 to gain access to important documentation.

4. That you were denied communication with members of staff whilst witnesses have stated they communicated with one another.

5. Despite allegations that you engaged inappropriately with students, not a single parent or student was interviewed.

6. Not all staff were interviewed in this process, certain female and male staff were not interviewed - management provided an incomplete picture of evidence and only interviewed those who would give credence to Ms Murray.

7. That not a single member of staff external to OLCVS was interviewed except for Anya Hiley. This means no male or female member of staff was interviewed to provide a full and balanced indication of your relationship with them.

8. That witnesses were coached by management and allowed to mingle with one another whilst waiting to be interviewed.

9. General comment - management did not pursue a certain line of questioning in respect of certain allegations. Management did not write to the theatre production company - you contacted the manager and there is evidence that will be provided as grievance. You asked the panel to consider the veracity of all of the other charges.

10. Ms Annabel Field's statement was not included in management's presentation.

11. Every witness was sent a statement to read and sign and you were not given the same opportunity.

The panel sought clarification from management on points 1,3,5,8 and 11 above which was as follows.

Point 1-The procedures do not state that the allegations cannot be forwarded onto the witnesses. Witnesses were sent a copy of the statement after they had already agreed to take part in the process. The complexity of the case and the number of people named in the allegations made this a necessity for management to be clear of the facts.

To send each member of staff a highly inflammatory document in which female pupils are described as "not so attractive", "attractive" and "very attractive" and other sexual allegations are made is an abuse of process. One example is the allegation of masturbation in the theatre. All of the staff read this allegation **before** they were interviewed. Had the process been entirely fair, the witnesses ought to have been sent notification that this allegation had, after all, been dropped and then **re-interviewed** once they had received this new information. But, of course, the damage had already been done by then by promulgating a libellous and inaccurate document.

Point 3—You were asked to refer to the suspension letter dated 8 December 2006. Management also stated that at a meeting on 20 April 2007 you were reminded about access to the office. At no time did you raise a request with management.

Brian Pead **did** raise a request with management for access to his office. This was immediately after his suspension on 8 December 2006. Gilhooly was always 'out of the office' when Pead called to arrange a visit to his office. He then sent in letters requesting visits, but still was denied access.

The reason, of course, is that his office had been ransacked on Twist's orders.

Point 5- Management stated that in child protection cases pupils under the age of 18 would be interviewed by social services not management. Further that it was not permissible to interview students under the age of 16 once the matter had become a disciplinary issue. You were advised that management were also mindful of adverse publicity for yourself and the OLCVS.

This is nonsense. Twist had claimed she couldn't call pupils as witnesses because of their age. In truth, she didn't call them because she knew she would have no case whatsoever.

Furthermore, why didn't Social Services interview pupils then?

And why weren't pupils interviewed **immediately prior** to it becoming a disciplinary matter. Both Twist and Hare had lied. They had not merely misled – they had deceived and lied.

Because Lambeth had dragged its feet, the pupils had, in any event, attained the age of 16 or over by the time the Disciplinary Hearing started.

With even stronger reason, why were no parents of pupils interviewed? Since they are all, obviously, over the age of 18, then no restrictions applied to them.

Hare claimed that any publicity might have damaged Pead's reputation. He knew this was impossible, since he was not guilty of any of the allegations. Anyone – he thought – whoever believed this nonsense without challenging it was a fool.

> Point 8- Management stated that they did not coach witnesses during the hearing and that had you brought witnesses you would have been allocated a room for you and your witnesses. Further witnesses had already given statements and did not add anything to the previous investigation.

The witnesses were clearly coached. They were all allowed to mingle. This is wholly improper practice.

The second sentence of Hare's point 8 serves no purpose whatsoever.

> Point 11 - You were given a copy of the disciplinary notes and had an opportunity to respond.

At no point was Brian Pead sent a copy of **his** four statements and asked to sign and return them. This means that the entire process was null and void.

Clearly Pead had not been sent copies of any person's statements in an abuse of process. He was entitled to have had sight of these statements before he was interviewed just as each member of his staff had been sent a copy of Murray's spurious allegations before being interviewed.

> "...The panel in consideration of these stated grievances were charged with the decision as to whether they impinged on the fairness of proceedings or not. The panel came to the view that in accordance with the disciplinary procedure you had the opportunity to present any witnesses or to submit any documentary evidence that would prove beneficial to you in the presentation of your case. The panel also found that other aspects of your grievance were either in accordance with procedure or otherwise management's actions were deemed to be a reasonable and not prejudicial to you in the circumstances. Accordingly your grievance is not upheld and the panel did not consider that the issues raised impinged on the fairness of the proceedings..."

Clearly Judith Hare does not understand the concept of fairness. The entire process was unfair according to the standards of the Court of Appeal.

You have a right of appeal on the grounds that are outlined in the Lambeth Council's Disciplinary Procedure, Section 9, specifically section 9.2.

The decision to dismiss you will be conveyed to the Executive Director of Children & Young Persons Service for ratification.

If you wish to appeal against this dismissal you may do so by writing to Phyllis Dunipace, Executive Director of Children & Young People's Service, 7th Floor, International House, Canterbury Crescent, London SW9 7QE, stating the grounds of your appeal within 5 working days of receipt of this letter.

As acknowledgment of receipt of this letter, please sign and return to me the enclosed copy within 5 working days. Failure to return the copy does not invalidate any possible subsequent procedures.

Judith Hare
Chair of Disciplinary Panel
cc: Cathy Twist - Assistant Director Inclusion Human Resources

And that was that.

124

decision ratified

On Saturday 4 August 2007, Brian Pead received a letter that he had to provide a signature for. He exchanged pleasantries with his usual cheerful postman, and went inside to open the letter. It was from Phyllis Dunipace – Executive Director for the Children and Young People's Service.

The letter read:

> Dear Brian Pead
>
> TERMINATION OF EMPLOYMENT CONTRACT
>
> I write with reference to the Disciplinary Hearing - Outcome letter dated 31 July 2007 and to inform you that I have made the decision to ratify the recommendation that you are dismissed from the post of Head of The Open Learning Centre for Vocational Studies.
>
> Your dismissal is as a result of a disciplinary hearing held over four days: 23rd, 24th, 27th and 30th July 2007, when the panel considered that charges of gross misconduct against you were found proven and that you should be summarily dismissed effective from 31 July 2007.
>
> cc: Cathy Twist - Assistant Director Inclusion
> Personal File

This was, in itself, a strange letter. The title 'Termination of Employment Contract' was ambiguous. He knew that his contract was due to end in any event, but Dunipace referred to Pead being dismissed as a direct consequence of the disciplinary hearing held over four days.

Thus Dunipace was complicit in the corruption that had taken place. By signing such a letter, she was implicating herself in the cover up of the racism and sexual grooming that had been carried out by Murray.

This may have been one of the reasons that Dunipace unexpectedly resigned from her post as Executive Director on 8 August 2010 and was replaced by Deborah Jones who received an annualised salary of £154,000. The year before that Chris Lee resigned from an Executive Director's position on 19 July 2009.

Lambeth's Executive Directors were in the habit of causing destruction and leaving havoc in their wake before conveniently resigning from their posts with a smile and a fat pension, courtesy of the Lambeth taxpayer. None are ever held accountable. None, that is, before the publication of this book.

Cowardice asks the question, "Is it safe?"
Expediency asks the question, "Is it politic?"
And Vanity comes along and asks the question, "Is it popular?"
But Conscience asks the question, "Is it right?"

And there comes a time when one must take a position that is neither safe, nor politic, nor popular, but he must do it because Conscience tells him it is right.

Martin Luther King, Jr.

125

the derek langan letter

On 30 December 2007, Derek Langan – a man of integrity - felt compelled to write to Cathy Twist about the perverse verdict that had removed Brian Pead.

The wily Langan had taught English to the refugee and asylum seeker pupils and he did an excellent job – ensuring that they not only secured GCSEs in the traditional subjects of Maths and English, but also in their own mother tongue.

Derek Langan has given permission for extracts of his letter to be reproduced here.

After the initial introduction in his letter, he gives an account of the parlous state of finances at the OLCVS:

> "...One afternoon, Sandra Roach had to take one of our students to St. Thomas' Hospital in a taxi when she started to bleed heavily. She was only fifteen and had been raped at the airport in Somalia before flying to London some months earlier. After the emergency Mrs Roach asked to be repaid from petty cash for the fare, only to be told that there was no petty cash, and Brian simply paid her from his own pocket..."

This episode is indicative of Gilhooly's mismanagement of the Unit. Brian Pead had asked Gilhooly for sight of a budget since he started the job in August 2005, but – more than a year later – Gilhooly had failed to produce such a basic document.

Langan continued to inform Twist of the failings of Lambeth:

> "...Brian was removed and no understandable explanation was given to the staff or students and the stage was set for the kind of vicious riot we had in March (2007)..."

Langan is referring to the knife fight that occurred in the Centre after Pead's suspension in which seven police officers attended.

This was under the Acting Headship of Colin Hill.

The Unit was clearly deteriorating in terms of ethos and discipline. A year before, the Unit had been described by Nadia Al-Khudhairy of King's College as "...the best pupil referral unit in London..."

Clearly there was something rotten in the state of Lambeth.

Langan continues to describe how Lambeth Council had largely been responsible for the lack of staff morale:

> "...The situation was not helped either by the treatment of Duane Maddison, who had a really excellent relationship with the students, being constantly denied an update of his contract demanded by his bank which resulted in his losing out on a move to a bigger family home..."

Brian Pead had written to Gilhooly about contracts as long ago as 7 May 2006 – and more than eighteen months later, the contractual problems still had not been resolved. Yet Brian Pead had been suspended a year before Langan's letter, so he could not possibly have been held responsible for the continuing problems.

He continues:

> "...As I was paid out of Lambeth's central budget, I wasn't too worried about my contractual situation, but I witnessed a situation where we were getting by on a wing and a prayer. Though generally happy with my own pay and conditions, I am still angry that I had to wait four months after I left its employ for Lambeth to finally pay me five days' pay owing to me. I'm also angry that my final three week employment (six days pay) with Lambeth were curtailed as this breached the original, clear understanding re my work..."

Thus Langan has provided a clear picture of wholesale inadequacy by Lambeth and ultimately by Gilhooly, who was responsible for overseeing the Unit.

After bringing to Twist's attention the appalling mismanagement of the Unit by Lambeth in terms of contracts and pay and conditions, Langan then focuses on the pupils:

> "...I have to say, too, that there was not enough awareness on the part of the Authority as to the very damaged minds of many of our mainstream (not refugee) students and to their need for stability and security..."

The emphasis is Derek Langan's.

This book has provided much evidence to show that Brian Pead had a sound understanding of the educational and emotional needs of the pupils in his care. His line manager, Barry Gilhooly, failed to understand the needs of these deprived pupils. Brian Pead fought for their rights as human beings. Gilhooly was not interested. Lambeth Council was not interested. This Unit, it appeared, had not been created for the needs of pupils: it had been created for a much darker purpose.

> "...The psychotherapeutic approach used by the Head within an on-going school situation operated whereby anti-social behaviour was dealt with on an immediate or at least same-day basis by bringing home to the student why he/she was acting in a certain way and how

they were damaging themselves most of all. There were elements of individual and group therapy involved here with the psychological problems of the students being addressed..."

This intelligent analysis of Pead's leadership and management of the Unit by Langan is important. He understood exactly what his line manager was achieving. His analysis is remarkably similar to that of Nadia Al-Khudhairy, the research therapist who had invited Brian to write a paper about his running of the Unit for a psychology journal.

But Langan was acutely aware that Pead's emphasis on running the Unit was not a psychotherapeutic one, but a learning one. He informs Twist:

"...You would have been surprised to witness the good, old fashioned teaching in Maths that took place in an atmosphere of sound discipline - Mr Johnson was a real stickler here - and a requirement for quite high standards in these subjects..."

Thus Twist is left in no doubt by Langan that there was considerable learning taking place within the Unit.

He continued to vilify the local authority:

"...I feel that the Unit lacked that element of close contact with the wider services and facilities of the authority..."

This confirms what Brian Pead had been saying about the lack of contact he experienced from Gilhooly. The Assistant Director had claimed in an interview with Twist that he was in regular contact with Pead, but this was not the case.

Langan expresses his feelings more deeply:

"...a significant number of students who couldn't get into any school in the borough or who were simply not cut out for a large school arrived punctually each day, worked quite hard and generally behaved like decent human beings..."

This is, of course, hugely complimentary towards Brian Pead and his management of the Unit.

Langan explains more about the success of the Unit under Pead:

"...Moreover most students (all in the case of the EAL students) went on to further education..."

This was factually correct. Brian Pead had taken a group of more than sixty disaffected, deprived and disillusioned pupils and given them hope and direction in their lives so much so that the majority went on to further education and to lead decent lives.

Why, then, had Lambeth been so keen to remove him?

Langan continues:

> "...I feel here that an audit of the school's work would be useful. Also the psychological approach being used could well be looked at by the appropriate services. Recently I discussed my experiences with an old acquaintance, Dr Gerald Wooster, formerly Psychiatric Advisor to the University of London, and he expressed a deep interest and excitement at what was attempted at the Virtual School..."

This is an extraordinary paragraph from Langan. Firstly, he has suggested to Twist that Lambeth should conduct an audit into the success of the Unit so that best practice could be disseminated throughout the borough.

Then he mentions that Dr Gerald Wooster, an eminent psychiatrist and author, expressed a deep interest and excitement at what was occurring at the OLCVS. Again, this interest in Pead's work reflects the interest shown by Al-Khudhairy from King's College.

Gerald Wooster is a member of The Institute of Psychoanalysis with a background in psychiatry, university student health and was an NHS Consultant in Psychotherapy at St George's Hospital, London, with responsibilities for group therapy. He would understand very well the way in which Brian Pead ran the Unit along group therapy lines.

Langan makes a final important comment:

> "...In my 30+years in teaching I have seen these kind of young people being sent to PRUs, suspended and expelled. However, this kind of therapeutic approach as an integrated part of sound school practice may well have something to offer and it would be a pity if the opportunity to assess it was lost in this instance..."

This is an intelligent piece of reflection from an intelligent teacher. Langan makes it clear that Pead's therapeutic approach to teaching was integrated with sound school practice. Colin Hill had also stated to Twist and White that there was a heavy emphasis on teaching and learning and, of course, this is borne out by the fact that every pupil left the OLCVS with at least one nationally recognised qualification. Twist attempted to impugn Pead by claiming that he had merely focused on the therapeutic aspect of the OLCVS instead of the teaching and learning. Clearly, the evidence proves otherwise.

However, Twist failed to enter Langan's letter as evidence into the forthcoming Employment Tribunal. Furthermore, Langan's letter cast considerable doubt on Murray's allegations. Twist had enough evidence in her possession to show that this entire case against Pead had been fabricated.

Yet Twist did not call a halt to the Tribunal. In fact, she did the opposite. What on earth could be compelling her to destroy an innocent man?

twist vilified

Brian Pead knew that he had been "stitched up" by Twist. He also knew – like his father had told him almost half a century before – "...if you give 'em enough rope, they'll hang themselves..."

Pead waited.

Then his moment came in August 2011. John Callow, his friend who had stated throughout their discussions that Pead should seek legal representation as the disciplinary procedures did not appear to be in line with those he had encountered, called him.

Callow: Hi Brian. Just letting you know that Lambeth Education is on the tv. They sacked a Head Master wrongly and he fought them and won his case. It sounds very similar to your experiences and you may find it useful to conduct some research into the case.

There were, indeed, many similarities.

The BBC ran the following story:

Headteacher James Walker gets Lambeth Council payout

James Walker was suspended months after being treated for cancer

Head teacher unfairly dismissed

A headteacher who won an unfair dismissal case after quitting a south London school has been given more than £100,000 in compensation.

James Walker resigned from Henry Fawcett Primary School in Kennington in 2010 after claims of bullying and financial mismanagement.

Lambeth Council's investigation was criticised by an employment tribunal.

The council said both parties had "agreed to draw a line under the matter and move forward".

Mr Walker, who was suspended in 2008 after returning to work following six months of chemotherapy, called for action to be taken against those responsible for his ordeal.

Public money 'wasted'

Ahead of the compensation hearing on Friday, he said: "...When I returned to work after cancer, instead of getting support, I felt victimised..."

"Having won my case in August I hoped the wrongful actions of those responsible for damaging my career, wasting public money and needlessly disrupting the education of my former pupils would be thoroughly investigated.

"Three months on there is little evidence of this... no action has been taken against them..."

On ruling his dismissal as unfair, the South London Employment Tribunal criticised the council's inquiry into the allegations, saying this "...amounted to a fishing exercise which focused on obtaining the most damaging information about the claimant..."

Several witnesses put forward by the council were not credible, the tribunal said.

It criticised Penny Bermingham, who was the acting head of the school during Mr Walker's sick leave; Matt Britt, who was the interim headteacher after Mr Walker's suspension; and two senior education officers - Cathy Twist and Claire Cobbold.

Barry Gilhooly, a former assistant director at Lambeth who carried out the investigation into the allegations against Mr Walker, was also criticised by the tribunal which found his investigation was flawed.

They chose not to respond to BBC London's report.

Following the ruling, the council stressed that the action taken against the headteacher was "completely unrelated to his illness".

A spokesman said: "...The matter has been complex and difficult and the parties have agreed to draw a line under the matter and move forward.

"The council fully accepts the criticism made in the tribunal judgement and has apologised to Mr Walker..."

It added that disciplinary procedures had been reviewed but it would not take action against any individuals.

Simon Hughes, MP for Bermondsey and Old Southwark, said: "...I have rarely found a tribunal as willing to condemn as many people, senior people who came before them, for not telling the truth. This is not good enough..."
Source: <http://www.bbc.co.uk/news/uk-england-london-16009828>

And Pead had been vindicated – at least in part. Twist and Gilhooly and Cobbold had been exposed as being corrupt.

The blog <http://conservativehome.blogs.com> ran an article on the dismissal of James Walker, stating that "...the local Labour MP, Kate Hoey, says the Council objected to Mr Walker for "resisting their policies." But an employment tribunal said the bullying allegations were a "stalking horse" to remove him and the investigation one-sided. The hostility of the council towards Mr Walker "bordered on callousness". He won his claim for unfair dismissal. Far from being the perpetrator of bullying, Mr Walker has been on the receiving end of astonishing municipal bullying..."

Phyllis Dunipace "...commissioned a report written by consultant Tom Walker in February 2009 outlining a strategy for removing James Walker from his post..." http://kenningtonnews.blogspot.co.uk/2011/08. No stone was left unturned as Dunipace malevolently ensured that a system would be put in place by which it appeared as though James Walker was the culprit rather than the innocent victim of municipal bullying. This was an exact echo of how Lambeth treated Brian Pead – they created a stalking horse of unfounded allegations against him in an effort to remove him from office. They claimed that "young, white female pupils" were in danger from him whereas they were in danger from Murray, whom Lambeth reinstated on the instructions of Dunipace. Phyllis Dunipace resigned as Executive Director of the Children and Young People's Service on 8 August 2010, immediately prior to the James Walker case being heard at the Employment Tribunal. She was awarded the OBE on 8 February 2011 by HRH Prince Charles. She was thus rewarded for the corrupt methods she employed whilst working as Executive Director in removing highly principled people from office, including James Walker and Brian Pead. The authors have written to HM The Queen asking that she strip Dunipace of her OBE, just as the Hillsborough families have asked that Sir Norman Bettison (Chief Constable of West Yorkshire) and Sir Irvine Patnick (former MP for Sheffield Hallam) be stripped of their knighthoods.

But the matter did not end there.

Much darker, deeper secrets were yet to be exposed.

an ealing comedy

The Machiavellian Murray claimed that she had been a Head of ICT at St. Augustine's School in Ealing. She claimed that she even turned down the offer of a permanent contract at the school to work at the Open Learning Centre for Vocational Studies.

Brian Pead was never convinced that this was true. He had been forced to dismiss Murray because of racism and bullying towards black male pupils and because she had been proven to have groomed young female pupils at the OLCVS.

Yet, despite sacking Murray for these transgressions, Lambeth reinstated **her** and wrongfully dismissed Pead.

But this was no ordinary dismissal of Pead. They had gone to **extraordinary** lengths to dismiss him. What warranted these extraordinary lengths?

Why would they do this? Why would they dismiss him when it was clear that Murray had been guilty of such offences?

pointless appeal against dismissal

Pead did appeal against his dismissal, but it was a complete waste of time. He and his colleagues and friends knew that the Appeal Panel would simply ratify the previous decision, but it had to be done for the sake of due process. Pead then made up his mind to take Lambeth to an Employment Tribunal and he set to work with Alex Passman on his case.

The Hearing was scheduled for 14 January 2008 at the Employment Tribunal Court at 101 London Road, West Croydon. This was also the scene of the James Walker and Lambeth Council case two years later.

a pupil's appraisal

A former pupil of Brian's, Shelaine Clarke-Kyaw-Zayya, had written a moving account of his teaching. It is reproduced in its entirety (save for her address):

> "...I am writing on behalf of Brian Johnson. Brian was a fantastic teacher. He did a lot for us at the OLCVS. He opened a place for students to learn and do GCSEs.
>
> I was out of school for two years after the Woodfield Centre was moved to Stockwell Park, which left me without a place to go. So when I got the letter saying that the centre was opening, I was so happy.
>
> I started in 2005-06 and the time I spent there was great. The staff were welcoming and we all got along. Brian was a funny and down-to-earth teacher. He got along with everyone. He never had favourites. He treated us all alike. He is like a child at heart which means that he can get on the individual student's wavelength and get more out of them, even the ones that haven't much confidence.
>
> If Brian was to leave, it would be Lambeth's and education's great loss. He is a very dedicated and professional teacher, which in this day and age is a very rare thing.
>
> Yours sincerely,
>
> Shelaine Clarke-Kyaw-Zayya..."

ofsted inspection

On Friday 11 January 2008, the OLCVS was inspected by an OfSTED inspection team led by Greg Sorrell. Their report provides some interesting facts that actually demonstrate that the entire process of Lambeth removing Brian Pead as Head Teacher of the OLCVS was a wholly unlawful move.

Under the heading 'Description of the school', Sorrell's report states that:

> "...In July 2007, the Open Learning Initiative for Vocational Education (OLIVE) changed its name from The Open Learning Centre for Vocational Studies (OLCVS). It is located within a self-managing and multi-purpose use community centre attached to a local secondary school. Two terms ago, after a period of management difficulties the executive headteacher and her seconded team took over the centre. **Since April 2007, the centre has been led and managed by the executive headteacher and the leadership team of a local secondary special school.** This arrangement is due to end officially in April 2008. A new assistant headteacher has recently been appointed..."

This introduction to the pupil referral unit is important for two reasons. Firstly, it brings attention to the change of name – this is the third name the Unit has had in three years. Why did Lambeth insist on changing its name each year? What were they trying to avoid or hide by changing its name on an annual basis? Was the Lambeth hierarchy misappropriating funds and hiding their losses under the guise of creating a new enterprise each year? Gilhooly – presumably acting upon instructions from Dunipace – had never presented Pead with a budget. Why not? In the Sunday Times, dated 30 May 1993, Brian Deer penned an article entitled 'Secret papers expose Lambeth as a borough rotten to the core'. Deer wrote: "...The real state of chaos within Lambeth council, believed to be Britain's worst-run local authority, is revealed this weekend after the completion of secret internal inquiries into financial scandals and rackets that have rocked the beleaguered London borough in recent months. Confidential papers obtained by The Sunday Times reveal a picture of fraud and mismanagement in the Labour-controlled borough on a far greater scale than previously suspected..."

The authors of this book put forward the view that Lambeth funds were being misappropriated by Dunipace, Gilhooly, Twist et al and call for a thorough and independent investigation into possible fraud.

Secondly, the emphasised sentence in the OfSTED report above demonstrates that a new Head teacher was in place whilst Brian Pead was still officially under suspension and whilst the investigatory hearings were still taking place.

This is clearly unlawful. It also demonstrates beyond any reasonable doubt that Lambeth's investigation was bound to find Pead guilty as charged and remove him from his post **because he had already been replaced!**

The OfSTED report continues to describe the Unit – now known as the OLIVE:

> "...The centre provides education for students in Years 10 and 11 who have no permanent secondary school place. **There is a wide range of need represented on the roll.** Some students have been excluded or are deemed to be at risk of exclusion. Other groups include students newly arrived in the borough having moved from other parts of the UK or abroad, refugee or asylum seekers and **a minority of students who have been out of formal education for up to four years.** No student has a statement of special educational need. **A substantial group of students speak English as an additional language with eleven different community languages represented.** Some students are at the early stages of learning English..."

The emphases are the authors'. The report shows that there was "...a wide range of need represented on the roll..." This clearly shows that Pead **had** to engage in meetings with certain pupils more often than other pupils. If he was to fulfil his role as Head of Centre and meet the wide range of needs of his pupils, then this inherently implies that he would spend more time with some pupils than with others. Yet Twist found Pead guilty of showing favouritism towards some pupils.

The report shows that some pupils had been out of education for **four years.** Put another way, **they had never been to secondary school before.** Wouldn't these pupils need extra help to acclimatise to a school setting? And wouldn't Pead need to spend extra time with these pupils in order to help them readjust to their new environment?

The report also highlights the language difficulties that existed at the Unit with more than eleven languages being spoken amongst the 60 pupils. It follows that Pead would have had to spend more time with some of these pupils in order to help them overcome their language difficulties. Yet Twist turned a blind eye to the obvious role that Pead was fulfilling and to the fact that he **would have to spend more time with some pupils than with others.**

Under the heading 'What the school should do to improve further', Sorrell's report suggests:

1. Make better use of assessment data to track students' progress in order to focus more sharply on the minority of underachieving students.
2. Improve attendance by more rigorous monitoring of absence and in liaison with the local authority seek increased support for persistent non-attenders.

3. In liaison with the local authority, continue to seek more appropriate premises that will enable students to have full access to the curriculum.

Brian Pead had already established a system to track the progress of pupils so that he could identify pupils who were weak in certain subjects and target the work to meet their specific needs. Again, this would have meant that he had to meet with certain pupils to discuss with them where they were going wrong and how to address their weaknesses. This is simply good management and sound educational practice. Yet Twist (and Murray) sought to turn this activity into something sordid.

Pead had commissioned a database to be built which would record every attendance (or non-attendance) of every pupil. His almost anal insistence on the collection of data from his days of writing his books on Liverpool FC had been turned to effective use in helping pupils and their parents understand the importance of regular attendance. In Pead's time at the OLCVS, there were no persistent non-attenders.

Pead had also been a thorn in Lambeth's side because he championed the acquisition of better premises with longevity of tenure.

Three years after Pead had created the OLCVS, it would seem that it had actually gone backwards after he was unlawfully removed from his post – something which Duane Maddison, Sandra Roach, Colin Hill and Derek Langan referred to when they were interviewed at the investigatory meeting.

Sorrell's report turned to Achievement and Standards – something which Cathy Twist was ultimately responsible for within Lambeth:

> "...pupils progress well in vocational programmes including the Award Scheme Development and Accreditation Network (ASDAN) and media studies. All students left in 2007 with at least one recognised qualification. The majority achieve grades A to F and one third of all students gained grades between A and C in GCSE English and mathematics..."

Sorrell particularly mentions the ASDAN awards. These were established by Pead and Colin Hill. It was one of these awards – office administration – that Pead had initially offered to Ashleigh Mills. A few months afterwards, Sorrell is praising the introduction of these exams. Murray, on the other hand – and with the full backing of Gilhooly, Twist and Dunipace – sought to turn a positive experience for the pupils into something altogether more sordid.

It can also be seen from the grades achieved the wide disparity between pupils. There were only 25 in number at the time of the report who took the exams. One might expect to see grades A – F in a cohort of, for example, 500 pupils, but to have such a wide range of grades in only 25 pupils shows the huge range of abilities at the

Centre. It is clear, therefore, that some pupils would need more one-to-one tuition than their more able peers.

The report provides evidence that "...all students left in 2007 with at least one recognised qualification..." yet Twist had attempted to engineer a report against Pead in which she claimed that his focus was on the creation of a "...therapeutic environment..." rather than the teaching and learning. Those who achieved the GCSE exams results in the summer of 2007 were those pupils who had been taught by Pead and his methods from September 2005. It is evident that the teaching and learning was every bit as successful as the therapeutic input – something that Nadia Al-Khudhairy had mentioned in her email of 19 December 2006. There can be no evidential basis, therefore, for Twist's myopic and one-dimensional account against Pead.

Under the heading 'Teaching and Learning', the OfSTED report states that:

> "...Plenary sessions at the end of lessons offer them and staff an opportunity to evaluate progress. Whilst this is usually effective, occasionally teachers say too much, reducing the students' opportunities to evaluate for themselves what they have learned..."

These 'plenary sessions' are what Pead introduced as 'Circle Time'. However, when he ran the Unit, the emphasis was always on the pupils having a forum to have their voice heard. Input from Pead and other teachers was always kept to a minimum. After Pead's unlawful removal from the Centre, it would seem that the new staff completely misunderstood what the nature of this time was about.

Sorrell's report makes mention of – though does not specifically name – the excellent work of Duane Maddison:

> "...The student liaison mentor has a very relevant understanding of the students' needs, offers good support and communicates well..."

Pead had worked hard with Maddison around this role. It would appear that his efforts had not gone to waste.

The report also praises 'regular tutorials' – something that Pead introduced in 2005 – which means that all pupils had regular one-to-ones, not some favoured pupils.

The report makes no mention of safeguarding measures at the Unit other than a single line: "...Do procedures for safeguarding learners meet current government requirements?..." The answer is given as "Yes", but absolutely no evidence is put forward to justify this response. This is a serious weakness in Sorrell's report.

It was the same weakness that allowed Maryn Murray to abuse children at the Unit, having come to the Centre from St. Augustine's School in Ealing, which also had equally negligent safeguarding measures.

passman email

The day before the Employment Tribunal Hearing, Pead emailed Passman and sought any last-minute advice. Passman's response is reproduced below in its entirety (except that typing errors have been corrected):

Re: Witness Statements
From: ETAS Direct London (etas.directlondon@googlemail.com)
Sent: 13 January 2008 12:56:44
To: Brian Pead (brian.pead@hotmail.co.uk)
Attachments: Brian Pead Schedule of loss.doc (35.4 KB) Security scan upon download

Dear Brian

The hearing details are within the first few pages of the bundle of documents, page 22. The location of the Tribunal is 101 London Road, West Croydon, Surrey, CR0 2RF.

The hearing starts at 10:00, although it would be advisable to arrive early at around 09:15 to hand the two additional copies of the bundle into the reception. I trust you have been able to hole-punch and place the documents that I sent you into files.

The main points to be concerned with are as follows:
1. The Tribunal have identified that they will be dealing with the claim as set out in the claim form, so you must be aware of the information in the claim form and the response.
2. It is our argument that the dismissal was unfair on both procedural and substantive grounds and therefore you should make that argument. The Respondent has tried to limit the issues to procedural grounds which had not been agreed by us and there is no basis for them to try to manipulate the tribunal into making such a ruling. The Tribunal will decide on what grounds the claim is brought and due to the fact that reference is made in the claim form to the test for unfair dismissal, (the BHS v Burchell test, as I have already sent you) the claim should be able to be brought on both procedural and substantive grounds. In any event the substantive issues go to the heart of the case as we do not believe that the Respondent has proven, on the balance of probabilities, that they have satisfied the test required of them to dismiss you. Their evidence appears to be based on hearsay and rumour. The fact that the bundle is over 500 pages, which the Tribunal will not like at all, goes some way to demonstrate that this has many issues over and above the procedural issues. My advice would be to suggest that we have suggested that the

bundle should be limited to the relevant documents but the Respondent wanted all these documents included. They will also be making an application to have further documents included which I would advise you to object to on the basis that you have prepared your case on the documents available to you. They requested this of me on Friday but I rejected their application.

3. It is the Respondent's case to prove and therefore you will be asked to give evidence first, you will be asked to read out your witness statement and then you may be asked further questions by the panel. You will then be cross examined by the Respondent's representative. Having seen the way in which you handled the questioning previously this is exactly what I would expect from the Respondent and as long as you keep your cool you should not have any problems. Your witness statement details that you do not consider the dismissal to be fair on the basis that you do not consider any of the charges to have been proven and there was no proper investigation.

4. If the Tribunal continues, you will then be asked to question the Respondent's witnesses on the content of their witness statements, Twist and Hare (although Hare may not be there). You may make reference to documents in the bundle and although this seems to be a massive task, there are not really that many relevant documents and you will have come across the majority before. Your case is based on the fact that the Respondent could not have held the belief that you had carried out such acts as they did not conduct a thorough investigation and therefore they could not have possibly discharged their burden of proof. This is on the basis that we have discussed in length, such as the fact that they did not present any evidence from students and they seem to have kept moving the goalposts with regard to these allegations from the start. Despite the fact that they seem to have collected together masses of information, such as witness statements etc, this does not prove that they conducted a full investigation and you should be keen to point this out, with such a wide range of charges, a wide ranging investigation would have been fair.

5. Ask when and where you were allowed to question the Respondent's witnesses, and ask if the Respondent considers that a dismissal based on unchallenged evidence is fair. If the Hearing does finish, you may be asked to present how much you consider you have lost as a result of the dismissal and therefore I have included a schedule of loss as an attachment. I advise you take six copies of this document along with six copies of your witness statement.

I will be looking through your file all day today and therefore I will be available on the phone if you have any questions. You really need to read and make notes in your copy of the file (one of the ones I sent to you). My main advice is to read through the notes of the hearings and the witness statements and base your questioning on the documents and the statements presented to you during the disciplinary hearings.

Main things to remember to take: your file, the two other files, 6 schedules of loss and 6 witness statements.

Kind regards,
Alex

132

first day at tribunal

On Monday 14 January 2008, Pead attended the London South Employment Tribunal Court in London Road, West Croydon. This Hearing was a year and a month after Pead's suspension from his post. This is an abuse of process in itself.

The waiting room was full. Many people had not enjoyed their Christmas holiday, it would seem.

Pead made an application for an adjournment based on two points:

(i)   that Lambeth had not provided him with full disclosure of documents
(ii)   that he told the Judge that his case would take more than one day to hear and probably at least fourteen days.

His application for an adjournment was not successful. Nor were his complaints about Lambeth handing in documents late listened to.

Furthermore, Lambeth entered a bundle of documents consisting of 616 pages – more than many bundles entered into complex criminal trials.

Forced to plough on by Judge Martin, he carefully explained that he had had to dismiss Murray for racism and child abuse.

Counsel for Lambeth, Miss S. Watson, challenged him about these statements and he provided chapter and verse about Murray's wrongdoing.

It fell on deaf ears. Judge Anne Martin did not want to hear this information. She employed the tactic of keeping the arguments within an extremely narrow line, like the corrupt Twist before her.

Pead had an opportunity in which to question Hare and Twist about the investigation and disciplinary hearing, but it was a kangaroo court, based on dishonesty and incompetence.

At the end of a long day, Pead fully expected to return the following day to continue the Tribunal Hearing.

Judge Martin had other ideas. She announced that the second day's hearing would not be for another **six weeks!**

Lambeth Council was continuing to buy time. The authors speculate whether Judge Martin was paid handsomely for her manipulation of time.

judge anne martin

News Release issued by the COI News Distribution Service on 04 September 2009:

The Lord Chancellor, the Right Honourable Jack Straw MP, has appointed Anne Martin to be a Salaried Part-time Employment Judge of the Employment Tribunals (England and Wales).

Mrs Martin will be assigned to the London South Region, working on an 80% pro rata basis, with effect from 1 October 2009.

Anne Martin is 50. She was admitted as a Solicitor in 1988 and was appointed as a Fee-paid Chairman of the Employment Tribunals (England and Wales) in 2001.

Anne Martin is also a trustee of the organisation Stem4Ed.
Source: <http://www.stem4.org.uk/eating_disorders/trustees>.

The Stem4Ed website states:

"...STEM4 encourages early identification and prevention of mental health illness in teenagers and young people. We provide this support and advice through our website and workshops. We do not provide a counselling service..."

How remarkable, therefore, that Martin is involved with the very work that Brian Pead was undertaking at the OLCVS.

The Stem4Ed website also provides help for young people affected by depression and suicide.

She is also a school governor. The role of a school governor, of course, brings people into contact with young children. It is a common theme throughout this book.

134

tribunal again

On Monday 25 February 2008, Pead once against found the waiting room at the Employment Tribunal in West Croydon full to capacity. He wondered just how many cases end up in Courts like this up and down the land each year. He did some simple maths in his head and was staggered at the result.

At 10:00am, Pead entered the room in the Employment Tribunal. He represented himself.

The original five charges first grew to seven, the seven then grew to fifteen, then the fifteen were reduced to fourteen. The goalposts moved more frequently than those at Lambeth Council's municipal football pitches.

He looked across at the other side. He saw a barrister (how much did she cost Lambeth tax-payers?) and **fourteen** Lambeth executive officers.

The lay person might see this as a show of strength by Lambeth to rid the teaching profession of a pernicious practitioner. The intelligent person will see that this was a show of strength: Lambeth wanted to win this case – had to win this case – and they wanted to know what Pead's response was and whether he would elaborate further on the reasons why he dismissed Murray.

The former Head ensured that the Judge knew that he had dismissed Murray for racism and child abuse, but Judge Martin simply admonished him and told him that the focus of the meeting was on whether the investigation had been fair and thorough.

In denying Pead his voice, she denied the rights of the abused children of Lambeth and Ealing.

The most bizarre aspect of the day was that Judge Martin decided that she had 'heard' all of the evidence in just the one day. This should be compared with the **18-day** hearing that James Walker had at the very same tribunal court in West Croydon. Brian Pead had been unlawfully suspended by Lambeth. He had been unlawfully dismissed. Now the employment tribunal – allegedly an independent court – was manipulating the law to suit its own ends.

The journey from West Croydon to New Eltham via London Bridge was a long one for Pead. He knew what the result of the tribunal hearing would be.

But he was not fighting merely for his job and reputation. He was fighting for his five-year-old self who had been sexually abused and he was fighting for the black pupils at the OLCVS whose rights had been denied, and he was fighting for Gemma Mandry and Ashleigh Mills, both of whom had been personally violated by Murray's grooming.

After the lunch break, only Twist, Hare and the barrister, Miss Watson, remained.

The arrogance and hubris of Lambeth executives was extraordinary. They had known they would win the case. They had the Judge in their pocket.

Despite it being a clear miscarriage of justice, Pead lost his case, though the decision was not made known to him for a further two months. This is in itself extremely strange. Pead could not possibly have lost. Passman had seen the case and knew Pead was innocent and that the entire process had been an abuse of process. John Callow – Pead's friend – said that it seemed to be a perverse verdict. Pead's counselling and business colleagues – who had all seen the spurious allegations against Pead – could not believe the ruling.

The entire process had been carefully stage-managed by people at the very top of the Lambeth tree. Whitmore, Hiley and Foster had all been wheeled out by the Lambeth hierarchy and used as pawns in a much higher game of chess than they could possibly have known they were involved in.

Barristers had been drafted in.

Lambeth had broken many Employment Law regulations; it had carried out an improper investigation; it had unlawfully suspended him; it had ransacked his office; it had entered false evidence into the hearing; it had prevented Pead from entering evidence; it had not interviewed any pupils; it had not interviewed parents; it had replaced him before the outcome of a disciplinary hearing and appeal – in short, it had failed in its Duty of Care to him.

The question has to be asked: why would Lambeth go to such extraordinary lengths to remove him from his post? Why would they not only support Maryn Murray's spurious allegations but also reinstate her, especially when they knew she had been dismissed for racism, bullying and child abuse?

Why would they wield such forces against an excellent and well-respected teacher in order to crush him and yet support Murray?

What power did Murray – who had come to the OLCVS from St. Augustine's Priory School in Ealing - hold over Lambeth executives?

tribunal judgment

It had taken the Employment Tribunal **seven months** to hear Pead's case following his unlawful dismissal in July 2007.

It took them only **five days** to produce a report. It claimed to have considered 616 pages and numerous reports, interviews and accounts.

The final judgment makes for astonishing reading. It would be hard to justify the inanity of such a decision – but Martin attempted such a feat.

The Report commenced with the finding: "...The unanimous Judgment of the Tribunal is that the Claimant's claim of unfair dismissal is unfounded and is dismissed..."

Having made such a decision, it then fell to Judge Martin to attempt to justify such crassness. The number of mistakes in an 8-page document is astounding.

The full judgment can be found online. It is précised here, with commentary by the authors:

> "...1. It is the Claimant's case that he has been dismissed unfairly as a result of the Respondent's failure to thoroughly investigate the allegations made against him in a series of letters, the final letter dated 3 July 2007..."

Pead never received a "...series of letters..." Nor did he ever receive a letter dated 3 July 2007.

> "...2. It is the Claimant's case that the Respondent could not have held the belief that he had carried out the acts alleged if a full and impartial investigation had been carried out. Furthermore, it is the Claimant's case that the investigation was pre-judged from its initiation and therefore was not reasonably conducted given the circumstances and the severity of the allegations made. The Respondent's case is that the investigation carried out was impartial, thorough and was not pre-judged..."

Of course Pead would state that the entire process was pre-judged – it was. The Greg Sorrell OfSTED Report dated January 2008 provides evidence that Pead had been replaced as Head of the OLCVS as early as April 2007 – before Pead had himself been interviewed in the Investigatory process, let alone the Disciplinary Hearing process. An OLCVS newsletter authored by Ginni Bealing also confirms that Pead had already been replaced before he had been dismissed.

Pead also claimed that the investigation was not thorough because no pupils or parents had been interviewed and more than a dozen other witnesses to Pead's management over a period of 18 months had also not been interviewed.

Twist had not visited the White Bear Theatre, nor did she visit the Old Library Centre in West Norwood. She also failed to visit the Redfearn Centre in Vauxhall.

The Court of Appeal has identified the need for investigating officers to visit what it refers to as 'the physical evidence'.

> "...4. The Tribunal heard from Ms Cathy Twist, Assistant Director Standards, and Ms Judith Hare, School Advisor for the Respondent, and from the Claimant himself. The Tribunal had before it an agreed bundle of documents comprising 616 pages. The Claimant made an application to amend his claim at the start of the hearing. He wanted to amend the claim to include substantive unfairness as well as procedural. When asked to explain further, the Claimant told the Tribunal that there was a number of allegations made against him and the investigating officer failed to carry out an investigation in a fair manner, that is, not at all. The Tribunal was satisfied that the Claim form covered this point. In any event the Tribunal was not prepared to allow an amendment at this late stage which would prejudice the Respondent in the hearing. The Claimant also made an application for an adjournment on the basis that the claim would take more than one day to hear. This application was adjourned as the issues that the Tribunal had to hear were narrow and although there may have been some documents delivered to the Claimant late, the Claimant was not prejudiced by this as the documents were not new to the Claimant. The Tribunal refused this application for a postponement as it did not consider that it was in the interest of justice to allow it..."

It will be seen that Pead was not given anything by Judge Martin. This paragraph is the footballing equivalent of an away team being fouled in every tackle and the referee awarding yellow or red cards **against** the away team and free kicks to the home side.

What is more worrying, of course, is that Judge Martin has got her facts wrong. Pead did not agree the 616-page bundle. The email he received from Alex Passman on 13 January 2008 (the day before the first day of the Employment Tribunal hearing) is evidence that Pead had not agreed the bundle.

Pead certainly **did not** want to amend his claim to include the substantive as well the procedural. This had already been done in the Claim Form – again, the Alex Passman email is evidence of this.

Furthermore, Lambeth had added pages to the bundle without Pead's knowledge or consent – Passman's email makes mention of the likelihood of such conniving tactics.

Judge Martin makes reference to the fact that Lambeth did not comply with due process by providing full disclosure within an agreed schedule. She claims that Pead was not prejudiced by this improper conduct on the part of Lambeth – but how could he fail to have been prejudiced? He did not have time to read all of the material, **some of which he had never seen before.**

Under the heading of "The facts", Judge Martin inadvertently assists Pead's case against Twist by stating that:

> "...6.1 This centre was set up in September 2005 to provide for pupils who had no secondary school place. The pupils were new arrivals to the country and young people who had not secured a place in the Borough. **A significant number of pupils had specific educational needs and were vulnerable...**"

With her use of the phrase "...a significant number of pupils had...", Martin implies that **not all** of the pupils had specific needs, but a number. This statement in itself provides a reason for Pead to have engaged in more one-to-one conversations with **some** pupils, but not all. Some did not need his input at a high level; others did.

Martin also emphasises that a significant number of pupils were "...vulnerable..." – again, this provides evidence of a need. Pead was meeting that need.

What Judge Martin records next is astonishing:

> "...On 6 December 2006, a written complaint was sent by Ms Maryn Murray, one of the Claimant's staff, to the Claimant's line manager Mr Gilhooly..."

This is astonishing for a number of reasons. Firstly, had Murray written to Gilhooly on 6 December 2006, why did Pead not receive the full list of complaints against him on the 8 December 2006 when he was suspended without being told any reasons for his suspension?

Why did Twist state that she did not receive the list of complaints until she actually interviewed Murray on 19 January 2007?

How did Judge Martin come by the date of 6 December 2006?

Was she privy to a document that Pead (and Passman) had never seen?

This is an alarming inconsistency in the entire process. Whichever date is correct (if either of them is correct, given the duplicity with which Lambeth acted), Lambeth are guilty of mismanagement of the entire process. If we were to assume that the date of 6 December is the correct date, then Gilhooly and Vaz ought to have informed Pead on 8 December 2006 of the reasons for his suspension, since they were aware of the Murray report.

Why would Gilhooly and Vaz keep that information secret from Pead?

If, on the other hand, the date of 19 January 2007 is correct, how did Judge Martin come by such a date of 6 December 2006? She clearly would not have made this date up – it can, therefore, only have come from a Lambeth document included in the 616-page bundle (which Pead did not receive a copy of).

Note the following:

> "...6.3   Ms Murray's letter of complaint appeared in the bundle at pages 93 to 107. [...] The allegations raised were numerous, many of them were serious and some raised child protection issues..."

Judge Martin has just sunk herself and Twist in one short sentence. The Judge stated on the public record that some of Murray's complaints "...raised child protection issues..." yet Twist had claimed that she didn't call pupils or parents in for interview because there were no child protection issues. For a similar reason, she stated that she did not inform Social Services. However, Judge Martin said that some issues of child protection **had** been raised – as Pead, Callow and Passman had known all along – and thus Twist was duty bound to involve Social Services and to interview pupils and parents.

This is an astonishing oversight on Twist's part. This book will call for her dismissal without pension for putting the safeguarding of children at risk and for conducting an improper and pre-judged investigation which she knew to be improper. This amounts to misfeasance in public office.

> "...6.4 In accordance with the Respondent's disciplinary procedure the Claimant was suspended from work on 8 December 2006. This was confirmed in writing. The first letter was dated 8 December 2006 and a follow up letter on 12 December 2006 (pg 112) set out the broad nature of the allegations..."

Why did the letter of 12 December 2006 only set out the "...broad nature of the allegations..." if, as Judge Martin has previously claimed, Lambeth were in possession of Murray's 8-page document against Pead?

Again, if we were to assume that Lambeth were, in fact, in possession of Murray's full document on 6 December, then why did Pead not receive a copy until late January 2007? Why would Lambeth seek to prejudice him by withholding such evidence – evidence which he was entitled to see, since they were allegations against him?

"...6.5 Ms Cathy Twist was appointed the investigation officer. The Tribunal is satisfied that Ms Twist was an independent person..."

Twist was far from independent as Martin claims. Twist conducted the investigatory meetings and the Disciplinary Meetings. This is improper practice. Furthermore, Twist knew that Pead had been replaced **before** he had even had his Disciplinary Hearing.

The next clause defies belief. If we are to assume that Judge Martin is a competent Judge and that she has sat on several Tribunal Hearings, her next comments are incredulous by their stupidity:

"...6.6 The Tribunal is satisfied that the investigation carried out by Ms Twist was extensive. In all, Ms Twist interviewed 13 witnesses including the Claimant and Ms Murray. The Tribunal considered the notes of these interviews which were produced to the Tribunal and which the Tribunal read carefully..."

To suggest – as Judge Martin does – that the investigation was extensive because thirteen people were interviewed defies belief.

The facts do not bear out Martin's assertion. Of the thirteen people interviewed, two were Pead and Murray. Two had been dismissed by Pead. Two (Duane Maddison and Annabel Field) were not called by Twist to the Disciplinary Hearing because their testimony was such that Twist would have no case. Pead had requested that Field and Maddison be present. Twist did not call them in an abuse of process.

It is possible to call 100 witnesses and not have a proper investigation. It is equally possible to call only one witness and have a thorough investigation.

The thoroughness and fairness of any investigation does not depend on numbers. It depends on the integrity of the questioning and of the process itself.

That a Tribunal Judge should be swayed by a mere number is reprehensible. Martin continues her judgment:

"...The Tribunal looked carefully at the interview notes made by Ms Twist and do not agree that the questioning was inappropriate. What is clear is that Ms Twist spent time exploring the allegations which had been made to elicit all the necessary information from the witnesses. A majority of the questions were open questions with closed questions being asked occasionally to pinpoint certain details..."

The table overleaf demonstrates that Judge Anne Martin had not studied the documents as she claimed. Note how Murray, Hiley and Whitmore are given substantially lengthy interviews in which to vent their spleen. Note, too, how Pead was interviewed on four occasions – all of the interviews being of considerable length.

Perhaps one of the most astonishing interviews was that with Rosa Vaz. She had not spent more than two hours in Pead's company over a period of some 18 months, yet she was asked an incredible 48 questions (in only 40 minutes – thus mostly closed questions as the table illustrates). Gilhooly's first interview (91%), his third interview (97%), Murray's second interview (91%) and Reynolds' interview (93.5%) highlight the incongruence of Judge Martin's comments:

Name	Number of questions asked	Length of Interview in minutes	Open questions	Closed questions	Leading questions
			expressed as % of total number of questions		
Field	35	100	40%	60%	14%
Foster	30	85	17%	83%	20%
Gilhooly 1	32	30	9%	91%	6%
Gilhooly 2	32	75	22%	78%	6%
Gilhooly 3	32	30	3%	97%	6%
Hiley	32	80	22%	78%	18%
Hill	24	75	25%	75%	24%
Langan	32	60	18%	82%	18%
Maddison	32	55	16%	84%	19%
Murray 1	40	135	40%	60%	15%
Murray 2	11	30	9%	91%	0%
Pead 1	82	175	18%	82%	7%
Pead 2	49	135	22%	78%	19%
Pead 3	78	140	19%	81%	6%
Pead 4	80	150	21%	79%	5%
Reynolds	31	25	6.5%	93.5%	6.5%
Roach	45	60	11%	89%	13%
Vaz	48	40	14.5%	85.5%	7%
Whitmore	36	120	33.3%	66.6%	14%
Averages	41	84	19%	81%	11%

It is clear from the above table that Twist had not explored the allegations. She had asked an average of 81% of closed questions. This demonstrates that she had an agenda (to dismiss Pead) and asked closed questions to seek answers that she could manipulate to ensure that she could dismiss him. Note how Murray was only asked 51 questions in two separate interviews, yet she had worked with Pead for a year and she had authored an 8-page document against him. Compare this with Rosa Vaz, who met Pead for a total of about two hours over a period of 18 months, and yet she was asked 48 questions, almost as many as Murray. Notice, too, the disproportionate time allotted to Pead's interviews: he had been hounded by Twist and White – Murray was let off lightly. This data analysis disproves Martin's perverse ruling.

Judge Martin continued:

> "...All witnesses checked the notes of their interviews to ensure that the written record was accurate..."

This is inaccurate. The authors are in possession of evidence to the contrary. Annabel Field, for example, stated that her interview notes were not accurate and Duane Maddison said the same.

No final draft interview notes exist in relation to Whitmore, Hiley, Foster, Hill, Langan, Roach, Vaz and Reynolds.

Brian Pead was interviewed on four separate occasions. **He never received the notes from his interviews for him to sign off.** He did, however, makes his own interview notes, as is his custom in meetings of any description.

Martin then states that Pead was invited to a disciplinary meeting on 15 July 2007. She does not record that he had already been replaced in April 2007. Incontrovertible evidence in the form of OfSTED reports and OLCVS newsletters exists in the public domain that shows that Pead had already been replaced **before** due process had been undertaken.

Martin's next clause is worrying in the extreme:

> "...6.7 One of the complaints which had been made by Ms Murray was in relation to inappropriate behaviour during a theatre visit. Following investigation she recommended that this was not part of the disciplinary process on the basis that this allegation was unproven..."

A solicitor since 1988, there can be no excuse for a Tribunal Judge not to ask why the masturbation incident was dropped. Where was the evidence? Furthermore, a solicitor of such experience would then be forced to question the veracity of the other allegations and the mind-set of Murray. That Murray had included such obvious lies about the theatre incident casts severe doubt on the veracity of her other allegations. Judge Martin does not entertain this thought process – yet she ought to have done had the Tribunal been a fair Hearing.

Martin staggers through the judgment like a drunk through a field of landmines, setting off explosion after explosion.

> "...6.8 The Tribunal is satisfied that the Claimant was able to suggest any witnesses that Ms Twist should interview, and/or to produce witness statements of witnesses, and/or any other documentation. The Claimant chose not to do so..."

The question has to be asked: Where is the evidence that Pead did not produce evidence of his own or did not suggest evidence?

The authors are in possession of documents which completely refute Martin's assertion. Three documents are of significance: (i) the Annabel Field email in which she praised Pead and thanked him for his support and (ii) the Ipek Yÿlmaz email which completely refuted the allegations of masturbation in the theatre and (iii) the Nadia Al-Khudhairy email in which she described Pead's unit as the best PRU in London.

Anne Martin obviously did not cast her eyes upon all of the available evidence. Nor did she examine a letter that Pead wrote to Twist asking for specific witnesses to attend the Disciplinary Hearings.

The authors are in possession of a copy of this letter. This letter and the above three emails demonstrate that the Martin judgment is perverse.

Perhaps the most incredible statement made by Martin in her reserved judgment was paragraph 6.10:

> "...During the investigatory process Ms Twist decided not to interview any student of the centre, any parent or carer and to limit investigations to those who were working or had worked at the centre who she believed to have been in daily contact with the Claimant. The Tribunal accepts the Respondent's reasons for not interviewing students and carers as a policy decision, in that it is not appropriate to bring these people into this type of investigation. The Tribunal further note, that the allegations relating to students were not proven at the final disciplinary procedure because the students had not been interviewed. **There was therefore no prejudice to the Claimant by not interviewing these witnesses...**"

This has to be one of the most inane summations ever produced by any Judge in any Court in the land.

To state that the Claimant – Brian Pead – was not prejudiced by Twist not calling a single pupil or parent defies belief. Of course he was prejudiced. Had the pupils and parents been called, they would have completely disproved Murray's allegations. And Hiley's. And Field's. And Whitmore's. And Foster's.

To state that it "...is not appropriate to bring these people into this type of investigation..." contradicts what she said at 6.3: "...The allegations raised were numerous, many of them were serious **and some raised child protection issues...**"

The emphasis is the authors'. If Martin believed that the allegations raised child protection issues, then Lambeth were legally bound to inform parents and carers. Lambeth failed to do so.

Furthermore, Lambeth were duty bound to call the named pupils and their parents or carers and Lambeth failed to do so.

That Martin supports such breaches of Child Protection Laws is deeply worrying.

Martin's perverse reasoning is also worrying at 8.2:

> "...There was no grey area here. It is rare for a Tribunal to see the extensive documents trail and steps taken as there is in this case. The steps taken by Ms Twist included nine days interviewing and 27 days in total. She also had the support of Ms White an HR advisor. Therefore it was going to be an uphill struggle for the Claimant to say that there was no reasonable investigation..."

The inept Martin seems to be in awe of numbers, rather like a child in a sweet shop is in awe of the delicious opportunities before it. To throw numbers around as if to impress is a worrying propensity for a judge to have. What matters is not quantity but quality and Twist's investigation lacked quality and integrity, just as her involvement in the James Walker case did.

Martin continued in her fantasy world:

> "...8.3 Ms Twist was an independent person. Therefore the Claimant's allegation that she pre-judged the situation was misconceived..."

That Martin can make such a statement is inconceivable. Pead had been replaced as Head of the OLCVS **before** the investigation and disciplinary hearings had even concluded. Of course the situation was pre-judged. Judge Martin's comment was misconceived.

Martin continues on her merry judgment:

> "...8.4 It was reasonable to send a copy of Ms Murray's complaints to the witnesses as the allegations were not simple and could not be divided up in order for the witnesses to comment, they needed time to think about the allegations made as the best use of time to give a copy of the allegations first the witnesses were told to keep the matter confidential..."

It is **never** reasonable to send witnesses you are about to interview a complete list of allegations against a person. This sows seeds of doubt in their minds (as Twist knew, hence her reason for sending them).

Throughout Martin's judgment she displayed such stupidity as rarely can have been heard in a Courtroom. Consider her next point:

> "...8.5 The Claimant had an issue with Ms Field as she didn't give evidence at the disciplinary hearing. The allegations of treatment to her were not proven because she did not give evidence and therefore there was no causative consequence to his dismissal..."

Of course there was a causative consequence to his dismissal by not calling Field. She would have proven that Murray lied about the theatre and the alleged bullying of Field. She would have shown that Murray had colluded with others, including Hiley and Whitmore. She would have drawn attention to the fact that she scribbled over her interview notes "...I did not say this..."

Martin's judgment continued:

> "...8.8 It was never going to be easy to investigate all the matters because of the number and nature of the allegations the steps taken by the Respondent were appropriate and if anything the Respondents went the extra mile. The resources and time committed to this matter is reflected in the documents..."

This is an appalling statement for Martin to make on a number of levels. Firstly, to say that it was not going to be easy to investigate all the matters undermines the legal process. Any employee has the right to receive a fair and thorough investigation. Brian Pead did not receive anything like a fair or thorough investigation. Judge Martin might be impressed by numbers, but the authors and most intelligent people are not. The 616 pages of 'evidence' that Lambeth entered into Court can be halved immediately because there were two copies of everything. This brings the 616 pages down to 308 pages. Given that there were more than 100 pages of Lambeth policies, such as grievance procedures, disciplinary hearings and the like, this reduced the number still further to a mere 208 pages. Given that 13 people were interviewed and the notes of these interviews typed up as double-spaced text, this gave 130 pages, which – typed differently – could conceivably have reduced the interview notes to a mere 65 pages. Had Judge Martin actually exercised any restraint, she would not have been quite so impressed by the 616 pages.

She also describes Twist as having gone the extra mile. She may well have gone the extra mile to pervert the course of natural justice, but she did not go the extra mile to ensure that the investigation was fair and thorough.

Neither did Twist go the extra mile to visit the White Bear Theatre in Kennington, or the Redfearn Centre in Vauxhall, or the Old Library Centre in West Norwood. Judge Martin's view of 'the extra mile' would seem to differ significantly from most intelligent people's perception of the term.

At 8.9, Martin erred again:

> "...The conclusions were reasoned and for those that were proven were based on corroborative evidence..."

There had been no evidence put forward by Lambeth in support of Murray's allegations apart from the statements produced by Murray, Hiley and Whitmore in collusion with one another.

In conclusion, Martin says the following:

> "...9.1 First the Tribunal is mindful that the remit of the issues is very narrow. The Tribunal is looking solely at the investigation carried out by the Respondent which led to the disciplinary process and the Claimant's subsequent dismissal. The Tribunal is mindful of the case of Sainsbury's Supermarket Limited-v-Hitt [2003] IRLR 23 Court of Appeal. This case related to the question of the investigation in a conduct case and held that the range of reasonable responses test (or to put it another way, the need to apply the objective standards of the reasonable employer) applies as much to the question of whether an investigation into suspected misconduct was reasonable in all the circumstances as it does to other procedural and substantive aspects of a decision to dismiss a person from his employment for a conduct reason. The objective standard of a reasonable employer did not require it to carry out forensic investigation into every possible aspect of the matter. What is required is that the Respondent carries out an investigation which is reasonable in all the circumstances..."

No reasonable person could – in all the circumstances of Brian Pead's case – say that there had been a fair and thorough investigation. Martin's judgment is utter nonsense. She attempts to justify her perverse ruling by referring to case law – in this instance the case of Sainsbury's and Hitt. She is quite correct to cite this case, stating that an employer must conduct an investigation that is reasonable in all the circumstances. So far, so good. The Hitt case established *ratio decidendi* – that is to say, the reasoned decisions of a Judge or Judges – in order to define in all subsequent cases the principle of what depth of investigation the Courts require employers to undertake.

Where Martin's legal expertise falls down, of course, is that she fails to make the link between the Court of Appeal's ruling in the Hitt case and the facts of Pead's case. Twist's investigation had not been "...reasonable in all the circumstances..." and this is the very yardstick that Courts require employers to adhere to. Quite obviously, the facts of each case differ considerably, so the Courts distilled each case down to the very essence of what is reasonable in **all the circumstances** of each case.

> "...9.2 Bearing this in mind, the Tribunal concludes that the investigation carried out by the Respondent was within the range of reasonable responses open to a reasonable employer. The amount of time and resources that the Respondent gave to the investigation is by any standard high. The Tribunal considered the extensive documents that the investigation process generated. The Tribunal is struck by the methodical and structured manner with which Ms Twist conducted and set out her investigation. This was by no means an easy investigation to conduct, there being so many different and serious allegations against a senior employee. The Tribunal note, that at every

step Ms Twist ensured that witnesses interviewed were happy with the notes that she had made. The witnesses were given the opportunity to check the notes and make any amendments if they wished..."

Again, this is palpable nonsense. Annabel Field and Duane Maddison, in particular, were **not** happy with their interview notes which were not included in the Tribunal bundle. This breaches the rules on disclosure of documents. Cathy Twist had been methodical – that much is true. She had been methodical in doctoring the evidence, in asking leading questions, in asking an average of 81% closed questions, in failing to call witnesses and in being unfair and unprofessional.

"...9.3 The Tribunal is satisfied that the choice of witness that Ms Twist chose to interview was reasonable..."

Twist failed to interview any pupils. She failed to interview any parents. She failed to interview Pead's counselling peers and supervisors. She failed to interview Lambeth consultants who had visited the OLCVS. She failed to interview Fraser Hall, the maths teacher. She failed to interview independent third party personnel such as Centre managers. She failed to interview Lambeth Detached Youth Workers. She failed to interview Nadia Al-Khudhairy. She failed to call Annabel Field and Duane Maddison to the Disciplinary Hearing. Yet, according to Martin, this was 'reasonable'.

"...9.4 Whilst the Tribunal can appreciate that the Claimant feels very strongly about his dismissal and may feel that his other aspects of his work at the centre have been ignored, the consideration for this Tribunal is not whether the Claimant was or was not a good manager and teacher, but whether in the light of the allegations which had been brought by Ms Murray that they are investigated in a reasonable way. The Tribunal is satisfied that the Respondent conducted itself during the investigatory process in a manner which was appropriate to the issues which it had to address and that the investigation fell within the band of reasonable responses. Consequently the Tribunal finds that the Claimant's claim of unfair dismissal is unfounded and is dismissed..."

Judge Martin had ratified in her closing statement the fact that the course of natural justice was perverted by Twist.

As Albert Einstein said, "...The world is a dangerous place, not because of those who do evil, but because of those who look on and do nothing..."

There were enough people in Lambeth looking on and doing nothing.

appeal

Brian Pead appealed but the Tribunal 'lost' the paperwork connected with his Appeal and then claimed that he was 'out of time'. He had sent the documents via recorded delivery and obtained a signature, but the Tribunal was not prepared to countenance his Appeal.

What possible reason could there be for such inhumane treatment of an innocent man?

Why had Pead's original Tribunal Hearing lasted only **one day** whilst former Lambeth Headteacher James Walker had been allowed **18 days** for his own Hearing?

This significant mismatch demonstrates the extremely dark forces that were behind the State's persecution of an innocent man.

Pead's contract ran out in July 2007. He had been suspended on the basis of spurious and unfounded allegations. Why would Lambeth go to such extraordinary lengths to dismiss him? Why didn't Lambeth merely let his contract expire? Why did Lambeth Council and the Metropolitan Police bring the full force of the State to bear upon a man who had – according to evidence in the public domain – been doing such an extraordinary job at the OLCVS that his work was being brought to the attention of eminent psychiatrists and researchers at King's College and elsewhere?

the st. augustine's connection

The answers can be found in the OfSTED Inspection Report undertaken on 3 and 6 July 2006 under Section 162A of the Education Act 2002 and the Independent Schools Inspectorate report of May 2010. Note the dates of these reports – compiled four years apart. It is safe to assume that a significant number of recommendations made to a school in 2006 ought to have been acted upon and eliminated by 2010.

Under the heading 'Information about the school', the OfSTED Report of 2006 described St. Augustine's Priory in Ealing as

> "...an independent Catholic day school for girls aged between 4 and 18 years. St. Augustine's Priory School Limited, a charitable company limited by guarantee owns the school. It is situated in Ealing, West London and occupies the buildings of an Augustinian priory. The school has a long established tradition.
>
> Originally founded in Paris, in 1634, by Lady Mary Tredway, it moved to its present purpose built premises in 1915. Generations of families have attended the school.
>
> Indeed, many staff, including the headteacher, are previous pupils. The school considers this long history of family association a unique characteristic and strength of the school.
>
> The school admits pupils from all religions. It has a distinctive Christian philosophical foundation based on the gospel values of truth, justice, compassion and forgiveness. The school's stated mission is to provide pupils with a 'full and balanced education in the Catholic tradition' in a caring and stimulating environment.
>
> It places great emphasis on 'individuality, originality and responsible care for others'.
>
> It aims to stretch those who are gifted both academically and in other ways to enable them to realise their full potential in the school or in the wider world.
>
> The school is organised into three departments, the preparatory (ages 4 - 7), junior (ages 7 - 11) and senior (ages 11 - 18) schools. Currently there are 509 pupils on roll. Although the school is culturally diverse, there are only eight pupils for whom English is not their principal language. The school gives additional learning support to 26 pupils including those with a statement of special educational need (SEN)..."

Whenever OfSTED or a similar organisation – such as the Independent Schools Inspectorate – produces a report of its findings after an inspection, it will provide a brief description of the school or unit.

The key facts to note here are that St. Augustine's is an all-girls school. The age range of the girls is from 4 to 18. Many staff – including the Head Teacher at the time of the report – were former pupils. There is great emphasis placed on forgiveness after sinful deeds. At the time of this report, there were a little over 500 pupils on roll.

Whilst these facts might make St Augustine's Priory appear to be some form of educational idyll, it provided a breeding ground for all the ingredients of abuse. Girls of all ages are a ready supply for those adults sexually interested in girls. Many staff were former pupils and abusive practices can breed in such an incestuous environment. The mantra that it's ok to sin because you will be forgiven after the event is a dangerous mantra. With 500 pupils on roll, there is considerable access to a large number of girls.

However, perhaps one of the most important aspects of any school is its ability to deal with the safeguarding of its pupils. The OfSTED inspection report showed the following under the heading of 'The suitability of the proprietor and staff':

> "...The school has a very large and highly qualified staff. Prior to confirming their appointment, the school carries out appropriate checks on the identity, medical fitness, qualifications, and employment history of all staff. The school ensures that staff and other adults, who come into regular contact with the pupils are checked by the Criminal Records Bureau at an appropriate level..."

When asking if the school met the requirements for registration, OfSTED was satisfied that it did. It published its report on St. Augustine's Priory on 3 August 2006.

The report was flawed.

Just as St. Augustine's safeguarding of children policy was flawed.

Quis custodiet ipsos custodes – who will guard the guards themselves?

Or, put another way, who will be the gatekeeper's gatekeeper?

The entire safeguarding policy at St. Augustine's was in the hands of just one person – the Head Teacher, Mrs Frances Jane Mariah Katrina Gumley-Mason. Just one person was totally responsible for deciding whether incidents of child abuse told to her by pupils or parents would be followed up or not. She, alone, was responsible for deciding whether teachers who had abused children should be reported to the authorities. She was also running a business with an income from fees alone each year in the £3-4million range, so the idea of reporting abusive teachers and having St. Augustine's brought to the attention of the press and wider public presented her with a conflict of interest of the highest magnitude. The Trustees and Governors should never have allowed this situation to occur.

Born on 28 January 1955, Gumley-Mason – who lists her interests as "playing with children's toys" - has been variously described in blogs and articles on the internet as either a saint or a mad woman or a combination of these and others.

She has an entry in Debrett's which reads:

> "...Career: journalist, broadcaster, radio & television producer and headmistress; Parly res 1974, braille transcriber 1975; Catholic Herald: editorial assistant 1975-76, staff reporter and literary editor 1976-79, editor 1979-81; senior producer religious broadcasting BBC 1981-88, series editor Channel 4 1988-89, acting executive producer Religion BBC World Service 1989, guest producer and scriptwriter BBC Radio 4 1989-95; headmistress St. Augustine's Priory Ealing 1995-; Mistress of the Keys (Catholic Writers' Guild) 1982-87..."
>
> Her books include: The Good Book, The Christian Centuries, The Pillars of Islam, Protestors for Paradise; Discovering Turkey (jtly)..."
> Source: <http://www.debretts.com/people/biographies/browse/g/70/Frances+Jane.aspx>

Thus, with no teaching career behind her, she became the Head teacher of St. Augustine's.

An article in the Times Educational Supplement dated 7 February 2012 described her thus:

> "...The school had been lead (sic) for the last 17 years by their first lay head, Mrs Frances Gumley-Mason. A former pupil of the school, Mrs Gumley-Mason was a blue print for a head that would be almost impossible to replicate. A larger than life character, to many people she was the school. Indeed, I don't think parts of the school community could imagine life beyond their first lay head..."
> Source: <http://www.tesprime.com/node/3930>

Gumley-Mason was the school's Designated Child Protection Officer (DCPO), yet was regarded by some pupils and teachers (and parents) as unapproachable. One of the pre-requisites of a DCPO is approachability. Another is detachment and it is inconceivable that a Head Teacher could be the DCPO for this reason alone. There are simply too many conflicts of interest.

An interesting and worrying comment was left on the 'Confessions of a Skeptic' blog, run by Jonathan West. This (anonymous) post stated:

"...Anonymous, 5 November 2011 18:06 ... You do realise that Mrs Gumley-Mason was an advisory governor at St. Benedict's prior to being appointed as headmistress of St. Augustine's?..."

St. Augustine's was subjected to an inspection in May 2010 by the Independent Schools Inspectorate following serial child abuse at St. Benedict's in Ealing.

The Independent Schools Inspectorate (ISI) is the body approved by the Government for the purpose of inspecting schools belonging to the Independent Schools Council (ISC) Associations and reporting on compliance with the Education (Independent School Standards) (England) Regulations 2003 as subsequently amended with effect from January 2005, May 2007 and February 2009.

This report was extremely damaging to St. Augustine's – so damaging, in fact, that Mrs Gumley-Mason took the ISI to the High Court to try to obtain an injunction against the ISI from publishing its damning report.

Yet all the ISI had done was draw attention to the alarming holes in the Child Protection measures at St. Augustine's, where parents were paying in the region of £3,000 per term in fees.

The ISI Report examines all aspects of the school's life. This particular report condemned the safeguarding of pupils. On page 4 of the report, the Inspection Team commented on significant failures:

> 2.4 At the time of the initial visit, the school did not meet all the requirements of the Independent School Standards Regulations 2003, as subsequently amended, and therefore it was required to:

- ensure that any persons whose services are no longer used because they are considered unsuitable to work with children are always reported fully to the Independent Safeguarding Authority within one month of leaving the school [Regulation 3.(2)(b), under Welfare, health and safety];
- ensure that appropriate checks and central register entries are made on staff appointed since 1st May 2007 [Regulations 4.(2)(a), 4.(2)(b), and 4C.(2)(b) and (d), under Suitability of staff, supply staff and proprietors];
- ensure that enhanced Criminal Records Bureau (CRB) checks are always obtained and recorded for proprietors as necessary [Regulation 4C.(7), under Suitability of staff, supply staff and proprietors];
- ensure that the central register of appointments is correctly completed regarding staff appointed before 1st May 2007 [Regulation 4C.(3), under Suitability of staff, supply staff and proprietors];
- ensure that the facilities provided for pupils who are ill are appropriate [Regulation 5.(1), under Premises and accommodation].

2.5 At the time of the final team visit, the school had rectified some of the above shortcomings, as noted in the text of the report. However, the following requirements remain unresolved, and therefore the school must:

- ensure that all appropriate checks are made on newly appointed staff [Regulation 4.(2)(a), under Suitability of staff, supply staff and proprietors];
- ensure that the central register of appointments is correctly completed [Regulation 4C.(3), under Suitability of staff, supply staff and proprietors].

It is clear from the above paragraphs that St. Augustine's was in breach of regulations in respect of the safeguarding of children. This is, obviously, an extremely serious range of offences. The ISI are unequivocal that St. Augustine's was putting children at risk because of lax safeguarding measures. This is not acceptable.

On page 10 of the Report, the ISI draws attention to the following:

4.6 The school's arrangements for welfare, health and safety, while good in some aspects, are unsatisfactory overall because the required appointment checks were not carried out and recorded and concerns about the suitability of two staff members were not reported to the appropriate authorities as required. The school acted quickly to take and act upon advice from safeguarding agencies in relation to the referrals. Good progress has since been made in the completion of the single central register of appointments.

Clearly two members of staff had given substantial cause for concern, but St. Augustine's failed in its duty to report these to the appropriate authorities.

Jonathan West wrote about this on his blog:

"...As for "the three people mentioned" in the entire ISI Report, one is the former chaplain and chairman of governors, not named in the Ealing Gazette but whom we all know is Father Gregory Chillman, and two are former teachers. Their current status does not reduce one bit the school's obligations to send referrals to the Independent Safeguarding Authority (ISA). If one of the teachers is no longer in the teaching profession, this is no thanks to Mrs Gumley-Mason, because this should have been ensured by her sending the proper report to the ISA..."

However, the ISI refer again to the lack of safeguarding at St Augustine's Priory:

4.8 [...] Safeguarding issues also feature as a standing item on governors' meeting agenda. The child protection policy, whilst good in some respects and containing useful guidance for staff, is unsatisfactory overall. In particular, it does not follow closely enough the statutory guidance in relation to the manner in which concerns are handled and reported, placing inappropriate emphasis on investigation by the school and not identifying clearly the proper threshold for referring concerns to other agencies such as the Local Authority Designated Officer (LADO). This has led to weaknesses in implementation. At the initial inspection visit, significant shortcomings in practice were identified with regard to the requirement to report to the appropriate authorities, within one month of leaving the school, any person whose services are no longer required because he or she is considered unsuitable to work with children.

The ISI draws attention to the fact that St. Augustine's seeks to deal with any allegations of improper conduct towards pupils 'in-house', which leaves a serious gap in the safeguarding procedures. The implication, of course, is that if improper conduct is dealt with 'in-house' there is a much greater risk of a cover-up.

On page 11 of the Report, the ISI added:

5.1 Governance of the school, whilst good in some aspects, notably in supporting the high attainment and excellent personal development of the pupils, is unsatisfactory overall because it does not monitor closely enough the school's arrangements for safeguarding.

5.2 A health and safety committee meets twice a year and provides comprehensive reports to the full governors' meetings. Governors have attended child protection training and as a body are concerned to ensure the well-being and protection of the school's pupils. However, the regulatory shortcomings found during the initial visit of the inspection indicate that the proprietors or their delegated governing body have not been sufficiently diligent in overseeing the school's child protection policy and its arrangements for checking, reporting and referring to the relevant authorities on the suitability of staff and others in contact with children. Several individuals had started work before their CRB certificates had been received, although these were eventually obtained as required. These individuals were not recorded as having a previous CRB check or List 99 clearance and supervision, and a few other checks were not complete. In a very small number of cases the recorded delay in checking was lengthy.

The ISI report thoroughly – and rightly – attacks the Child Protection measures at St. Augustine's.

5.4 Leadership at the highest level has relied heavily on informal procedures to identify and implement improvements. This approach, whilst effective for some management processes, does not provide a consistent mechanism for evaluating the success of new initiatives, for monitoring the implementation of policies or for driving strategic development based on earlier achievements. Weaknesses in the operation of recruitment checks and in the drafting and implementation of the child protection policy have resulted in inadequacies in safeguarding practice.

Information in the public domain is that the Child Protection Policy at St. Augustine's was authored by the husband of the Head teacher!

The report draws attention to serious weaknesses in recruitment checks on new staff coming into the school.

The inspectors – led by Mrs Colette Culligan - observed lessons, conducted formal interviews with pupils and examined samples of pupils' work. They held discussions with senior members of staff and with the chair of governors and governors, observed a sample of the extra-curricular activities that occurred during the inspection period, and attended registration sessions and assemblies.

Inspectors visited the facilities for sick or injured pupils. The responses of parents and pupils to pre-inspection questionnaires were analysed, and the inspectors examined regulatory documentation made available by the school.

Mrs Culligan had an impressive team at her disposal: Mrs Lynne Horner, Team Inspector (Headmistress, SHMIS school), Mr Paul Baker, Team Inspector (Former Head of Department, IAPS school), Mr Stephen Callaghan, Team Inspector (Headmaster, GSA school), Mrs Nicola Fortune, Team Inspector (Director of Studies, IAPS school), Mrs Deborah Leonard, Team Inspector (Deputy Head, GSA school) and Mrs Anne McConway, (Early Years Lead Inspector).

Culligan's team was incredibly experienced and the combined wisdom of the team of seven made significant – and accurate – criticisms of the safeguarding measures at St. Augustine's.

The authors assert that the white South African, Maryn Murray, was guilty of child abuse at St. Augustine's and she had left under a cloud to take up a post at the OLCVS, where she went on to abuse young girls – all white and blonde. The authors also assert that Mrs Gumley-Mason covered up Murray's abuse and failed to report her to the appropriate authorities. Gumley-Mason has previously been guilty of failing to report instances of sexual impropriety by her teachers. She has since resigned her post as Head teacher at St. Augustine's.

Rosa Vaz – of Lambeth Human Resources – admitted in her interview with Twist and White that: "...We [Lambeth HR] wouldn't know if agency staff were CRB checked or not..."

Murray had come from South Africa via the ClassroomTeachers organisation, which was affiliated to the agency of the same name in London.

Thousands of teachers came across to the UK via this operation, many of them unqualified and – more importantly – unchecked in terms of CRB and other background checks including, for example, List 99 checks (now referred to as the Vetting and Barring Scheme). Those teachers with a sexual proclivity towards children were then allowed unfettered access to thousands of children. If any 'incidents' arose they could simply leave the school in a hurry, contact their agency for a new posting and move on. Their actions never caught up with them, but they left a trail of destruction. They could even leave the UK and return to their country of origin.

And Lambeth were made aware of this by Pead, and Lambeth reinstated Murray.

high court action

Mrs Gumley-Mason did not take kindly to the Independent Schools Inspectorate report about her safeguarding policies. In fact, she was incensed by the report so much so that she took the ISI to the High Court, hoping to seek an injunction to prevent the publication of the report.

In any Court hearing, there will be what are called the Statement of Grounds. In layman's terms, this simply means the grounds on which you are bringing your case against your opponent. Below are the grounds on which Gumley-Mason sought to obtain an injunction:

> 1. St. Augustine's Priory School Limited is a registered charity which operates an independent Catholic day school for girls under the name St. Augustine's Priory ("the School").
>
> 2. The Independent Schools Inspectorate ("ISI") is a body approved by the Secretary of State for Education under section 163 of the Education Act 2002 (as originally enacted) for the purpose of conducting inspections of independent schools and making reports on such schools.
>
> 3. ISI conducted an inspection of the School on 23rd and 24th March and 4th to 6th May 2010 and concluded inter alia, in a report ("the Proposed Report") intended to be published on 2nd November 2010 pursuant to the provisions of the applicable inspection framework, that the quality of governance, leadership and management, whilst good in some aspects, is unsatisfactory overall because it has not ensured that safeguarding procedures and practice meet the required standards.
>
> 4. The School objects to that judgment on the grounds that it is based on errors of fact and law, is unfairly inconsistent with other reports and is a judgment which no reasonable inspecting body could have reached.
>
> 5. The School accordingly seeks orders directing ISI to reconsider the terms of the Proposed Report. On 1st November 2010 the School obtained an interim Order from Mr. Justice Butterfield restraining publication until trial of this claim or further order.

That was the basic outline of her case. Gumley-Mason felt that the ISI report was 'unfair'. This is a woman with more than 500 girls at her school. She appears to have failed to grasp the idea that the safety of those girls is of paramount importance and not the reputation of the school.

Having outlined her case, Gumley-Mason's solicitors present the facts (as they see them):

6. In the course of the initial inspection on 23rd and 24th March 2010, the inspectors, led by Mrs. Culligan, the reporting inspector, assessed whether the School complied with the requirements set out in the Education (Independent Schools Standards) (England) regulations 2003, S.I. 2003 No. 1910, as amended ("the regulatory requirements").

7. The Proposed Report states that the inspectors concluded that at the time of the initial inspection the School failed to comply fully with the regulatory requirements because, inter alia:

(1) the School failed to ensure that any persons whose services were no longer used because they were considered unsuitable to work with children were always reported fully to the Independent Safeguarding Authority within one month of leaving the School;

(2) the School failed to ensure that appropriate checks and central register entries were made, an alleged failure which was said to include failing to ensure that enhanced Criminal Records Bureau ("CRB") checks were always obtained and recorded for a governor as necessary.

8. The Proposed Report further states, having regard to those conclusions, that:

(1) the School's arrangements for welfare, health and safety are inadequate;

(2) the child protection policy is unsatisfactory overall and at the initial inspection significant failures in referral practice were identified;

(3) governance of the school is unsatisfactory overall because it does not monitor closely enough the School's arrangements for safeguarding;

(4) leadership and management of the educational aspects of the School are mostly good but weaknesses in safeguarding practice make them unsatisfactory overall.

9. The Proposed Report therefore sets out in one of the three paragraphs recording the inspector's main findings that the quality of governance, leadership and management, whilst good in some aspects, notably in supporting high attainment and excellent personal development, is unsatisfactory overall because it has not ensured that safeguarding procedures and practice meet the required standard.

It is worth noting at this point that Gumley-Mason and her legal team are not focussing at all on the safety of the pupils at St. Augustine's – she is merely trying to save the reputation of the school and her legal team are assisting her. They should, of course, in Jonathan West's and the authors' opinions, have been more diligent in ensuring that the lax safeguarding measures were improved.

10. The concerns expressed to the headmistress of the School, Mrs. Frances Gumley-Mason ("the Headmistress") by Mrs. Culligan at the time of the initial inspection as to failure always to make full referrals to the Independent Safeguarding Authority within one month related to (a) [Teacher A] (b) [Teacher B] (c) Father Gregory Chillman.

11. [Teacher A], employed at the School from 1st September 2007, was suspended from 7th February 2008 (at which time she was already on sick leave) and her employment ended on 31st May 2008. The suspension was imposed on the ground that [Teacher A]'s CRB disclosure contained information relating to her husband and son which she said was inaccurate and was pending an amended disclosure. The Headmistress decided that under the statutory and guidance provisions then applicable referral was not required or appropriate. After speaking to Mrs. Culligan, the Headmistress made inquiries of the Independent Safeguarding Authority and was informed that [Teacher A] was "definitely not referral material". The Headmistress subsequently informed Mrs. Culligan of this.

12. [Teacher B] was employed at the School from 1st September 2007 and was suspended on 3rd December 2008 following written complaints from two groups of sixth form pupils on 1st and 3rd December 2008. He responded to the complaints by e-mail received on 5th December 2008 and subsequently, having sought advice from the Association of Teachers and Lecturers, resigned on 18th December 2008. The Headmistress decided that under the statutory and guidance provisions then applicable, referral was not required or appropriate.

After speaking to Mrs. Culligan, the Headmistress made inquiries of the Independent Safeguarding Authority and was informed that it was "up to her" whether or not she made a referral in respect of [Teacher B]. The Headmistress decided in all the circumstances to do so. The Headmistress subsequently informed Mrs. Culligan of these matters.

13. For many years Father Gregory Chillman was the School's chaplain and a governor. The appointment to the office of chaplain was made not by the School but by the Abbot of St. Benedict's Abbey, a monastic foundation connected with St. Benedict's School, a nearby Catholic school originally for boys which has recently become co-educational. At the time of the initial visit the School was aware of one

allegation only relating to Father Gregory's conduct at the School, involving a conversation in January 2004 with two sixth form students in the sixth form common room in the presence of other students. No complaint was made by the students involved in the conversation themselves. On investigation by the Headmistress it appeared that Father Gregory had made an ill-judged remark and it was agreed that he should receive further training on child protection issues. The Headmistress decided that under the statutory and guidance provisions then applicable referral was not required or appropriate.

14. At about the same time the School became aware of an allegation of historic abuse, taking place in the 1970s, newly made by a former male pupil of St. Benedict's against Father Gregory. The School had no knowledge of this matter, save that the allegation had been made. The School was advised by the relevant local authority, the London Borough of Ealing, on 10th April 2010 that there was no reason to be concerned for the safety of students at the School.

15. The Headmistress informed Mrs. Culligan of these matters. Further, the Headmistress has been advised by both the Independent Safeguarding Authority and by the London Borough of Ealing that since Father Gregory has never been employed by the School it is not for the School to make any referral.

16. In those circumstances, the School contends that:

(1) there has been no failure on its part to ensure that any persons whose services are no longer used because they are considered unsuitable to work with children are always reported fully to the Independent Safeguarding Authority within one month of leaving the School;

(2) there have been no cases in which the School has been obliged to make a referral to the Independent Safeguarding Authority.

CRB and other checks

17. The regulatory requirements were amended with effect from 1st May 2007 to require schools to keep a central register recording checks made on staff and proprietors and amending the requirements as to who should be checked and in what manner.

18. Mrs. Culligan required the School to obtain an enhanced CRB disclosure in respect of a governor, Brigadier Cantley, although he was appointed a governor before 1st May 2007 and thus before such a requirement applied to governors who were not the chair of the governing body.

19. Mrs. Culligan criticised the checking procedures undertaken in relation to [Teacher A] although:

(1) the regulatory requirements did not oblige the School to obtain a CRB disclosure in respect of a person (such as [Teacher A]) who had worked in a school in England in a position bringing her regularly into contact with children or young persons during a period ending not more than three months before the date of appointment;

(2) the School had obtained references in respect of [Teacher A] from her previous school stating that there was no reason why she should not work with children and that CRB checks had been undertaken prior to her previous appointment;

(3) the School itself (consistently with the applicable regulatory requirements if a CRB disclosure was required) appointed her for a probationary period subject to CRB checks which were applied for on 18th May 2007. The regulatory requirement was to obtain a disclosure before or as soon as practicable after appointment;

(4) although no disclosure document was produced for [Teacher A] until December 2007, that delay was outside the School's control.

20. In those circumstances, the School contends that standards which are erroneous in law have been applied in determining whether or not the School complied with the regulatory requirements relating to CRB and other checks.

Unfair inconsistency

21. It is demonstrable from other reports on the Defendant's web site that on an initial inspection visit schools are frequently found to have failed in complying with the regulatory requirements in some respects. Typically, where such errors are comparatively minor and improved procedures for the avoidance of such errors in future have been instituted, the failures and the improved procedures are both noted and there is no main finding which adversely reflects on the governance, leadership and management of the school.

22. The report on the School departs from this pattern, despite the inspectors' finding that the governors had identified a number of specific and appropriate procedures to be put into action with immediate effect and the further fact that Mrs. Culligan informed the School that its amended child protection policy was "watertight". The School is thus at a loss to know what more is still required.

23. The tenor of the report is to treat regulatory failures as continuing (as shown by the terms of paragraph 8 above) instead of as having been remedied (as illustrated by the matters set out in paragraph 22 above).

24. St. Benedict's itself was inspected by the Defendant in November 2009 and received a favourable report in respect of its child protection policies. It was re-inspected in April and May 2010 because a member of the public had drawn the Defendant's attention to public records of six prosecutions or civil actions brought in connection with the Abbey and St. Benedict's School. On re-inspection the Defendant recorded a number of failings in St. Benedict's approach to safeguarding and expressed the judgment that the governors' commitment to St. Benedict's rule of love and forgiveness "appears on occasion to have overshadowed responsibility for children's welfare". Notwithstanding that criticism, there was no revision of the overall assessment of governance as good and leadership as excellent.

25. This is of particular relevance because on publication of the Proposed Report the School will come under an obligation to send copies to parents and guardians, many of whom also have children at St. Benedict's. The favourable assessment of St. Benedict's is liable to be compared with the unfavourable assessment of the School.

Legal basis of challenge

26. The School respectfully submits that the Defendant is amenable to judicial review because in inspecting schools it is carrying out a statutory function in the public interest on behalf of the Department for Education under the terms of an agreement with that Department. Its reports are published on its web site and supplied to the Department and are available to be read by any member of the public. A principal purpose of the reports is to determine whether an independent school is satisfying the statutorily prescribed standards for independent schools in England.

27. It is the School's case that:

(1) the Defendant's conclusions as to the School's compliance at the initial visit with the regulatory requirements relating to safeguarding are based on errors of fact and law in relation to referral and checking obligations and cannot be supported;

(2) the Defendant's conclusions as to the School's continuing failures to comply with the regulatory requirements (if as the Proposed Report appears to imply, it is alleged that there are continuing failures) are

based on no material and are contrary to statements made to the School by the Defendant;

(3) the Defendant's conclusions as to the governance, leadership and management of the School are unfairly inconsistent with the conclusions reached in other cases and as such are in breach of the Defendant's own guidelines for preparing reports;

(4) having regard to all the matters set out above, the conclusions reached as to the governance, leadership and management of the School are conclusions which no reasonable body of inspectors could have reached.

28. In the premises, the Defendant should be directed to reconsider the terms of the Proposed Report in the light of the matters set out above.

st. augustine's cover-up

The blogger Jonathan West has valiantly attempted to draw parents' - and the wider public's - attention to the lackadaisical and inept child protection policies at both St. Augustine's and at St. Benedict's.

He added the following important message to parents on his blog on 18 March 2011:

> "...Based on what is in the ISI report, St. Augustine's has been breaking the law on child protection for years. They employed teachers before their CRB checks had been done. Anybody could have been working there.
>
> They didn't report staff to the Independent Safeguarding Authority who left because they were unsuitable to supervise children, so abusive teachers might have gone on to other teaching jobs.
>
> The child protection policy didn't even ensure that all allegations of abuse are reported to the authorities so that they could be properly investigated.
>
> These are really serious and basic child protection failures. Similar failures at St. Benedict's have resulted in child sexual abuse there lasting for a long time, even after a former teacher had been sent to jail for abuse.
>
> We have no way of knowing if children at St. Augustine's have been abused and it has gone unreported. It's outrageous that the school tried to stop publication of the report and keep parents in the dark about all this. Their priority is obviously protecting the school's reputation rather than keeping children safe..."

the school governors

In a remarkable coincidence, research has shown that Phyllis Dunipace (former Executive Director of Lambeth), Glenice Lake (Anya Hiley's line manager) and Judge Anne Martin are all school governors, giving them considerable access to children and the opportunity not to report to the safeguarding authorities instances of child abuse (in whatsoever format) brought to their attention in the schools in which they are Governors.

Dunipace is a Governor at La Retraite Girls' School in Lambeth. La Retraite is a Catholic girls' school – just as St. Augustine's is. Maryn Murray worked at St. Augustine's. Brian Pead dismissed Murray for racism and for the sexual grooming of young, white girls. Lambeth re-employed her. Phyllis Dunipace ratified the re-employment of Murray.

Judge Anne Martin is also a school governor. Martin is also listed as a Director of Stem4ED, a charity for eating disorders amongst vulnerable teenagers. The address for Stem4ED is Unit 1, 49 Pelham Road, London, SW19 1SU.

SW19 is the postal address for Wimbledon. Less than a mile away is Morden – where Maryn Murray claimed to live.

Glenice Lake is a School Governor at the Priory School in Croydon, some three miles from Morden.

lord carlile of berriew

On Monday, 9 July 2012, Jonathan West composed an important blog. This blog should – in the authors' opinion – be read by **every** parent throughout the land.

West writes:

> "...The "Annual Report and Accounts" for The Trust of St Benedict's Abbey, Ealing to the end of August 2011 have recently been published on the Charity Commission website.
>
> They do make very interesting reading. The point that I most wanted to see was how much Lord Carlile's fees had been for his report issued in November last year.
>
> The accounts don't have a separate heading for "Lord Carlile", but it is pretty clear under what heading his fees have been placed under. Page 35 of the report contains section 7 "Governance costs". This section contains just one item "Professional fees and charges". In 2010 these totalled £20,392; in 2011 they were a whopping £256,372, an increase of just under £236,000. The vast majority of this increase will have gone on Lord Carlile, with perhaps a modest additional fee for the school solicitors through whom he was engaged.
>
> Of course, the total cost may be considerably higher. Lord Carlile didn't issue his final report until November 2011, so I'm sure his final bill will appear in the accounts for the current financial year, so we won't see those on the Charity Commission website for another 12 months or so.
>
> But let's just consider the £230,000 that appears on last year's accounts. As the school has about 1000 pupils, that's the equivalent of about £230 on the fees, probably somewhat more since a proportion of the pupils are on scholarships and bursaries. Or it can be thought of as 70% of the parish collections and donations for the year, which were £341,322.
>
> Back in September 2010, I estimated that the school wouldn't see much change out of a quarter of a million pounds.
>
> They are spending a sum probably of the order of a quarter of a million pounds on an exercise in reassurance. As the headmaster's comments at the safeguarding meeting amply showed, there is no evidence of any interest in actually improving safeguarding, but they want to give the impression that Something Is Being Done. Lord Carlile's name will of

course appear on the cover page of the report in letters rather larger than the title. And of course a glossily printed copy will be sent to each parent. The aim is to provide a reassurance to parents that All Is Well Really, if with some minor tweaks to procedures.

I'm gratified that my estimate of the cost was so close to the mark. Let's have a look as to my estimate of the aims of the exercise back then, that it wasn't to improve safeguarding, but rather that it was an exercise in reassurance.

A glossily printed copy of the report was of course printed and sent to all parents, and Lord Carlile's name wasn't merely larger than the title, it was the title, or most of it.

Recall that Lord Carlile made no new recommendations concerning safeguarding in the course of his report, he merely repeated recommendations which others had already made. His only new recommendation concerned governance, the proposal to split the governance of the school from that of the abbey and parish. The annual report includes just one paragraph from Carlile's report, as follows:

"...I believe that St. Benedict's School, Ealing, is an excellent place for boys and girls to be educated in safety today and for the future. No school is perfect, and 'never' is a dangerous word and a hostage to fortune. However, if those responsible for the School adopt the advice offered in this Report, and advice from the agencies referred to above, I consider that St. Benedict students will be as well safeguarded as anywhere else in the country, without in any way losing the Benedictine connection and ethos..."

The annual report also lists "Objectives for the year". The first of these is as follows:

"...Over the next year the School will be responding to the two main recommendations of the Lord Carlile Report (see above). Firstly, ensuring that its Safeguarding Policy is not only a model of excellence but that implementation of the Policy is given top priority by all those working in the School. Secondly, it will be working towards setting up a new educational charity, separate from the main Trust, for the School's operations. This will ensure that the governance of the School is separate from that of the Trust of St Benedict's Abbey, Ealing..."

As far as the first of these points is concerned, "ensuring that its Safeguarding Policy is not only a model of excellence but that implementation of the Policy is given top priority by all those working in the School", the wording is so vague that no tangible and measurable objective can be obtained from it. There is no sign of any progress with regard to safeguarding. I have raised continuing concerns with the school concerning its safeguarding policy, and its latest version still contains language that is far too full of holes to give confidence that safeguarding really is a priority.

Looking to make the safeguarding policy "a model of excellence" is meaningless unless there is some external yardstick against which excellence is measured. None has been provided, so there is no means of telling whether this objective will have been met by the end of the year.

Looking to see that "implementation of the Policy is given top priority" is also meaningless. Priority doesn't matter at all, what matters is tangible achievements, and none are stated..."

for whom the bell tolled

But if Brian Pead thought that he was simply the victim of an improperly held investigation and disciplinary process and an Employment Tribunal perverse ruling, he was very much mistaken.

Within the next six months he would be arrested twice on two separate criminal charges and he would beaten up in the street by four Bexley Police officers ... he would be vilified in the press and he would be found guilty of a criminal offence by a Jury that wasn't sworn in. Key witnesses to his innocence were not called by Dominic Bell, his barrister. A computer belonging to a friend was illegally seized by the police and the hard drive burnt out.

Research proving his innocence had been wiped off by the police. Two illegal searches of his house took place and research materials were unlawfully removed.

Mother and daughter Adrienne and Victoria Tear - witnesses to his beating up in the street by four officers - were then visited by the Police and forced to withdraw their complaints of police brutality.

He lost his job again – this time working as a counsellor. His office was ransacked and his computer at work wiped clean, in an echo of the methods employed by Lambeth Council.

'For Whom the Bell Tolled' is a highly-explosive account of top level police corruption, crooked barristers and a Judge who threatened to jail a man he knew to be innocent.

143

dunipace resigns

Phyllis Dunipace resigned as Executive Director of the Children and Young People's Service on 8 August 2010.

At the time of writing, Dunipace is 62 years old and first became a director 16 years ago at the age of 46. In total, Dunipace has held 6 directorships, 2 are current directorships, and 4 are previous.

Source: <https://www.duedil.com/director/906161154/phyllis-dunipace>

Did she declare her outside financial interests to Lambeth?

Did these outside directorships cause conflicts of interest?

phyllis dunipace, obe

Royal Investitures:

Miss Phyllis Dunipace from London is made an OBE by The Prince of Wales at Buckingham Palace on 8 February 2011.

The case of James Walker v Lambeth Council – which commenced on Dunipace's watch – is progressing through the Employment Tribunal system at the very same time that Dunipace receives a royal investiture.

Dunipace had commissioned a report written by consultant Tom Walker of Lambeth Council in February 2009 outlining a strategy for removing James Walker, who had been suspended in November 2008, from his post.

The reward for such treachery, it would seem, is an OBE.

As a direct result of the publication of this book, the authors have written to Buckingham Palace asking that Dunipace forfeits this royal award. It is impossible to imagine that HM The Queen would be happy to learn of such misfeasance in public office by someone she has given such an award to.

allaroundjustice.com

Living in a country that claims that it has freedom of speech, Brian Pead and friends put together a website in order to draw the wider public's attention to corruption within Lambeth Council, within the police service and within the judicial system at barrister and Judge level.

No civilised society should ever treat a citizen in the way that it has treated Brian Pead. The website was constructed by people who were extremely sympathetic to Pead's cause – they could see the top level corruption that had taken place – but they asked to remain anonymous and the authors have respected their wishes.

The website merely pointed out all of the legal abuses that the police and the justice system have perpetrated against Pead, including unlawfully sending him to jail in 2011 for a period of seven weeks. Those in authority who had a lot to hide thought that they would silence him. They totally mis-judged him and his love for his beloved grand-children. He had vowed to get the truth – THE REAL TRUTH – to them, not the truth peddled by the police, social services, politicians and corrupt lawyers and judges.

The website highlighted all of the human rights abuses the State was guilty of in respect of Pead. Every comment was supported by robust evidence. Pead is not the type to rant. Everything with him has to have the professional and well-considered touch.

The website highlighted all of the abuses against him in a calm and considered manner.

The police sought to have it taken down from the internet.

doreen lawrence

On 16 June 2012, Doreen Lawrence said she was pleased that there would be an independent review into allegations that police corruption may have shielded suspects in her son's racist murder. The Home Secretary, Theresa May, ordered the probe on 1 June, just a day after reviews from the Metropolitan Police and watchdog, the Independent Police Complaints Commission (IPCC), said they found no evidence of corruption.

In a statement, Mrs. Lawrence, who had expressed disappointment with the reviews by the Met Police and IPCC, said: "...I am pleased that the Home Secretary has taken my concerns seriously about allegations of corruption in the investigations into my son's murder..."

Mrs. Lawrence had written to the Home Secretary in March after a large number of media reports alleged one investigating officer had links to the father of one of two suspects, who were jailed for Stephen's murder in January 2012.

The reports also claimed that the Met Police failed to disclose certain evidence to the Macpherson Inquiry into the police's handling of the original investigation into the teenager's 1993 murder.

A Home Office spokesperson told reporters that May had ordered "...a QC-led review of the work the Metropolitan Police has undertaken into investigating claims of corruption in the original Stephen Lawrence murder investigation..."

Mrs. Lawrence continued: "...Whilst I asked for a public enquiry into these allegations my discussions with the Home Secretary have reassured me that the independent review she has ordered will seek to deal with my concerns. This is because firstly, it will be conducted by someone independent of both the police and the IPCC, organisations in which I have little faith and confidence and secondly, the person conducting the review, Mark Ellison QC, is someone who has already shown his commitment in getting justice for me and my family..."

She added: "...I see this review as only the start of a process which, should it reveal matters which need further exploration, will be done without hesitation..."

On May 31, the Met Police said its internal review, carried out by the Met's Directorate of Professional Standards (DPS), showed officers did not withhold evidence linked to corruption from the Stephen Lawrence inquiry.

The Met claimed that its internal review "...concluded that no investigations, nor the inquiry, have uncovered evidence of corruption or collusion which could have adversely affected or otherwise influenced the path of the original investigation or subsequent investigations..."

Despite its name, the Independent Police Complaints Commission is anything but independent. It is staffed by police officers and operatives. It simply cannot claim to be independent.

In a strange quirk of fate, Brian Pead was unlawfully imprisoned in Belmarsh Prison on 23 September 2011 where David Norris and Gary Dobson – found guilty of the murder of Stephen Lawrence - were also inmates.

Pead had been imprisoned on a charge of witness intimidation when he said "Hello" to his grand-daughter, Emily Birch, then aged 13, at a bus-stop near Sidcup station in Kent. Emily Birch was, and had never been, a witness in any trial.

Brian Pead had been incarcerated not because of anything he had done but once again for what he knew.

john terry - 1

On Friday 13 July 2012, Brian Pead was at the City of Westminster Magistrates' Court in London for the trial of John Terry.

Chief Magistrate Howard Riddle found Terry not guilty of a racially aggravated public order offence after four days of bitterly disputed evidence and argument. Brian Pead had attended every single day at Court.

This was the very same Court at which a Magistrate – not Riddle – allegedly signed a search warrant on a house belonging to a friend of Pead in a criminal trial in 2009. The Magistrate did not, in fact, sign the warrant – it had been forged by the Metropolitan Police Service.

Terry, on the other hand, received the highest standard of legal representation.

The Football Association, the Metropolitan Police and the Crown Prosecution Service had gone to great lengths to prosecute Terry for racist language said in the heat of battle. (The authors do not condone such language, but the point needs to be made that it was said in the heat of battle in an important Premier League football match).

Why, then, did Lambeth Council, the Metropolitan Police Service and the Crown Prosecution Service **fail** to act when Brian Pead informed Barry Gilhooly of Murray's racist language and behaviour towards three young black men during their school lessons?

148

alleged complaint about allaroundjustice.com

On 27 July 2012, AllAroundJustice received an email from its webhosts UK2Net, claiming that a Mr Paul Birch of Sidcup had been libelled on the website and that, as a result, the web hosts were withdrawing the service and taking the website down.

Naturally AllAroundJustice asked for a copy of the alleged complaint.

None was forthcoming.

Scotland Yard had a hand in this ridiculous communication.

Mr Paul Birch is Brian Pead's son-in-law. He is a director in a garage known as Foxberry Garages and other related ventures.

The Metropolitan Police Service has been the largest customer of the garage for a number of years.

john terry - 2

Having been cleared in a criminal court of racially abusing Anton Ferdinand, a black player with Queen's Park Rangers football team, John Terry was then subjected to a Disciplinary Hearing by the Football Association in September 2012.

He was, as has been widely reported, found guilty of using racist language towards Mr Ferdinand, a millionaire.

If the law of England and Wales exists to protect all of its citizens, why was a case involving racially aggravated behaviour taken to Court when it involved a millionaire and not when it involved three innocent (and poor) young black men who had gone to a pupil referral unit to be educated and not racially abused by Maryn Murray?

The Football Association was not concerned with how it would be perceived as an organisation by bringing such action against Mr Terry – it merely focused on righting the wrong that is racism.

Lambeth Council, on the other hand, was more concerned with its public image than it was with eradicating racism from its schools.

allaroundjustice.com website taken down

from: UK2.net support@support.uk2.net Jul 28, 2012

to: office@allaroundjustice.com

Hello,

Thank you for contacting UK2 Support. I am sorry if you have misunderstood the Terms of Service to which you agreed. Please refer to our Service Agreement, section 9, which allows UK2 to suspend an account if there is reasonable suspicion that you may have been in violation of the Terms of Service. The technician who suspended your account had reason to believe this was the case.

Also, we do not arrange a face-to-face meeting with the CEO. Rather, you can submit a stage one complaint by emailing us (opening a ticket). If you are not satisfied with the response, the complaint can be updated to a stage two complaint, at which point a senior manager will review the email. If you continue to be dissatisfied, the email can be forwarded to the UK2 Management Team and CEO for review.

Please let me know if you need help with anything else!

Regards,

Adam Jensen
Technical Support
UK-2 Ltd

AllAroundJustice had not violated any terms and conditions of their web hosting package. The long arm of the law was certainly **very** long.

institutional corruption

On 12 September 2012, Brian Pead heard, along with all other Liverpool fans, what he and they had known for 23 years – that the police had been involved in a cover-up of immense proportions. The media, and especially The Sun, had been controlled by Margaret Thatcher's government to lay the blame for Hillsborough at the feet of the Liverpool fans.

The fans were **not** to blame.

Just as Brian Pead had not been to blame at the OLCVS, where Lambeth Council embarked upon a smear campaign of an innocent man who had uncovered child abuse and inadequate safeguarding procedures within Lambeth and who witnessed Lambeth's cover-up of institutionalised corruption.

Just as Brian Pead knew that his brother, Robert William Pead, had not been guilty of causing his own death on board a Lowestoft trawler in 1972 but that the Coroner had claimed that Robert had caused his own death in order to save the insurance company paying out his widow and two sons, Jason and Shaun.

Through the Hillsborough enquiry, the police tactic of disinformation has become more widely known. Brian Pead had known about this strategy used by the police since he had attended the FA Cup semi-final at Hillsborough on 15 April 1989.

On that fateful day, he attended the game with a friend, Mark Golledge, a Liverpool FC shareholder. They had seats facing the halfway line, and they naturally looked across to the Liverpool fans gathering behind the goal at the Leppings Lane end of the ground.

At 2.30pm, just thirty minutes before kick-off, Pead and Golledge commented on the unusual pattern of crowd control in the pens behind the goal. Pens 3 and 4 were obviously becoming exceedingly crowded, whilst the pens either side were less than half-empty. The two men exchanged the view that it was an odd way to manage the Liverpool fans.

At 2.40pm Mark Golledge's whole body shuddered. Pead turned to him and asked him, "What's wrong?" and Golledge replied, "Something terrible is going to happen today."

Not quite understanding what his friend meant, Pead said, "What do you mean? You think we're going to be beaten?"

"I don't know," replied Golledge.

At 2.50pm, the Liverpool fans slowly filtered into the ground and pens 3 and 4 were filled to capacity.

At 2.52pm, the inept and inexperienced Chief Superintendent David Duckenfield ordered gate C to be opened and fans made for the tunnel leading directly to pens 3 and 4, with the result that dozens of fans were crushed to death against the metal fences preventing fans from encroaching on to the pitch.

Pead and Golledge watched the horror unfold. Golledge's shudder had been an ominous portent of the tragedy that was Hillsborough.

On the following Monday after the match, Brian Pead, teaching at Bexleyheath School in Kent, organised a Variety Show in which pupils sang or danced or told jokes to raise money for the Hillsborough Disaster Fund.

The shows – held over three evenings – were a resounding success and more than £600 was raised by the pupils, a not insignificant sum of money in 1989.

Pead called Ray Clemence, the former Liverpool, Tottenham and England goalkeeper, who was coaching at Tottenham Hotspur.

Clemence agreed to come to the school to accept a cheque on behalf of the Hillsborough Disaster Fund. The brilliant goalkeeper held the whole school enthralled in a magnificent assembly in which Clemence found the right tone when addressing his young audience. Brian Pead marvelled at Clemence's ability to say the right thing in the right way.

Pead was shocked at the headlines in The Sun and other newspapers. He was a Liverpool season ticket holder and ventured north to Anfield every other week to watch home matches and he mixed with many Liverpudlians who felt huge resentment against Thatcher and Murdoch in their malevolent manipulation of what was supposed to be a free press.

At this period of time in his life, Brian Pead came to learn at first hand the ways in which a government can manipulate the press by disseminating disinformation. He had studied the role of propaganda within the Nazi regime during his English degree, and he learnt how Goebbels - and others within that political party - used the media, particularly the radio, by which to manipulate the masses.

Hitler's Nuremberg rallies were deliberately held at night – so that men, after working long hours, would be more susceptible to adopting the Nazi credo when tired.

The way in which Thatcher's government manipulated the ordinary man and woman in the street through disinformation was appalling in Pead's view. He studied it carefully. He noted particularly how the police lied. How they doctored evidence.

How they had tried to turn the blame for their own inadequacies on to the victims – just as the Lowestoft coroner had done at his brother's inquest.

Pead studied how the police immediately set about disinforming the public. Misinformation, of course, is one thing. Anybody can misinform another by mistake. But the act of disinformation is a cold, calculated tactic which is meant to deliberately provide false information to people in order to get them to think or feel a certain way. At the time of Hillsborough, the police wanted the ordinary person in the street to believe that the Liverpool fans had been the architects of their own deaths because of their alleged behaviour. But Pead and Golledge knew – just as thousands of other fans knew – that this was simply not true.

Pead had witnessed the way that the Government and the police had treated the miners and their families during the infamous miners' strikes of the 1980s. He had been disgusted at the treatment of decent, hard-working people.

But Hillsborough was the unacceptable face of police corruption – the very institution that is charged with protecting the public had immediately set about vilifying the dead and dying at Hillsborough, who had been accused of being drunken or ticketless. It has now become widely known that the police sought to defame the dead by ordering checks on the police national computer and taking blood samples.

It has also become known that 41 of those who died might have been saved had the emergency services actually done what they were paid to do. More time was spent trying to disparage the dead and dying than on trying to save fans from dying.

Over the years, it also became known that police had doctored evidence and completely changed statements. Pead had seen this happen in the famous cases of the Guildford Four and the Birmingham Six and other such cases of gross miscarriages of justice.

Little was Brian Pead to know that he would become the target of disinformation, doctored evidence, smear campaigns, unlawful imprisonment and his own miscarriages of justice simply because he had uncovered corruption and a cover-up on an industrial scale.

The Independent has reported on Hillsborough that:

> "...The report of the independent panel into the Hillsborough disaster is a political, legal and social milestone. It has not only brought out the truth about the unnecessary deaths of 96 football fans which the victims' families have struggled for 23 long years to discover. It has also - finally - revealed the shocking reality that the police, politicians, coroner, local councils and even a full judicial inquiry failed to disclose.

The findings make chilling reading. In addition to the serious failures of the public authorities, the panel also exposes a massive cover-up to protect the institutional reputation of the police. It discloses flaws, too, in the competence of the ambulance and emergency services. And it shows that officials at both football club and the local council knew that safety standards at the Sheffield stadium were inadequate and that lessons had not been learned from previous incidents at Hillsborough and also at other football grounds.

Taken together, then, the evidence lays bare if not a conspiracy then certainly a confluence of establishment interests in which some journalists enthusiastically peddled sensational lies to denigrate the deceased and suggest the fans were the authors of their own demise. It confirms as erroneous the decision by the coroner not to take evidence on the deaths past the time of 3.15pm on the day of the disaster – which would have revealed that as many as 41 of the 96 people might have been saved had the police and ambulance services done their jobs properly. And it raises questions about how key documents were withheld from the inquiry led by Lord Justice Taylor which neglected the shortcomings in the ambulance system and focused on the "failure of police control".

The Taylor report gave no sense of the systematic nature of the cover-up and the mud-slinging in which the police engaged. We now know that 164 police statements were "significantly amended" of which 116 were edited to "remove negative comments" about the operation. Officers ran checks on the police national computer to try to find information to impugn the reputations of those who had died. The coroner ordered alcohol checks on the dead in search of evidence for the false assertion that the tragedy had been caused by drunken fans arriving late without tickets.

And so a narrative of hooliganism was created, against a background of times when football was perceived as a national disease thanks to the behaviour of supporters who routinely invaded pitches or fought in the streets. Football fans were treated as second-class citizens and regarded by the police with hostility. Politicians concurred and stadium terraces were turned into wire-caged pens. It was against these that innocent fans were crushed to death.

Another shocking disclosure is that when the police mendacity began to emerge, Prime Minister Thatcher was briefed by her press secretary that the "close to deceitful" behaviour of senior officers was "depressingly familiar" – a phenomenon which has not since diminished, as the cases of Jean Charles de Menezes and Ian Tomlinson show. One MP told Parliament yesterday that the "criminal conspiracy" among the police was so shocking "it completely takes your breath away".

After truth should come justice, David Cameron told the Commons. That must mean re-opening the inquests into the Hillsborough deaths. It must mean criminal proceedings against senior police officers and others, for perverting the course of justice or misconduct in public office. But it also raises questions about why it took an independent panel to succeed where police, lawyers, judges, journalists and politicians failed. What has been revealed is a stain on Britain's reputation that no amount of scrubbing can remove..."

© The Independent 13 September 2012

Brian Pead knows only too well the corruption at senior levels of the Metropolitan Police. He has been subjected to false criminal proceedings brought against him. He had been subjected to police brutality in the streets. He has been falsely imprisoned. He has been lied about. He has had elected politicians including James Brokenshire and James Duddridge fail to represent him. Duddridge could not bear to read about so much police and political corruption that he wrote to Pead and told him "...never write to me again..." So much for politics.

Brian Pead cannot order a new inquest into the death of his brother, aged 21 and married with two young sons. The Coroner and those on board the St Kitts trawler which was working off the east coast of Scotland on Tuesday, 11 April, 1972, will have to live with their own lack of personal responsibility after Robert suffered catastrophic head injuries. Brian Pead cannot seek compensation for his widow and sons. Just like those responsible for Hillsborough cannot bring back the dead, Brian Pead cannot bring back his brother. But Robert left behind an enduring legacy to his younger brother – that of an unquenchable thirst for justice and truth. Out of the older brother's death came the younger brother's life and driving force to expose corruption at every level.

On 1 November 2011, whilst being unlawfully held in Belmarsh Prison, Brian Pead was illegally found guilty of the harassment of his daughter, Sorrel Pead, and grand-daughter, Emily Birch, for sending Emily a card for her birthday. Neither Sorrel nor Emily was in Court. No evidence was put forward, but the corrupt magistrate still found Pead 'guilty' of harassment.

The police would stop at nothing to disrupt the life of a man they not only knew to be innocent, but whom they regarded as an enemy because of his desire to expose corruption at whatever level.

In January 2012, Brian Pead was forced by Judge Robinson to represent himself at Woolwich Crown Court on yet another false allegation. Bexley Police were represented by PC John Brown, who was clearly a stooge to take the blame for his superiors at Scotland Yard.

Full of resentment, Judge Robinson was forced to stop the case halfway through and send the Jury home due to Brown's "demonstrable lies" and because he had entered "demonstrably false evidence" into Court.

To date, Judge Robinson has failed to report PC Brown for perverting the course of justice. She failed to apologise to Pead. Such is the arrogance of many within the legal profession.

In January 2012, Pead attended each day of the Harry Redknapp trial at Southwark Crown Court – the scene of an improper trial that Pead suffered where his Jury was not sworn in.

In July 2012, Pead attended every day of the John Terry trial at the City of Westminster Magistrates' Court.

Both high profile cases had shown significant abuses of power in his own cases and serious corruption. To date, no-one has been held responsible – echoes of Hillsborough.

152

david cameron

Eschewing politics *per se*, however difficult it is in the circumstances that surrounded Hillsborough, and focussing entirely on the legal implications of that disaster, prime minister David Cameron addressed the House of Commons on 12 September 2012, the day of the publication of the Hillsborough Report.

Cameron's speech has some important parallels with the case of Brian Pead and Lambeth Council.

"...The families have not heard the truth and have not found justice," said Cameron in the House of Commons.

The family of Brian Pead was lied to by officers from the Metropolitan Police, who sought to impugn him **after** he brought evidence – incontrovertible evidence – of Murray's racism and sexual grooming of young girls to their attention.

Cameron continued: "...this government insisted that no stone should be left unturned and that all papers should be made available to the Bishop of Liverpool and his team..."

Why, then, has the present government and the Metropolitan Police Service failed to make available all of the documents to which Brian Pead is fully entitled?

Cameron then highlighted "...the failure of the authorities to help protect people and the attempt to blame the fans..."

Lambeth Council, the Metropolitan Police Service and the Crown Prosecution Service have all failed to protect the people – the innocent pupils at the OLCVS and three innocent grand-children of Brian Pead. Racism by Murray went unpunished. The sexual grooming of young women similarly went unpunished.

Moreover, Lambeth Council **with the knowledge of Murray's misdemeanours** reinstated her and placed hundreds more pupils at risk.

Notwithstanding such blatant misfeasance, Lambeth Council then attempted to blame Brian Pead for **their** (and Murray's) **wrongdoing**. Just as the police had attempted to lay the blame for the Hillsborough Disaster on to the shoulders of the dead, Lambeth – and subsequently the police – attempted to blame Pead for their wrongdoing in not punishing Murray and bringing her to the attention of the police and safeguarding authorities. The police then published defamatory newspaper and internet articles about Pead's 'crimes' when he was, in fact, an innocent man all along. But Pead had uncovered their corrupt methods and he had to be silenced.

Cameron then informs the House that "...There is a trail of new documents which show the extent to which the safety of the crowd at Hillsborough was 'compromised at every level'..."

The authors are urging Mr Cameron and his government to produce the trail of documents that proves that Brian Pead was innocent and that, by failing to notify the police, Lambeth Council is guilty of compromising the safety of hundreds of pupils in its schools.

Cameron refers the House to "...these despicable untruths...". This book highlights "the despicable untruths" told by Gilhooly, Twist, White, Murray, Hiley, Whitmore and Martin.

Shades of Hillsborough.

Furthermore, Mr Cameron refers to the fact that "...we already know that police reports were significantly altered..."

Lambeth Council significantly altered witness statements when they interviewed some of Brian Pead's staff. Annabel Field – once her conscience returned to her – wrote to Lambeth and informed them that the statement they had sent her was not an exact representation of what had been said at interview. It had been altered and redacted. Just as 164 police statements had been altered in the Hillsborough disaster.

As a direct result of this Lambeth case, the Metropolitan Police then brought false charges against Brian Pead and in several different courts of law, they introduced as 'evidence' false documents and police were found to have lied on oath.

Further shades of Hillsborough.

Mr Cameron then highlights the excellent work of Andy Burnham, MP for Leigh and agrees that "...governments then and since have simply not done enough to challenge publicly the unjust and untrue narrative that sought to blame the fans..."

This present government has simply not done enough to challenge publicly the unjust and untrue narrative that sought to blame Brian Pead after he brought corruption and cover-up to the attention of first Scotland Yard and then Cameron and Home Secretary, Theresa May. Their response? To bring false allegations of witness intimidation against him and then jail him for seven weeks. In an attempt to silence him.

The prime minister then informs the House of "wrongs" perpetrated by previous governments, local authorities and the police:

"...It was wrong that the responsible authorities knew Hillsborough did not meet minimum safety standards and yet still allowed the match to go ahead..."

Similarly, it was wrong that Lambeth Council knew that Murray did not meet minimum safeguarding children standards and yet still allowed her to work in schools.

"...It was wrong that the families have had to wait for so long - and fight so hard - just to get to the truth..."

Similarly, it is wrong that Brian Pead and his family have had to wait so long for the truth about Murray to be made public. It is wrong that Pead has had to fight so hard just to get to the truth.

"...And it was wrong that the police changed the records of what happened and tried to blame the fans..."

Similarly, it was wrong that Lambeth officials – principally Cathy Twist, Claire Cobbold, Barry Gilhooly and Mary White **all under the watchful eye of Phyllis Dunipace** changed written statements and invented others. It was also wrong that the Metropolitan Police did likewise and tried to blame Pead for the crimes perpetrated by themselves and others.

David Cameron then rightly and nobly tells the House that "...we do the many, many honourable police men and women a great disservice if we try to defend the indefensible..."

For this reason, the authors have contacted the relevant authorities (the Prime Minister, the Metropolitan Police, the Home Secretary, the Attorney General, the Minister for Justice and others) in order that they no longer defend the indefensible. The authors are calling for a Judicial Review and expect that certain individuals are brought to justice through the Court system.

The prime minister then told the House that "...the new evidence that we are presented with today makes clear that these families have suffered a double injustice.

The injustice of the appalling events - the failure of the state to protect their loved ones - and the indefensible wait to get to the truth..."

Just as with Hillsborough, Brian Pead has suffered a double injustice. He was sexually abused in a children's home from the age of five and, then when he brought to the attention of the appropriate authorities examples of the sexual grooming of young girls by a female teacher, he was blamed for something he had never done. The full force of the state was brought to bear against him when it should have been protecting him.

And there has been an indefensible wait for his loved ones to get to the truth.

The wait is now over. This book is the truth. The REAL TRUTH.

jimmy savile

On Monday 8 October 2012, The Times ran an editorial which is reproduced in its entirety below:

> "...The Jimmy Savile affair provides Lord Patten with a test and an opportunity
>
> For George Entwistle, the new Director General of the BBC, and Lord Patten of Barnes, the fairly new Chairman of the BBC Trust, the gathering momentum of the allegations about Sir Jimmy Savile and his sexual abuse of young girls must seem like the worst of corporate nightmares.
>
> It is now obvious that the truth of Savile's behaviour and the culture that surrounded him is very dark indeed. Moreover, the BBC's response over many years to rumours, suspicions and widespread and apparently well-founded beliefs was entirely inadequate.
>
> Yet the worst of these outrages happened long ago and the incumbents have little to reproach themselves for. In such circumstances, it would be easy to succumb to self-pity. Mr Entwistle and Lord Patten may reasonably wonder at their being assailed for something that was not their fault and for which they cannot make historical amends.
>
> But Mr Entwistle and Lord Patten should see the scandal as an opportunity. The BBC has many strengths, but one of its weaknesses has always concerned its ability to accept and respond to criticism and to police itself as vigorously as it polices others. The terrible allegations against their former star, and the obvious implication that many in the BBC knew about this and did nothing, provide a chance to address this weakness.
>
> The right response is for the BBC to own up its mistakes, be the first to root them out and be the most aggressive seeker of the truth. Lord Patten, in particular, should use his position from outside the staff to demand answers, and insist that the BBC has procedures that would never allow such a thing to happen again..."
> © The Times 8 October 2012

The Times' suggestion that Patten instigate procedures that would never allow such abuse to occur again is interesting. Lord Patten of Barnes is a Catholic. He is a former pupil of St. Benedict's School in Ealing. He is also a School Advisor at St.

Benedict's. Jonathan West has blogged about the links between Chris Patten, the Catholic church, St. Benedict's and sexual abuse of children:

> "...Chris Patten is an old boy of St. Benedict's School. He has the Christopher Patten Cup for "Outstanding Performance at GCSE" named after him, and he is on the board of School Advisors.
>
> This of course is the school where Father David Pearce enjoyed a 36 year paedophile career, whose child protection policy remains a shambles, and where the Abbot, who is also is Chairman of Trustees, refuses to attend a meeting called by the Diocesan Safeguarding Advisor to discuss these matters, and where a supposedly independent review has managed to avoid reviewing almost the whole of the time David Pearce was a monk at the Abbey, and managed to avoid reviewing anything of his career as a teacher at the school.
>
> It is also the school at which John Maestri taught, who has been convicted three times of sexual offences whose victims were boys at the school, and who was sent on his way as he was about to take over as headmaster of the Middle School.
>
> This is the school where the Independent Schools Inspectorate has had to withdraw its most recent inspection report because of concerns over the accuracy of the information provided to it by the school.
>
> This is the school about which the Charity Commission conducted two Statutory Enquiries, the report of which was "severely critical of the Trustees".
>
> This is the school where Father Gregory Chillman has recently mysteriously resigned as a trustee.
>
> This is the school where, according to evidence given in court and not denied, Father Stanislaus Hobbs sexually assaulted a pupil while on a school trip to Italy.
>
> This is the school which in 2006 contested a civil case in respect of accusations of abuse by Father David Pearce and lost, with the judge awarding damages of £43,000.
>
> And Chris Patten is a member of the Board of School Advisors. So he has some degree of responsibility for running the school.
>
> In the light of all this, it seems to me that either:
>
> • He isn't aware of all these problems, in which case he's not doing much of a job as a School Advisor, or

• He is aware of all these problems, and has chosen not to do anything about it, in which case I had better not offer my opinion of him, or

• He is aware of all these problems, and has tried to do something about it and failed, coming up against the intransigence of the Abbot. If this is the case the honourable thing to do would be to publicly resign as a School Advisor, since his name at present is providing cover to a deplorable state of affairs.

It would be nice if Chris Patten would use his present position to help ensure that St. Benedict's does properly clean up its safeguarding procedures, and does set up a proper enquiry..."

Jonathan West posted that on his blog "Confessions of a Skeptic" on Friday 9 July 2010. He drew the public's attention over two years ago to the fact that Chris Patten failed to 'clean up' child safeguarding procedures at St. Benedict's School in Ealing. Why, then, would The Times suggest that Patten 'clean up' the BBC when it is clear – from a historical glance into the most recent past – that Patten is not being held to account and actually 'cleaning up' organisations with which he is associated?

like the hillsborough families, seeking justice

After one of the most significant cover-ups in the history of the UK, those affected by the Hillsborough Disaster are now rightly seeking justice. This will not be the justice that the Government and the police think they will have, but the very real Justice that they deserve and that the nation expects.

In a similar vein, the authors of this book have brought the corruption and cover-up in this book to the attention of the Government and the police.

Those involved with the Hillsborough tragedy are rightly involved in making certain demands that will hopefully bring mendacious individuals to account.

Similarly, the authors of this book are seeking to bring these individuals to account.

Just as there are calls for Sir Irvine Patnick to be stripped of his knighthood, the authors expect that Phyllis Dunipace will be stripped of her OBE since not only was she instrumental in the unlawful dismissal of James Walker, Headteacher of Henry Fawcett Primary School in Lambeth, but also that of Brian Pead, Headteacher of the Open Learning Centre for Vocational Studies in Vauxhall, Lambeth. There may have been countless other unfair or unlawful dismissals that Dunipace knew about and even ordered. She does not deserve to have been rewarded for such corrupt practices at worst, or inept management at best. Furthermore, she gave permission for Murray to be reinstated when she must have known – through Gilhooly – that Murray had been racist and groomed young girls.

Dunipace also knew that pupils at the OLCVS and their parents or carers were deliberately kept in the dark, despite the fact that there were allegations of sexual impropriety made against Pead. This is not acceptable. Nor is it acceptable that Dunipace allowed the course of justice to be perverted.

At the time of publication, Barry Gilhooly appears to have retired. Dunipace resigned in 2010, and Gilhooly has left. This is just one way in which Local Authorities and the police distance themselves from accountability - they either allow corrupt individuals to resign or retire or they promote them or transfer them to another department. However, the inept Gilhooly is in receipt of a considerable pension and the authors will press for this to be returned to the Lambeth taxpayer. He is also guilty of perverting the course of justice, so it is expected that he undergoes a criminal trial.

Cathy Twist was vilified in the case of James Walker. Her investigatory skills were called into question. In the case of Brian Pead, she deliberately perverted the course of justice, and the authors are calling for her to be held to account in a criminal prosecution. The authors also expect that she is dismissed with immediate effect and that her pension is withheld.

Mary White – an alleged Human Resources consultant to Lambeth – also needs to be held to account for aiding and abetting the conniving Twist. She should never be allowed to work for Lambeth – or any other Local Authority – in any capacity whatsoever. She is also guilty of perverting the course of justice, so it is expected that she undergoes a criminal trial.

Rosa Vaz was shown to have lied in a Disciplinary Hearing. The authors believe that she, too, should be dismissed without pension and not allowed to ever work in a local authority again.

Anya Hiley – the Connexions Personal Advisor who worked in close partnership with Maryn Murray – must also be dismissed from her post without any financial rights whatsoever. She should be reported to the Independent Safeguarding Authority and to the Vetting and Barring Scheme (List 99) and not allowed to work with young people ever again. She is also guilty of perverting the course of justice, so it is expected that she undergoes a criminal trial.

All of the Disciplinary Panel members – Carol Palmer, Brian Netto and Paul Barraclough – should also be held to account for ratifying a perverse verdict when they knew, or ought to have known, that they were involved in corrupt practices. The authors are calling for them all to be dismissed with immediate effect.

Paul Waters – aka Ermina aka Mina – should never be allowed to work in schools again. She forged a strong alliance with Murray **after** Murray had been dismissed for racism and sexual impropriety towards young girls. Clearly, this is wholly unacceptable and Waters must now be reported to the Independent Safeguarding Authority and to the Vetting and Barring Scheme.

Annabel Field is also guilty of perverting the course of justice. She deliberately lied to Twist in an investigatory meeting on 23 February 2007 when she claimed that Pead had bullied her and that he had been masturbated in the White Bear Theatre during a play in which she was acting. Her behaviour has been reprehensible.

Eloise Whitmore will also be reported to the police for conspiracy to pervert the course of justice with her entire statement against Pead.

Maryn Murray, of course, is guilty of racism and the grooming of young girls. Lambeth Council allowed her – on Dunipace's watch - to continue to work in schools as an ICT consultant. Murray is also guilty of slander and libel and of perverting the course of justice. She has been reported to the Independent Safeguarding Authority and to the Vetting and Barring Scheme. It is imperative that she never works with young people again. She is a highly dangerous individual. Furthermore, she has been reported to the Attorney General, Dominic Grieve, with a view to her being prosecuted in a criminal trial.

FOR WHOM THE BELL TOLLED

1

Verdict

23 December 2009

6:41pm

PROSPECT CLOSE, SOUTHEND, ESSEX

Michael Bird receives a mobile call from Brian Pead calling from 89 Days Lane, Sidcup, Kent DA15 9JP

BRIAN: Hi Michael, I'm just calling to let you know the verdict.

MICHAEL: Great! Not Guilty I take it?

BRIAN: No. On the Exposure case, not guilty ... on the Incitement case, Guilty by 10-2.

MICHAEL: [Silence] No fucking way! That's impossible. The Judge clearly said to the Jurors that you could not be found guilty because there was no victim. That woman Juror even asked the Judge the question, "Are you saying that if there is no victim, then we can't find him guilty?" and he said, "Yes, that is exactly what I'm saying."

BRIAN: Well, it gets worse. When I return for sentencing on 27 January [2010], they said I must sign the Sex Offenders' Register. The judge said that he would send me to jail if I continued to protest my innocence.

MICHAEL: Under no circumstances must you sign that register, regardless if they send you to prison for years, you never sign to say you did something that you didn't do. It's irreversible once you've signed and said you're guilty.

BRIAN: Well, I am innocent, so I'm not gonna sign it.

MICHAEL: Brian, this will be a turning point in your life. If you do say you're guilty just to stay out of prison, you will never be able to prove your innocence. But if you stick to your guns now, however difficult they may make it for you, you will always be able to look at yourself in the mirror.

BRIAN: Well, I want to be able to look at my grand-children and get the truth to them. I'm gonna write a letter to my daughter and put it

467

through their letterbox tomorrow. As you know, my grand-children mean everything to me and they have to learn the truth. Whatever their parents have told them, it must be lies. I want them to grow up with the truth, not with lies.

MICHAEL: Well, let them bring it on. It's gonna be hard for you, but let them bring it on.

BRIAN: Ok. Well, I'll call you again over Christmas. Take care, bye.

MICHAEL: Yeah, good luck, bye.

2

trial day one – 14 december 2009

Brian Pead left his house in Days Lane, Sidcup at 7.45am. On his way to the station he saw Adrienne and Victoria Tear at the bus-stop outside their house in Halfway Street. He asked them if they had heard back from the police and they said that the police had told them that Pead was a "wanted man" and that he had resisted arrest. Clearly the Tears knew this to be a lie, because they had witnessed his brutal beating by four police officers outside their house on 18 July 2009.

He caught a fast train from New Eltham to London Bridge, found a Pret near the station and bought a hot chocolate and a *pain au raisin*.

He felt anger, frustration and fear at the pointlessness of this trial and the police lies.

A friend, Christine Morgan, called him on the Sunday and that meant a lot to him. Another friend, Mandy Rawsthorne, called at 8.50 and wished him luck.

His lover, Maya Walker, said that she felt the result was in his destiny. She also said that she had got the dates wrong – she thought that the trial was in January. This did not make sense to Brian Pead. She had let him down.

An overwhelming feeling was that Pead wanted to be little Brian's parent/representative and lawyer: the nice little lad who was feeling so much pain and hurt 50 years ago and who never got the help and support that he needed. The adult Pead felt that he wanted to be a good parent to the little Brian; he wanted to represent himself well and he wanted closure on an unhappy half century without unconditional love.

Yesterday, Kirsty McIntyre – a former pupil of Pead's at Bexleyheath School – texted him to ask if he needed her to accompany him to Southwark Crown Court.

At 9.15am, Pead received a telephone call from Bromley County Court regarding the fence dispute with his neighbour – the police informant, Susan Ann Pool. They claimed they hadn't received his letter of exemption and verification of unemployment. This was additional stress that he neither deserved nor needed at this present time. This was part of the police's wider campaign against him. The fence had, of course, been repaired several months earlier.

Thoughts of his dead brother, Robert, and his late mother floated into his mind.

Pead arrived at Court 4 and called his barrister, Dominic Bell. His solicitors said that he was not at court, but on his way.

One of the females in the Exposure case against Pead arrived. She was apparently unable to turn up at Woolwich Crown Court in February, but here she was in December.

A tannoy called out the name of Dominic Bell.

Pead felt at that moment that his barrister was not performing properly and the trial had not even started.

At 10:03, Bell arrived. "We need to chat," he said to his client, but then disappeared into Court 4.

Pead felt that he was being overlooked and neglected by Bell, who was now in discussion with Timothy Forster, the Prosecutor.

Then Bell came and spoke with his client.

"I need more information regarding the calls the girls made to the police," he told Pead. So, some 23 months after first being charged with exposure, Bell had failed to secure some vital evidence in his client's interests. The report of the conversation the girls allegedly made to the police to report exposure was not part of the defence bundle of documents.

It was not to be the only missing document in the trial.

"This fellow, what's his name? – Erm, Geoffrey Bacon, the fellow whose computer was seized and his hard drive burnt out by the police ... erm, I don't think I'll call him."

"But that's nonsense," replied Pead. "He needs to be called as a witness. He wants to be called as a witness."

But Bell failed to take instructions from his client, saying "I'm not calling him. He won't add anything to your case."

The Authors

Michael Bird

I first met Brian in July 2006 when he came for interview as a trainee counsellor in the Drug Agency of which I was supervisor.

Little was I to know at that time what an impact on my life that that first meeting with Brian would have. Between 2006 and the publication of this book, I came to learn that this man would be beaten up in the street by police officers, falsely imprisoned at Belmarsh and Wandsworth prisons and taken to court on more than fifty occasions within six years. I also attended Crown Court hearings where invisible warrants ensured that he was unlawfully held in prison when he should have been released.

This left me wondering what this man had done to warrant such attention from the authorities. This is the first in a series of books that have been written which explain the level of corruption that he had uncovered.

As a child in the playground, whenever I saw injustice – usually in the form of bullying – I felt compelled to do something about it. On many occasions that left me battered and bruised but it never deterred me from defending what I felt to be right. This part of my nature has never left me and as I saw Brian's story unfold, I was once again compelled to do something about the grave injustices that I saw being carried out against him.

I am sure that my inclusion in this book will once again see me battered and bruised by the authorities but it will never deter me from exposing such corruption.

The information contained in this and subsequent books, has led me to my current position in demanding Government change in the laws around the statutory obligations of schools to report **any** allegation of child abuse.

The current laws in the UK are not prescriptive enough and several loopholes exist which mean that many teachers – particularly foreign teachers – can be placed in schools by Local Authorities without the necessary Criminal Records Bureau (CRB) or other relevant checks such as the Vetting and Barring Scheme in place.

For more information about my work in seeking to change the laws around safeguarding children, please visit: <www.statutoryobligation.com>

Brian Pead

At the age of 5, having been sexually abused in a children's home, I developed a great interest in the psychology of perpetrators and their victims, as well as the concept of survivors of abuse.

At 14, I began writing my first book on the history of Liverpool Football Club which was published almost twenty years later. I went on to write five books on the entire history of Liverpool FC from 1892 to the present.

At 19, I witnessed the Coroner at the inquest of my late brother attempt to lay the blame for his death on board a Lowestoft trawler on to my brother's shoulders when I instinctively knew him to be innocent. Shades of the Hillsborough Coroner.

At 27, I brought corporate lies and mismanagement to the attention of the Chairman of Unilever, the late Sir David Orr, who instigated an enquiry.

At 36, I attended the football match which came to be known as the Hillsborough disaster, when the three pillars of society – the police, the legal system and a free press – conspired to lay the blame for the unnecessary deaths of Liverpool fans on to the fans themselves. I baulked at the police lies and the obvious cover-up and I dedicated my book 'Ee Aye Addio – We've Won the Cup!' to those who had died at Hillsborough and their families and friends.

At 39, I spent half a day with one of the most humble – yet successful – men I have ever met in my entire life: Bob Paisley. In his foreword, he kindly referred to the depth of research that I had undertaken to write 'Champions of Champions', my fourth book on the history of the club that I love.

At 47, I was involved in a legal fight of David and Goliath proportions with the Football Association and the Premier League who tried to blacken my name when I legally purchased the domain names of Premier League clubs. Having taken advice from my MP, the late Sir Edward Heath, I beat the legal action against me when the Premier League settled out of court.

All my life, I have been drawn towards lies, corruption and cover-ups and felt that it was my duty to expose them wherever possible.

At the age of 53, I was forced to dismiss a female colleague for racism and the sexual grooming of female pupils. Three weeks later, I was unlawfully suspended from my post as Head teacher and she was reinstated by Lambeth Council **with the full knowledge of her misdemeanours** - and placed in an all-girls' school.

This book is the true story of local authority corruption and a cover-up of inadequate child safeguarding policies which currently give *carte blanche* to those teachers who have a sexual interest in children to perpetrate their crimes in the knowledge that if they are reported to the Head teacher, their crime will usually not get reported outside of the four walls of the school.

As the survivor of child sexual abuse, this story is for all those who have suffered wrongly and for all those who have been the victims of a cover-up. And for the 96.